Why We Pray What We Pray

Why We Pray What We Pray

The Remarkable History
of Jewish Prayer

Rabbi Dr. Barry Freundel

URIM PUBLICATIONS
Jerusalem ◆ New York

Why We Pray What We Pray: The Remarkable History of Jewish Prayer
by Rabbi Dr. Barry Freundel

Copyright © 2010 by Barry Freundel

Printed in Israel
First Edition

ISBN: 978-965-524-034-4

Urim Publications, P.O. Box 52287, Jerusalem 91521 Israel
Typeset by Ariel Walden, Bookraft

Lambda Publishers Inc.
3709 13th Avenue Brooklyn, New York 11218 U.S.A.
Tel: 718-972-5449 Fax: 718-972-6307, mh@ejudaica.com

www.UrimPublications.com

CONTENTS

שבע ביום הללתיך
"Seven times a day I praise you"

(Psalms 119:164)

This book tells the story of six prayers.
The seventh chapter is the muse,
the שבע for whom I praise You every day.

Special thanks to the pillars on whose gifts this book stands:

Stuart Bloch

Stuart and Lotta Brafman

Ambassador Jaime and Gina Daremblum

Liebe Diamond

Baruch and Karen Fellner

Eli and Eva Genauer

Jerry Gontownick

Bernardo and Gladys Hirschman

Louis and Manette Mayberg

Alfred Moses and Fern Schad

Elia and Anna Roumani

Barry Schochet and Gail Weiss

ACKNOWLEDGMENTS

MANY PEOPLE CONTRIBUTED in very different ways to this volume. This includes those who did the nitty-gritty work of typing and proofreading, those who challenged with their questions, those who encouraged and facilitated the work and those who offered financial support. I list them below in alphabetical order with a few exceptions at the beginning and at the end.

David Levin, my friend and the most hospitable person I know, spent hours as a volunteer proofreader. So, too, my very special congregation, Kesher Israel, the Georgetown Synagogue, tolerated and even encouraged bimonthly discussions of the history of the prayers that we recite. My students at George Washington University and at Baltimore Hebrew University (now the Baltimore Hebrew Institute at Towson University) contributed a great deal, with their insights and their questions.

That brings me to this alphabetical list with profound thanks to those mentioned here and heartfelt apologies to anyone I forgot: Avidan Ackerson, Beth Allen, Rosa Alonso, Alfred and Lynn Altschul, Amtrak, Anne Ashbaugh, Kate Bailey, David and Sarah Barak, Claudia Barrientos, Chana Black, Stuart Bloch, Stuart and Lotta Brafman, Allison Bush, Cafe Hillel, Cafe Tal Bagels, Channah Charlton, Rose Ann Christian, Jim Cleeman, Adam Cohen and Linda Safran, Leah Covel, Carrol Cowan and Comet, Ambassador Jaime and Gina Daremblum, Liebe Diamond, Robbie and Shari Diamond, Channah Delisle, Courtney Egelhoff, David Epstein, Dino Feigelstock, Mort Feigenbaum, Baruch and Karen Fellner, Sheldon Fischer, Susanna Garfein, Jay and Renee Garfinkle, Michael and Edith Gelfand, Eli and Eva Genauer, Rami and Rebekah Genauer, Barry Gittlen, Jerry Gontownick, Aviva Gottlieb, Jessie Grauman, Hana-Bashe

Himelstein, Bernardo and Gladys Hirschman, Mat and Bruchie Hoffman, Matt Horowitz, Andrew and Elanit Jakabovics, Aimee Jones, Jeremy and Jana Kadden, Martin Katz, Hannah Kaye, Dan Klein, Max and Suzette Klein, Phillipp Klein ob"m and Charlotte Klein, Harpaul Kohli, Gamliel Kronemer, Valerie Lamotte, Joy Langley, Fred and Kathy Lawrence, Lacey Leblanc, Ari Leifman, Rozzie Liss, Elaine Mael, Adrienne Marks, Tzvi Mauer, Louis and Manette Mayberg, Aylana Meisel, Jesse and Elana Mendelson, D'alizza Mercedes, Jess Minnen, Alfred Moses and Fern Schad, Asher Namenson, Seth and Rena Opert, Rabbi Yoel and Rebecca Oz, Michael Perkins and Shoshana Danon Perkins, Harry Peters (Mo Pete's Dad), Suzanne Peyser, Ben Pick, Steven and Nava Pickman, Jonathan and Joan Pincus, David and Paulina Plotinsky, Jeremy and Rhoda Rabkin, Jennifer Reed, Daniel and Adela Renna, Bracha Reznik, Esther Rinde, Judah Rose and Lisa Schreier, Howard Rosen, Sara Rosenbaum, Sue Tedmon Rosenfeld, Daniel Roth, Gabriel Roth, Elia and Anna Roumani, Candace Ryan, Barry Schochet and Gail Weiss, Erica Schon, Roz Singer, David and Deb Sloan and Rami, Howie Slugh, Dov and Ellen Spolsky, Clate and Talia Stansbury, Andrew and Miriam Stein, Moises and Perla Steren, Carolan Sudol, Olympia Nowicka Sulla, Marcela Sulak, Amalia and her illustrations, Susan Taylor, Jose and Adelaide Tennenbaum, Rivka Turk, Evelyn Volk, Gary Waxman, Ilan and Jessica Weinberger, Ken Weinstein and Amy Kauffman, Sheldon and Mindy Weisel, Leon Wieseltier and Jennifer Bradley, Gary and Shanna Winters, Herman Wouk, Rebecca Zimmerman.

My precious family deserves unique mention of its own.

First, my wonderful wife, Sharon, who defines an Orthodox woman in a leadership role, and who allowed me the time, space and support to write this book.

My children: Dan with his beautiful davening voice , JoJo with his remarkable analytical mind and Arielle with her deep spirituality, all raised questions about every new chapter in the Connections series.

My mother, Alice, a Ba'alat Teshuva of simple faith, in her ability to communicate with God, and my father, Oscar, of blessed memory, who dedicated himself to attending services every day of his life:

All of my precious family are represented in every word I wrote in this book.

B. F.

INTRODUCTION

THE IDEA FOR this book probably began with Dave Kinsberg. Mr. Kinsberg (ob"m) was a powerful figure in the synagogue I attended as a child and teenager. He was the President of the shul for decades. He had a beautiful voice and was our most frequent Hazzan (prayer leader), particularly at the various high points of the year, such as the High Holidays. He also personally educated many of the young people of the community in synagogue skills. In my case, beginning around age seven, he taught me how to sing and chant Anim Zemirot and the conclusion of the Sabbath services (see ch. 4 below), with great patience and tolerance for my very tone-deaf ear. For the next ten years or so he instructed me in every aspect of how to lead the synagogue liturgy from Torah reading to daily, Sabbath and holiday services, to how to function as a Gabbai who calls individuals to be part of Torah reading and then blesses them and their families for doing so. I owe him a great and unpayable debt of gratitude.

Through all of this he played another role in the "J" (our synagogue) as well. He was one of those, in this very Germanic house of worship, who was a vocal guardian of our prayer customs. There was a way that we did things week after week and year after year, and he, along with a few others, was going to make "darn sure" that no "young Turks" were allowed to change our practices. (I guess I was included in that category, particularly because I once had the temerity to suggest a different melody for some part of the service that he was teaching me.) That is, until a very interesting thing happened.

Mr. Kinsberg had a son named Aaron who was a few years older than me. Aaron went to Yeshiva University and then spent his sophomore year in Israel. Dave went to visit him (actually several times, as I recall), and when he returned, suddenly things were very different. When Mr. Kinsberg got up to lead services the Friday night after he got back, he began to sing *Yedid Nefesh*, a medieval mystical composition sung in most synagogues at this point in the services today, but virtually unheard of outside of Israel in the mid-1960s, when this all took place.

This was the first of several changes, all instituted by this former "rock of our tradition," and all following the emerging practices of the then, roughly, twenty-year-old State of Israel. The power of the hoary history of our synagogue customs that withstood those "young Turks" for years, proved remarkably fragile when hit with the right hammer – Zionism, and the pride of a father for his son studying in an Israeli venue who happened to have the clout and voice to make these changes happen.

I remember thinking, as this was going on, that there must be other places and other examples where these kinds of ex-Cathedra influences had impacted on Jewish liturgical custom. Sure enough, over the years I heard or read indications that this was true far more often than people realize.

When I entered the pulpit rabbinate, I resolved to explore this question. The Public Broadcasting System was running a series on TV called *Connections* that took pivotal moments in human history and showed all the influences – social, scientific, technological, philosophical, even interpersonal – that went into things happening as they had. I found the broadcasts fascinating and used them to launch an ongoing series of talks in my synagogues (over the years there have been three), called "Connections in the Siddur" (Jewish prayer book). Once every six weeks or so I take some aspect of the liturgy and try to discover and describe the influences (including the Dave and Aaron Kinsbergs of history where I can find them) that shaped this particular aspect of the prayers into what it is today. I then used this material to teach a course on the subject at Baltimore Hebrew University and at George Washington University.

Over the years I have been encouraged to publish these talks and here – in expanded and more complete form than one can accomplish in a fifteen- or twenty-minute presentation on a Saturday morning to congregants who want to get on to lunch and other activities – is my first attempt at doing so. Not all the influences on the Siddur are as personal and warm as the story of my dedicated teacher and his son (by the way, I should mention that he would get angry at any suggestion of financial remuneration for his labor of love with me and others), but virtually all speak to and enhance the emotional depth of the prayers.

Limiting myself only to the six texts discussed in this volume, we can see that Jewish liturgy has been influenced by the need to respond to devastating persecutions, great internecine ideological and philosophical battles and yearnings for communal unity, the coming of the messiah, and the ability to stand before God and experience His glory. At the same time Jewish prayer has also been a place for nervous bridegrooms to find solace, for people to make liturgical decisions that are musically sound but thematically and structurally wrong, and for fascinating historic errors and inconsistencies that lead to unintended consequences, but which often work out just fine in the end. In short, the liturgy is an area of Jewish life where all the vagaries – great and small – of Jewish existence make their mark. So whether it is the most profound of ideas or a small interaction in a father's relationship with his son, the study of Jewish liturgy in all its richness and fullness is both fascinating and an important doorway to spirituality and transcendent meaning. And after all, isn't that what prayer is about anyway?

This volume explores prayers that occupy prominent positions in Jewish liturgy. They are a cross section of different types of texts across the Jewish spectrum. Anim Zmirot has a single author. Others (e.g. Birkat haHodesh) was contributed to over the centuries by many different hands. The purposes of these texts are also very different. In this way I hope to give the reader a sense of the remarkable breadth that Jewish literacy encompasses. The chapters follow the order of the prayer service on a Sabbath morning in many synagogues with the exception of Kriyat Shma which because of its central role in Jewish thought and worship comes first. Anim Zemirot appears where it does because different congregations recite it at different points in their services. While Aleinu and Kaddish are always concluding liturgies.

The approach of this book is scholarly and not anecdotal. While there has been a significant amount of academic work done on the history of Jewish liturgy beginning some years before Ismar Elbogen's 1906 classic opus *Der Yiddeshe Gottesdeinst* (since translated into both Hebrew and English) and continuing until today, the discussions below add three elements generally lacking from these other works. First, this book tries to present the history of each prayer more completely and with greater nuance and detail – while reflecting the complex and interlocking, though often contradictory forces that shaped it – than has been done before.

Second, our discussion highlights the critical influence of Heikhalot or Merkavah mysticism on the prayer book. This ancient mysticism, now shown to have been around since no later than the first or second century BCE, was not investigated by many who have written on Jewish prayer. Given the dramatic impact that this esoteric material had on Jewish worship, this lack needs to be rectified.

Third, and to my mind, perhaps most importantly, many of those who have written on Jewish liturgy have left out the dimensions of theology and religious belief and ideology from their discussion of the history of the prayers. One need not believe in the Jewish God or in the common principles of Judaism's belief system to recognize that the prayers were written and recited by people who did. These beliefs shaped those prayers – in fact, it is axiomatic that they are at the core of those prayers. To not investigate the faith elements that moved Jewish believers to speak to their God as they did is to miss the heart and soul of what one is investigating. Historical and communal forces were certainly important factors in shaping the Siddur, but ideology and belief were simply more important. The discussions that follow try to make this abundantly clear.

At the end of the day, no one can describe the full history of any prayer; too much of the story is lost or was never written down. Dave Kinsberg's contribution to one community's customs has only found its way into print because of the accident of who authored this book. Other Dave Kinsbergs and even many of the larger influences on Jewish worship were not that lucky. But all of the contributors and influences share one common characteristic. They all impacted on a community seeking to make the best and most personal connection to God that it could, given the contemporary existential reality of the world in which it functioned. As such, the Siddur and the history of its liturgy is a story of people and the things that shaped their lives in a way that no other Jewish sacred text can match precisely because, unlike any other of Judaism's sacred texts, it was so open to these influences. That is why understanding this history simply adds a depth, texture, and pathos to words that are already meaningful and spiritually stimulating without such an understanding. With this knowledge, even if academically produced, the Siddur becomes more of a text that records and expresses the deepest aspirations and emotions of a people trying to find meaning in the universe by connecting with their God than it is without knowing why we pray what we pray.

BARRY FREUNDEL
Washington, DC 2010

Note to the Reader

THROUGHOUT THIS VOLUME, reference is made to page numbers where specific prayers appear. The references are to the texts listed below. They are largely from Mesorah Publication's ArtScroll series. This should not necessarily be seen as an endorsement of those texts, but simply as a recognition that they are the most frequently encountered in the synagogues I am familiar with (though they are not the primary prayer books in my own congregation), and, therefore, the most accessible to likely readers of this volume:

"Siddur" refers to *Sidur Ḳol Ya'akov: The complete ArtScroll siddur* (Brooklyn, NY: 1984).

"Sephardic Siddur" refers to *Sidur Ets Hayim: The complete ArtScroll siddur* (Brooklyn, NY: 1985).

"Ari Siddur" refers to *Sidur Tehilat Hashem: al pi nusah ha-Ari, zal* (Brooklyn, NY: 2001).

"Mahzor Rosh Hashanah" refers to *Mahzor Zikhron Re'uven le-Rosh ha-Shanah: The complete ArtScroll machzor: Rosh Hashanah* (Brooklyn, NY: 1985).

"Mahzor Yom Kippur" refers to *Mahzor Zikhron Yosef le-Yom Kipur: The complete ArtScroll machzor: Yom Kippur* (Brooklyn, NY: 1986).

"Selihot" refers to *Divre Rivkah: Selihot le-Yamim Nora'im: The complete ArtScroll Selichos* (Brooklyn, NY: 1993).

"Kinnot" refers to *Zekhor le-Avraham: The complete Tishah b'Av service* (Brooklyn, NY: 1989).

CHAPTER I

It is Not Your Great Grandfather's Keriyat Shema

In private prayer add: Lord, faithful King.

Hear, Israel; God our Lord; God is One.

Inaudibly – Blessed be the Name of His glorious kingdom for ever and ever.

And you shall love God your Lord with all your heart, and with all your soul, and with all your might.

And these words, which I command you this day, shall be in your heart;

And you shall teach them diligently to your children, and shall talk of them when you sit in your house, and when you walk on the way, and when you lie down, and when you rise up.

And you shall bind them for a sign upon your hand, and as frontlets between your eyes.

And you shall write them upon the posts of your house, and on your gates.

And it shall come to pass, if you shall diligently follow My commandments which I command you this day, to love God your Lord, and to serve Him with all your heart and with all your soul,

יחיד אומר: א־ל מֶלֶךְ נֶאֱמָן:

שְׁמַע יִשְׂרָאֵל ה' אֱלֹהֵינוּ ה' אֶחָד:

בלחש - בָּרוּךְ שֵׁם כְּבוֹד מַלְכוּתוֹ לְעוֹלָם וָעֶד:

וְאָהַבְתָּ אֵת ה' אֱ־לֹהֶיךָ בְּכָל לְבָבְךָ וּבְכָל נַפְשְׁךָ וּבְכָל מְאֹדֶךָ:

וְהָיוּ הַדְּבָרִים הָאֵלֶּה אֲשֶׁר אָנֹכִי מְצַוְּךָ הַיּוֹם עַל לְבָבֶךָ:

וְשִׁנַּנְתָּם לְבָנֶיךָ וְדִבַּרְתָּ בָּם בְּשִׁבְתְּךָ בְּבֵיתֶךָ וּבְלֶכְתְּךָ בַדֶּרֶךְ וּבְשָׁכְבְּךָ וּבְקוּמֶךָ:

וּקְשַׁרְתָּם לְאוֹת עַל יָדֶךָ וְהָיוּ לְטֹטָפֹת בֵּין עֵינֶיךָ:

וּכְתַבְתָּם עַל מְזֻזוֹת בֵּיתֶךָ וּבִשְׁעָרֶיךָ:

וְהָיָה אִם שָׁמֹעַ תִּשְׁמְעוּ אֶל מִצְוֹתַי אֲשֶׁר אָנֹכִי מְצַוֶּה אֶתְכֶם הַיּוֹם לְאַהֲבָה אֶת ה' אֱ־לֹהֵיכֶם וּלְעָבְדוֹ בְּכָל לְבַבְכֶם וּבְכָל נַפְשְׁכֶם:

That I will give you the rain of your land in its due season, the first rain and the latter rain, that you may gather in your grain, and your wine, and your oil.

And I will send grass in your fields for your cattle that you may eat and be full.

Take heed to yourselves, that your heart be not deceived, and you turn aside, and serve other powers, and worship them;

And then God's anger be kindled against you, and He close the skies, that there should be no rain, and that the land yield not her fruit; and lest you perish quickly from off the good land which God gives you.

Therefore shall you place these My words in your heart and in your soul, and bind them for a sign upon your hand, and frontlets between your eyes.

And you shall teach them to your children, speaking of them when you sit in your house, and when you walk by the way, when you lie down, and when you rise up.

And you shall write them upon the door posts of your house, and upon your gates;

That your days may be multiplied, and the days of your children, in the land which the Lord swore to your fathers to give them, as the days of heaven upon the earth.

And God spoke to Moses, saying,

"Speak to the people of Israel, and say to them that they make for themselves fringes, at the corners of their garments, throughout their generations, and that they put upon the fringe of the corner a thread of blue;

And it shall be to you for a fringe, that you may see it, and remember all the commandments of God, and do them; and that you seek not after your own heart and your own eyes, which

וְנָתַתִּי מְטַר אַרְצְכֶם בְּעִתּוֹ יוֹרֶה וּמַלְקוֹשׁ וְאָסַפְתָּ דְגָנֶךָ וְתִירֹשְׁךָ וְיִצְהָרֶךָ:

וְנָתַתִּי עֵשֶׂב בְּשָׂדְךָ לִבְהֶמְתֶּךָ וְאָכַלְתָּ וְשָׂבָעְתָּ:

הִשָּׁמְרוּ לָכֶם פֶּן יִפְתֶּה לְבַבְכֶם וְסַרְתֶּם וַעֲבַדְתֶּם אֱלֹהִים אֲחֵרִים וְהִשְׁתַּחֲוִיתֶם לָהֶם:

וְחָרָה אַף ה' בָּכֶם וְעָצַר אֶת הַשָּׁמַיִם וְלֹא יִהְיֶה מָטָר וְהָאֲדָמָה לֹא תִתֵּן אֶת יְבוּלָהּ וַאֲבַדְתֶּם מְהֵרָה מֵעַל הָאָרֶץ הַטֹּבָה אֲשֶׁר ה' נֹתֵן לָכֶם:

וְשַׂמְתֶּם אֶת דְּבָרַי אֵלֶּה עַל לְבַבְכֶם וְעַל נַפְשְׁכֶם וּקְשַׁרְתֶּם אֹתָם לְאוֹת עַל יֶדְכֶם וְהָיוּ לְטוֹטָפֹת בֵּין עֵינֵיכֶם:

וְלִמַּדְתֶּם אֹתָם אֶת בְּנֵיכֶם לְדַבֵּר בָּם בְּשִׁבְתְּךָ בְּבֵיתֶךָ וּבְלֶכְתְּךָ בַדֶּרֶךְ וּבְשָׁכְבְּךָ וּבְקוּמֶךָ:

וּכְתַבְתָּם עַל מְזוּזוֹת בֵּיתֶךָ וּבִשְׁעָרֶיךָ:

לְמַעַן יִרְבּוּ יְמֵיכֶם וִימֵי בְנֵיכֶם עַל הָאֲדָמָה אֲשֶׁר נִשְׁבַּע ה' לַאֲבֹתֵיכֶם לָתֵת לָהֶם כִּימֵי הַשָּׁמַיִם עַל הָאָרֶץ:

וַיֹּאמֶר ה' אֶל מֹשֶׁה לֵּאמֹר:

דַּבֵּר אֶל בְּנֵי יִשְׂרָאֵל וְאָמַרְתָּ אֲלֵהֶם וְעָשׂוּ לָהֶם צִיצִת עַל כַּנְפֵי בִגְדֵיהֶם לְדֹרֹתָם וְנָתְנוּ עַל צִיצִת הַכָּנָף פְּתִיל תְּכֵלֶת:

וְהָיָה לָכֶם לְצִיצִת וּרְאִיתֶם אֹתוֹ וּזְכַרְתֶּם אֶת כָּל מִצְוֹת ה' וַעֲשִׂיתֶם אֹתָם וְלֹא תָתוּרוּ אַחֲרֵי לְבַבְכֶם וְאַחֲרֵי עֵינֵיכֶם אֲשֶׁר אַתֶּם זֹנִים

20

incline you to go astray;
That you may remember and do all My commandments, and be holy to your Lord.
I am God your Lord, Who brought you out of the land of Egypt, to be your Lord; I am God your Lord." Truth

The prayer leader repeats and says:
God your Lord. Truth

אַחֲרֵיהֶם:
לְמַעַן תִּזְכְּרוּ וַעֲשִׂיתֶם אֶת כָּל מִצְוֹתָי וִהְיִיתֶם קְדֹשִׁים לֵא-לֹהֵיכֶם:
אֲנִי ה' א-לֹהֵיכֶם אֲשֶׁר הוֹצֵאתִי אֶתְכֶם מֵאֶרֶץ מִצְרַיִם לִהְיוֹת לָכֶם לֵא-לֹהִים אֲנִי ה' א-לֹהֵיכֶם. אֱמֶת:

הש"ץ חוזר ואומר:
ה' א-לֹהֵיכֶם אֱמֶת:

I N THIS CHAPTER, we will examine how the prayer known as *Keriyat Shema* developed. Our journey through the story of its development will carry us to a discussion of a good number of noteworthy ideas and significant events from the pages of Jewish history that each left their mark on this liturgy. Some of these elements are actually quite remarkable, and every one of these factors is a piece of an elaborate jigsaw puzzle that needed to come together for this prayer to be what it is today.

Included here we will find a discussion of what prayer looked like before 70 C.E. and the destruction of the Second Temple. In that connection we will examine the role that *Keriyat Shema* played in ancient Jewish liturgical practice. We will also look at incontrovertible evidence that the text of this prayer is radically different today than it was in antiquity, and we will explore the ideological and philosophical battles that brought these changes into reality. As part of that discussion we will encounter other suggested alternatives to the content of *Keriyat Shema*, which were rejected, but that help us explain the changes that did occur.

A major focus of our discussion will be early Jewish mysticism and its stories of mystics – such as the famous Rabbi Akiva – journeying through the seven heavens to stand before God's throne. Those stories, and the visions of the celestial realm that these mystics included in their tales, will have a dramatic effect on *Keriyat Shema* over the centuries. This is true not only for the text of the prayer itself, but also for the choreography that surrounds it in the synagogue service. In this way the worship conducted in the synagogue will be made to look like the prayers offered by the angels in heaven.

Ultimately, we will come to understand *Keriyat Shema* from this mystical vantage point as a celebration of the human being – in all of his or her physical reality – as the greatest of God's creations. But before we get to all of that please allow for a few pages describing some basic facts about *Keriyat Shema*.

Keriyat Shema is one of the most important parts of the *Siddur* (the Jewish Prayer book). Its name means "the *reading* of the *Shema*," with *Shema* being the first word of the text to be recited. Finding a prayer with this title is surprising, because offering supplication to God is usually understood as constituting an entirely different activity than reading or studying Scriptural passages.[1] This may explain why this liturgy is often referred to colloquially, simply as *Shema*. Nonetheless, the connection between the full name and the prayer itself will emerge as we present the history of this pivotal ritual practice.

Keriyat Shema is unique in that it is the only part of the daily synagogue service understood by the Rabbis to be Biblically mandated.[2] In keeping with the Torah text found in the prayer itself that requires "speaking of the words of Torah ... when you lie down and when you get up" (וְדִבַּרְתָּ בָּם ... וּבְשָׁכְבְּךָ וּבְקוּמֶךָ), it is recited every day of the year in the morning, and again at night.[3] One should also attempt to recite this prayer as one's soul leaves this world and enters the next, according to rabbinic tradition.[4]

The first verse of *Shema* has a liturgical life all its own. It is taught to young

---

1   Cf. B. Berakhot 32b. The day to day rituals in the contemporary synagogue makes this abundantly clear. At some morning services (Sabbaths, holidays, other special days, Mondays and Thursdays), and at some afternoon prayers (Sabbaths and fast days), and (for many), *Simhat Torah* at night, a Biblical text (and sometimes two, three or more Biblical texts) are read publicly. The experience, choreography and meaning of these readings seems to be very different than the prayer rituals that precede, follow and sometimes are interspersed with the reading of these texts. *Keriyat Shema* is always part of the prayers that precede these readings and, in no way is it experienced as a "reading." Also, at the majority of services of the year, though prayers are always recited, no public reading of a Biblical text occurs. This is true, even though *Keriyat Shema* is said twice, every day of the year. Compare Siddur pp. 90–94 with pp. 142–147.

2   B. Berakhot 14a, Rabbi Moses ben Maimon (Rambam, Maimonides 1138–1204): *Sefer ha-Mitsvot*: Mitsvat Aseh #10.

3   Deuteronomy 6:7, 11:19, Maimonides, *Mishneh Torah*, Hilkhot Keriyat Shema 1:1. This is the premise behind M. Berakhot 1:1–2.

4   Based on the story of Rabbi Akiva, B. Berakhot 61b. This is actually a late tradition as Rabbi Joseph ben Ephraim Karo (1488–1575), *Shulhan Arukh* (the Code of Jewish Law), *Yoreh Deah* 338 does not include it as part of the deathbed confessional, and see Siddur p. 796.

children as one element of their initial exposure to Torah study,[5] and this sentence appears along with בָּרוּךְ שֵׁם כְּבוֹד מַלְכוּתוֹ לְעוֹלָם וָעֶד (Blessed be the Name of His glorious kingdom forever and ever) – the second line of the prayer – at the very beginning of the morning service each day.[6] It is also loudly and publicly proclaimed when taking the Torah from the ark on Sabbaths and festivals.[7] Finally, it appears on some occasions in *Kedushah*, a prayer that describes the liturgy of the angels as they serve God.[8] There is simply no more important and far-reaching a section of the prayer book than *Keriyat Shema*.

The prayer as we know it today consists – in largest measure – of three Biblical sections: Deuteronomy 6:4–9; Deuteronomy 11:13–21; and Numbers 15:37–41. Most of the people who regularly recite *Keriyat Shema* assume incorrectly that this must have been its content and structure from the time that Moses brought the Torah and its teachings to the Jewish people.

However, closer inspection of the contemporary *Shema* reveals that this picture is too simplistic. Daily Jewish prayer may be recited by an individual alone, or it may be offered (and this is preferable) in a *minyan*, a group of ten that is considered to be a community at worship.[9] These three Biblical paragraphs are introduced with a phrase [אֵ־ל מֶלֶךְ נֶאֱמָן (God the faithful King)], that does not appear in the Bible. This phrase can be found in the Talmud – but not in the context of *Keriyat Shema*.[10] These words preface the *Shema*; but only

---

5 B. Sukkah 42a.

6 Siddur p. 28. This is a very early practice. We find it in both the earliest Sefardic prayer book that we have, the Siddur (or Seder) of Rav Amram Gaon (9th century), *Birkhot ha-Shahar*, and in the earliest Ashkenazic prayer book, Rabbi Simhah of Vitry, *Mahzor Vitry* (12th century), #89. The second line does not appear in either of these early prayer books.

7 Siddur p. 436; *Mahzor Vitry*, #527.

8 See discussion below. It also is recited just before going to sleep (Siddur pp. 288–291), at the end of the *Yom Kippur* liturgy (Mahzor YK p. 762), and in *Tahanun* on Mondays and Thursdays (Siddur p. 132). In some communities it also appears at other points in the liturgy. These uses are not essential to our discussion here.

9 B. Megillah 23b and Gittin 46a. Also cf. Rabbi Aharon ben Jacob Ha-Cohen (13th–14th century; there is some doubt about the authorship), *Sefer Kolbo*, #11, that communal prayers are always heard. Traditionally, ten men are required to constitute a community (or *minyan*) at prayer.

10 See Shabbat 119b and Sanhedrin 111a. These texts see אֵ־ל מלך נֶאֱמָן as the meaning of אמן. Since אמן is normally said at the end of a prayer and אֵ־ל מֶלֶךְ נֶאֱמָן is recited at the beginning of Shema, the connection here is certainly less than obvious.

when one recites it as part of individual prayer.[11] This phrase is not said when joining a community in its devotion.

The first paragraph is also interrupted after the peripatetic first verse with *Barukh shem kevod malkhuto le-olam va-ed* (Blessed is the Name of God's glorious kingdom forever), another non-Biblical passage found first in the Mishnah – again not in a *Shema* context.[12] It is recited in an undertone, except on the Day of Atonement (*Yom Kippur*) when it is said aloud.[13] In short, these three paragraphs were *not* treated as completely inviolable over the course of Jewish liturgical history. Instead additions and modifications were made to them.

Further, the word *emet* (truth), is appended to the end of *Shema*, "borrowed" from the next paragraph of the prayers in both the nighttime and morning liturgies. The "next paragraph" in the morning is actually quite different than the "next paragraph" at night except that each begins with the word *emet*.[14]

This word then, along with the last two words of the *Shema* itself (i.e., ה' א-להיכם אמת "God, your Lord, truth"), is recited twice by the prayer leader (*shaliah tsibur*) at communal services, once silently and a second time aloud.[15] When praying in private these three words are said only once by the individual supplicant.[16]

The usual practice of the prayer leader when ending a paragraph or a liturgy is to recite the last words out loud – but that is normally his only recitation of these words. This allows him both to fulfill his own personal obligation to recite the prayer while also cuing the congregation to begin the next paragraph. Only here, in all of Jewish practice, do we find this mandated doubling of words at the end of a section by the *shaliah tsibur*.

Also, the prayer leader is normally not constrained as to how many words to recite out loud to indicate that a particular paragraph has been concluded. Here, however, the *shaliah tsibur* is expected to recite precisely these three

---

11 See Moses b. Nahman (Nahmanides 1194–1270), *Hidushei Ramban*: Berakhot 11b, who discusses the halakhic problems attendant on adding א-ל מלך נאמן at this point in the prayers.

12 M. Yoma 3:8, 4:1–2, 6:2.

13 Cf. Rabbi Yom Tov ben Avraham Ashvili (Ritva 13th–14th century). *Hidushei Ritva*: Yoma 35b,

14 Siddur p. 94 and p. 260. See B. Berakhot 12a.

15 *Shulhan Arukh: Orah Hayim* 61:3.

16 Rabbi Moses b. Israel Isserles (16th century), Rema, ad. loc.

words and only these three words.[17] This despite the fact that the original Biblical phrase, אני ה' א-להיכם – I am God, your Lord," has been all but lost in the liturgically created and grammatically difficult ה' א-להיכם אֱמֶת – God, your Lord, truth."

While all of this indicates that some historical development of the prayer did occur, none of what we have seen so far does more than touch indirectly on the three core paragraphs and their recitation. Nonetheless, the key to understanding the origin, purpose and meaning of these more peripheral alterations lies in the less obvious, but far more seismic changes that affected the body of *Keriyat Shema* itself, over the course of Jewish liturgical history.

We begin our discussion of those changes by asking three central questions that surround the early development of this prayer. What was the nature and purpose of this liturgy in its most ancient iteration? What Biblical paragraph or paragraphs served as the constituent parts of *Keriyat Shema* at the earliest point in history for which we have any record of it? If these paragraphs were not the same as the ones we have today, how did the changes occur that brought us to the text that appears in our prayer books?

To start to answer these questions we must take note of an opinion held by many contemporary scholars of Jewish liturgy. They claim that before the destruction of the Second Temple in 70 C.E., there were no formal prayers to speak of.[18] Even the "eighteen (blessings)," or *Shmoneh Esrei*, the central liturgy of each of the daily services, appears to post-date 70 as the Mishnah itself attributes the requirement for its recitation to Rabban Gamaliel II, patriarch in Yavneh after the Temple was destroyed.[19] Instead, according to these scholars, the activity of the early synagogue centered on study – specifically on Torah reading and interpretive exposition of that reading.[20]

---

17 See discussion below and the lengthy discussion of this issue in Joseph Karo. *Bet Yosef.* 61:3, and see B. Berakhot 14a-b.

18 See my dissertation, "Formalization of Individual Prayer Around the Shmoneh Esrei in the Talmudic Period; Patterns of Acceptance, Rejection and Modification," for discussion of these issues. See also Maimonides: *Mishneh Torah: Hilkhot Tefillah*: 1:1, 4. Maimonides dates the transition to a formal text to the beginning of the Second Temple period.

19 M. Berakhot 4:3.

20 Fleischer, Ezra. "Bein Arai le-Kevah bi-Tefillat ha-Rabim be-Eretz Yisrael ha-Keduma." In ed. M. Benayahu, *Rabbi Isaac Nissim Memorial Volume*, Jerusalem: 1985, 5:7–33; "Le-Kadmoniyut Tefillot ha-Hovah be-Yisrael." In *Tarbits* 59, 1990, pp. 397–441; "Tefillat Shmoneh Esrei: Iyunim be-Ofya, Sidra, Tokhana, Umagamoteha."

If this is so, calling our prayer *Keriyat Shema* may well indicate that the Torah paragraphs included in the *Shema* were part of a fixed set of Biblical texts to be studied every day (perhaps they constituted the entire set of fixed texts to be read), to which were added other passages that were particular to individual days of the liturgical calendar. These would include special readings for holidays, the new moon or the section from the regular (in those days probably triennial) Torah reading cycle.[21]

My own understanding of late second Temple era liturgical practice is somewhat different. I think we can show that the *Shmoneh Esrei* does pre-date the second Temple's destruction. Before Rabban Gamaliel, however, it was mandatory only as part of communal prayer. This was usually an activity practiced by small groups of pietists in this era. Individual prayer in this time period, on the other hand, was unstructured, and not formalized. When praying alone each individual spoke to God as he or she chose. Rabban Gamaliel's decree expanded the requirement to recite the *Shmoneh Esrei* into the realm of individual personal supplication. In other words, in the aftermath of the Temple's destruction he declared that – in addition to the community – every individual was also to recite the formal "eighteen" each day.[22]

On the other hand, *Keriyat Shema* was part of both personal and communal ritual activity even in the pre-destruction era. At that time, it served as part of daily Torah study, not as prayer per se. When the *Shmoneh Esrei* and its

In *Tarbits* 62(2), 1993, 179–223. See also Zeitlin, Solomon. *An Historical Study of the First Canonizaton of the Hebrew Liturgy*. Philadelphia: 1933; Zahavy, Tzvee. "Three Stages in the Development of Early Rabbinic Prayer." In ed. Jacob Neusner, Ernest Frerichs, Nahum Sarna, *From Ancient Israel to Modern Judaism: Intellect In Quest of Understanding: Essays in honor of Marvin Fox*, Atlanta, Georgia: 1989, 1:233–265; Elbogen, Ismar. *Jewish Liturgy: A Comprehensive History*. Philadelphia: 1993; Kugelmass, Harvey J. "Jewish Liturgy and the Emergence of the Synagogue as House of Prayer in the Post-Destruction Era." In ed. Jean-Claude Petit, *Où demeures-tu*, Quebec: 1994, pp. 289–303; Levine, Lee I. "The Development of Synagogue Liturgy in Late Antiquity." In ed. Eric M. Meyers, *Galilee Through the Centuries: Confluence of Cultures*, Winona Lake: 1999, pp. 123–144.

21   Heinemann, Joseph. "The Triennial Lectionary Cycle." In *Journal of Jewish Studies*, 19, 1968, pp. 41–48; Charnov, B.H. Shavuot. "Matan Torah and the Triennial Cycle." In *Judaism* 23, 1974, pp. 332–336; Bloom, Norman. "The Torah Reading Cycle Past and Present." In *Journal of Jewish Music and Liturgy*, 1996, 18:37–59.

22   See n. 18. The context and wording of M. Berakhot 4:3 supports this approach as do many other rabbinic sources.

supplicatory nature became part of everyone's daily liturgical reality, *Keriyat Shema* began to be treated as prayer as well. This is true according to either of the theories of the nature of prayer in late second Temple times, presented here.

The following text is particularly instructive in this regard:

A–Rabbi Ami said:	א–אמר רבי אמי:
B–From the words of Rabbi Jose we learn	ב–מדבריו של רבי יוסי נלמוד,
C–Even though a man learns but one chapter [of the Torah] in the morning and one chapter in the evening	ג–אפילו לא שנה אדם אלא פרק אחד שחרית ופרק אחד ערבית,
D–He has fulfilled the precept of "This book of the law shall not depart out of your mouth."[23]	ד–קיים מצות לא ימוש ספר התורה הזה מפיך.
E–Rabbi Johanan said in the name of Rabbi Simeon b. Yohai,	ה–אמר רבי יוחנן משום רבי שמעון בן יוחי:
F–Even though a man only reads the *Shema* morning and evening	ו–אפילו לא קרא אדם אלא קרית שמע שחרית וערבית
G–He has thereby fulfilled the precept of "[This book of the law] shall not depart."[24]	ז–קיים לא ימוש

In this teaching Rabbi Simeon b. Yohai, who lived some eighty or so years after the destruction of the Temple, evokes the – for him – older practice of treating *Keriyat Shema* as Torah study, even though it was part of daily supplication in his time. Nonetheless, in his opinion it can still be used for its original purpose, even after it had taken on this new liturgical reality.

One can find other rabbinic comments that retain an understanding of *Shema* as Torah study.[25] But the common view today is that it is part of the prayers. The fact that it is recited by the Cantor and the congregation, and not by the Torah Reader – from a *Siddur,* and not from a Torah scroll – certainly supports that point of view.

---

23 Joshua 1:8.

24 B. Menahot 99b.

25 Cf. B. Berakhot 10b. See Tabory, Joseph. "Prayers and Berakhot." In ed, Shmuel Safrai, *The Literature of the Sages II*, Philadelphia: 2006, pp. 290–291 for a source in the Letter of Aristeas that speaks of "meditating on the ordinances of God on going to bed and on rising." Tabory also finds something similar in the Dead Sea Scrolls, p 292. He also cites references to twice-daily prayer in Philo, Josephus and the Dead Sea Scrolls.

The name *Keriyat Shema* reflects the older understanding of the ritual. That name was retained even when the liturgy was no longer understood to serve primarily as a Scriptural reading.[26] This is an important indication that whichever approach to the early history of prayer is correct, it is certainly true that our understanding of the nature and purpose of the *Shema* paragraphs has changed over time.[27]

One of our earliest rabbinic texts strongly supports this suggested history of the changing liturgical understanding of *Keriyat Shema*. This text is found in a Mishnah that describes the daily sacrificial service in the Temple (the *Beit ha-Mikdash*). It tells of the priests, their study and liturgical behavior in that venue, and it will carry us into the next stage of our discussion in dramatic fashion.

The text reads:

A–The superintendent said to them [the priests in the Temple]:	א–אמר להם הממונה:
B–Recite one blessing,	ב–ברכו ברכה אחת
C–And they did so	ג–והן ברכו
D–*Read*: the Ten Commandments, the first, second and third paragraphs of the *Shema*,	ד–קראו: עשרת הדברים שמע והיה אם שמוע ויאמר
E–Bless the people with three benedictions;	ה–ברכו את העם שלש ברכות:
F–True and firm, *Avodah* and the priestly benedictions.[28]	ו–אמת ויציב ועבודה וברכות כהנים

Comparing contemporary practice with this text reveals both similarities and differences. *Keriyat Shema,* which is certainly understood here as part of a Biblical reading and not as a supplication, is preceded in this Mishnah by an introductory blessing. Current practice, already described elsewhere in the

---

26 A similar phenomenon can be found in regard to the *Tahanun* supplication, which retains the name *Nefilat Apayim* (falling on one's face), despite the fact that no one today follows the custom of prostrating oneself on the ground when reciting this prayer, Siddur p. 132. See Gartner, J. *Ha-Hatayah be-Nifilat Apayim be-Tefillah*. Sinai, 122, 1998, pp. 94–112, who traces the history of the body position to use when reciting this prayer from the time when prostrating oneself was in use.

27 Another supportive passage is M. Berakhot 2:1 where Torah reading and study are equated with recitation of the *Shema*.

28 M. Tamid 5:1. For discussion of this text in terms similar to my understanding of it see Tabory, p. 290f.

Mishnah, is to recite two such introductory benedictions.[29] These blessings speak of God's two revelations. The first (the blessing that ends, יוֹצֵר הַמְּאוֹרוֹת – Who creates the lights [in the sky] in our contemporary liturgy) focuses on nature and creation through which humankind is able to know God in the same way that the artist is known through his paintings or the sculptor through his sculptures.[30] The second revelation is embodied in God's Torah, the ultimate source of Jewish law and teaching. This revelation is celebrated in the second benediction (the blessing that today concludes with הַבּוֹחֵר בְּעַמּוֹ יִשְׂרָאֵל בְּאַהֲבָה – "He who chooses His nation Israel with love").[31]

Later Rabbinic sources debate which one of these two blessings the Priests actually recited.[32] But either – and particularly the second one – could easily serve as a lead-in to the reading of a series of Biblical texts.[33] These texts would either illustrate the revelation of God's Torah that is praised in the second benediction, or complement and supplement the revelation through nature praised in the first blessing.

Moving to the end of the citation: the priestly *Keriyat Shema* is followed by the same paragraph that comes after the contemporary morning *Shema* that begins with the word "truth" and speaks of God's steadfastness, and by two items that appear in some fashion in the current *Shmoneh Esrei* – the priestly blessing, and the *Avodah*. The latter is similar to the paragraph in our contemporary liturgy that begins with the word *retsei* (probably best translated as "accept"), which asks God to look favorably on what has been offered to Him.[34] While the former, which represents fulfillment of the Biblical command that the priests bless the people, is really its own free-standing ritual, though it has now been incorporated into the communal repetition of the "eighteen,"[35] the rest – and much larger part – of the *Shmoneh Esrei* does not appear here.

---

29 M. Berakhot 1:4.

30 Siddur p. 88.

31 Siddur pp. 88–91. For a discussion of this blessing and of the blessing that follows *Keriyat Shema* see Liebreich, Leon J. "The Benediction Immediately Preceding and the One Following the Recital of the Shema." In *Revue des Etudes Juives* 125, 1966, pp. 151–165.

32 B. Berakhot 11b-12a.

33 See B. Berakhot 11b, that this benediction can replace the daily ברכת התורה (the blessing of the Torah), that is to be said before one begins Torah study each day, Siddur p. 16.

34 Siddur p. 110.

35 Siddur p. 116, Numbers 6:22–27. On holidays in the diaspora, when the priests actually

These three items are described in the Mishnah as "blessings" directed by the priests at the community. While the Priestly Blessings retain that function today, the other two elements are supplications offered by the people to God in the contemporary liturgy. This again indicates that parts of the early morning ritual took on new identities when the Temple was destroyed and the liturgy was restructured in its aftermath. The change from *Keriyat Shema* as a Biblical reading to *Shema* as a supplication is part of this historical development, and we see it reflected in this citation from the Mishnah.

The central part of this text is the most important for our analysis. There is a *Keriyat Shema* described here, but it has *four* paragraphs – the three that we know plus the Ten Commandments (*Aseret ha-Dibrot* or *Aseret ha-Devarim*).[36] As indicated, these paragraphs constitute a reading and not a supplication. In fact nothing in this text is called a prayer or supplication. There are only blessings and readings.

This source tells us that even the body of the *Shema* was not inviolate having once contained the *Aseret ha-Dibrot*. There is some archeological evidence for this connection between *Shema* and the Ten Commandments. One of the important Second Temple era documents that we possess is called the Nash Papyrus. It was acquired by W. L. Nash in Egypt in 1898. A fragment of this artifact contains two Biblical paragraphs: the Ten Commandments and the beginning of the first paragraph of the *Shema* (Deuteronomy 6:4–9, this paragraph is itself called *Shema* because of its first word). Scholars now date the Nash Papyrus to approximately 150–100 B.C.E. It has long been assumed to be a liturgical document that reflects some iteration of the service described in the Mishnah that we are discussing.[37] It, therefore, provides evidence for what part of *Keriyat Shema* looked like in the second Temple period.

The second piece of archeological evidence comes from the *tefillin* (phylacteries) worn on the head (*tefillin shel rosh*) found by Yigal Yadin at Qumran, the

---

bless the people, this section is expanded though it is still part of the repetition of the *Amidah*, Siddur pp. 694–701.

36 Exodus 20:2–13 and Deuteronomy 5:6–17. The two texts have some differences in how they are worded.

37 Burkitt, F. C. "The Hebrew Papyrus of the Ten Commandments." In *The Jewish Quarterly Review*, 1903, 15, pp. 392–408; Albright, William F. "A Biblical Fragment from the Maccabean Age: The Nash Papyrus." In *Journal of Biblical Literature* 56, 1937, p. 145–176.

site where the Dead Sea Scrolls were discovered.[38] Contemporary head *tefillin* consist of leather boxes divided into four compartments that each contain a Biblical portion written on parchment. Following the order of the Torah, these four sections are Exodus 13:1–10; 13:11–16, and Deuteronomy 6:4–9; 11:13–21.[39] The last two are the same as the first two paragraphs of the contemporary *Shema*.

Yadin found an ancient *tefillin shel rosh* in which three of the original four portions remained. However, unlike contemporary *tefillin* parchments which contain only the requisite Torah section, these texts have additional Biblical verses both before and after the Biblical paragraph that serve, apparently, to highlight and expand on the themes of the portion.

Interestingly, above the *Shema* paragraph, among these "supportive" verses in the *tefillin* found by Yadin, are the Ten Commandments. This is apparently another indication of the ancient connection between *Shema* and the *Aseret ha-Dibrot*.

There may yet be one more artifact related to the Ten Commandments that remains on the contemporary *tefillin*. The head *tefillin* bear the Hebrew letter *shin* [ש] on two sides of the leather box. On one side this is a normal *shin*, with three heads ש. On the other side, however, the *shin* appears this way, with four heads ש.[40] My sainted teacher, Rabbi Joseph Dov Soloveitchik zt"l, theorized that the *shin* can be found here in the three indentations and not in the four areas that protrude. In this way, said Rabbi Soloveitchik, this *shin* symbolizes the carving of the Ten Commandments on the two tablets of stone given to Moses at Sinai.

If, as we shall see shortly, the Ten Commandments were removed from the *Shema* (and possibly from the *Shema* section of the *tefillin*) because of ideological challenges, it would not be surprising to find a symbolic remnant that served to recall their original presence in these important rituals of Jewish life. Perhaps that reminder can be found in the unique and unusual four-headed shin.

We have now introduced a truly remarkable idea: that the very presence of the Ten Commandments in the *Shema* somehow created an ideological problem that forced their removal from the liturgy. Our next source from B.

---

38   Yadin, Yigael. *Tefillin from Qumran* (X Q Phyl 1–4), Jerusalem: 1969.

39   Cf. Kaplan, Aryeh. *Tefillin: G-d, Man and Tefillin*. New York: National Conference of Synagogue Youth, 1973.

40   Naiman, Mosheh Hanina and Oratz, Dovid. *Tefillin: An Illustrated Guide*. New York: 1995, p. 37.

Berakhot 12a not only supports that suggestion, it tells us that the defenders of the Ten Commandments put up a multi-generational fight to keep them as part of *Keriyat Shema*, only to eventually be defeated in their quest.

A–They read the Ten Commandments, the first, second and third paragraphs of the *Shema*, true and firm, *Avodah* and the priestly benediction.[41]	א–וקורין עשרת הדברות שמע והיה אם שמוע ויאמר אמת ויציב ועבודה וברכת כהנים.
B–Rav Judah said in the name of Samuel:	ב–אמר רב יהודה אמר שמואל:
C–Even outside the Temple they wanted to do the same [to say the Ten Commandments as part of the *Shema*],	ג–אף בגבולין בקשו לקרות כן,
D–But they were previously *abolished* because of the slander of the *Minim* [sectarians].	ד–אלא שכבר בטלום מפני תרעומת המינין.
E–Similarly it has been taught:	ה–תניא נמי הכי,
F–Rabbi Nathan says:	ו–רבי נתן אומר:
G–They sought to do the same outside the Temple,	ז–בגבולין בקשו לקרות כן,
H–But they had previously *been abolished* because of the slander of the *Minim*.	ח–אלא שכבר בטלום מפני תרעומת המינין.
I–Rabbah b. Bar Hanah thought of re-instituting this in Sura,	ט–רבה בר בר חנה סבר למקבעינהו בסורא,
J–But Rav Hisda said to him:	י–אמר ליה רב חסדא:
K–They had previously *been abolished* because of the slander of the *Minim*.	כ–כבר בטלום מפני תרעומת המינין.
L–Amemar thought of re-instituting it in Nehardea,	ל–אמימר סבר למקבעינהו בנהרדעא,
M–But Rav Ashi said to him:	מ–אמר ליה רב אשי:
N–They had previously *been abolished* because of the slander of the *Minim*.	נ–כבר בטלום מפני תרעומת המינין.

It is important to recognize that all of the names cited in this source are Babylonian. Chronologically they range from Rabbi Nathan (c. 150 C.E.) who lived in the next-to-last *Tannaitic* generation (the era of the Mishnah, which was redacted in approximately 200 C.E.), through Amemar (c. mid-5th century C.E.), who was part of the sixth *Amoraic* generation (the era of the Gemarah,

---

41   Citing M. Tamid 5:1 discussed above.

which was completed sometime between 600 and 800 C.E.) – covering a period of nearly 500 years.

There are no Palestinian sources from any point in the Talmudic era that indicate any resistance at all to removing the Ten Commandments from *Keriyat Shema*. This strongly suggests that the problem, whatever it was, occurred and was confronted in Palestine where the decision was reached to delete the Ten Commandments from the daily readings. On the other hand, the Babylonians, who apparently did not have first-hand experience with these sectarian challenges, struggled unsuccessfully to resist this profound change in religious practice.

But who were these sectarians, and what was their "slander"? The Babylonian Talmud (or Bavli) is silent on both of these questions while the Jerusalem Talmud responds only to the second one.

A–Said Rabbi Ba:	א–אמר רב בא
B–From here one can understand nothing else but	ב–אין מן הדא לית ש"מ כלום
C–That the Ten Commandments	ג–שעשרת הדברות הן הן גופה
are the very essence of *Shema*.	של שמע
D–For Rav Matnah and Rabbi	ד–דרב מתנה ורבי שמואל בר
Samuel b. Nahman both said:	נחמן אמר תרויהון אמרין
E–Logically we should read the Ten	ה–בדין הוה שיהו קורין עשרת
Commandments every day.	הדיברות בכל יום
F–But why don't we read them,	ו–ומפני מה אין קורין אותן
G–Because of the claims of the *Minim*	ז–מפני טענת המינין
H–So that they not say	ח–שלא יהו אומרין
I–Only these were given to Moses at Sinai.[42]	ט–אלו לבדם ניתנו לו למשה
	בסיני

This text tells us that the Ten Commandments were once considered the essence of the *Shema* (גופה של שמע), and were to be read every day. It also shows us that the claim that God's revelation at Sinai was quite limited was taken as a very serious threat to normative belief when it was raised. Only a truly dangerous and dynamic challenge could possibly lead to the "essence of the *Shema*" being removed from the prayer in this way. Given that conclusion

---

42   J. Berakhot 1:5 (3c).

we should date the challenge, and the change in the liturgy, to a period when such a claim would have posed a significant theological problem.

One small digression to an incorrect identification of our "dangerous" sectarians is in order at this time. It comes from Rashi's commentary to the text from B. Berakhot 12a discussed above, as it appears in some talmudic manuscripts. Unfortunately, this reading was censored from our printed editions. We will cite both the uncensored text and a second important comment by Rashi to B. Tamid 32b concerning the presence of the Ten Commandments in *Keriyat Shema*.

Says Rashi:

A–They wanted – To establish the Ten Commandments as part of *Keriyat Shema*	א–בקשו – לקבוע עשרת הדברות בקריאת שמע.
B–Because of the slander of the Sectarians – that they not say to the common people, "The rest of the Torah is not true."	ב–מפני תרעומת המינין – שלא יאמרו לעמי הארץ: אין שאר תורה אמת,
C–And you should know that they read only what God said that they [actually] heard from His mouth at Sinai.	ג–ותדעו שאין קורין אלא מה שאמר הקדוש ברוך הוא ושמעו מפיו בסיני.
D–The Sectarians – Idolators	ד–המינין – עכו"ם
E–[Deletion of the censor]: The students of Jesus.	ה–השמטת הצנזורה: תלמידי ישו

And then in the second comment he says:

A–And when they said: Read the Ten Commandments every day	א–ומה שאמרו קראו עשרת הדברות בכל יום
B–Because they are the essence of the faith and its beginning.	ב–לפי שהם עיקר הדת וראשיתו
C–And they also had already said:	ג–וכבר אמרו
D–Even outside the Temple they wanted to do the same,	ד–בגבולים בקשו לומר כן
E–But they were previously *abolished* because of the slander of the *Minim* [sectarians].[43]	ה–אלא שכבר בטלום מפני תרעומת המינין
F–But the Babylonian Talmud does not	ו–ולא באר הבבלי מה היא

---

43   Citing B. Berakhot 12a.

explain what the slander of the Minim is,   תרעומת המינין

G–However it is explained in the beginning of   ז–אלא שנתבאר בתחלת ברכות

tractate Berakhot in the Jerusalem Talmud: בירושלמי

H–They said: Logically we should read the   ח–ואמרו בדין היה שקורין

Ten Commandments every single day.   עשרת הדברות בכל יום ויום

I–But why don't we read them?   ט–אלא מפני מה אין קורין

    אותם

J–Because of the *Minim*   י–מפני המינין

K–So that they not say only these alone   כ–שלא יהיו אומרים אלו לבדם

were given to Moses at Sinai.   ניתנו למשה מסיני

Rashi here provides an even stronger reason for inclusion of the Ten Commandments in *Keriyat Shema*. They are the *"essence and beginning of the Jewish faith"* and, therefore, appropriately, should be read (or recited) each day. Whether in the era when *Shema* was considered mandatory Torah study, or in an era when it is seen as requisite prayer, the Ten Commandments would seem to belong in *Keriyat Shema*. Again, only the strongest of concerns could lead to their removal.

The censored text of Rashi blames the early Christians for having created the climate in which the Ten Commandments were displaced, but that is unlikely to be true. We have no record of any group of early Christians claiming only a limited Biblical revelation. In fact, the founder of Christianity claims in the Christian Bible to have come "not to change one jot or one tittle of the law."[44] Further, Christians saw themselves as heirs to the entire Biblical revelation that, for them, served to predict the coming of their Messiah and with him a new covenant or testament.[45] Undermining the "old" revelation in this way would not help their cause. It would remove most of the claimed "Old

---

44 Mathew 5:18. Kimelman, Reuven. "The Shema Liturgy: from Covenant Ceremony to Coronation." In *Kenishta* 1, 2001, p. 213, n. 4 proves the point that Christians did not take this position. His mention of one group that claimed that the Ten Commandments would have been the totality of the law had the sin of the Golden Calf not occurred – despite his suggestion to the contrary – does not meet the criteria here. Even this group saw all the commandments as Divine, they just saw most of them as being part of a post-Golden Calf second revelation.

45 Cf. Nicole, Roger. "New Testament Use of the Old Testament." In Carl. F.H. Henry ed., *Revelation and the Bible*. Grand Rapids: 1958, pp. 137–151.

Testament" proofs for Christianity from consideration as they would no longer be considered Divinely revealed.

The more likely candidates to be the sectarians mentioned here are the Hellenized Jews who were the opponents of the Maccabees, the Pharisees, and later of the Rabbis.[46] Greek philosophy had trouble accepting the possibility of any personal interaction between God and human beings such as prophetic revelation – God was simply too far removed and too sublime for such things.[47] Limiting Divine revelation as much as possible would, therefore, serve the ideological interests of Jewish Hellenizers as it would bring Jewish thought more in line with Greek philosophy.

Further, if only the Ten Commandments were from God, then circumcision and *kashrut* (kosher food restrictions) – problematic areas in the confrontation between Jews and Greeks – would not fall in the category of Divinely revealed law.[48] As such these areas of ritual performance could more easily be ignored. That again would support the agenda of the Hellenizers, who wanted to subscribe to Greek ideas of the beauty of the body in its natural state, and who wanted to take part in Greek feasts where pork was a staple.

This confrontation between Hellenizing Jews trying to create a Judaism more in line with Greek thought and practice, and more traditionalist-minded Jews – who wanted to maintain their ancestral customs – was the central catalyst in the Maccabean revolt. The Hasmonean (or traditionalist) victory in that conflict is celebrated on *Hanukah*.

If we date the removal of the Ten Commandments to some time in the early part of the reign of the Maccabees (164–63 B.C.E.)[49] that would make it early enough in historic time, central enough to the national memory of the Jewish people, and Palestinian enough in its location to explain why some later Babylonian authorities (dating from the mid-second to the mid-fifth century C.E.) might have tried to reverse the decision to remove the Ten

---

46 Cf. Bickerman, Elias. *The God of the Maccabees: Studies on the Meaning and Origin of the Maccabean Revolt.* Leiden, 1979; Kampen, John. *The Hasideans and the Origin of Pharisaism: a Study in 1 and 2 Maccabees.* Atlanta: 1988.

47 Cf. Kenny, Anthony. *The God of the Philosophers.* Oxford, 1979.

48 Gruen, Erich. *Diaspora: Jews Amidst Greeks and Romans.* Cambridge: 2002, p. 51.

49 These are the years when the Hasmoneans or Maccabees were in power. The war that led to the rededication of the Temple began in 167 B.C.E. with the actual rededication of the Temple occurring several years later.

Commandments from *Keriyat Shema*, but also why they were unsuccessful in doing so.

On the other hand, an anti-Christian liturgical change, as suggested by the uncensored text of Rashi, would have been unlikely to strike such deep roots in Babylonian soil where there was no Christian presence in the Talmudic period, and where the need to combat Christianity's influence was likely to be too new and too unfamiliar to command communal loyalty. The Babylonian reaction to an actual Christian challenge to the liturgy that we will encounter below offers strong support for what we have said here.

Having done our best to determine both the philosophical and historical underpinnings of the removal of the Ten Commandments from *Keriyat Shema*, we still must explore the question of what exactly was the content of the original recitation. While the Mishnah cited above tells us that the three paragraphs that we know today were present in the Temple along with the Ten Commandments, that source may only reflect the final stage in the development of *Keriyat Shema* as recited in the *Beit ha-Mikdash*, and not its earlier history.

In truth, from across the centuries, Jewish texts present several different possibilities as to the original formulation of the *Shema*. For example, two relatively late sources read as follows:

A–And thus said Rabbi Jose b. Durmaskit in the name of Rabbi Akiva:	א–והכי אמר רבי יוחנן בן נורי אמר רבי יוסי בן דורמסקית, משמיה דרבי עקיבא,
B–The early pious ones decreed *Keriyat Shema* in place of the Ten Commandments.[50]	ב–חסידים הראשונים תקנו קריאת שמע כנגד עשרת הדברות.
A–Rabbi Hiyya b. Abba said:	א–אמר רבי חייא בר אבא
B–Anyone who fulfills *Keriyat Shema*,	ב–כל המקיים קריאת שמע
C–It is as if he fulfilled the Ten Commandments	ג–כאלו קיים עשרת הדברות
D–For the Ten Commandments were given at the time that *Keriyat Shema* [is to be recited].	ד–שבשעת קריאת שמע נתנו עשרת הדברות.

---

50 Zohar Hadash: *Midrash Ruth*: 2:30b, New York: 1981. The text was composed (or revealed according to some) in the 13th century.

E–The Sages wished to establish the Ten Commandments in *Keriyat Shema* (presumably after they had been removed, or else this would contradict the earlier sources cited above)	ה–בקשו חכמים לקבוע עשרת הדברות בקריאת שמע,
F–And why did they not establish them?	ו–ומפני מה לא קבעום
G–Because they are all included in them . . . (What follows is a series of parallels drawn between each of the Ten Commandments and a phrase in *Keriyat Shema*.)[51]	ז–לפי שכולם כלולים בו:

These sources suggest that originally only the Ten Commandments were read, later to be replaced by the three paragraphs that are presently recited. Within the *Beit ha-Mikdash* a combination of both practices then became the rule. However, these sources are late, coming from the medieval period long after talmudic times, and as such are not our most reliable witnesses.

The most likely early history of the *Shema* is embodied in this passage from the Jerusalem Talmud:

A–For what reason do we read these *two* portions each day?	א–מפני מה קורין שתי פרשיות הללו בכל יום
B–Rabbi Levi and Rabbi Siman,	ב–ר' לוי ור' סימון
C–Rabbi Siman said: Because lying down and rising up [nighttime and morning, the times when *Shema* is recited] are mentioned in them.	ג–ר' סימון אמר מפני שכתוב בהן שכיבה וקימה
D–Rabbi Levi said: Because the Ten Commandments are included in them.[52]	ד–ר' לוי אמר מפני שעשרת הדברות כלולין בהן

The two portions referred to here are Deuteronomy 6:4–9 (that begins with the words *Shema Yisrael* – "hear, Israel," and represents the Jew's acceptance of the authority of God's rule), and Deuteronomy 11:13–21 (that commences with *Ve-Haya Im Shamoa* – "and it will be if you shall listen," which offers the promise of reward for obedience to God's word and punishment for violation of it), both of which mention "lying down and rising up." These words do not appear in the current third paragraph that we will refer to as the *Tsitsit* para-

---

51   Eisenstein, Judah. *Otsar ha-Midrashim*. Tel Aviv: 1969, *Pesikta* p. 489.
52   J. Berakhot 1:5 (3c).

graph. This source would, therefore, indicate that the original *Keriyat Shema* included *Shema, Ve-Haya* and the Ten Commandments. We will find a good deal of additional textual support for this conclusion as we proceed.

Before examining that evidence we will analyze the ideological implications of this suggested structure for *Keriyat Shema*. Thematically speaking this arrangement makes a great deal of sense. If what we say here is correct and if we include the introductory blessings and the paragraph that follows the *Shema* discussed above, the ritual would then have the following structure: a blessing evoking God's revelation to the world through creation and nature; a blessing evoking God's revelation to the Jewish people through Torah; the Ten Commandments – the first or central statement of that second revelation; the *Shema* paragraph in which the supplicant accepts the authority of God's rule, revelation and laws; and *Ve-Haya Im Shamoa*, which promises reward for adhering to God's commandments and warns of punishments if one fails to do so. This is then followed by a declaration that this is all true and in place (אֱמֶת וְיַצִּיב – true and steadfast).[53] The liturgy then concludes with a blessing not yet discussed, that speaks of perhaps the prototypical example of the benefits that accrue to the Jewish people because of their relationship with God – the emergence of the people as a nation at the Exodus from Egypt (גָּאַל יִשְׂרָאֵל – "Who redeemed Israel.")[54] In this way *Keriyat Shema* and its attendant liturgies would truly be a recitation of the essence of what it means to be a believing and committed Jew – which appears to have been its fundamental purpose.

Looking at *Keriyat Shema* in this way challenges the presence of the current third paragraph. This section, like many parts of the Bible, evokes the Exodus, but also has a strong focus on *Tsitsit* (the fringes of a four-cornered garment), which would seem not to be thematically relevant to *Keriyat Shema* at all. In keeping with Rashi's comment concerning *Keriyat Shema*, one would be looking for a section that embodies "the essence of the faith and its origins." This is an appropriate description for the Ten Commandments. It also fits the two paragraphs that focus on accepting God's authority and the doctrine of reward and punishment. These are certainly foundational principles of Judaism.

On the other hand, there does not seem to be anything specific about *Tsitsit*

---

53 The nighttime paragraph similarly speaks of all of this as being "true and faithful." Faith is a characteristic that is necessary in the dark, while steadfastness is visible during the day B. Berakhot 12a.

54 Siddur p. 96.

or about the *Tsitsit* paragraph that appears to advance the supposed agenda of *Keriyat Shema* any more than many other Biblical texts. While *Tsitsit* is an important commandment, it does not intuitively seem more foundational than many other aspects of Judaism. It therefore seems most reasonable to conclude that the original structure for *Keriyat Shema* was the Ten Commandments, *Shema* and *Ve-Haya Im Shamoa*, with Numbers 15:37–41 being added only after sectarian claims forced the traditionalist leadership to remove the Ten Commandments from the recitation.

Further indication that the third or *Tsitsit* paragraph is a later addition comes from this well-known Mishnah.

A–The Exodus from Egypt is to be mentioned [in *Keriyat Shema*] at nighttime.	א-מזכירין יציאת מצרים בלילות
B–Said Rabbi Eleazar b. Azariah:	ב-אמר רבי אלעזר בן עזריה
C–Behold I am about seventy years old,	ג-הרי אני כבן שבעים שנה
D–And I have never been worthy to [find a reason] why the Exodus from Egypt should be mentioned at nighttime	ד-ולא זכיתי שתאמר יציאת מצרים בלילות
E–Until Ben Zoma expounded it:	ה-עד שדרשה בן זומא
F–For it says:	ו-שנאמר
G–"That you may remember the day when you left the land of Egypt *all* the days of your life."	ז-למען תזכור את יום צאתך מארץ מצרים כל ימי חייך
H–"The days of your life" indicates [only] the days;	ח-ימי חייך הימים
I–But "*all* the days of your life" indicates the nights [as well].	ט-כל ימי חייך הלילות
J–But the Sages say:	י-וחכמים אומרים
K–"The days of your life" indicates this world;	כ-ימי חייך העולם הזה
L–But "*all* the days of your life" brings this into the next world.[55]	ל-כל ימי חייך להביא לימות המשיח:

Though some may remember this text from the Passover *Haggadah*, this Mishnah actually comes from the discussion of *Keriyat Shema* found in tractate

---

55 M. Berakhot 1:5. Some suggest that Josephus's statement (Antiquities 4:7:13: ln. 212), requiring that the Jews offer thanks for the Exodus from Egypt in the morning and at night is a reference to the *Tsitsit* paragraph and to *Keriyat Shema*. I do not find Josephus's statement explicit enough to make that leap, though the dating (Josephus lived from 37C.E.–c.100C.E.) would fit nicely, particularly if he were highlighting

Berakhot. It records a late first- or early second-century C.E. (post-second Temple destruction), discussion of whether the *Tsitsit* paragraph should be recited in the nighttime reading of the *Shema* or only in the morning.

Apparently Rabbi Eleazar b. Azariah was unsure of what to do, while Ben Zoma and the Sages were in debate on this question. If this was still an issue that had not been settled at this late date, it is reasonable to suggest that this was because the *Tsitsit* paragraph was a relatively recent addition to the liturgy as far as Rabbi Eleazar b. Azariah, Ben Zoma and the Sages were concerned. If so, then it was a relative latecomer to *Keriyat Shema* which, as we have seen, is much older.

We can take a major step forward in our discussion with our next source that tells us that before the *Tsitsit* paragraph, a very different Biblical section was a candidate for inclusion in *Keriyat Shema*.

The Babylonian Talmud, Berakhot 12b reads:

A–Rabbi Abbahu b. Zutrathi said in the name of Rabbi Judah b. Zebida:	א–אמר רבי אבהו בן זוטרתי אמר רבי יהודה בר זבידא:
B–They wanted to include the section of *Balak*[56] in *Keriyat Shema*,	ב–בקשו לקבוע פרשת בלק בקריאת שמע,
C–But why did they not do so?	ג–ומפני מה לא קבעוה?
D–Because it would have meant too great a burden for the congregation [because it is too long] ...	ד–משום טורח צבור ...
E–Why [did they want to insert it]? ...	ה–מאי טעמא? ...
F–Said Rabbi Jose b. Abin:	ו–אמר רבי יוסי בר אבין:
G–[The reason is] because it contains this verse:	ז–משום דכתיב בה האי קרא:
H–"He couched, he lay down as a lion, and as a lioness; who shall rouse him up?"[57] (The reason is that it mentions lying down and rising up – the times when *Shema* is recited.)[58]	ח–כרע שכב כארי וכלביא מי יקימנו.
I–Let us then say this one verse and no more?	ט–ולימא האי פסוקא ותו לא?
J–We have a tradition:	י–גמירי:

the requirement to mention the Exodus because it was a relatively new custom. Cf. Cohen, Shaye. *From the Maccabees to the Mishnah*. Louisville: 2006, p. 69.

56   Numbers 22–24.

57   Numbers 24:9.

58   See J Berakhot 1:5, 3(c) discussed above.

K–That every section which our master, Moses, has divided off	כ–כל פרשה דפסקה משה רבינו
L–We may divide off,	ל–פסקינן,
M–But that which our master, Moses, has not divided off,	מ–דלא פסקה משה רבינו
N–We may not divide off (this refers to the breaks in the text and excludes the divisions into chapters and verses).[59]	נ–לא פסקינן
O–Why did they include the section of *Tsitsit*? ...	ס–פרשת ציצית מפני מה קבעוה? ...

Apparently the first reaction of the Sages to the removal of the Ten Commandments from *Keriyat Shema* was to replace them with Numbers 22–24.[60] This Biblical section tells the story of King Balak of Moab's frustrated attempt to hire Bilam, the evil prophet, to curse the Jewish people. The story culminates, after two attempts at uttering such curses were transformed by God into blessings, with Bilam himself choosing to bless the Jews – a blessing that begins with the well-known phrase, מה טבו אהליך יעקב ("How goodly are your tents, Jacob ...").[61]

The three Biblical chapters that tell this story have no section breaks that would allow for reading only part of the text, and taken together they are rather lengthy. As such it was felt that it would impose too much of a burden on the community for *Parshat Balak* to become part of a twice-daily mandatory

---

59 This seems to be violated by the many uses of just the first verse of *Shema* in the liturgy, see discussion towards the end of this chapter. This may mean that at the point in time when the Ten Commandments were removed, reciting only entire paragraphs was the accepted practice, and that later, a different opinion held sway. Or – and this is more likely – it may be that this discussion dates from the era when *Shema* was seen as Scriptural reading and study. As such only a complete section could be used. When *Shema* began to be used in prayer, borrowing a single line from its text, or even interrupting its text to add a response to the first line as discussed below, became acceptable.

60 See Sifrei: Deuteronomy 34:7, that Exodus 13:1–10 and 11–16 were also considered as candidates for inclusion in *Keriyat Shema*. This section is a post-facto hermeneutic rationalization of why *Keriyat Shema* existed as it did when this text was written, and not as Kimelman, loc. cit., pp. 9–105 suggests, an indication of the triumph of *Shema* over the decalogue.

61 Numbers 24:5.

recitation and, so, this suggestion was rejected.[62] Subsequently, as indicated in this source, the *Tsitsit* paragraph was included in *Keriyat Shema* and it became a permanent part of the ritual. This process – that begins with the removal of the Ten Commandments and ends with the acceptance of the *Tsitsit* paragraph and the determination of whether it is to be recited at night or only in the morning – may have taken many years to complete. Our available evidence suggests removal of the Ten Commandments in the Hasmonean era, an attempt to add *Parshat Balak* shortly thereafter, acceptance of the *Tsitsit* paragraph some decades before the Temple's destruction, and the final decision that it be recited at night in the early 2nd century C.E.

But why was the story of Balak and Bilam suggested in the first place? What recommends its becoming part of a set of readings that speak of fundamental Jewish beliefs? How does it respond to the sectarian challenge that led to the removal of the Ten Commandments from *Keriyat Shema*? And how can it help us understand why the *Tsitsit* paragraph was eventually accepted, when it, too, comes with these same challenges to its inclusion? The answers to these questions are not immediately obvious from the story of the King and the evil prophet.

We can see that the Babylonian Talmud itself struggles with these or similar concerns when it asks, "Why [did they want to insert it]?" The portion of this source that deals with this question was abbreviated above for the sake of easier comprehension. The complete text is necessary here and it reads:

A–Why [did they want to insert it]?	א–מאי טעמא?
B–If you want to say, because it contains the words	ב–אילימא משום דכתיב בה:
C–"God Who brought them forth out of Egypt,"	ג–א־ל מציאם ממצרים
D–Then let us say the section of usury or of weights	ד–לימא פרשת רבית ופרשת משקלות
E–In which the going forth from Egypt is [also] mentioned?	ה–דכתיב בהן יציאת מצרים?
F–Said Rabbi Jose b. Abin:	ו–אמר רבי יוסי בר אבין:
G–Because it contains this verse:	ז–משום דכתיב בה האי קרא:
H–"He couched, he lay down as a lion, and as a lioness; who shall rouse him up?"	ח–כרע שכב כארי וכלביא מי יקימנו.

---

62   For discussion of this concept see, Encyclopedia Talmudit, Jerusalem: 1947 (and ongoing), vol. 20, sv. *tirha de-tsibuta*.

The initial suggestion is that reference to the Exodus from Egypt in the *Balak* chapters led to the proposal that it be included in *Keriyat Shema*. The Exodus is, after all, the founding moment of the Jews as a people, and the embodiment of the belief that God involves Himself in the historic process on behalf of the children of Israel. However, many Biblical portions include such a reference, so why not choose them? This is the same question we asked in relation to the *Tsitsit* paragraph above. This source then concludes that this Biblical section was preferred because of an oblique reference to lying down and rising up – the points in time each day when the *Shema* is to be recited.

With due respect to this source, on its face, it is somewhat difficult to understand. The reference to lying down and rising up in the *Balak* story is very different from the way the same idea is evoked in *Shema* and in *Ve-Haya Im Shamoa*. In the *Keriyat Shema* paragraphs these actions appear as part of the central imperative of these texts; that the words that God has commanded be part of our conversation in many different venues and at many different times. That can easily be understood to refer to *Keriyat Shema*, with the implicit claim that these are the words that need to be repeated under these different circumstances. In *Parshat Balak*, on the other hand, lying down and rising up is part of a description of the Jews as a powerful lion, with no reference to any requirement to recite God's words. There is no apparent or implicit connection to *Shema* here.

In addition, the verse in *Balak* is remarkably similar to a part of the blessing that Jacob, on his deathbed, gives to his son Judah. That verse reads:

| Judah is a lion's whelp; from the prey, my son, you are gone up; he stooped down, he couched as a lion, and as a lioness; who shall rouse him up?[63] | גור אריה יהודה מטרף בני עלית כרע רבץ כאריה וכלביא מי יקימנו. |

which is very much the same as the verse from Balak:

| He couched, he lay down as a lion, and as a lioness; who shall rouse him up? | כרע שכב כארי וכלביא מי יקימנו. |

yet no one suggests including Jacob's blessing in *Keriyat Shema* even though the entire section that includes this line is only five verses long, and would,

---

63   Genesis 49:9.

therefore, not be a burden on the community if it were a required recitation each day.

Therefore, there may well be another reason for the suggested inclusion of the *Balak* section into this ritual. That reason will bring us back to our search for the historic forces that shaped *Keriyat Shema* as we know it.

The section of *Balak* or *Bilam*, as it is also known, occupies an interesting and prominent place in another rabbinic source. In the Babylonian Talmud, Tractate *Baba Bathra* 14b, one finds a discussion of who was responsible for bringing each of the Biblical books to its written form, i.e., for taking God's prophetic words and visions and formalizing them into the Biblical text. The section begins:

A–Who wrote them [the Scriptures]?	א–ומי כתבן?
B–Moses wrote his own book and the portion of [*parshat*] *Bilam* and *Job*.	ב–משה כתב ספרו ופרשת בלעם ואיוב;

Moses's "book" refers to the Pentateuch. Mention of Job is appropriate here as that book is found in a different part of the Bible, i.e., the third section, the *Ketuvim* or Writings. Also, the subsequent discussion in the *Bavli* preserves several other opinions as to who might have been Job's author.[64]

The problem in the text is the mention of *Parshat Bilam*. The difficulty is that this section would have been known to the Rabbis of the Babylonian Talmud – as it is to us – *only* from the Pentateuch. It is not immediately obvious, therefore, what we gain by being told that it, too, along with the Pentateuch, was brought to written form by Moses. If Moses wrote the entire Pentateuch including *Parshat Bilam* and we have already been told that this is the case, the second mention of this section is simply redundant.

One of the rules of Rabbinic Biblical exegesis is that when a general principle is enumerated and then a specific part of that general principle is restated, this is done not to teach us something about the specific element, but rather to teach us something about the entire general principle.[65] If we extend that rule to this case, this means that the specific mention of *Parshat Bilam* teaches us

---

64 B. *Baba Bathra* 15a-b.

65 See the Beraita of Rabbi Ishmael, the introduction to Sifra, also found at the end of the section of the sacrifices recited at the very beginning of morning prayers, Siddur pp. 48–53.

something about the entire Pentateuch (the general principle), and not simply about *Parshat Bilam* (the specific exceptional case).

If so, what does *Parshat Bilam* teach us about the entire Pentateuch? I believe that, as far as the Rabbis were concerned, they saw this section as providing the best independent proof that the entire Torah was the revealed word of God. In fact, for them, *Parshat Bilam* was a central pillar on which they rested that critical belief that stands at the core of traditional Judaism.

To explain how this section provides such a proof, we turn to the scroll of Esther, best known from its recitation on the holiday of *Purim*, and to part of the rabbinic discussion concerning whether this scroll too, was revealed by God (i.e., written under the inspiration of the Divine spirit).[66] Says the Babylonian Talmud:

A–It has been taught: Rabbi Eleazar said:	א–תניא, רבי אליעזר אומר:
B–Esther was composed under the inspiration of the holy spirit,	ב–אסתר ברוח הקודש נאמרה,
C–As it says,	ג–שנאמר
D–"And Haman said in his heart . . ."[67]	ד–ויאמר המן בלבו.
E–Rabbi Akiva said:	ה–רבי עקיבא אומר:
F–Esther was composed under the inspiration of the holy spirit,	ו–אסתר ברוח הקודש נאמרה,
G–As it says,[68]	ז–שנאמר
H–"And Esther obtained favor in the eyes of all that looked upon her . . ."[69]	ח–ותהי אסתר נשאת חן בעיני כל ראיה . . .

The rationale for both Rabbi Eliezer's and Rabbi Akiva's proofs is that the information they cite would be unavailable to the author of the book without

---

66 Esther was a controversial book. The people in Qumran did not include it in their Biblical canon, and no remnant of it has been found in the Dead Sea scrolls. They also did not include the holiday of *Purim* in their calendar, presumably because they did not think that the book was Divinely inspired. See Schiffman, Lawrence. *Reclaiming the Dead Sea Scrolls: the History of Judaism, the Background of Christianity, The Lost Library of Qumran.* New York: 1995. For Talmudic indication of doubt about the book of Esther see, in addition to the source we are about to cite, B. Megillah 7a.

67 Esther 6:6.

68 Esther 2:15.

69 B. Megillah 7a.

God's revelation. How could any human being possibly know what was in Haman's heart or in the hearts of all who saw Esther unless God revealed these hidden thoughts? Hence, the presence of these sentences in this book indicates that they (and therefore that the entire book) must have been Divinely inspired.

This talmudic text continues with other Sages offering other verses from Esther that are claimed to prove that the book originates with God and not with human beings. This same rationale, in one way or another, runs through the rest of the suggested proofs, as they all involve information included in the Book of Esther that is normally unavailable to the mortal man or woman. The only reasonable conclusion – as far as this text in the *Bavli* is concerned – is that Esther was written through the Divine spirit.

Turning our attention back to *Parshat Bilam* or *Balak*, it, too, provides the same scenario. The Rabbis of the talmudic period accepted as axiomatic that the Pentateuch was a completed work by the close of the Jewish wanderings in the desert. How then could the Jews have known about the detailed descriptions of events and conversations between King Balak and the prophet Bilam preserved in *Parshat Balak*? The only human beings who might have known about this story – Balak, his people, Bilam and his people, ever the sworn enemies of the Jews during this period – would not have shared intimate details of their defeat at the hands of the Jewish God with those they disliked so much. At the very least such a disclosure would have been unacceptably humiliating for them. In addition, from their perspective it would have meant giving aid and comfort to their enemies, the Jewish people.

Let us look at the story of Balak and Bilam from the vantage point of the Jews in the desert. Given that no one who knew the details would have told them what occurred, their only possible contemporaneous knowledge of the events described in the Bible might have been seeing some people gathered on the cliffs above them offering sacrifices[70] – hardly the detailed description one finds in the Bible. Again, the story could only be known to the Jews by Divine inspiration.

This explains why the list of Moses's authored texts in Tractate *Baba Bathra* contains both *Parshat Bilam* and the Pentateuch. That which is true about the smaller specific section –*Parshat Bilam* – is also true about the larger text – the Torah. What the source in tractate *Baba Bathra* is trying to tell us is that

---

70   Cf. Numbers: 22:41.

Moses wrote both *Parshat Bilam* and "his book" (the Pentateuch), all under the aegis of Divine revelation.

Our intellectual journey now returns us to the *Shema*. The sectarians – likely Hellenistic Jews – were philosophically constrained to limit Divine revelation, meaning Divine interaction with "lowly" humans, as much as possible, while retaining some connection between the Jews and their God. It was also important for them to remove the Divine imprimatur from the laws of circumcision and *kashrut*. As part of that theological agenda, they claimed that only the Ten Commandments were Divinely revealed. They then attempted to prove this assertion from the fact that the Ten Commandments were part of the daily *Keriyat Shema* and, therefore, held a uniquely honored place in Jewish practice.

This "slander of the sectarians" presented such a serious threat that the Sages removed the Ten Commandments from the *Shema* as part of their battle against the Hellenizers. In its place they initially proposed recitation of the strongest proof for Divine revelation of the *entire* Torah. That suggested replacement was *Parshat Balak* (*Bilam*) – a direct, linear response to the philosophical and theological challenge of the Hellenizers.

On second thought however, this section proved to be too long for daily recitation, and it was abandoned. In its stead the next proposal for which we have evidence was Numbers 15:37–41 – the *Tsitsit* portion. This portion has found a home in *Keriyat Shema* ever since.

But, again, this raises the question of – why? There appears to be nothing in this section that speaks to a proof for the revelation of the entire Torah. Nonetheless, the continuation of the Bavli text cited above, offers five reasons why the *Tsitsit* portion was chosen. At least some of these five are also something of a linear response to the challenge of the sectarians.

The text reads:

A–[w]hy did they include the section of fringes?	א–פרשת ציצית מפני מה קבעוה?
B–Rabbi Judah b. Habiba said:	ב–אמר רבי יהודה בר חביבא:

---

71   Numbers 15:39.
72   Ibid., 38.
73   Ibid., 41.
74   Ibid., 39.
75   Psalms 14:1, 53:2
76   Numbers, 15:39.

C–Because it makes reference to five things: ג–מפני שיש בה חמשה דברים:

D–The precept of fringes, the Exodus from Egypt, ד–מצות ציצית, יציאת מצרים,
the yoke of the commandments, [a warning against] עול מצות, ודעת מינים, הרהור
the opinions of the *Minim*, the hankering after עבירה, והרהור עבודה זרה.
sexual immorality and the hankering after idolatry.

E–The first three, we grant you, are obvious: ה–בשלמא הני תלת מפרשן;

F–The yoke of the commandments [as it is ו–עול מצות וראיתם אתו
written]: "That you may look upon it and וזכרתם את כל מצות ה',
remember all the commandments of the Lord";[71]

G–The fringes, as it is written: "That ז–ציצית דכתיב: ועשו להם
they make for themselves fringes";[72] ציצית וגו',

H–The Exodus from Egypt, as it is written: ח–יציאת מצרים דכתיב: אשר
"Who brought you out of the land of Egypt."[73] הוצאתי וגומר,

I–But where do we find [warnings against] ט–אלא דעת מינים, הרהור
the opinions of the heretics, and the עבירה, והרהור עבודה זרה
hankering after immorality and idolatry? מנלן?

J–It has been taught: "After your own י–דתניא: אחרי לבבכם זו מינות,
heart":[74] this refers to heresy;

K–And so it says: כ–וכן הוא אומר:

L–"The fool hath said in his ל–אמר נבל בלבו אין א-להים,
heart, There is no God."[75]

M–"After your own eyes":[76] this refers מ–אחרי עיניכם זה הרהור
to the hankering after immorality; עבירה,

N–And so it says, נ–שנאמר:

O–"And Samson said to his father, 'Get her ס–ויאמר שמשון אל אביו אותה
for me, for she is pleasing in my eyes.'"[77] קח לי כי היא ישרה בעיני,

P–"After which ye use to go astray":[78] this ע–אתם זונים זה הרהור עבודה
refers to the hankering after idolatry; זרה,

Q–And so it says, פ–וכן הוא אומר:

R–"And they went astray after the Ba'alim."[79] צ–ויזנו אחרי הבעלים.

The five reasons given for inclusion of this section are that the paragraph includes the laws of *tsitsit*, the Exodus from Egypt, the yoke of the commandments,

---

77   Judges 14:3.
78   Numbers, 15:39.
79   Judges 8:13.

a response to the sectarians, a response to sinful thoughts, and a response to idolatry. If this paragraph was chosen to challenge the philosophical claims of the Hellenizers, most of these things are relevant to that enterprise.

The Exodus dramatically embodies God's personal involvement with the Jewish people that goes far beyond a single limited revelation of the Ten Commandments. The "yoke of the commandments" makes the claim that all the laws are binding – not just the ten.

Certainly a direct response to the *Minim* is in place here. The particular verse cited as providing that response condemns those "who follow their hearts." Using this verse in this way brands sectarianism as a subjective, human-created doctrine, which, from the perspective of the Rabbis is, therefore, completely inauthentic as religious teaching. Adding responses to sexually sinful thoughts and idolatry rounds out the picture, as these items challenge the debauchery that the Rabbis saw in the Greco-Roman world, and labels sectarianism with the ultimate degradation for any Jew – "idolatry."

The careful reader will note two things: first that I left out one of the reasons listed in the talmudic passage, and, second, that there are actually six reasons (not five) on this list. The remaining item is the one that figures most prominently in the Biblical paragraph – i.e., the *tsitsit*. Perhaps the author and editors of this passage realized that the laws of *tsitsit* do not constitute a linear response to the sectarians. They are no different from any other imperative that does not appear in the Ten Commandments. *tsitsit* would seem to be just another law that – for the *Minim* – did not come through God's revelation.

Nonetheless, the pivotal importance of *tsitsit* in this context cannot be overstated. In my opinion, these ritual fringes – or, more correctly, one aspect of them – is the central reason for the inclusion of this paragraph in *Keriyat Shema*.[80] But the understanding of that part of our story lies elsewhere, beyond the world of Talmudic literature as we shall now hopefully come to understand.

We begin by restating the remaining question as starkly as possible. Why the emphasis on *tsitsit*? What does this one law add to the conflict against the Hellenizers that, from a traditionalist perspective, would truly respond once and for all to their "slander"? We have seen some answers in the Talmudic passage just discussed as to why this *paragraph* was included. These answers come

---

80   Tabory p. 291f recognizes that the *tsitsit* aspect is the most important reason for the inclusion of this paragraph in *Keriyat Shema*, but because he does not reference the *Heikhalot* material, his explanation seems quite forced.

from the universe of rationalist Judaism and respond to our question to some extent, but they do not discuss *tsitsit* per se. That is because the reason that *tsitsit* was chosen as the best rejoinder to the *Minim* comes from the world of early Jewish mysticism – but the text we are discussing does not include any mystical elements.

Before we develop this esoteric answer we must take note of the fact that some mystical influence has touched and shaped virtually every Jewish prayer in some way – at some point in its history. There is almost always strong rationalist influence on the history of each part of the liturgy; but there is also, almost always, an esoteric level that must be explored as well. To understand that second level and its impact here, we again need to take a bit of an intellectual journey.

The *Bavli* – in its discussion of *Parshat Balak* as a possible replacement for the Ten Commandments – laid down a principle that one may not divide a Biblical section, except where breaks already appear in the Torah text. It was for this reason that *Parshat Balak*, which lacks any such break, was too long to use in the daily liturgy.

The contemporary *Keriyat Shema* tells us that this rule has its exceptions. As we described at the beginning of this chapter, the first verse, שְׁמַע יִשְׂרָאֵל ה' אֱ-לֹהֵינוּ ה' אֶחָד ("Hear O Israel the Lord our God the Lord is One"),[81] is recited; then, despite the fact that there is no section break after this sentence in the Biblical text, the phrase בָּרוּךְ שֵׁם כְּבוֹד מַלְכוּתוֹ לְעוֹלָם וָעֶד (Blessed be the Name of His glorious kingdom forever and ever) is inserted at this point.

The Mishnah and the *Bavli* tell us that there was opposition to this practice. Says the Mishnah:

A–Six things were done by the people of Jericho:	א–שׁשׁה דברים עשו אנשי יריחו
B–Three they [the Sages] forbade them,	ב–על שלשה מיחו בידם
C–And three [they] did not forbid them.	ג–ועל שלשה לא מיחו בידם
D–And it is these which they did not forbid them: . . .	ג–ואלו הן שלא מיחו בידם . . .
E–They wrapped up the *Shema* . . .[82]	ד–וכורכין את שמע

---

81   Deuteronomy 6:4.
82   M. Pesahim 4:8.

The Bavli explains the obscure term כורכין "wrapped up" as follows:

A–Our Rabbis taught:	א–תנו רבנן:
B–How did they wrap up the *Shema*?	ב–כיצד היו כורכין את שמע?
C–They recited, "Hear O Israel the	ג–אומרים שמע ישראל ה'
Lord our God the Lord is One"	א־להינו ה' אחד
D–And they did not make a pause:	ד–ולא היו מפסיקין,
E–This is Rabbi Meir's view.	ה–דברי רבי מאיר.
F–Rabbi Judah said:	ו–רבי יהודה אומר:
G–They did make a pause,	ז–מפסיקין היו,
H–But they did not recite, Blessed be the Name	ח–אלא שלא היו אומרים ברוך
of His glorious kingdom forever and ever.	שם כבוד מלכותו לעולם ועד.

This text gives us an indication that – as with many liturgical practices – there was originally less than universal agreement concerning whether this extra line should be said.

This same section of the *Bavli* then proceeds to a more rationalist/historical explanation for the insertion of this extra phrase than the reason we will encounter somewhat further on in our discussion.

A–And what is the reason that we do recite it?	א–ואנן מאי טעמא אמרינן ליה?
B–Even as Rabbi Simeon b. Lakish expounded.	ב–כדדריש רבי שמעון בן לקיש,
C–For Rabbi Simeon b. Lakish said:	ג–דאמר רבי שמעון בן לקיש:
D–And Jacob called unto his sons, and said:	ד–ויקרא יעקב אל בניו ויאמר
E–"Gather yourselves together, that I may tell you [that which shall befall you in the end of days]."[84]	ה–האספו ואגידה לכם.
F–Jacob wished to reveal to his sons the End of Days.	ו–ביקש יעקב לגלות לבניו קץ הימין,
G–Whereupon the *Shekhinah* [the Divine presence] departed from him [so he could not receive prophecy].	ז–ונסתלקה ממנו שכינה.
H–Said he, "Perhaps, Heaven forefend, there is one unfit among my children,	ח–אמר: שמא חס ושלום יש במטתי פסול,

---

83   Pesahim 56a.
84   Genesis 49:1.

I–Like Abraham, from whom there issued Ishmael,	ט–כאברהם שיצא ממנו ישמעאל,
J–Or like my father, Isaac, from whom there issued Esau."	י–ואבי יצחק שיצא ממנו עשו.
K–His sons said to him:	כ–אמרו לו בניו:
L–"Hear O Israel, the Lord our God the Lord is One";[85]	ל–שמע ישראל ה' א־להינו ה' אחד.
M–They said: "Just as there is only One in your heart,	מ–אמרו: כשם שאין בלבך אלא אחד
N–So is there in our heart only One."	נ–כך אין בלבנו אלא אחד.
O–In that moment our father Jacob opened [his discourse] and exclaimed:	ס–באותה שעה פתח יעקב אבינו ואמר:
P–"Blessed be the Name of His glorious kingdom for ever and ever."	ע–ברוך שם כבוד מלכותו לעולם ועד.
Q–Said the Rabbis:	פ–אמרי רבנן:
R–How shall we act?	צ–היכי נעביד?
S–Shall we recite it,	ק–נאמרוהו
T–But our Teacher Moses did not say it [it is not included in the text in Deuteronomy].	ר–לא אמרו משה רבינו,
U–Shall we not say it?	ש–לא נאמרוהו
V–But Jacob said it.	ת–אמרו יעקב.
W–[Hence] they enacted that it should be recited quietly.	אא–התקינו שיהו אומרים אותו בחשאי.

While this offers a possible explanation for the presence of our extra phrase, it does not help in the search for an esoteric origin for the *tsitsit* paragraph as a replacement for the Ten Commandments in *Keriyat Shema*. It also does not adequately explain contemporary liturgical practice. While it is true that ברוך שם כבוד מלכותו לעולם ועד is generally recited *soto voce* on most days of the year, on *Yom Kippur* (the Day of Atonement), Jews all over the world proclaim this phrase out loud throughout the day. Nothing in this source offers any explanation of why this occurs.

Happily there is a rabbinic text that will respond to both of these questions. Before introducing that text, we will cite the rest of the source presently under discussion. This material is interesting both because it contains some additional

---

85   Dueronomy 6:4.

information about the questions we are exploring and because it tells us some more about the history of *Keriyat Shema* in general.

A–Rabbi Isaac said, The School of Rabbi Ammi said:	א–אמר רבי יצחק, אמרי דבי רבי אמי:
B–"This is to be compared to a king's daughter who smelled a spicy pudding.	ב–משל לבת מלך שהריחה ציקי קדירה,
C–If she reveals [her desire], she suffers disgrace;	ג–אם תאמר –יש לה גנאי,
D–If she does not reveal it, she suffers pain.	ד–לא תאמר –יש לה צער.
E–So her servants began bringing it to her in secret."	ה–התחילו עבדיה להביא בחשאי.
F–Rabbi Abbahu said: They [the Sages] enacted that this should be recited aloud, on account of the slander of the sectarians.	ו–אמר רבי אבהו: התקינו שיהו אומרים אותו בקול רם מפני תרעומת המינין.
G–But in Nehardea, where there are no sectarians, until now they have always recited it quietly.	ז–ובנהרדעא דליכא מינין – עד השתא אמרי לה בחשאי.

The spicy pudding reference will be explained shortly. We will focus first on the intriguing sectarian slander mentioned here. This time the outcome of the challenge from the ideological opponents of the Rabbis was different. The Babylonians (Nehardea was a major Babylonian Torah-study center) resisted the proposed liturgical change because "they had no sectarians."

The texts that we discussed previously indicated that the sectarian claims regarding the Ten Commandments also had no contemporary reality in the Amoraic period in Babylonia. Nonetheless, many rabbinic leaders in that community accepted the assertion that the Ten Commandments could not be re-instituted in *Keriyat Shema* because "they had previously been done away with as a result of the slander of the *Minim*." Why, then, was this second sectarian challenge successfully resisted, while the first one was not?

The most likely answer to this question, and one that supports what we said earlier, is that we are dealing with two different groups of "sectarians" and two different historical periods. As indicated, the claim that God's revelation was limited only to the Ten Commandments that caused the Sages to alter *Keriyat Shema*, came from the hellenized Jews of the Greek period.

On the other hand, in this case the sectarians were the Christians from the later Roman era, particularly those who were more Trinitarian in their orientation. Those groups, who believed in a tripartite godhead, found themselves theologically challenged by the assertion of God's singularity that appears in the first verse of the *Shema* ("Hear Israel God our Lord God is *One*").[86] Since this verse was followed by an inaudible recitation almost every time it was offered in prayer by Jews, they might well suspect that those praying were silently adding an attack on their beliefs at this point.

As Rashi says

| That they not say about us that we are adding something inappropriate.[87] | שלא יהו אומרים עלינו שאנו מוסיפין דבר שאינו הגון |

Significantly, this would have been a Palestinian problem because Christians and Christian persecutions of the Jews were an ever-increasing concern in that community during the Amoraic period.[88] In Babylonia, however, there were no Christians and no such threats to the Jews and the Jewish community in this era. As such, Jews in Palestine were forced to say the phrase ברוך שם כבוד מלכותו לעולם ועד out loud – every day – to avoid suspicion and attacks. In Babylonia, on the other hand, there would have been no compelling reason to change the usual practice of silent recitation. In fact, the Babylonian tradition has been maintained as the custom of essentially all of the Jewish communities that exist today.

This later sectarian slander was treated very differently by the Amoraim of Babylonia than the way in which they reacted to the events that led to the removal of the Ten Commandments from the *Shema* in an earlier era. For Babylonian Amoraim, the non-recitation of the Ten Commandments was a long-standing practice with roots in the stories of the Maccabees. When some in Babylonia chose to challenge that practice by trying to bring the Ten Commandments back into the *Shema*, the historical precedent and communal memory were too strong, and the ancient way of doing things remained in place.

Bringing back the Ten Commandments simply could not occur in the late Mishnaic or Amoraic periods, centuries after they had been removed under such celebrated circumstances. The weight of historical precedent was simply

---

86   Cf. Jan Pelikan, Jaroslav. *The Christian Tradition: A History of the Development of Doctrine*. Chicago: 1971–1989, p. 202f.

87   Rashi, Pesahim 56a, sv. *Mipnei Tarumot ha-Minim*.

88   See the chapter on *Birkhat ha-Hodesh* in this volume.

too great. On the other hand, resisting a proposed liturgical change whose origin was contemporary, and that responded to ideological challenges not present in Babylonia at that time, was both easy and the obvious course to take.

Finally, this record of a failed sectarian challenge following on the heels of the much more successful one, which we have described, probably helps strengthen Jewish self-image. I am certain that many Jews will be glad to know that those making the decisions as to what customs to follow did not ultimately succumb to every sectarian challenge that came along by changing Judaism's traditional ritual practices.

We can now move back into the esoteric/mystical realm with the next source that we discuss, which will help us answer our remaining questions:

A–And why does Israel recite it ["Blessed be the Name of His glorious kingdom forever and ever"] in a whisper?	א–ולמה ישראל אומרים אותו בלחישה?
B–When Moses ascended to heaven	ב–אלא כשעלה משה למרום
C–He stole it from the ministering angels	ג–גנב אותו מן המלאכים
D–And taught it to Israel.	ד–ולימדה לישראל.
E–Rabbi Samuel b. Nahman said,	ה–אמר רבי שמואל בר נחמן
F–"To what may this be compared?	ו–למה הדבר דומה?
G–To the son of the daughter of a king	ז–לבן בתו של מלך
H–Who had a young daughter,	ח–שהיתה לו בת בתולה,
I–And who saw beautiful clothing [in the king's home].	ט–והיתה רואה בגדים נאים
J–She said to him:	י–ואומרת לו
K–Take these clothes,	כ–קח את הבגדים הללו,
L–And he took them for her.	ל–והיה לוקח לה,
M–One time he entered the palace of the King	מ–פעם אחת נכנס לפלטין של מלך
N–And saw the tiara of the Mistress of the house.	נ–וראה קוזמירין של מטרונה
O–He stole it	ס–וגנב אותה
P–And gave it to his daughter.	ע–ובא ונתנה לבתו,
Q–He began to command her and said to her,	פ–מתחיל מצוה ואומר לה,
R–"All the clothes that I acquired for you, go and wear in public,	צ–כל הבגדים שלקחתי ליך לבוש אותן בפרהסיא,
S–But this tiara is stolen;	ק–אבל קוזמירין זה גנוב הוא,
T–Do not wear it except within the	ר–אל תלבשי אותו אלא מן

56

doorway [i.e., only in the house]."

הדלת ולפנים,

U–So, too, Moses said to Israel,

ש–כך אמר משה לישראל,

V–"All of the commandments that I gave you
are from what I received from the Torah,

ת–כל המצווה שנתתי לכם
ממה שקבלתי מן התורה,

W–But this Name is what I heard
from the ministering angels.

אא–אבל השם הזה ממה
ששמעתי ממלאכי השרת

X–Through its use they praise the
Holy One Blessed Be He.

בב–שבו הם משבחים להקדוש
ברוך הוא

Y–And I took it from them.

גג–ונטלתי אותו מהם,

Z–Therefore, recite it only in a whisper,

דד–לכך תהיו אומרין אותו
בלחישה,

AA–'Blessed be the Name of His
glorious kingdom forever and ever.'"

הה–ברוך שם כבוד מלכותו
לעולם ועד.

BB–But on the Day of Atonement
why do they recite it publicly?

וו–למה הן אומריו אותו ביום
הכפורים בפרהסיא?

CC–Because they are like the angels;

זז–אלא שהם כמלאכים,

DD–They wear white,

חח–לובשין לבנים

EE–They do not eat, they do not drink,

טט–ולא אוכלין ולא שותין

FF–And there is in them no sin
and no transgression,

יי–ואין בהם לא חטא ולא עון

GG–For God forgives them all of their misdeeds.

כב–שהקדוש ברוך הוא סולח
להם כל עונותיהם.

This source claims that our extra phrase is angelic in origin, and that recitation of this sentence *out loud* only on *Yom Kippur* is in sync with Jews taking on angelic ways on this one very special day of the year. It also explains the metaphor of the spicy cake, which is here transposed into the symbolism of a magnificent tiara. In both cases the woman – who is Israel – has encountered something beautiful; the knowledge of which she must keep hidden except on *Yom Kippur* when it is appropriate to be on display.

We can understand this source, and the discussion that follows, more completely, if we take a moment to describe the esoteric study and practices of the Rabbinic (and perhaps even earlier) period, called the *Heikhalot* or *Merkavah* mysticism (the mysticism of the sanctuaries or of the chariot).[90] A large part of

---

89   Deuteronomy Rabbah: 2:36.

90   There are parallels between this mysticism and material in the Dead Sea Scrolls, see

this literature describes the journeys of adepts such as Rabbi Akiva and Rabbi Nehuniah b. Hakaneh, as they travel through the seven heavens to stand before the throne of glory (כסא הכבוד) where they experience the Divine presence.[91]

It is a journey that demands truth, purity and courage. Along the way the traveler encounters dangers and potentially hostile angelic creatures. One must use proper mystical crowns, Divine Names and prayers if one is to reach one's goal unharmed. At the end – for the successful mystical adventurer – he can experience being part of the celestial choir of the angels, singing God's praises in His holy presence before His Divine throne. For the spiritually sensitive, the possibility of such an experience is so religiously motivating that likening something brought back from such a journey to a beautiful tiara or a food with a compelling taste and smell, is perfectly appropriate.

The literary origin of this mysticism lies in the first through third chapters of the Biblical book of Ezekiel and in the sixth chapter of the book of Isaiah, where the prophets experience visions of heaven and hear the prayers of the celestial servants of God. Rabbinic Midrash expands on those texts in works called *Heikhalot Rabbati*, *Heikhalot Zutarti*, and *Alphabeta De-Rabbi Akiva*, along with a significant number of other compositions. Reference to elements of this esoteric material and texts that come from it can also be found in the Mishnah, the Tosefta, the Babylonian and Palestinian Talmuds and in various classic Midrashim such as the works known as *Midrash Rabbah*.[92]

The well-known tale of the four Sages who enter *Pardes*, which tells of Elishah b. Abuya becoming an apostate, Ben Zoma becoming mentally impaired, Ben Azai dying, and only Rabbi Akiva emerging successfully – having grown from the experience – is a story about this mystical journey through the seven heavens.[93] That story is only fully understood by comparing the Babylonian Talmud's presentation of it with the relevant sections of *Heikhalot*

"The Dead Sea Scrolls and Merkavah Mysticism." In T.H. Lim, ed., *The Dead Sea Scrolls in their Historical Context*, Edinburgh: 1999, pp. 246–64; Halperin, David. *The Faces of the Chariot: Early Jewish Responses to Ezekiel's Vision*. Tübingen: 1988.

91   See the discussion and notes in the chapter on *Aleinu*, which is a prayer that plays an important role in *Heikhalot* literature.

92   These Midrashim exist to the Five books of Moses and to the Five Megillot; They are not from one author or one time period as they date from the 5th to the 12th century.

93   Tosefta Hagigah 2:1–5 and Hagigah 14b.

literature.[94] But even the Bavli's presentation reminds us that the journey of the *Heikhalot* mystics was both dangerous and potentially infinitely spiritually rewarding.

Though this literature has not been included in the usual course of study in *Yeshivot* or other schools of higher Jewish learning, nor has it even been referenced in Jewish texts for many generations in most traditional circles,[95] its impact on all parts of Jewish liturgy is profound. Virtually every section of the prayer book finds its parallel in *Merkavah* literature, and has been influenced by it.[96]

To give us a sense of this literature as it relates to *Keriyat Shema* and ברוך שם כבוד מלכותו לעולם ועד, we cite this Midrash from Deuteronomy Rabbah: *Parshat va-Ethanan.*

A–When Israel recites, "Hear O Israel,"	א–כשישראל אומרים שמע ישראל,
B–They are then silent and recite in a whisper,	ב–דוממים ואומרים בלחישה
C–"Blessed be the Name of His glorious kingdom for ever and ever."	ג–ברוך שם כבוד מלכותו לעולם ועד.
D–At that moment they [the angels] praise [God].	ד–באותה שעה הן מקלסין,
E–And so Ezekiel says as well,	ה–וכן יחזקאל אומר,
F–"I heard after me,[97]	ו–ואשמע אחרי
G–After I praised, the ministering angels praised,	ז–מאחר שקלסתי קלסו מלאכי השרת,
H–[Saying,] 'Blessed be the Name of His glorious kingdom . . .'"	ח–ברוך שם כבוד מלכותו.

In this text, the human recitation of ברוך שם כבוד מלכותו לעולם ועד is really

---

94 The story is told several times in this literature, cf. Schaefer, Peter, *Synopse zur Heikhalot Literatur, Tubingen.* 1981, par. 345f. For discussion see: Scholem, Gershom Gerhard (1897–1982). *Jewish Gnosticism, Merkabah Mysticism, and Talmudic Tradition*, 1960. ch. 3.

95 See discussion of the place of this material among *Hasidei Ashkenaz* in the chapter on *Anim Zemirot* in this volume.

96 I did a research paper in graduate school that explored the parallels between the contemporary Siddur and the *Heikhalot* literature. That research serves as the basis for this comment.

97 Ezekiel 3:12.

a this-worldly whispered echo of the heavenly exclamation by the angels as they proclaim this verse out loud. On the Day of Atonement, as discussed above, both the heavenly and earthly worshippers say the phrase so that all can hear it. In fact, the usual synagogue practice on that day is that these words are fairly shouted by those gathered for prayer as believers in this world strive to become part of the heavenly chorus. In short, the angelic activity described in these texts, which come from early Jewish mystical literature, has become part of contemporary Jewish ritual practice.[98]

One other piece of this puzzle appears in a comment of Rashi's that is based on, among other sources, a passage from Mishnah Yoma 6:2 familiar from the *Yom Kippur* liturgy.[99] The Mishnah reads as follows:

A–He then came to the goat that was sent out,	א–בא לו אצל שעיר המשתלח
B–Laid his two hands upon it and made confession.	ב–וסומך שתי ידיו עליו ומתוודה
C–And this is what he said:	ג–וכך היה אומר
D–"Please, God,	ד–אנא השם
E–Your people the house of Israel have failed, committed iniquity and transgressed before you.	ה–עוו פשעו חטאו לפניך עמך בית ישראל
F–Please, in Your Name,	ו–אנא בשם
G–Atone the failures, the iniquities and the transgressions which your people, the house of Israel,	ז–כפר נא לעונות ולפשעים ולחטאים
H–Have failed, committed and transgressed before You,	ח–שעוו ושפשעו ושחטאו לפניך עמך בית ישראל
I–As it is written in the Torah of Moses, Your servant, saying:	ט–ככתוב בתורת משה עבדך לאמר
J–'For on this day shall atonement be made for you, to purify you from all your sins. You shall be purified before God,'"[100]	י–כי ביום הזה יכפר עליכם לטהר אתכם מכל חטאתיכם לפני ה' תטהרו
K–And when the priests and the people standing in the Temple court	כ–והכהנים והעם העומדים בעזרה
L–Heard the explicit Name	ל–כשהיו שומעים שם המפורש

---

98 See above footnote 13.

99 Mahzor YK, p. 566; see also p. 560 and p. 562.

100 Leviticus 16:30.

M–Come forth from the mouth of the High Priest,	מ–שהוא יוצא מפי כהן גדול
N–They knelt, bowed down, fell	נ–היו כורעים ומשתחוים
on their faces and said:	ונופלים על פניהם
O–"Blessed be the Name of His glorious	ס–ואומרים ברוך שם כבוד
kingdom forever and ever."[101]	מלכותו לעולם ועד:

And Rashi, in tractate Berakhot explains:

A–They shall bless Your glorious Name	א–ויברכו שם כבודך – במקום
– in place of responding *Amen*.	עניית אמן,
B–Because in the Temple they said, "Blessed be the	ב–שבמקדש אומר ברוך שם
Name of His glorious kingdom forever and ever."	כבוד מלכותו לעולם ועד.

ברוך שם כבוד מלכותו לעולם ועד was not only the angelic response; it was the people's response – but only in the Temple. In fact, in *Merkavah* mysticism, the lowest of the seven heavens – the lowest *heikhal* or sanctuary – is often the *heikhal* of the *Beit ha-mikdash* from which both *tefillot* (prayers) and mystics could enter the higher realms.[103] The use of ברוך שם כבוד מלכותו לעולם ועד in the Temple served as an indication for the *Merkavah* mystic that this esoteric understanding of reality was correct. It was here, at this lowest level of heaven, that an angelic response began to be useable by those who had entered its precincts, while this same response was significantly restricted outside this realm.

Given this background, the inclusion of ברוך שם כבוד מלכותו לעולם ועד in *Keriyat Shema* and the way this sentence is recited at different times of the year forces us to recognize the mystical dimension that exists in what until now appeared to us to be an entirely rationalistic prayer. Instead of simply being a statement of the essential principles of the Jewish faith – which is

---

101   Lines K–N may not be original to the Mishnah and may have entered because of the influence of *Heikhalot* literature and the *Avodah* liturgy of *Yom Kippur*. See *Dikdukei Soferim*, ad. loc. See also M. Yoma 3:8, 4:1–2; Tosefta Yoma 2:1; J. Yoma 6:2, 43b, 3:7, 40b; Rabbi Yitshak ben Rabbi Moshe of Vienna (12th–13th century). *Or Zarua* 2 "Hilkhot Yom ha-Kippurim," 281; Rabbi David ben Solomon ibn Avi Zimra (15th–16th century). *Responsa Radbaz* 2:810.

102   B. Berakhot 53b.

103   Davies, W.D., et al. *The Cambridge History of Judaism*. Cambridge, New York: Cambridge University Press, 2006, pp. 758–759. See also the chapter on *Aleinu* in this volume.

profound enough – the recitation of *Shema* now begins to take on elements of a coordinated choreography involving both the Jews praying below and the angels praising God above.

Perhaps the most dramatic evidence for this second level of meaning appears in the simple, but almost universal custom of changing prayer leaders in the synagogue just a few paragraphs before reciting *Keriyat Shema* in the morning liturgy. I can find no reason for this practice except in this passage from *Heikhalot Rabbati*:

A–Rabbi Akiva said:	א–אמר רבי עקיבא:
B–Every single day, an angel stands in the middle	ב–בכל יום ויום מלאך אחד
of the *rakia* [one of the levels of heaven]	עומד באמצע הרקיע
C–And begins [to pray] and says:	ג–ופותח ואומר:
D–"God rules..."[104]	ד–ה' מלך
E–And all the hosts of heaven respond after him	ה–וכל צבא מרום עונין אחריו
F–Until he reaches [the prayer called]	ו–עד שמגיע לברכו
Barekhu [understood as the call to communal prayer in the contemporary liturgy].[105]	
G–Once he reaches *Barekhu*,	ז–כיון שמגיע לברכו
H–There is a *hayah* [an angel described as a wild beast] whose name is "Israel" –	ח–חיה אחת יש ששמה ישראל
I–And carved on its forehead is *ami li* [my people are mine] –	ט–וחקוק על מצחה עמי לי
J–Which stands in the middle of the *rakia* and says:	י–עומד באמצע הרקיע ואומרת:
K–"*Barkhu et Ha-Shem ha-me-vorakh*" [Bless God, Who is blessed – this is the prayer called *Barekhu*).	כ–ברכו את ה' המבורך
L–And all the officers on high respond after her:	ל–וכל שרי מעלה עונין אחריה:
M–"*Barukh Ha-Shem ha-me-vorakh le-olam vaed*" [Bless God, Who is blessed forever – the	מ–ברוך ה' המבורך לעולם ועד,

---

104 A prayer that appears at the beginning of *Psukei Dezimrah* (the early morning liturgy called the "verses of song" Siddur p. 58–83), in the Sephardi (Sepharad Siddur p. 64) and Ari (Ari Siddur p. 29) rites, starts with this phrase. In Ashkenazi custom this phrase appears in the paragraph called *yehi khavod* that also comes early in the services (Siddur p. 64–67). There is also a *piyut* recited on the High Holidays that is built around it.

105 Siddur p. 84, cf. Barukh Halevi Epstein (19th–20th centuries), *Torah Temimah*: Deuteronomy 32, Note 33–34.

usual communal response to *Barkhu*].[106]

N–Even before he completes his words,	נ–עד שלא יגמור דבריו
O–The angelic spheres quake and shake	ס–רועשים ורועדים האופנים
P–And cause the whole world to tremble	ע–ומרעידים את כל העולם
Q–And they say:	פ–ואומרים
R–"Bless the Glory of God from His place."[107]	צ–ברוך כבוד ה' ממקומו,
S–And that *hayah* stands in the middle of the *rakia*	ק–ואותה חיה עומדת באמצע הרקיע
T–Until all the officers on high,	ר–עד שרועדים כל שרי מעלה
U–The celestial dignitaries, the bands of angels and all the angelic camps all tremble.	ש–וטפסרים וגדודים וכל המחנות
V–And each one as it stands says to the *hayah*:	ת–וכל אחד ואחד בעמדו אומר לחיה
W– "Hear, Israel: the Lord our God the Lord is One" [the *Shema*].[108]	אא–שמע ישראל ה' א'להינו ה' אחד

The choreography of the synagogue – the usual changing of prayer leaders at this point in the services – follows the lead of this ancient mystical text from *heikhalot* literature. This, despite the fact that the vast majority of contemporary worshippers are unfamiliar with this source, and have no idea why the prayer leaders change when and how they do. In this way the *Shema* ritual, as it is known today, again displays the influence of mystical/esoteric speculation and teaching.

This also explains why the paragraphs in the contemporary liturgy known as *Kedushah de-Yotser* that are recited after *Barekhu* and before the two blessings that introduce the *Keriyat Shema* describe the great noise made by the heavenly hosts as they praise God.[109] As we now know from this text, this is precisely what occurs in heaven at this point in the angelic service according to *Merkavah* mysticism's description, and Jewish worshippers follow that lead

---

106 Siddur, ad. loc.

107 Ezekiel 3:12; see Siddur p. 88.

108 See Synopse par. 296 and par. 406. Eisenstein loc. cit p. 501 has a somewhat expanded version of this text.

109 Siddur pp. 84–89. This section concludes with the verse that appears in line R in the source we are discussing. The two introductory blessings of the *Shema* follow this line in the liturgy.

"down below." In this way, the earthly congregation strives to be in sync with the choreography of the "celestial" services.[110]

But what has all of this to do with the commandment to wear *tsitsit*, and with responding to our hellenistic sectarians? To finally settle that question, we must focus on an essential part of the ancient manufacture of *tsitsit* that was long unavailable to us for use or study. Intriguingly, it has been revitalized in some circles by those who claim to have rediscovered how it is to be done.[111]

The Bible describes the physical reality of *tsitsit* in the *tsitsit* paragraph as follows:

A–Speak to the people of Israel,	א–דַּבֵּר אֶל בְּנֵי יִשְׂרָאֵל
B–And say to them	ב–וְאָמַרְתָּ אֲלֵהֶם
C–That they make for themselves fringes,	ג–וְעָשׂוּ לָהֶם צִיצִת
D–At the corners of their garments,	ד–עַל כַּנְפֵי בִגְדֵיהֶם
E–Throughout their generations,	ה–לְדֹרֹתָם
F–And that they put upon the fringe of the corner	ו–וְנָתְנוּ עַל צִיצִת הַכָּנָף
G–A thread of blue [*tekhelet*];	ז–פְּתִיל תְּכֵלֶת:
H–*And it shall be to you for a fringe,*	ח–וְהָיָה לָכֶם לְצִיצִת
I–That you may see it,	ט–וּרְאִיתֶם אֹתוֹ

---

110 Seder Rav Amram Gaon, *Keriyat Shema u-Virkhoteha*, cites this *Heikhalot* text as he describes this part of the morning service and comments:

בוא וראה כמה חביב לפני הקב"ה מה שישראל אומרין לפניו קדוש. שהרי הזהיר ליורדי מרכבה ללמדנו באיזה ענין נאמר לפניו קדוש. ויש לנו להזהר ולעשות נחת ליוצרנו ולהעלות לפניו לריח ניחוח.

"Come and see how beloved before God is Israel's recitation of *Kadosh* before Him. For He has commanded the Merkavah mystics [*yordei merkavah* – those who descend into the chariot], to teach us *in what manner* to say Kadosh before Him. And we must be careful and give comfort to our Creator so that we rise before Him as a sweet savor."

It is not just the words, but the choreography that is important. This section in Seder Rav Amram Gaon includes other similar comments.

111 Spanier, Ehud, ed. *The Royal Purple and the Biblical Blue – Argaman and Tekhelet: the Study of Chief Rabbi Dr. Isaac Herzog on the Dye Industries in Ancient Israel and Recent Scientific Contributions.* Jerusalem: Keter, 1987; Twerski, Chaim E., "Identifying the Chilazon." In *Journal of Halacha and Contemporary Society* 34, 77–102, 1997; Singer, Mendel E. "Understanding the Criteria for the 'Chilazon.'" In *Journal of Halacha and Contemporary Society* 42, 5–29, 2001; Sterman, Baruch. *The Source of "Techelet"*; response to Dr. Singer. Ibid., 43, 112–124, 2002; Singer, Mendel E. *Criteria from the "Sugya" of "Techelet"* [response to Baruch Sterman]. Ibid., 44, 97–110, 2002; Greenspan, Avi. "The Search for Biblical Blue." In *Biblical Research* 29, 1 32–39, 2003.

J–And remember all the commandments of the Lord,	י–וּזְכַרְתֶּם אֶת כָּל מִצְוֹת ה'
K–And do them,	כ–וַעֲשִׂיתֶם אֹתָם
L–And that you seek not after your own heart and your own eyes,	ל–וְלֹא תָתוּרוּ אַחֲרֵי לְבַבְכֶם וְאַחֲרֵי עֵינֵיכֶם
M–Which incline you to go astray.[112]	מ–אֲשֶׁר אַתֶּם זֹנִים אַחֲרֵיהֶם:

A simple reading of these verses makes the blue color critical to this ritual object, as it is only with the placing of the thread of *tekhelet* on the garment that the Bible declares: וְהָיָה לָכֶם לְצִיצַת (And it shall be to you for a fringe (*Tsitsit*). Unfortunately, the knowledge of how to manufacture the necessary blue dye for this thread was lost for many centuries, and so the Jewish community made due without it. As indicated, some are now using the blue color again, but there is controversy as to whether they are making the dye in accordance with Jewish law (*halakhah*) as it was done in ancient times.

Regardless of how one decides the historical and legal questions concerning *Tekhelet*, nothing in this debate takes away from the over-arching mystical meaning of the blue thread. As the Babylonian Talmud indicates in Tractate Sotah 17a:

A–But what is [the meaning of] the thread of blue?	א–אלא חוט של תכלת מאי היא?
B–As we learned: Rabbi Meir used to say:	ב–דתניא, היה רבי מאיר אומר:
C–How different is blue from all the varieties of colors.	ג–מה נשתנה תכלת מכל מיני צבעונין.
D–Because the blue resembles the sea,	ד–מפני שהתכלת דומה לים,
E–And the sea resembles heaven,	ה–וים דומה לרקיע,
F–And heaven resembles the Throne of Glory,	ו–ורקיע דומה לכסא הכבוד,
G–As it is said:	ז–שנאמר:
H–"And they saw the God of Israel and there was under His feet, as it were, a paved work of sapphire stone, and as it were the very heaven for purity,"[113]	ח–ויראו את א-להי ישראל ותחת רגליו כמעשה לבנת הספיר וכעצם השמים לטהר,
I–And it is written:	ט–וכתיב:

---

112 Numbers 15:38–39.

113 Exodus 24:10.

J–"The likeness of a throne as the appearance of a sapphire stone."[114]   י–כמראה אבן ספיר דמות כסא.

This "color" commentary on the meaning of the blue thread embodies the quest of the *Merkavah* mystic: to stand before the throne of God, to experience His presence and to sing His praises along with the angels. It is here, in the mention and description of the *tekhelet*, that the section of *tsitsit* would have its greatest power for the rabbinic-era mystic.

Looking at the blue thread and evoking the similes described in this passage would give that mystic an intimation of standing before God's throne as he recited the daily *Keriyat Shema*. That would only reinforce the symbolism of the other mystical elements that appear in and around the recitation of the *Shema* as it is currently formulated. In other words, along with the importance of *Keriyat Shema* to rationalistic thinkers, who see this recitation as central to Judaism in a theological sense, more mystical believers would also find a dramatic and powerful connection to this text that would speak to them in performing this liturgy.

It is certainly quite profound to offer a proof for the Divine origin of the entire Torah within the liturgy as was suggested by those who wanted to use *Parshat Balak* to replace the Ten Commandments. As we have said, that would also have been a powerful, linear response to the hellenistic sectarians.

Nonetheless, for those who understood and accepted the mystical meaning of *tekhelet* as we have described it here, the presence of the *tsitsit* paragraph in *Keriyat Shema* would have served the same purpose, but in a very different and non-linear way. For the mystic, this paragraph effectively says to the Hellenist, "You who claim that God's interactions with inconsequential humans are dramatically limited, look to the *tekhelet*. Its symbolism – the very essence of its purpose in appearing in *tsitsit* – is to tell us that we all can stand before God's throne, in His presence, whenever we want."

In fact – as Jewish liturgy developed over the course of history – Jews act as if they are standing there among the angels every day of the year in their prayers. The possible interactions with God are, therefore, essentially unlimited and, consequently, the Hellenists are profoundly and fundamentally mistaken in what they believe.

Both the symbolic statement that God is accessible to all Jews at all times and

---

114   Ezekiel 1:26. See Synopse par. 371.

the response that this provides to the sectarian slander that we are discussing makes this paragraph a very good candidate to replace the Ten Commandments in *Keriyat Shema*. Once *Parshat Balak* was found unsuitable for daily use, the *tsitsit* paragraph – which is significantly shorter – became the replacement of choice, both for rationalistic reasons and even more profoundly for its mystical significance. As we have said, the response to the Hellenistic sectarians embodied in the mystical understanding of *Tekhelet* is not as direct a response to their challenge as that provided by *Parshat Balak*. Nonetheless, it may – in a religious sense – be even more important.

In a non-linear way this paragraph is telling the long-ago sectarians, as well as those who understand its esoteric meaning today, that people are consequential to God and that He welcomes their presence as they pray and recite texts from His Torah. In an ontological sense this would be a perfect response to the challenge of the sectarians, who saw human life – as it were – as less than a fly-speck on God's lapel.

It is to combat that view that I believe that the Rabbis finally settled on the *Tsitsit* paragraph as the replacement for the Ten Commandments. For Judaism, people are absolutely significant and essential to God and His plan for the universe. For Hellenistic thought and for many other systems of belief, the opposite is true.

As important as Divine revelation is to the traditional Jew, the belief in human significance before God may be even more important. It both explains why God would give His precious revealed law to puny humans, and it underlies much of how Jewish teaching approaches life in this world. Critical themes in Judaism such as "reward and punishment," repentance, Divine providence and the coming of the Messiah – which are not all explicitly detailed in the five books of Moses that constitute the Biblical text portion of the Sinaitic revelation – all rest on the idea that God cares about the fate of His children. In this way, the *Tsitsit* paragraph also fits the description of *Keriyat Shema* as containing "the essence of the faith and its beginning."

We will yet discover another important usage of the *Shema* that affirms this "cosmic significance of the human being" in perhaps an even more profound way. Before we move to that part of our story, let us summarize the mystical elements we have found thus far in looking at the history of *Keriyat Shema*.

The *tsitsit* and their threads of *tekhelet* embody the fulfillment of the mystical quest to stand before God. The choreography and liturgy of the synagogue service parallel the mystical description of the actions and sounds of the angels during morning services in heaven. The insertion of ברוך שם כבוד מלכותו לעולם ועד – the angelic/Temple response – into *Keriyat Shema*, parallels Ezekiel's experience of praising God and then hearing the angels respond to him with this phrase embodying their praise of the Creator. This sentence also has the effect of separating the first verse of the *Shema* paragraph from the rest of the text under angelic and heavenly precedent and imprimatur. That will have far-reaching implications because once it was recited in this way, the Rabbis felt free to use this first verse as a stand alone phrase in many different circumstances.

The theme of human significance has other important implications for the history of *Shema*. To explore another aspect of the relationship between this concept and this prayer, we turn our attention to the connection between *Keriyat Shema* and *Kedushah,* a section of the liturgy based entirely on *Heikhalot* traditions and whose name itself means "holiness."[115]

Kedushah is recited in the contemporary synagogue during the prayer leader's public repetition of the *Amidah* – the liturgy's central supplication. These repetitions usually occur during the morning (*Shaharit*), afternoon (*Minhah*) and additional (*Musaf*) services. In the *Musaf Kedushah* of *Shabbat* (the Sabbath), *Yom Tov* (holidays) and in all services on *Yom Kippur* (*Shaharit, Musaf, Minhah* and *Neilah* (the special concluding service recited in the contemporary liturgy only on *Yom Kippur*), the first verse of *Shema* is added to *Kedushah*.[116]

Why should this be? After all, the core of *Kedushah* is two verses that were heard by the prophets Isaiah and Ezekiel as part of Divinely inspired visions that the Bible describes.[117] These verses: קדוש קדוש קדוש ה' צבאות מלא כל הארץ כבודו (Holy, holy, holy, is the Lord of hosts; the whole earth is full of His glory), and ברוך כבוד ה' ממקומו (Blessed be the glory of the Lord from His place), are experienced by them in these visions as central to the prayers of the angels.[118] On the other hand, שמע ישראל, "Hear O Israel ..." is clearly a text directed at and recited by human beings who are part of the Jewish people.

There are those who try to explain the appearance of *Shema* in *Kedushah* as resulting from a nasty practice employed by some who persecuted the Jews.

---

115   Cf. Siddur p. 100. The central verses of *Kedushah* come from the chapters in Isaiah and Ezekiel that are the basis of *Heikhalot* mysticism, and they are frequently quoted in *Heikhalot* texts, cf. the source from Synopse par. 296 and par. 406 cited above, and par. 419.

116   Siddur pp. 464, 676; Mahzor YK pp. 408, 536, 672, 730.

117   Isaiah 6:3, Ezekiel 3:12.

118   Isaiah ch. 6, Ezekiel ch. 1–3.

They would send soldiers or spies into the synagogue to insure that *Keriyat Shema*, which embodies the basic credo of Judaism, not be recited by Jewish worshippers. In response, the *Shema* was "hidden" in *Musaf Kedushah* to fool these foreign agents, who were engaged in theological censorship. Since *Keriyat Shema* was – under normal circumstances – recited much earlier in the services, by the time the congregation reached the *Musaf Kedushah* these agents of the enemies of the Jewish people were long gone and so *Shema* could be recited here with significantly less fear of reprisal.[119]

This may well explain the presence of the first sentence of *Shema* in the initial prayers of the morning service where it appears and when it is recited within the first three minutes of the community's daily worship.[120] This is unlikely, however, to explain its presence in *Musaf Kedushah* and on the Day of Atonement. Like all military personnel assigned to tedious, non-hazardous duty such as standing in a synagogue and making sure that certain parts of an unfamiliar service were not recited, the soldiers assigned to the tefillah detail would very quickly begin to show up late to their post. This is particularly true since they know that the normal recitation of *Keriyat Shema* does not take place until the worshippers are well into the services. Their absence at the very beginning of the prayers would provide an opportunity right at the start of the liturgy to sneak these words into the daily supplication.

On the other hand, if the various appearances of "Hear O Israel ..." in *Kedushah* were designed to find a home for the "prohibited" *Shema*, then the sentence should appear in *Kedushah* every day, either in *Shaharit*, or if that was too close in time to the original *Shema* recitation, then at the completely separate afternoon service – *Minhah* – by which time these agents of anti-semitism would certainly no longer be in attendance. In fact, why not recite the entire *Keriyat Shema*, not just one verse, at the very end of the *Musaf* service? This would be a more complete recitation of the liturgy, at an even later point in time in the *Shabbat* and holiday worship, when these infiltrators would have been even more likely to have left the building.

Limiting *Shema* only to the *Kedushah* of *Musaf* means that it would not be said at all on the vast majority of the days of the year. It also should appear only once on Yom Kippur, in *Musaf*, and not four times as it does. Given the

---

119 See *Mahzor Vitry*, #138, Rabbi Israel ben Rabbi Joseph Al-Nakawa (14th century), Menorat Hamaor: *Tefillot shel Shabbat*, p. 188.

120 Siddur p. 28

importance of the Day of Atonement to Jews, which would have been known to any of their enemies savvy enough to understand the significance of *Keriyat Shema*, the repeated recitation throughout the day would have made discovery of this subterfuge much more likely. This is particularly true as one would expect heightened scrutiny in the synagogue on the part of the enemies of the Jews on this, the most significant annual holiday of the Jewish year.

Again, *Heikhalot* literature provides us with a dramatic and radically different answer to these questions.

A–Beloved is Israel before the Holy One blessed is He.	א–חביבין ישראל לפני הקדוש ברוך הוא
B–More than the ministering angels.	ב–יותר ממלאכי השרת,
C–For Israel is worthy to mention the Name, may He be blessed, after [only] two [preparatory] words	ג–שישראל ראוים להזכיר השם יתברך לאחר שתי תיבות
D–As it says: (1) Hear (2) Israel, God (the tetragramaton or four letter personal Name of God appears here),	ד–שנאמר: שמע ישראל ה'
E–But the ministering angels are not worthy of mentioning the Name	ה–אבל מלאכי השרת אינם ראוים להזכיר השם
F–Except after three [preparatory] words	ו–אלא לאחר ג' תיבות
G–As it says: (1) Holy (2) holy (3) holy is the God (again the tetragramaton; appears here as well) of hosts.[121]	ז–שנאמר קדוש קדוש קדוש ה' צבאות

To appreciate the import of this text we must note that scholars of this literature understand prayer in *Heikhalot* mysticism as being a numinous experience.[122] In saying this they are claiming that the specific meaning of the words of the liturgies in these sources is not all that important. Rather the words of these prayers are used like a mantra, often repetitively, to help the mystic transcend this world and enter heaven as a spiritual presence.

If that is correct then the number of words needed before one achieves the desired mystical epiphany becomes a very important measure of the spiritual quality of the individual supplicant. The fact that Jews in their most important

---

121 Eisenstein, loc. cit., p. 486.

122 Cf. Elior, Rachel. "Mysticism, Magic, and Angelology: The Perception of Angels in Hekhalot Literature." In *JSQ*, vol. 1, 1993, p. 52.

utterance to God – שמע ישראל ה' א-להינו ה' אחד – take only two words to reach God's Name, while the angels take three in theirs – קדוש קדוש קדוש ה' צבאות מלא כל הארץ כבודו – indicates the superiority of human beings over the angels. In short, people can take less time and need less effort than the celestial creatures to enter God's presence, even though the latter are physically so much closer to the seventh heaven where God's throne resides.

This "superiority of the human being over the angels" is a significant and central theme throughout *Heikhalot* literature, and provides an important corrective to this angelic-centered mysticism.[123] The message of these texts is that although the goal of the mystic is to stand with (or above)[124] the angels before God's throne in praise and prayer, one must not lose oneself in angelic pursuits because the full range of the human experience is simply more important. In prayer, the worshipper joins with the angels in singing the praises of God, but there are other important endeavors in life where the human being stands alone and unique.

In that regard, any sectarian looking to claim that God takes little or no notice of human beings must contend with the fact that – certainly in this literature – God is aware of both angels and people, and that human beings are simply more important than God's heavenly entourage, the celestial hosts. As such it is unreasonable to deny God's involvement with this world and its inhabitants.

The *Musaf Kedushah* on *Shabbat* and holy days is different in its wording and format than the other *Kedushah* recitations of those days. It is this *Musaf* form of the *Kedushah* that appears in all the services of *Yom Kippur*. This variation of the prayer is the most mystical and angelic of all the *Kedushah* forms.[125] This is particularly evident in the Ari and Sephardic (Spanish and Mediterranean area Jews) versions of the liturgy, but it is also true among

---

123   This is a major point that the author makes in Schaefer, Peter. *The Hidden and Manifest God: Some Major Themes in Early Jewish Mysticism*. Albany: 1992.

124   The fact that the angels ask: איה מקום כבודו ? ("Where is His holy place?" cf. Siddur p. 464, Eisenstein, loc. cit., p. 377), or that they are described as having an icy firmament over their heads so that they cannot see God's throne (Ezekiel 1:22–28), while the mystic is able to get to the point where he can look directly at that throne (Ezekiel 1: 26–28, Isaiah 6: 1), again indicates human superiority (see Schaefer).

125   See Rabbi David ben Rabbi Yosef Abudraham (13th century), Abudraham, *Shaharit shel Shabbat*, sv. *Keter Yitnu*.

Ashkenazim (European Jews) as well.[126] Again *Yom Kippur* is the day when the worshippers are said to be most like angels. Not surprisingly, this more angelic *Kedushah* is recited all day long.

It, therefore, becomes particularly important on the occasions when this more mystical *Kedushah* appears, to bring the worshippers back to earth, as it were, by specifically adding the first verse of *Shema* into the prayer. It is this verse that reminds the supplicant of human superiority over the angels even as he recites the angels' own liturgy.

Again, this constitutes a dramatic affirmation of the centrality of the human being in traditional Jewish thought. This also supports our contention that *Keriyat Shema* as presently constituted serves as a non-linear response to the claim of the sectarians that humans are inadequate to receive Divine attention. If the first line of the liturgy affirms human ontological significance to the degree that it does, the sectarian claims "don't have a prayer" of being even remotely correct.

Before we leave this theme, one last aspect of *Keriyat Shema's* import and two additional sources should be introduced.

A–Said Rabbi Mani:	א–אמר רבי מני:
B–Let not *Keriyat Shema* be treated lightly in your eyes,	ב–לא תהא קריית שמע קלה בעיניך,
C–Because it contains 248 words,	ג–מפני שיש בה רמ"ח תיבות,
D–Parallel in number to the limbs that are found in the human being.[127]	ד–כנגד אברים שבאדם,
E–And "Blessed be the Name of His glorious kingdom for ever and ever" is included in that number.	ה–ומהם ברוך שם כבוד מלכותו לעולם ועד,
F–Said the Holy One blessed be He:	ו–אמר הקדוש ברוך הוא:
F–If you protected Mine to read it as established,	ז–אם שמרתם שלי לקרותה כתיקנה,
G–I, too, will preserve yours.[128]	ח–אף אני אשמור את שלכם,

---

126 See Rabbi Yaakov ben Yehuda Landa (15th century). *Sefer ha-Agur*: Laws of Shabbat, #394.

127 This is a frequent theme found in rabbinic literature, cf. B. Eiruvin 54a. It is also claimed to be the number of affirmative commandments in the Torah, cf. *Yalkut Shimoni*: Torah #271.

128 Midrash Tanhuma (Buber): Kedoshim #6.

A–And thus said Rabbi Johanan b. Nuri citing Rabbi Jose b. Durmaskit in the name of Rabbi Akiva:	א–והכי אמר רבי יוחנן בן נורי אמר רבי יוסי בן דורמסקית, משמיה דר' עקיבא,
B–The first pious ones decreed *Keriyat Shema*	ב–חסידים הראשונים תקנו קריאת שמע
C–As against the Ten Commandments	ג–כנגד עשרת הדברות.
D–And as against the number of limbs in the human being.	ד–וכנגד מנין איבריו של אדם.
E–But are there not three [words] lacking [from the necessary number]?	ה–והא חסרו מהם שלשה.
F–They, therefore, decreed that the prayer leader should repeat and complete them.	ו–תקנו שיהא ש"צ חוזר ומשלים אותם.
G–And which are they?	ו–ומאי נינהו.
H–"God your Lord, truth."[129]	ז–ה' א-להיכם אמת:

These two sources explain three anomalies associated with *Keriyat Shema* that we mentioned as we began this chapter. The word אמת ("truth") may have originally been appended to the end of the *tsitsit* paragraph as a statement of affirmation of the veracity of the texts and ideas included in the three paragraphs of *Shema*. This might well have been particularly important after the Ten Commandments were removed from the recitation as an additional element in the Sages' response to the sectarians and their denial of the divinity, and therefore of the truth, of much of the Torah.[130] Nonetheless, in these two sources, אמת takes on a different meaning. It becomes part of a numerological claim that associates the human body with *Keriyat Shema*.

So, too, the need for the doubled recitation of the last three words of *Keriyat Shema* by the prayer leader in communal worship, which is replaced by a single recitation of that phrase and by the requirement to add אל מלך נאמן at the beginning of the liturgy in private devotion, are all explained in these sources. One needs all of these extra elements along with the angelic ברוך שם כבוד מלכותו לעולם ועד, to get to two hundred forty-eight words. Two hundred forty-eight is traditionally understood as the the number of limbs and organs in the body,

---

129 See above n. 50.

130 See Midrash Agadah: Deuteronomy ch. 5:11, which adds אל מלך נאמן to the number of words in the Ten Commandments in order to get to 613, the number of Biblical commandments. The numbers do not equate with the actuality even if one includes the three paragraphs of Shema with the Ten Commandments.

and with all of these additions and liturgical maneuvers in place, *Keriyat Shema* has precisely that number of words. At first glance this all appears to be an interesting numerological exercise without much significance.

Underlying this explanation however, is a profound statement validating the physical aspects of human existence. Even those organs that are used for sex, or for elimination of waste, are valued in this association between *Keriyat Shema* and the human body. In short, once again we have an affirmation here of the totality of the human experience, even in regard to aspects of man's existence that we would not intuitively have thought would be part of that spiritual approbation. Nonetheless, it is clear that expressing the importance of the human being in totality is central to the mystical structure placed on *Keriyat Shema* by the Sages.

Shema begins as the "essence of our faith" in God, and concludes as God's affirmation of the essence of His faith in humankind. This appears to be the import of the phrase "if you protected Mine to read it as established, I, too, will preserve yours," which concludes one of the texts we are discussing.

At the end of the day, *Keriyat Shema* reminds us, in a number of important ways, just how consequential human beings really are to Jewish thought. This is true even in the customs and practices just discussed that we labeled as peripheral at the beginning of this chapter. Though they may be secondary customs that became associated with the recitation of *Keriyat Shema* – coming later in Jewish history and being less central to this liturgy than the primary question of which paragraphs to recite – they are well in line with what we have seen previously. In many ways they mirror the impact and meaning of the more central and profound changes embodied by the removal of the Ten Commandments and their replacement by the *tsitsit* section. At the end of the day, all of these things bring us back to the true profundity of *Keriyat Shema* that celebrates the centrality of God and the human being to Judaism and Jewish belief.

We now return from our intellectual travels through the heavens of early Jewish mysticism to some last issues concerning *Keriyat Shema* that fall within the rubric of more rationalist Judaism. The severing of the first verse of *Shema* from its connection to the rest of the paragraph allows it to be used as one of two basic texts in early childhood education.

| A–If he is able to speak, | א–יודע לדבר |
| B–His father must teach him | ב–אביו לומדו תורה וקריאת |

Torah and *Keriyat Shema*.	שמע.
C–What is meant by Torah?	ג–תורה מאי היא?
D–Rav Hamnuna said:	ד–אמר רב המנונא:
E–[The verse] "Moses commanded us Torah, an inheritance for the congregation of Jacob."[131]	ה–תורה צוה לנו משה מורשה קהלת יעקב.
F–What is meant by *Keriyat Shema*?	ו–קריאת שמע מאי היא?
G–The first verse.[132]	ז–פסוק ראשון.

Further, the *Shema*, and particularly the first verse of the liturgy, become the text of choice with which to affirm one's commitment to God as one leaves this world. Though one can find other texts used in this way in Jewish history,[133] given the central beliefs of Judaism embodied in *Keriyat Shema* this usage is not surprising.

Also, the memory of the famous Rabbi Akiva reciting this prayer and this verse as he was martyred, made this recitation into an even more dramatic act of unending faith in God. So, too, the interpretation by Rabbi Akiva – at the time of his martyrdom – of the second Biblical verse of *Shema*, "You shall love God your Lord with all your heart, and with all your soul, and with all your might" to mean that loving God with all your soul entails giving up your life for Him, made this the expression of choice for Jews at their final moments of existence in this world.[134]

Using the first sentence of *Shema* to affirm one's basic belief in and commitment to God is also done by Jewish worshippers when the Torah is taken out of its ark on Sabbaths and holidays. Those gathered in the synagogue repeat the words of this sentence in response to the prayer leader who chants the verse while holding the Torah scroll that contains God's revelation.[135] The words of the Torah are understood by Jews to be the source of how they are to live their lives and structure their beliefs. As such, using the verse that begins the prayer that incorporates the most important and basic Jewish principals into its text, certainly makes sense at this point in the services.

---

131 Deuteronomy 33:4.

132 B. Sukah 42a.

133 See the chapter on *Aleinu* in this volume.

134 B. Berakhot 61b. See my beloved congregant Herman Wouk's dramatic memory of reciting this verse as he thought he was going to be swept overboard while serving in the U.S. Navy in World War II in his *This is My God*. N.Y.: 1959.

135 Siddur p. 436.

Finally, for one very important Sage, the entire history and meaning of *Keriyat Shema* was embodied in just this one verse.

A–Our Rabbis taught:	א–תנו רבנן:
B–"Hear Israel, God our Lord, God is One":	ב–שמע ישראל ה' א-להינו ה' אחד
C–This was Rabbi Judah the Prince's *Keriyat Shema*.	ג–זו קריאת שמע של רבי יהודה הנשיא.
D–Rav said to Rabbi Hiyya:	ד–אמר ליה רב לרבי חייא:
E–"I do not see Rabbi [Rabbi Judah the Prince], accept upon himself the yoke of the kingdom of heaven [i.e., recite the *Shema*]."	ה–לא חזינא ליה לרבי דמקבל עליה מלכות שמים.
F–He said to him:	ו–אמר ליה:
G–"Son of Princes!	ז–בר פחתי!
H–In the moment when he passes his hand over his eyes,	ח–בשעה שמעביר ידיו על פניו
I–He accepts upon himself the yoke of the kingdom of heaven [because he uses that moment to recite the first sentence].	ט–מקבל עליו עול מלכות שמים.
J–Does he finish it, or does he not go back and finish it?"	י–חוזר וגומרה, או אינו חוזר וגומרה?
K–Bar Kappara said:	כ–בר קפרא אומר:
L–"He does not go back and finish it";	ל–אינו חוזר וגומרה,
M–Rabbi Simeon son of Rabbi said:[136]	מ–רבי שמעון ברבי אומר:
N–"He does go back and finish it."	נ–חוזר וגומרה.
O–Said Bar Kappara to Rabbi Simeon the son of Rabbi:	ס–אמר ליה בר קפרא לרבי שמעון ברבי:
P–"On my view that he does not go back and finish it,	ע–בשלמא לדידי דאמינא אינו חוזר וגומרה
Q–There is a good reason why Rabbi always is anxious to give a lesson in which there is mention of the Exodus from Egypt [to compensate for the lack of the third paragraph that mentions this event].	פ–היינו דמהדר רבי אשמעתא דאית בה יציאת מצרים,
R–But on your view that he does	צ–אלא לדידך דאמרת חוזר

---

136   It is interesting that someone would debate with Rabbi's son about Rabbi's liturgical practices.

go back and finish it,	וגומרה,
S–Why is he anxious to give such a lesson?	ק–למה ליה לאהדורי?
T–So as to mention the going forth from Egypt at	ר–כדי להזכיר יציאת מצרים
at the proper time [since he will only finish *Shema*	בזמנה.
after the lesson is over, and that will be after	
the mandated time for reciting *Keriyat Shema*,	
which is relatively early in the morning]."[137]	

Rabbi Judah the Prince, the editor of the Mishnah (c. 200 C.E.) was a pivotal figure in rabbinic history. The fact that he was called simply Rabbi or "Our holy Rabbi" in talmudic texts makes this abundantly clear.[138]

With the precedent of this source in place, we can understand more completely, why we have so many appearances of just the first verse of *Keriyat Shema* included at so many different points in Jewish prayers. At each of these points it can and did serve to represent the entire substance and meaning of the *Shema* liturgy and the "essence of the faith" that is included in it.

Keriyat Shema may be contemporary Judaism's best-known prayer. It is recited twice a day in its entirety, both in *Shaharit* and again in *Ma'ariv*. However, for it to have achieved its present stature and structure, and to be used in all the places that are familiar to us today, sectarian challenges, concerns about lengthy Biblical passages, mystical journeys into heaven, angelic and Temple liturgies, affirmation of Biblical truths, numerological parallels to the number of bodily organs, belief in the superiority of human beings over angels, the presence of prayer-censoring soldiers in the synagogue and freeing the first verse of *Keriyat Shema* to stand and function alone, have all connected with one another across Jewish history to give us the prayer that we know.

This liturgy, at its most basic level, also needed traditional Jews to engage in a paradigm shift. This change of perception took this ritual that originally was understood as a *Keriya* – a reading and study of a series of Biblical texts – and transformed people's understanding of it after the destruction of the second Temple into a supplication and a prayer of praise before God. As with

---

137 B. Berakhot 13b. For the timing of *Keriyat Shema* see M. Berakhot 1:2.
138 See M. Shabbat 118b, B. Gittin 59a, B. Sanhedrin 36a.

all aspects of Jewish liturgical practice – and particularly in regards to the *Siddur's* most important components – the long and varied history of Judaism's ritual customs has taken this critically important early element of the liturgy in directions never anticipated by the community at its moment of origin, and only dimly remembered, if at all, by its contemporary adherents.

CHAPTER 2

Nishmat: The Soul, the Song, Shabbat and the Pope

Nishmat (Siddur p. 400)

נשמת

The soul of all that lives will bless Your Name, God our Lord, and the spirit of all flesh shall beautify and exalt the memory of You, our King at all times.

נִשְׁמַת כָּל חַי תְּבָרֵךְ אֶת שִׁמְךָ ה' אֱ-לֹהֵינוּ. וְרוּחַ כָּל בָּשָׂר תְּפָאֵר וּתְרוֹמֵם זִכְרְךָ מַלְכֵּנוּ תָּמִיד:

From one end of the world to the other, You are God, and other than You we have no king, who redeems, saves, releases, rescues, sustains and is merciful in every time of difficulty and distress; we have no king, but You.

מִן הָעוֹלָם וְעַד הָעוֹלָם אַתָּה אֵ-ל. וּמִבַּלְעָדֶיךָ אֵין לָנוּ מֶלֶךְ גּוֹאֵל וּמוֹשִׁיעַ. פּוֹדֶה וּמַצִּיל וּמְפַרְנֵס וּמְרַחֵם בְּכָל עֵת צָרָה וְצוּקָה. אֵין לָנוּ מֶלֶךְ אֶלָּא אַתָּה:

Lord of the first and of the last, Lord of all creatures, Master of all Generations, Who is renowned by many praises; Who guides His world with kindness and His creatures with mercy.

אֱ-לֹהֵי הָרִאשׁוֹנִים וְהָאַחֲרוֹנִים. אֱ-לוֹהַּ כָּל בְּרִיּוֹת. אֲדוֹן כָּל תּוֹלָדוֹת. הַמְהֻלָּל בְּרֹב הַתִּשְׁבָּחוֹת. הַמְנַהֵג עוֹלָמוֹ בְּחֶסֶד וּבְרִיּוֹתָיו בְּרַחֲמִים:

And God neither slumbers nor sleeps. He awakens those who are sleeping and rouses those who are slumbering. He gives speech to the mute, sets free those who are bound, supports those who fall and straightens those

וַה' לֹא יָנוּם וְלֹא יִישָׁן. הַמְעוֹרֵר יְשֵׁנִים. וְהַמֵּקִיץ נִרְדָּמִים. וְהַמֵּשִׂיחַ אִלְּמִים. וְהַמַּתִּיר אֲסוּרִים. וְהַסּוֹמֵךְ נוֹפְלִים. וְהַזּוֹקֵף כְּפוּפִים. לְךָ

79

who are bent. To You alone we give thanks.

Were our mouths full of song as the sea, and our tongues produced music as the multitude of its waves, and our lips brought praise as the wide expanse of the heavens, and our eyes giving light as the sun and the moon, and our hands spread as the eagles of the sky and our feet as swift as the deer, we would not be sufficiently able to thank You, God, our Lord and Lord of our fathers, and to bless Your Name for even one out of a thousand of the thousand, thousands of thousands and multiple tens of thousands of times. For the good things you have done for our ancestors and for us.

From Egypt You redeemed us, God our Lord, and from the house of slaves You released us; In famine You fed us, and in plenty You provided for us. From the sword You saved us and from plague You gave us escape; and from severe and chronic diseases You spared us.

Until now Your mercy has helped us, and Your kindness has not abandoned us. Do not abandon us, God our Lord, forever.

Therefore the organs that You set aside within us and the spirit and the soul that You breathed into our nostrils, and the tongue that You placed in our mouth, all of them shall thank, bless, praise, beautify, exalt, revere, sanctify and establish the rule of Your Name, our King.

For every mouth shall offer thanks to You, every tongue shall take an oath to You, every knee shall bend to You; every one who is erect shall bow before You. All hearts shall be in awe of You, and all innermost selves shall sing to Your Name, as it is written: "All my bones shall say, God, who is like You? You save the poor man from one who is stronger than he, the

לְבַדְּךָ אֲנַחְנוּ מוֹדִים:

אִלּוּ פִינוּ מָלֵא שִׁירָה כַּיָּם. וּלְשׁוֹנֵנוּ רִנָּה כַּהֲמוֹן גַּלָּיו. וְשִׂפְתוֹתֵינוּ שֶׁבַח כְּמֶרְחֲבֵי רָקִיעַ. וְעֵינֵינוּ מְאִירוֹת כַּשֶּׁמֶשׁ וְכַיָּרֵחַ. וְיָדֵינוּ פְרוּשׂוֹת כְּנִשְׁרֵי שָׁמָיִם. וְרַגְלֵינוּ קַלּוֹת כָּאַיָּלוֹת. אֵין אֲנַחְנוּ מַסְפִּיקִים לְהוֹדוֹת לְךָ ה' אֱ-לֹהֵינוּ וֵא-לֹהֵי אֲבוֹתֵינוּ. וּלְבָרֵךְ אֶת שְׁמֶךָ עַל אַחַת מֵאֶלֶף אַלְפֵי אֲלָפִים וְרִבֵּי רְבָבוֹת פְּעָמִים. הַטּוֹבוֹת שֶׁעָשִׂיתָ עִם אֲבוֹתֵינוּ וְעִמָּנוּ:

מִמִּצְרַיִם גְּאַלְתָּנוּ ה' אֱ-לֹהֵינוּ. וּמִבֵּית עֲבָדִים פְּדִיתָנוּ. בְּרָעָב זַנְתָּנוּ. וּבְשָׂבָע כִּלְכַּלְתָּנוּ. מֵחֶרֶב הִצַּלְתָּנוּ. וּמִדֶּבֶר מִלַּטְתָּנוּ. וּמֵחֳלָיִם רָעִים וְנֶאֱמָנִים דִּלִּיתָנוּ:

עַד הֵנָּה עֲזָרוּנוּ רַחֲמֶיךָ. וְלֹא עֲזָבוּנוּ חֲסָדֶיךָ וְאַל תִּטְּשֵׁנוּ ה' אֱ-לֹהֵינוּ לָנֶצַח:

עַל כֵּן אֵבָרִים שֶׁפִּלַּגְתָּ בָּנוּ. וְרוּחַ וּנְשָׁמָה שֶׁנָּפַחְתָּ בְּאַפֵּינוּ. וְלָשׁוֹן אֲשֶׁר שַׂמְתָּ בְּפִינוּ. הֵן הֵם. יוֹדוּ וִיבָרְכוּ וִישַׁבְּחוּ וִיפָאֲרוּ וִירוֹמְמוּ וְיַעֲרִיצוּ וְיַקְדִּישׁוּ וְיַמְלִיכוּ אֶת שְׁמֶךָ מַלְכֵּנוּ:

כִּי כָל פֶּה לְךָ יוֹדֶה. וְכָל לָשׁוֹן לְךָ תִשָּׁבַע. וְכָל בֶּרֶךְ לְךָ תִכְרַע. וְכָל קוֹמָה לְפָנֶיךָ תִשְׁתַּחֲוֶה. וְכָל לְבָבוֹת יִירָאוּךָ. וְכָל קֶרֶב וּכְלָיוֹת יְזַמְּרוּ לִשְׁמֶךָ. כַּדָּבָר שֶׁכָּתוּב. כָּל עַצְמוֹתַי תֹּאמַרְנָה ה' מִי כָמוֹךָ. מַצִּיל עָנִי מֵחָזָק מִמֶּנּוּ. וְעָנִי וְאֶבְיוֹן מִגּוֹזְלוֹ.

poor and the destitute from the one who would rob him." [Psalms 35:10]

Who is similar to You? Who can be compared to You? Who can be valued like You? The great, mighty and terrible Lord, the highest Lord, the Creator of heaven and earth.

We will praise You, we will exalt You, we will beautify You, and we will bless Your holy Name, as it says: "For David: My soul bless God and all my innards His holy Name." [Psalms 103:1]

[On Festivals the Cantor begins with: "The Lord . . ."]

The Lord in the power of Your strength, the Great One in the glory of Your Name, the Powerful One forever, the Terrible One in Your awesomeness,

[On Rosh Hashanah and Yom Kippur the Cantor begins with: "The King . . ."]

The King Who sits on a high and lofty throne.

[On Sabbaths the Cantor begins with: "Who abides . . ."]

Who abides forever, exalted and sanctified is His Name, and it is written: "You righteous, sing about God, for the upright praise is appropriate." [Psalms 33:1]

By the mouth of the upright You are praised (exalted*), and by the words of the righteous You are blessed, and by the tongue of the pious You are exalted (sanctified*), and in the innards of the holy ones You are sanctified (praised*).

And in the assemblies of tens of thousands of Your people, the House of Israel, Your Name, our King, will be beautified with song in all generations. For this is the duty of all creatures, before You, God our Lord and God of our fathers, to give thanks, to laud, to praise, to

מִי יִדְמֶה לָּךְ. וּמִי יִשְׁוֶה לָּךְ. וּמִי יַעֲרָךְ לָּךְ. הָאֵ־ל הַגָּדוֹל הַגִּבּוֹר וְהַנּוֹרָא אֵל עֶלְיוֹן. קוֹנֵה שָׁמַיִם וָאָרֶץ:

נְהַלֶּלְךָ וּנְשַׁבֵּחֲךָ וּנְפָאֶרְךָ וּנְבָרֵךְ אֶת שֵׁם קָדְשֶׁךָ. כָּאָמוּר, לְדָוִד, בָּרְכִי נַפְשִׁי אֶת ה'. וְכָל קְרָבַי אֶת שֵׁם קָדְשׁוֹ:

ביום טוב מתחיל החזן "האל בתעצומות":

הָאֵ־ל בְּתַעֲצֻמוֹת עֻזֶּךָ. הַגָּדוֹל בִּכְבוֹד שְׁמֶךָ. הַגִּבּוֹר לָנֶצַח וְהַנּוֹרָא בְּנוֹרְאוֹתֶיךָ:

בראש השנה ויום הכפורים מתחיל החזן "המלך":

הַמֶּלֶךְ הַיּוֹשֵׁב עַל כִּסֵּא רָם וְנִשָּׂא:

בשבת מתחיל החזן "שוכן עד":

שׁוֹכֵן עַד מָרוֹם וְקָדוֹשׁ שְׁמוֹ. וְכָתוּב רַנְּנוּ צַדִּיקִים בַּה'. לַיְשָׁרִים נָאוָה תְהִלָּה:

בְּפִי יְשָׁרִים תִּתְהַלָּל (י"נ תתרומם). וּבְדִבְרֵי צַדִּיקִים תִּתְבָּרַךְ. וּבִלְשׁוֹן חֲסִידִים תִּתְרוֹמָם (י"נ תתקדש). וּבְקֶרֶב קְדוֹשִׁים תִּתְקַדָּשׁ (י"נ תתהלל):

וּבְמַקְהֲלוֹת רִבְבוֹת עַמְּךָ בֵּית יִשְׂרָאֵל. בְּרִנָּה יִתְפָּאַר שִׁמְךָ מַלְכֵּנוּ בְּכָל דּוֹר וָדוֹר. שֶׁר חוֹבַת כָּל הַיְצוּרִים. לִ־,ךְ ה' אֱ־לֹהֵינוּ וֵא־לֹהֵי אֲ־וֹתֵינוּ. לְהוֹדוֹת לְהַלֵּל לְשַׁבֵּחַ לְפָאֵר

beautify, to exalt, to adorn, to bless, to raise high, and to sing praises, beyond all the words of the songs and praises of David, the son of Jesse, Your servant, Your anointed one.	לְרוֹמֵם לְהַדֵּר לְבָרֵךְ לְעַלֵּה וּלְקַלֵּס. עַל כָּל דִּבְרֵי שִׁירוֹת וְתִשְׁבְּחוֹת דָּוִד בֶּן יִשַׁי עַבְדֶּךָ מְשִׁיחֶךָ:

*This version used on the High Holidays.

THE SOUL OF all that lives will bless Your Name (נשמת כל חי תברך את שמך): this prayer, whose history we are about to examine, describes the praise that is naturally offered to God in His role as the Deity. It does so in remarkably powerful and compelling ways. The text mixes descriptions of God's eternity and uniqueness, His kindness and His protective concern for the Jewish people, with historic examples of the Almighty's mercy and providence. It also includes dramatic words that express how ultimately inadequate human beings are in actually portraying all the accolades that are due to the Creator. The outside influences, associated customs and changing understanding of the text of this prayer that shaped its use over the last two millennia make up the intriguing story that we will tell here.

Nishmat is most familiar today from the early morning service of Sabbath and holidays where it appears at the end of the section called פסוקי דזמרה (Pesukei Dezimrah; verses of song and praise, which itself comes toward the beginning of the prayers).[1] It marks the transition point where the prayer leader for *Shaharit* (the central part of the morning service) begins his sacred task. In *Ashkenazi* circles this occurs when the words שוכן עד (Shokhen ad, Who abides forever), which appear toward the end of the prayer, are recited. For Sepharadim, the Cantor starts with the words *Nishmat kol hai* at the beginning of this beautiful text.[2]

This liturgy can also be found in the Passover *Haggadah* (the special ritual service for that holiday), where it is recited toward the conclusion of the *Seder* (the festive meal that is the central ceremony of the holiday at which the *Haggadah* is read and studied).[3] *Nishmat* appears in a secondary or supportive role as part of a series of songs and praises of God that make up the *Hallel*

---

1   Siddur p. 400. פסוקי דזמרא for Sabbaths and Festivals occupy pp. 368–404.
2   In fact, the Sephardic liturgy does not include the words שוכן עד.
3   Haggadah p.192.

section of the *Hagaddah*.[4] I describe *Nishmat's* role as secondary because *Hallel*, in this context, specifically refers to Psalms 113–118,[5] and *Nishmat* does not appear in those Psalms, nor can it be found in any other Biblical text. Instead, *Nishmat*, along with some other paragraphs, serves to offer additional praises to God as a kind of liturgical counterpoint to the actual *Hallel* recitation on the night of Passover.

From early in my childhood I remember that whenever we reached *Nishmat* on Passover eve, someone would comment on how remarkable it was to find "morning" prayers being recited in the middle of the night. In response, someone else would suggest that this must be a sign of the coming "dawning of the Redemption," either in our reliving the story of the exodus from Egypt at the Passover *Seder* – or in the contemporary hope for the coming of the Messiah.

Nice sentiments! But from a chronological perspective, incorrect. The available historical evidence shows us that *Nishmat* of Passover night was not borrowed from the morning prayers of *Shabbat* and holidays; instead *Nishmat* of the morning liturgies was borrowed from Passover. Jewish tradition did not bring a prayer celebrating daybreak into the nighttime *Seder*; instead it brought a less-than-primary prayer that was part of the Passover experience into a more central role in the Sabbath and holiday morning services.

Speaking more generally. Often in examining Jewish liturgy we find the same text appearing in different places where it is used in very different ways.[6] When that occurs we can only understand its history if we uncover the accurate chronology of the different uses of the prayer and how the understanding of the meaning of the text changed as it moved from one venue in the liturgy to another.

If we follow that approach then the story of *Nishmat* as told in our extant sources begins with Mishnah: Pesahim 10:7. This entire chapter in the Mishnah describes the Passover *Seder* as it began to develop in the era following the destruction of the Second Temple. The relevant text for our purposes reads:

---

4   Ibid., pp. 174–201.

5   Haggadah pp. 150–153, 178–189; Siddur p. 632f. *Hallel* can also refer to Psalm 136 (Siddur p. 384), which is called *Hallel Hagadol* (the great *Hallel*), cf Tosefta Ta'anit: 2:17. The original *Hallel* may have been the Song of the Sea (Exodus 15: 1–19), cf. Pesahim 117a.

6   Cf. the origin of the first paragraph of the Blessing for the New Moon, which derives from a personal post-*Amidah* prayer, apparently recited every weekday by its author, and discussed in the chapter on *Birkat ha-Hodesh* in this volume.

A–They filled the third cup for him (at the Passover *Seder*). He then recites grace after meals.	א–מזגו לו כוס שלישי –מברך על מזונו.
B–Over the fourth [cup] he concludes the *Hallel*, and recites the blessing of the song.	ב–רביעי –גומר עליו את הלל, ואומר עליו ברכת השיר.

The Talmud Bavli is unsure as to what constitutes this "blessing of the song."

A–What is the Blessing of the Song?	א–מאי ברכת השיר?
B–Rav Judah said: "They shall praise Thee, O Lord our God";	ב–רב יהודה אמר: יהללוך ה' א–להינו,
C–Rabbi Johanan said: "The soul of all that lives."[7]	ג–ורבי יוחנן אמר: נשמת כל חי

Our present practice at least since the geonic period (c. 800–1000 C.E.) is to include both suggested texts in the *Haggadah*.[8]

Moreover, from the wording of the talmudic passage we are discussing it would seem that *Nishmat* was a known prayer that was even older than its first appearance at the *Seder*. Both Rabbi Johanan and the community for whom the Talmud *Bavli* was redacted are assumed by this text to know what liturgy is meant by the designation נשמת כל חי. Unfortunately, the other uses the text may have had predate its inclusion in the *Haggadah* and appear to be lost in the mists of history.

The Mishnah was edited in the late second or early third centuries CE, while Rabbi Johanan was in his prime some fifty years or so later.[9] These citations from rabbinic texts show us that *Nishmat* had developed its association with Passover eve no later than the third century and possibly even earlier.

In contrast, it is not until the medieval period that we first find mention of anyone reciting *Nishmat* in the morning on *Shabbat* and special days – and even then there was some opposition to the practice. On the one hand, Maimonides (1138–1204), who, among many other things, was a *Sephardic*

---

7   B. Pesahim 118a.

8   Compare *Seder Rav Amram Gaon, Seder Pesah,* Bnai Berak: 1984, with *Teshuvot ha-Geonim ha-Chadashot,* Jerusalem: Simcha Emanuel, 1995, #36.

9   His actual dates were 180–279 C.E.

scholar (Jews from Spain or the Mediterranean countries are called Sephardic), says:

A–On the Sabbath the entire nation is accustomed to add before this blessing (*Yishtabah*, which is the concluding benediction of פסוקי דזמרה (*Pesukei De-Zimrah*),[10] this liturgical language:	א–בשבת נהגו כל העם להוסיף לפני ברכה זו נוסח זה:
B–"The soul of all that lives will bless Your Name."[11]	ב–נשמת כל חי תברך את שמך

In comparison, *Kol Bo*, an early *Ashkenazic* (the designation for Jews who come from European countries other than Spain) compilation of laws and customs that was written by Rabbi Aharon b. Jacob Ha-Kohen of Narbonne, France (13th–14th century), tells of a more dramatic history for this prayer.

A–But the custom of Narbonne is that on the Sabbath they do *not* say *Nishmat Kol Hai* and also *not* *Ve-ilu Finu* (the second paragraph of *Nishmat*. Some *Siddurim* lack the conjunctive *ve* and record the text as *Ilu Finu*),	א–ומנהג נרבונה שבשבת אין אומרים נשמת כל חי ולא ואלו פינו
B–But rather *Yishtabah* and the *Yotser* (the pre-*Shema* liturgy that comes after *Pesukei De-Zimrah*)[12] of weekdays . . .	ב–אלא ישתבח ויוצר של חול ...
C–But we do not act in this fashion.[13]	ג–ואנו לא כן נהגו ,

In all likelihood those who objected to *Nishmat* did so out of concern that reciting it at this point would be an interruption (a *hefsek*) in the proper order of the prayers. Such an interruption is not allowed by Jewish law.[14]

Whatever the reason for the objection, the debate found in medieval sources

---

10   Siddur p. 404. *Pesukei De-Zimrah* for Shabbat appears on p. 368–405.

11   Maimonides: Mishneh Torah: *Seder Tefillot Kol ha-Shanah*.

12   Siddur pp. 406–413. *Yotzer* is the section that describes the great noise of the angels in heaven that precedes recitation of *Shema Yisrael* discussed in the chapter on *Keriyat Shema*.

13   Jerusalem: 1997 #114. There is some doubt as to whether he is actually the author of this work.

14   See Rabbi Chalfon Moses Ha-Kohen, Responsa *Sho'el Ve-Nishal*, *Orah Hayim*, 2:14,

as to whether *Nishmat* should or should not be recited as part of the *Shabbat* and holiday morning liturgy indicates that hundreds of years after this prayer took its place in the Passover *Seder*, it was not yet a fixture in the Sabbath and holiday morning services in all Jewish communities.

Kol Bo, in this source, mentions *Ilu Finu* (if our mouths were . . .) – the "second paragraph of *Nishmat*" – as if it were a separate liturgical text. In truth, this paragraph appears in all known iterations of *Nishmat* as an inseparable, integral part of the prayer. As we shall see, however, there was a time when this second paragraph was used for a different ritual purpose that has also largely disappeared from Jewish collective communal memory. Nonetheless, it is this second paragraph that provided the key that opened the door for *Nishmat's* move to the morning services of these special days.

The *Ilu Finu* paragraph incorporates and redeems a theme that has Biblical roots. The prophet Jeremiah, in describing his overwhelming sorrow at the destruction of the first Temple, says:

Who can make my head change into water, and my eyes into a fountain of tears, so that I might cry day and night for the slain of the daughter of my people?[15]	מי יתן ראשי מים ועיני מקור דמעה ואבכה יומם ולילה את חללי בת עמי:

This precise imagery is used in one of the *Kinot* (poetic dirges) of the Ninth of Av, when many of the tragedies of Jewish history are memorialized.[16] It expresses the community's utter inability to adequately mourn the losses it has suffered over the centuries due to persecution and violence.[17]

Remarkably, Jewish perseverance also managed to transform this theme of

---

(early 20th century), who discusses this issue and offers an explanation as to why it is not an interruption.

15 Jeremiah 8:23.

16 Kinot p. 270. This *Kinah* speaks specifically of the tragedies associated with the Crusades. See the chapter on the Song of Glory in this volume.

17 The *Kinah* we are referencing begins:

מי יתן ראשי מים ועיני מקור דמעה ואבכה יומם ולילה על חללי בת עמי

"Who can make my head change into water, and my eyes into a fountain of tears, so that I might cry day and night *concerning* the slain of the daughter of my people" citing the verse we are discussing, but with a minor variation in the wording; see David and Hillel Altschuler in their commentaries *Metzudat David* and *Metzudat Zion*, ad. loc., who translate את as על in this verse.

unending weeping in the face of tragedy into an image that could be used to praise God. This far more positive formulation speaks of the human inability to describe the glory of the Almighty's attributes regardless of how many tools and how much effort one invests in such an enterprise.

In the *Ilu Finu* paragraph this is expressed as:

A–Were our mouths full of song as the sea,	א–אִלּוּ פִינוּ מָלֵא שִׁירָה כַיָּם.
B–And our tongues produced music as the multitude of its waves,	ב–וּלְשׁוֹנֵנוּ רִנָּה כַּהֲמוֹן גַּלָּיו.
C–And our lips brought praise as the wide expanse of the heavens,	ג–וְשִׂפְתוֹתֵינוּ שֶׁבַח כְּמֶרְחֲבֵי רָקִיעַ.
D–And our eyes giving of light as the sun and the moon,	ד–וְעֵינֵינוּ מְאִירוֹת כַּשֶּׁמֶשׁ וְכַיָּרֵחַ.
E–And our hands spread as the eagles of the sky	ה–וְיָדֵינוּ פְרוּשׂוֹת כְּנִשְׁרֵי שָׁמָיִם.
F–And our feet as swift as the deer,	ו–וְרַגְלֵינוּ קַלּוֹת כָּאַיָּלוֹת.
G–We would not be sufficiently able to thank You, God, our Lord and Lord of our fathers,	ז–אֵין אֲנַחְנוּ מַסְפִּיקִים לְהוֹדוֹת לְךָ ה' אֱ־לֹהֵינוּ וֵא־לֹהֵי אֲבוֹתֵינוּ.
H–And to bless Your Name	ח–וּלְבָרֵךְ אֶת שְׁמֶךָ
I–For even one out of a thousand of the thousand, thousands of thousands and multiple tens of thousands of times.	ט–עַל אַחַת מֵאֶלֶף אַלְפֵי אֲלָפִים וְרִבֵּי רְבָבוֹת פְּעָמִים.
J–For the good things you have done for our ancestors and for us.	י–הַטּוֹבוֹת שֶׁעָשִׂיתָ עִם אֲבוֹתֵינוּ וְעִמָּנוּ:
K–From Egypt You redeemed us, God our Lord,	כ–מִמִּצְרַיִם גְּאַלְתָּנוּ ה' אֱ־לֹהֵינוּ.
L–And from the house of slaves You released us;	ל–וּמִבֵּית עֲבָדִים פְּדִיתָנוּ.
M–In famine You fed us,	מ–בְּרָעָב זַנְתָּנוּ.
N–And in plenty You provided for us.	נ–וּבְשָׂבָע כִּלְכַּלְתָּנוּ.
O–From the sword You saved us	ס–מֵחֶרֶב הִצַּלְתָּנוּ.
P–And from plague You gave us escape;	ע–וּמִדֶּבֶר מִלַּטְתָּנוּ.
Q–And from severe and chronic diseases You spared us.	פ–וּמֵחֳלָיִם רָעִים וְנֶאֱמָנִים דִּלִּיתָנוּ:
R–Until now Your mercy has helped us,	צ–עַד הֵנָּה עֲזָרוּנוּ רַחֲמֶיךָ.
S–And Your kindness has not abandoned us.	ק–וְלֹא עֲזָבוּנוּ חֲסָדֶיךָ
T–Do not abandon us, God our Lord, forever.	ר–וְאַל תִּטְּשֵׁנוּ ה' אֱ־לֹהֵינוּ לָנֶצַח:

Liturgically, one also finds the same theme in the Aramaic poem *Akdamut* that is chanted as an introduction to the Torah reading on the first day of the holiday of *Shavuot* in many Jewish communities.[18] The Biblical section read on that day tells of the revelation at Sinai and of the giving of the Ten Commandments.[19] As part of reliving that seminal moment in Jewish history, many synagogues add this poem. It, too, incorporates the theme of the inability to properly express gratitude to God no matter what tools are used. Similar expressions appear in some medieval philosophical and ethical works such as Bahya Ibn Paquda's *Duties of the Heart* (חבות הלבבות).[20]

As indicated, *Ve-ilu Finu* (or *Ilu Finu*) appears as part of *Nishmat* in all of our current texts. Nonetheless one important appearance of this liturgy as a separate and independent prayer is recalled in rabbinic literature.

A–Regarding the coming of the rain [in the rainy season], should one recite the blessing "Who is good and does good"?[21]	א–ועל הגשמים הטוב והמטיב מברך?
B–But Rabbi Abbahu said, while some say it has been taught in a Baraitha:[22]	ב–והאמר רבי אבהו, ואמרי לה במתניתא תנא:
C–"From when do they say the blessing over rain?	ג–מאימתי מברכין על הגשמים
D–*From the time that the bridegroom goes out to meet his bride* [when the raindrops begin to rebound from the puddles that the rain has caused and move up toward the rain that is still coming down]."	ד–משיצא חתן לקראת כלה.
E–What blessing do they say?	ה–מאי מברכין?
F–Rav Judah said: "We give thanks to You for every single drop which You have caused to fall for us";	ו–אמר רב יהודה: מודים אנחנו לך על כל טפה וטפה שהורדת לנו,
G–And Rabbi Johanan concluded the prayer with: "If our mouths were full of song like the sea . . . we could not sufficiently give thanks unto You, God our Lord, etc." up to "bow before You."[23]	ז–ורבי יוחנן מסיים בה הכי: אילו פינו מלא שירה כים וכו' אין אנו מספיקין להודות לך ה' אלהינו . . . עד תשתחוה

---

18 Siddur 714f. *Akdamut* was composed by Rabbi Meir b. Yitzchak of Worms, Germany, who lived in the 11th century.

19 The Biblical reading is Exodus ch. 19–20.

20 Cf. *Sha'ar ha-Yihud* 1:10, Jerusalem: 1928.

21 This is the blessing recited in response to good news, M. Berakhot 9:2.

22 A teaching from the period of the Mishnah not recorded in the Mishnah.

23 B. Berakhot 59b.

To the best of my knowledge this prayer is not recited in this way today.

It is not clear from the wording of this text whether *Ilu Finu* was originally a paragraph unto itself that was added both to *Nishmat* and – in the view of Rabbi Johanan, who seems to be a champion of this liturgy – to the rain prayer as well, or if Rabbi Johanan simply borrowed this paragraph from its original home within *Nishmat* and included it here. In either case it expresses the unlimited gratitude that people have when precious life-giving rain begins to fall in the land of Israel.

In that same vein, the imagery of unlimited praises accompanying a groom going out to meet his bride[24] is not only relevant to rain – reflecting the yearning of the land of Israel and the people who live on it for the life and sustenance that comes with precipitation[25] – it is also a redemptive, Messianic vision. In the Bible, God and the Jewish people are portrayed as marriage partners.[26] The sinning of the Jews, and particularly their worshipping of other gods, is portrayed as adultery.[27] Exile and diaspora, in this metaphor, become a marital separation, and the coming of the Messiah and the attendant redemption of the Jews is parallel to a loving reconciliation.[28] That is the moment when the Groom (God) again goes out to meet His bride (the Jewish people), and He again deserves unlimited accolades for being willing to do so.

This explains the original appropriateness of the prayer to the themes of Passover night when Jews celebrate being saved from Egypt and pray for the messianic salvation of the "end of days."[29] The *Seder* is a moment filled with the potential that God will use the opportunity of a celebration of freedom and redemption – which evokes the time when we were first connected with Him as a nation – to make His reappearance as He returns to His "bride." In short, both the beginning of the rainy season and Passover evoke enough of the same type of imagery, that this paragraph can, appropriately, be shared between them.

Further, and this is the key that I mentioned above, the phrase "from when

---

24 Cf. *Yalkut Shimoni* I Kings 201; B. Ketuvot 17a; and Baruch Epstein (1860–1942), *Torah Temimah*: Shir Hashirim 4:11 n. 138.

25 Cf. Deut. 11:11–12.

26 Cf. Isaiah 54:5.

27 Cf. Hosea 1:2.

28 Cf. Isaiah 49–50, Hosea 1–2.

29 Cf, the very end of the *Seder*, Haggadah, p. 200, and the words: לשנה הבאה בירושלים (Next year in Jerusalem).

the groom goes out to meet his bride," which refers to large drops of rain falling on puddles of water and creating a corresponding splash that moves upward toward the still descending precipitation. It is an imagery that one also finds in connection with bringing the spiritual experience of *Shabbat* into one's life. The Sabbath, too, is a divine gift worthy of unlimited praise.

The Babylonian Talmud, in two similar but somewhat different sources, details for us the Friday afternoon practices of some of the ancient sages.

A–For Rabbi Hanina said:	א–דאמר ר' חנינא:
B–"Come, let us go out to meet the bride, the queen!"	ב–בואו ונצא לקראת כלה מלכתא;
C–Some say:	ג–ואמרי לה:
D–"To meet Sabbath, the bride, the queen."	ד–לקראת שבת כלה מלכתא.
E–Rabbi Jannai, would wrap himself [in his clothes or his *tallit* (prayer shawl)],	ה–רבי ינאי מתעטף,
F–Remain standing and say: "Come the bride, come the bride!"[30]	ו–וקאי ואמר: בואי כלה, בואי כלה.

A–Rabbi Hanina wrapped himself and stood at sunset of Sabbath eve;	א–רבי חנינא מיעטף וקאי אפניא דמעלי שבתא,
B–He said, "Come and let us go forth to welcome the Queen Sabbath."	ב–אמר: בואו ונצא לקראת שבת המלכה.
C–Rabbi Jannai put on his robes on Sabbath eve	ג–רבי ינאי לביש מאניה מעלי שבת,
D–And said, "Come, the bride; come, the bride."[31]	ד–ואמר: בואי כלה בואי כלה.

Many will recognize that these sources are the earliest historical underpinnings of the current Friday evening *Kabbalat Shabbat* (acceptance of the Sabbath) service and its *Lekha Dodi* song whose well known refrain is:

"Let us go, my beloved, toward the bride; let us receive the presence of the Sabbath!"	לכה דודי, לקראת כלה, פני שבת נקבלה

that carries this same imagery.[32]

---

30   B. Baba Kama 32a-b.

31   B. Shabbat 119a.

32   See Siddur p. 308–329 for *Kabbalat Shabbat*; *Lekha Dodi* appears on p. 316–319.

A chronological perspective concerning all of this is critical to our understanding of *Nishmat*: *Kabbalat Shabbat* and *Lekha Dodi* are products of the mystics of 15th–16th century *Tsefat*, a city in northern Israel, whereas *Nishmat* as a Sabbath morning prayer appears in some sources at least 800 years earlier.[33] These later developments, therefore, have no impact on the early history of *Nishmat* and its various uses in Jewish liturgy.

Now, to summarize that early history: because of the rainfall "bride-and-groom" imagery that is also Sabbath imagery, and because both *Shabbat*[34] and the coming of the rainfall are moments of high praise to the Creator, *Nishmat* and *Ilu Finu* were moved from being liturgies said in response to rain or on Passover night to Sabbath morning. By extension they were then moved to holiday morning services whose prayers are very similar to those said on *Shabbat*.[35] The theological and spiritual synergy between Passover, rain and the Sabbath allowed this liturgy to find a home in each of those three venues.

Nishmat's inclusion in the Shabbat morning liturgy came about over some rabbinic objection, but also with strong rabbinic support. In this way *Nishmat*, which began, in our sources, as a blessing of song and redemption recited on Passover – and which included a section that was also recited in response to God's sending rain to the land – became the first *Kabbalat Shabbat* service, hundreds of years before the ritual that carries that name today was even being contemplated. It continues to be recited just before *Shaharit* on Sabbath and Festivals despite the fact that many people who offer this prayer in the contemporary Jewish community are generally unaware of its original purpose and meaning.

We have previously encountered Narbonnean opposition to the *Shabbat* morning recitation of *Nishmat* that was described by Aharon b. Jacob Ha-Kohen around the turn of the 14th century. What we have yet to discuss is the opposite side of that coin; our earliest indication of acceptance of the use of this prayer on the Sabbath. That appears in the geonic period in the text of the most ancient *Siddur* that we possess – *Siddur* (or more correctly *Seder*) *Rav Amram Gaon*.[36] This work, which is named after its author, was written in Babylonia in the ninth century in response to a request for instruction as

---

33　See the discussion of *Nishmat's* appearance in Seder Rav Amram Gaon below.
34　Cf. *Teshuvot ha-Geonim ha-Chadashot*, #36.
35　See *Kol Bo #37*.
36　Bnai Berak, 1994.

to what to pray each day that came from a community of Jewish merchants who were living in Spain at that time.

Amram Gaon sets the tone for those who accepted the use of *Nishmat* on Shabbat morning in this way:

"And the prayer leader *stands* and recites, *Nishmat kol hai* . . ."[37]	ועומד שליח צבור ואמר, נשמת כל חי

Just these seven words alone allow Amram Gaon to indicate to his readers that he considers this liturgy to be particularly important. He is telling us here that the sacred role of the *Shaharit* prayer-leader on *Shabbat* mornings begins with recitation of this prayer, and, therefore, that *Nishmat*, which is technically part of *Pesukei De-Zimrah*, has a higher status than the other liturgical elements that make up that section of the Sabbath prayers. Instead of being offered in the same way that the rest of the preliminary or introductory section of the services is recited, in terms of the one leading the prayers, it is treated as belonging to the more central and essential component of the liturgy: *Shaharit*.

Seder Rav Amram Gaon, written as it was to Jews in Spain, is an important source – perhaps the most important single source – from which *Sephardic*, liturgical practice as we know it, developed. What then was the status of *Nishmat* in early *Ashkenazi* prayer books?

Mahzor Vitry by Rabbi Simhah of Vitry (12th century), our earliest *Ashkenazi siddur*, discusses the recitation of *Nishmat* in the *Shabbat* morning service. That discussion contains a lengthy analysis of the meaning of the text of this liturgy and a determination of the correct reading of many of its words.[38] The tone of this analysis strongly suggests that it embodies a defense of the practice of reciting this prayer on *Shabbat* mornings. One senses, therefore, that this defense is presented because the recitation of *Nishmat* was a relatively new and controversial practice in European circles in Simhah of Vitry's time. Since we know of Narbonnean opposition to that recitation that existed a century or so later, these comments in *Mahzor Vitry* would appear to have been written in response to similar opposition in this earlier time period.

In contrast, later in *Mahzor Vitry* when the discussion turns to the Passover *Seder, Nishmat* – as part of the "Blessing of Song" – is described as a "decree

---

37 Sv. *Shaharit shel Shabbat*.
38 #161, Nurnberg 1923. Rabbi Simhah of Vitry was a student of Rashi's.

of the Men of the Great Assembly."[39] This institution is thought to have guided the Jewish people from some time after the return from Babylonia to build the 2nd Temple in 516 BCE until the Greek conquest of the Middle East by Alexander the Great in the late 330s BCE. That is certainly a long time before *Mahzor Vitry* was written and would indicate that use of this prayer in the *Haggadah* was a well-established practice when Simhah of Vitry wrote these words.

Also, if the Passover night *Nishmat* had such a noble past, that would have aided in the attempt to have it become a fixed and universal part of the Sabbath morning services.[40] As such this comment may also indicate that the issue of the recitation of *Nishmat* on *Shabbat* was being joined in earnest in the 12th century C.E. in Europe, and that *Mahzor Vitry* was an important defender of this fairly new liturgical custom.

Siddur Rashi, from the same era and school as *Mahzor Vitry*, does not offer any of the justifications or defenses that are found in *Mahzor Vitry*. Instead, it parallels *Seder Rav Amram Gaon* and introduces the recitation of *Nishmat* as an accepted liturgical practice on Shabbat and holiday mornings with the words:

At *Shaharit*, the prayer leader *stands* and says before the Torah Ark, "*Nishmat*…"[41]	שחרית עומד שליח צבור ואמר לפני החיבה נשמת …

Nonetheless, just as with Amram Gaon's similar choreography, the prayer has been raised in importance by this bit of rabbinic stage direction. That, too, may have been part of the attempt to have it gain universal acceptance as a *Shabbat* morning ritual.

We can find yet another attempt to defend this practice in *Kol Bo*, the work that first told us about the controversy that came with *Nishmat*'s move to *Shabbat* morning. The author of this work, Aharon b. Jacob Ha-Kohen cites a certain Rabbi Nathan son of Rabbi Judah who says that anyone who does

---

39   Hilkhot Pesah #73.

40   Cf. *Teshuvot ha-Geonim ha-Hadashot*, #36. Jerusalem: Simcha Emanuel, 1995. The author speaks of the noble history of *Nishmat* as he provides additional support for recitation of this prayer on *Shabbat* morning. He cites the opinion of Rabbi Johanan that *Nishmat* is the *Birkat ha-Shir* of Passover. He claims that this prayer was "'minted' by the first ones, the sages of the Talmud" (מטבע ראשונים חכמי התלמוד) and that it was a tradition in their (the sages of the Talmud's) hands (מסורת היה בידם).

41   Rashi, #213. Freiman, 1912.

not recite *Nishmat* in its proper place on Shabbat morning has "sinned" (פשע pasha).[42] This comment can only indicate that there were some who did not accept this practice at this point in history.

Aharon b. Jacob Ha-Kohen also adds his own similar stage direction to what we have seen in *Seder Rav Amram Gaon* and *Mahzor Vitry*. He says:

And after that, the prayer leader goes down before the ark and begins in a loud voice, "*Nishmat kol hai* [the soul of all that lives]."[43]	ואחר כך יורד שליח צבור לפני התיבה ופותח בקול רם נשמת כל חי

Again this would indicate specific support for this prayer, presumably against the opposition that he, himself mentions.

So, too, this comment in *Sefer ha-Itim*, authored by Judah b. Barzilai (Barcelona 11th–12th century), also supports adding *Nishmat* to *Shabbat* morning services.

A–It is required of everyone that they say *Nishmat kol hai*	א–ומיבעי ליה לאיניש למימר נשמת כל חי
B–As the world is accustomed to do on Sabbaths and holidays	ב–כמו שנהגו עלמא למימריה בשבתות ובימים טובים
C–Because *Nishmat kol hai* was established from the days of the Rabbis who had the power to decide the law [the Rabbis of the Talmud].	ג–משום דנשמת כל חי מימי רבנן דהוראה איתקן

[He then cites the "Blessing of the Song" discussion from tractate Pesahim as proof].[44]

All of this supports my contention that the inclusion of *Nishmat* in the Sabbath liturgy came in the face of some significant opposition in the medieval period. At the same time we can also see that in defending its recitation, many sages made claims, or gave indication, that the prayer was quite significant, and that it had a very important pedigree. That helps explain how the meaning and understanding of this liturgy was allowed to undergo the profound change that we have described as it moved from Passover eve to *Shabbat* morning.

---

42 *Kol Bo* #5.
43 Ibid., #37.
44 #170. Cracow: 1903.

These rabbinic statements may also have eased the way for another change in the meaning of this prayer that occurred in the later part of the middle ages.

Once the prayer became accepted in its *Shabbat* morning role, it was then given an expanded esoteric importance in the literature of the 14th–16th centuries as *kabbalah* – the mysticism that captured the community's interest in that period – became both more public and more popular. The fact that this liturgy was given such importance in earlier texts probably helped focus mystical interest on this prayer.

The next change in understanding of the prayer's meaning emerged from the following Rabbinic passage:

A–For Rabbi Simeon b. Lakish said:	א–דאמר רבי שמעון בן לקיש:
B–On Sabbath eve the Holy One, blessed be	ב–נשמה יתירה נותן הקדוש
He, puts an extra soul into the human being.	ברוך הוא באדם ערב שבת,
C–And at the going out of the Sabbath	ג–ולמוצאי שבת נוטלין אותה
it is taken away from him.[45]	הימנו,

Isaac Tyrnau (14th–15th century) in his *Sefer Minhagim* draws the connection:

And *Nishmat* [is to be recited] because each	ונשמת לפי שיש לכל יהודי
Jew has an extra soul on the Sabbath.[46]	נשמה יתירה בשבת.

This leads to the claim that the Ari, the great 15th–16th century mystical master and teacher, went a significant step further:

A–We have heard from the "proper intentions"	א–שמענו מכוונות רבנו האר"י
of our teacher the Ari of blessed memory,	זלה"ה
B–That one must receive the additional	ב–שצריך לקבל תוספת הנפש
spiritual element of the Sabbath day	דיום שבת בנשמת כל חי,
when reciting *Nishmat kol hai,*	
C–And the additional spirit [of the Sabbath	ג–ותוספת הרוח אחר פסוק ה'
day] after the verse, "May God open my lips,"	שפתי תפתח שקודם עמידת
which precedes the morning *Amidah*[47]	שחרית,

---

45   B. Beitzah 16a.

46   *Minhag shel Shabbat*. Jerusalem: 1979.

47   Siddur p. 420; the verse itself comes from Psalms 51:17.

D–And the [additional] soul [of the Sabbath day] with the word "where"[48] of *Keter* [the *Musaf* (additional service) *Kedushah* in Sephardic and *Nusah Ari* practice].[49]

ד–והנשמה במילת איה של
כתר מוסף,

In medieval sources dividing the soul into three parts or aspects, the *nefesh*, the *ruah* and the *neshamah*, is a frequently encountered conceptualization of the divine elements that God has placed in the human being.[50] The Ari, in keeping with this spiritual taxonomy, finds that each of the three parts of a Jew's soul receives an additional component on the Sabbath. The arrival of these extra divine aspects occurs at different places in the prayer service. The first of these moments takes place at *Nishmat*. The Ari, in this way, presents *Nishmat* as *Kabbalat Shabbat* in mystical, spiritual and soulful terms.

Yet another step follows on this analysis. The claim is then made that singing the first line of *Nishmat* with the chant familiar in most synagogues allows the people praying to open themselves up to receiving this extra soul of the Sabbath day.[51] As such it is not just the words, but it is also the music that make the recitation of *Nishmat* into a *Kabbalat Shabbat* moment and then into a mystical *Kabbalat Shabbat* event.

Finally, the prayer becomes so associated with the extra soul of *Shabbat* that Yihya b. Joseph Tsalakh, a Yemenite teacher of the 18th century, makes this comment and asks this question:

A–We find in the Code of Jewish Law: Orah Hayim: 624,[52] that one does not say the blessing over the spices after the conclusion of the Day of Atonement.

א–בשולחן ערוך אורח חיים סי'
תרכ"ד איתא שאין מברכין על
הבשמים במוצאי יום הכיפורים

---

48 Nusach Sefard Siddur, p. 502. The word "where" (איה) in *Musaf Kedusha* appears in Ashkenazi practice as well (Siddur p. 464).

49 Rabbi Joseph Haim ben Elijah al-Hakam, Responsa *Torah le-Shmah* #118. (The author lived in the 19th century.) See also Idem, *Sefer Ben Ish Hai, Hilkhot Shanah Shni'ah, Parshat Toldot*, Jerusalem, 1992.

50 Cf. Sa'adiah ben Yosef Gaon. *Emunot Ve-De'Ot, Ma'amar* 6. Jerusalem: 1970; Abraham ibn Ezra. *Sefer Yesod Mora, Sha'ar* 7. Prague: 1833.

51 Several *Hassidic* Rabbis have told me that this is what they have been taught, and one can find reference to this belief online at several websites that discuss this prayer.

52 Paragraph 3.

B–And the reason is because there is no extra
soul [the spices used after *Shabbat* are said to
gladden the human spirit that is sad because
the extra soul of the Sabbath has left][53] since
there is no food being eaten [on this day] ...
C–And we must examine how it is that we
say *Nishmat Kol Hai* etc. [on this day]
D–Since it relates to the extra soul that
descends on the human being.[54]

ב–והטעם שאין כאן נשמה
יתרה כיון שאין כאן מאכל ...

ג–וצריך עיון איך אנו אומרים
נשמת כל חי
ד–דקאי על הנשמה היתירה
ששורה על האדם.

As a non-mystical Sabbath song – for all the reasons discussed above –
Nishmat is absolutely appropriate to *Yom Kippur*, which is called שבת שבתון (a
Sabbath among Sabbaths) in the Bible.[55] It is a holiday on which the relationship between God and Israel is particularly strong and under close scrutiny.[56]
Repentance or reconciliation of that relationship is what that day is all about.[57]
Praising God on *Yom Kippur* is certainly in order and many parts of the Day
of Atonement liturgy do just that.[58] It certainly is a time when contemplating how inadequate human beings are to sing the praises due to God fits well
within the themes of the day.[59]

On the other hand, as a song of the "extra soul," its presence in the liturgy
is problematic. *Yom Kippur* as a fast day, when the body is weak and not joyous, does not provide an appropriate environment for this additional spiritual
presence. *Shabbat* – when the menu for the meals is usually expansive and joy
for that week is at its peak – finds the extra soul happy to be here.

Hence Yihya b. Joseph Tsalakh asks his question. Why is *Nishmat* recited
on *Yom Kippur*? This question arises, however, only after the third and latest
understanding of *Nishmat* takes hold within the religious imagination of, at

---

53 Cf. *Mahzor Vitry* #151.
54 Responsa *Pe'ulat Tsadik*: 3:17.
55 Leviticus 16:31, 23:32.
56 Cf. the *Piyut* סלח נא (Mahzor YK p. 112).
57 Cf. Leviticus 16:30.
58 Cf. the *Piyut* אמרו לא־להים, ibid., p. 390.
59 Since *Yom Kippur* is "life and death" Judgement Day, there are many parts of the
   service that speak of feelings of inadequacy, cf. the sentences beginning with the
   words מה אנו (ibid. p., 420), which include the words: מה נאמר לפנך (what can we
   say before You?).

least, some parts of the Jewish community. Before that point in time – when *Nishmat* actually entered the *Yom Kippur* liturgy – no one would have even begun to think about this as an issue of concern.

Yet another element – perhaps the most intriguing of all, since it involves claims that the first Pope was both Jewish and a counterspy – also enters into the history of *Nishmat*. Let us return to the confluence of the introductory phrases that we find in *Seder Rav Amram Gaon*, in *Mahzor Vitry* and in *Kol Bo*. Apparently, the original practice in both *Sephardic* and *Ashkenazic* circles, was to have the *Shaharit* prayer leader or *Hazan* (Cantor) begin at the beginning of *Nishmat*, the "*Kabbalat Shabbat*" paragraph, and not in the middle with the words שוכן עד (Who abides forever), as is generally done in *Ashkenazi* synagogues today.

Given the history of the prayer as we have described it to this point, having the Cantor start at the beginning of the liturgy is both logical and appropriate. Starting at *Nishmat Kol Hai* emphasizes the significance granted to this text by those who, over the centuries, came to recite it on *Shabbat* mornings.

I have memories of my own third-grade teacher, Mr. Ben-Ezra, who fancied himself as having quite a good voice (correctly, as I recall), describing this custom as the one to be followed. Several times over the course of the year that I studied with him, on Friday afternoons as he taught us about the *Shabbat* prayers, I remember him saying in Hebrew that at this point *ha-Hazan ha-gadol* (the great Cantor) would begin to sing. He would then chant *Nishmat* from the beginning to illustrate, and to use his voice as an educational tool. I have also heard that some few *Ashkenazi* synagogues still maintain this custom.

Further, the current, more common *Ashkenazi* practice of having the Cantor begin at שוכן עד is remarkably atypical in that the new prayer leader begins mid-liturgy, which in and of itself is surprising. Also, given the point where this *Hazan* begins, his introduction into the services interrupts the flow and rhythm of the prayer in dramatic fashion. Citing the sentences that incorporate the contemporary introduction of the *Shaharit* Cantor shows us that he begins his task right in the middle of an idea:

A–The Lord in the power of Your strength,	א–האל בתעצמות עזך
B–The Great One in the glory of Your Name,	ב–הגדול בכבוד שמך
C–The Powerful One forever,	ג–הגבור לנצח
D–The Terrible One in Your awesomeness,	ד–והנורא בנוראותיך
E–The King Who sits on a high and lofty throne	ה–המלך היושב על כסא רם

On Sabbaths the Cantor begins with: "Abides forever…"	ונשא
	בשבת מתחיל החזן "שוכן עד":
F–Abides forever, exalted and sanctified is His Name,	ו–שוכן עד מרום וקדוש שמו

This is hardly the most logical place for such a change to occur. Certainly, only something quite significant could allow for interrupting the liturgy in this way.

It seems to me that the origin of this practice comes from a remarkable belief that is not based in fact, but that captured Jewish popular imagination throughout the Middle Ages anyway. I will introduce this belief by way of a heavily censored text from the previously discussed "oldest *Ashkenazi* siddur." *Mahzor Vitry*, in a version that seems to be at least fairly close to the original reading:[60]

A–And there are those who say concerning that reprobate Simon Peter the jackass, who is the error of Rome,	א–ויש שאומרים על אותו נבל שמעון פטר חמור שהוא טעות של רומה
B–That he established this prayer [*Nishmat*] first	ב–יסדו אותו תחילה
C–Along with other prayers when he was *on the rock.*	ג–ושאר תפילות כשהיה על הסלע.
D–But God forbid, no such a thing should occur in Israel.	ד–וחס ושלום שלא תהיה זאת בישראל.
E–And any one who says this thing,	ה–וכל האומר דבר זה.
F–When the Temple is built, he shall bring a fat sin offering.[61]	ו–כשיבנה בית המקדש יביא חטאת שמנה:

First, the phrase "Simon Peter the jackass" needs explanation. It is a pun based on Exodus 13:13:

---

60   This is very close to the version found in Issur ve-Heter le-Rashi, #33. Berlin: 1938. Mahzor Vitry includes much of this work in its text.

61   *Hilkhot Pesah*, #66. The full version of this text in Mahzor Vitry shows the hand of the censor. It reads:

יש שאומרי' על אותו (כבל) [נבל] שמעון פטר חמור שהיא טעות של (דומה) [רומה] יסדו (עם אותו תחילה) [אותה תפילה]. ושאר תפילות כשהיה על הסלע. וחס ושלום שלא תהיה זאת בישר'. (ולכל האומות דיבר) [וכל האומר דבר] זה , כשיבנה בית המקדש (יביאו) [יביא] חטאת (שמצה) [שמנה]:

And every *firstling* [*"peter"*] *of an ass* you shall redeem with a lamb; and if you will not redeem it, then you shall break its neck;	וכל פטר חמר תפדה בשה ואם לא תפדה וערפתו

This unflattering nickname was designed to degrade Simon Peter the first Pope of Rome. Since Peter as written in Hebrew consists of the same letters as the word פטר, the term used by the Bible here when it speaks of the first-born of a donkey, Simhah of Vitry, the author of *Mahzor Vitry* chose to use this coincidental spelling to denigrate the Papal leader and his church.

Second, Simhah of Vitry lived during the era of the crusades and their consequences. The crusaders perpetrated many murderous acts against the Jewish people in Europe.[62] A literary response like this, that demeans someone who was an important historical leader of those responsible for this terror is not surprising coming as it does from among Jews who suffered so much and who had few, if any, outlets to express their pain, anger, and frustration.

The mention of Rome in this context is actually a reference to the Church. Referring to the Church as "the error of Rome" appears to be a similar attempt to denigrate the tormenters of the Jews. In a moment we will see that this expression actually means quite a bit more for our discussion of the history of how *Nishmat* was understood in the Jewish community.

To get to that next step in our study, we must understand the Christian Bible background to this expression. Two relevant passages are (Mark 8:31–33):

A–He began to teach them that the Son of Man must suffer greatly

B–And be rejected by the elders, the chief priests and the scribes,

C–And be killed,

D–And rise after three days.

E–He spoke this openly.

F–Then Peter took him aside and began to rebuke him.

G–At this he turned around and, looking at his
disciples, rebuked Peter and said,

H–"Get behind me, Satan. You are thinking not as
God does, but as human beings do."

---

62   See the chapters on *Anim Zemirot* and *Aleinu* in this volume.

and (Matthew 16:13–19):

A–When Jesus went into the region of Caesarea Philippi
B–He asked his disciples,
C–"Who do people say that the Son of Man is?"
D–They replied,
E–"Some say John the Baptist, others Elijah, still
    others Jeremiah or one of the prophets."
F–He said to them,
G–"But who do you say that I am?"
H–Simon Peter said in reply,
I–"You are the Messiah, the Son of the living God."
J–Jesus said to him in reply,
K–"Blessed are you, Simon son of Jonah.
L–For flesh and blood has not revealed this to you,
M–But my heavenly Father.
N–And so I say to you,
O–You are Peter,
P–And upon this rock I will build my church,
Q–And the gates of the netherworld shall not prevail against it.
R–I will give you the keys to the kingdom of heaven.
S–Whatever you bind on earth shall be bound in heaven;
T–And whatever you loose on earth shall be loosed in heaven."

Peter (or Simon Peter) is here portrayed as originally being a doubter of Jesus, and then as the first Pope building the Church "on the rock," a key phrase that appears in both *Mahzor Vitry* and the Christian Bible. This history of Simon Peter's changing attitude toward fundamental Christian doctrine – despite its brevity – opens the door to some interesting speculation.

In the Crusader period some Jews came to believe that Simon Peter never actually gave up his opposition to Jesus's mission, and that, in fact because of this, he was specifically sent by the Rabbis to become Pope in Rome.[63] The

---

63   Lerner, David Levine. "The Enduring Legend of the Jewish Pope." In *Judaism*, 40:2, 1991, pp. 148–170, particularly p. 163–164; David, Abraham. "Notes on the Legend of the Jewish Pope." In *Immanuel*, 15, 1982/1983, pp. 85–96; Bekkum, Wout Jacques van. "The Rock on which the Church is Founded: Simon Peter in Jewish Folktale." In Marcel Poorthuis, Joshua Schwartz, ed., *Saints and Role Models in Judaism and Christianity*, Leiden, 2004, pp. 289–310. There are other Jewish Pope legends that

Rabbis were concerned that early Christianity looked too much like Judaism, making it easier for the evangelists of their day to bring Jews into the Christian faith. It was Simon Peter's task to make changes in the Church. He was to move the Sabbath to Sunday for example, or to get Christians to celebrate different holidays than those described in the Hebrew Bible, so that the lines of demarcation between the faiths were clearer. This would allow those contemplating changing their allegiance from Judaism to Christianity to realize that they were truly moving into a different faith community. That understanding would – or so it was believed – prevent many conversions out of Judaism.[64]

As indicated, there is no evidence that this story is at all historical, but it was accepted as true by many Jews in the Crusader period. There is probably a good psychological reason for the popularity of this belief at that time. The Franco-German community had lived in relative serenity for many centuries prior to the events we are discussing. The Crusades – particularly the first Crusade – shattered the community in a physical sense. But along with the material destruction and loss of life, from a psychological perspective, these events robbed the Jews of any sense of well being. Worse, it became clear to the Jews that they were very much at the mercy of their Christian neighbors who were showing them anything but Christian kindness.

One of the possible ways to gain a measure of control in such a situation is not only to argue that Christian doctrine is theologically in error, but also

---

have nothing to do with *Nishmat*. For the story we are discussing see the three versions of this tale in Eisenstein, Judah David. *Otsar ha-Midrashim*, 1915, Tel-Aviv: pp. 557–559. The written records that present the story of the Jewish Pope vary dramatically in the tale that they tell. I have presented the most robust report of the legend gleaned from various sources, because that approach helps capture the full flavor of its impact. But even the more limited versions of the tale contain at least some of these elements, and any one of them would fit into the story of the history of *Nishmat* being told here.

64 The texts also see him as working to get the Christians to stop persecuting and massacring the Jews – but our focus here is more theological than pragmatic. Since the story of the Jewish Pope is not true in a historic sense, it is the ideological underpinnings of the tale that tell us what was going on in the Medieval period that made this story so popular. The desire for Christian persecution to end was certainly real in the era of the Crusades. But a story like this, which would have been offensive to Christians, was not going to help with that problem. Instead, this aspect of the Jewish Pope legend should also be seen as Jewish self-expression of the community's most heartfelt feelings at this point in history.

to claim that this error came though purposeful Jewish action. If one adopts this understanding of history, then the Jewish community can be empowered by its implications. After all, it is *we* who, through our conscious and clever planning, took them to the place of ultimate failure – to profound theological error.[65] They may be controlling us and even physically injuring us in significant ways, but we have gotten the better of them in the most important arena: the realm of God and the spiritual.

Though this all may sound strange to modern ears, in an era like the Medieval period in Europe – when the belief that one was living according to *the* one correct religious truth was essential to many people's self-identity regardless of their faith – this was a truly compelling narrative. Given Jewish physical weakness at this juncture in history, something like this tale was absolutely necessary for many Jews to maintain any sense of self-worth.

Christians could and did attempt to show that their understanding of God was correct by saying that it must be He who is giving them the power to dominate the Jews.[66] In response the Jews said, "but in the end, you live a lie because our God gave us the power to trick you into fundamental theological misunderstanding." It is, at least in part, for this reason that the claim that Simon Peter was a Jew sent by the Rabbis on a mission to expose and accentuate the false underpinnings of Christianity became so popular. This popularity endured despite the lack of any historical evidence that such a mission actually occurred, and despite the condemnation by Simhah of Vitry of those who believed it.

Instead, support was found for the claim that Simon Peter composed *Nishmat* while he was Pope from the text of the liturgy itself. This prayer contains these words:

A–*And other than You* we have no *king*, Who *redeems, saves, releases, rescues, sustains and is merciful* [One might also read this as "no *king*, *Redeemer, Savior, One Who Releases, Rescuer,*	א–וּמִבַּלְעָדֶיךָ אֵין לָנוּ מֶלֶךְ גּוֹאֵל וּמוֹשִׁיעַ פּוֹדֶה וּמַצִּיל וּמְפַרְנֵס וּמְרַחֵם בְּכָל עֵת צָרָה וְצוּקָה. אֵין לָנוּ מֶלֶךְ

---

65   Even in those versions of the tale of the Jewish Pope in which Simon Peter acted on his own initiative, it is still a Jew who outsmarts the Christians in this way.

66   See in this regard the complete title to Yehudah Halevi's famous work, the Kuzari. The full title is *Book of Responses to Allegations Against the Downtrodden Faith*. Also see Treatise 1:4 in this work.

Sustainer, Merciful One"][67] *in every time of difficulty and distress; we have no king, but You.*

אֶלָּא אָתָּה:

B–Lord of the first and of the last, Lord of all creatures, Master of all Generations, Who is renowned by many praises; *Who guides His world with kindness and His creatures with mercy.*

ב–אֱ־לֹהֵי הָרִאשׁוֹנִים
וְהָאַחֲרוֹנִים. אֱ־לוֹהַּ כָּל בְּרִיּוֹת.
אֲדוֹן כָּל תּוֹלָדוֹת. הַמְהֻלָּל בְּרֹב
הַתִּשְׁבָּחוֹת. הַמְנַהֵג עוֹלָמוֹ בְּחֶסֶד
וּבְרִיּוֹתָיו בְּרַחֲמִים:

This entire section can be read as an anti-Christian polemic (note the italicized words) challenging both the belief that Jesus is God, king, messiah and/or savior, and the claim that he performed miracles – particularly miracles of help and salvation.[68] It also challenges the Christian assertion that their Deity is more benevolent and loving than the "vengeful" Jewish God.[69]

Reading *Nishmat* in this way was part of developing a narrative built around Simon Peter that was remarkably poignant, powerful and comforting for many Jews. They came to see Simon Peter as a believing co-religionist with a secret, committed Jewish identity – a *Converso* in high office. While in this office, functioning publicly as the leader of the Church of Rome, he purposefully directed that institution away from Judaism to accomplish the Rabbis' plan. And Simon Peter did all this while clandestinely sending prayers "over the wall"

---

67   Cf. the Artscroll Siddur's translation of this section. Though grammatically this reading is not as sustainable, it makes the passage even more anti-Christian in content, since Jesus is referred to by many of these terms in Christian literature.

68   Note the commentary of Rabbi Eleazar of Worms (1160–1230), *Peirushei Siddur ha-Tefillah le-Rokeah*, 44 (*Ezrat Avoteinu* p.305), who, in commenting on *Nishmat* writes וכן מפרש לפני לא נוצר אל, לפני שולחי נביאי ואחר שלוחי אותם לא נוצר אל ... לא נוצר אל, ואין אלוה זולתי.

אחרי עבדי אשר בחרתי, גם מיום עמידתי בהר סיני אני הוא המצוה אתכם.

And so, too, He explains: Before Me no god was created [Isaiah 43:10]. Before I sent My prophets and also after I sent them *no god was created* ... No god was created, and *there is no god other than Me* [compare Isaiah 45:5]. After My servant whom I chose [Jacob; see Isaiah 41:8] and also from the day that I stood on Mt. Sinai, it is I Who command you.

69   Cf. my revered teacher, Rabbi Dr. Norman Lamm, "Did Auschwitz Ever Happen?" At http://brussels.mc.yu.edu/gsdl/collect/lammserm/index/assoc/HASH010e/d9cc4c5e.dir/doc.pdf

for Jews to recite, which would affirm his and their continuing commitment to the Jewish God and to His Torah.[70]

For those suffering persecution during the crusades, the tale of Simon Peter's courage in the face of adversity would offer much encouragement for them to face their own burdens as well. This might be yet another, less public, reason for the significant popularity that *Nishmat* enjoyed within the Jewish community in this era.

There are those who see an "encoded" indication of Simon Peter's authorship in the text of *Nishmat* itself, but it takes some imagination to find it. At essentially equal distances throughout the prayer, we can discover an acrostic spelling out the name "Shimon" – ש, מ, ע, ו, ן – (Simon) ... but only if one goes backward through the prayer. The name is said to appear as follows: the Shin ש is the first letter of שוכן עד (Who abides forever); the mem (מ) marks the beginning of מי ידמה לך (Who is similar to You?); the ayin ע appears in על כן אברים (Therefore the organs); the vav (ו) starts ואילו פינו (And were our mouths),[71] and the nun (נ) is there in the prayer's first word, נשמת כל חי (the soul of all that lives).[72]

For some, this was proof-positive of Simon Peter's authorship. In fact the very obscure and hidden nature of the hint added to its authenticity. This would be precisely the only kind of clue that a secret Jew living as the Pope could possibly dare to leave for his co-religionists. Anything else was simply too dangerous as it might lead to his discovery, his death and, therefore, to his work being undone.

This remarkable story appears to be the source for the introduction of the *Shaharit* prayer leader in European (*Ashkenazi*) circles on *Shabbat*, not at the beginning of *Nishmat* as described in our earliest sources, but at שוכן עד (Who

---

70 All three versions of the story cited in n. 63 mention the prayers supposedly composed by Simon Peter and their liturgical use by the Jewish people. See Bekkum for details of *piyutim* that are said to have been written by the Jewish Pope.

71 The *Ashkenazi* version of the prayer reads אילו פינו which lacks the ו, but there are several phrases that begin with a ו within a line or two of this phrase that can serve to complete the acrostic.

72 Some claim that this acrostic refers to Shimon b. Shetah a second Temple era leader of the *Sanhedrin* and the Jewish people (2nd–1st century BCE), and that he was the author of the liturgy. Cf. Nulman, Macy. *The Encyclopedia of Jewish Prayer*, Northvale: 1993, p. 255. There is nothing in the text of this prayer that particularly recommends him as the author.

abides forever), where we find the first letter of Simon's name.[73] There is no other reason that I can find for making the switch at this point in the prayer – effectively in the middle of a paragraph. In contrast, Jews whose origins are not in Europe, who did not experience the Crusades in the same murderous and destructive ways and to whom the legend of the Jewish Pope was either unknown or nowhere near as powerful, have retained the original custom of letting the *Hazan* begin at the beginning of *Nishmat*.

The sources that speak of introducing the *Shaharit* prayer leader found in very early mystical literature – predating the move of *Nishmat* to Sabbath morning[74] – speak of switching to the new *Hazan* before *Barkhu* (the call to worship) that comes after *Nishmat* in contemporary liturgy.[75] The early *Siddurim* that accept *Nishmat* as the morning *Kabbalat Shabbat* liturgy speak of the new prayer leader beginning as the paragraph commences. Nonetheless most contemporary *Ashkenazi* congregations change at שוכן עד, right in the middle of things.

The only reference I can find to שוכן עד as an important independent element within the prayer is in the discussion of the reverse acrostic of Simon's name in which these words mark the beginning of his hidden appearance. It would seem that many in the Jewish community are still commemorating Simon Peter's claimed authorship of this liturgy by having the *Hazan* begin his chanting of *Shaharit* here.

In this case, probably because the connection between this practice, the claimed Papal history and the text was not well known (the acrostic was, after all meant to be hidden), there is no recorded opposition to this custom, except in the case of my third grade teacher and the communities that follow the practice that he taught. Nonetheless, I am sure that those who have the prayer leader begin at *Nishmat*, including my third grade teacher, are generally unaware of

---

73   For those who follow the contemporary *Sephardic* rite, the *Hazan* begins at the beginning of the prayer. The *Sephardic* version of the prayer also lacks the words שוכן עד, though in their place we find the phrase: שועת עניים אתה תשמע [You hear the cry of the poor]. This phrase also begins with a ש, but it does not have the polemical power of the claim that God "abides forever," which implies that He does not change the rules by sending His "son" to grant salvation to those who accept this manifestation of the godhead as "Savior."

74   See the chapter on *Keriyat Shema* in this volume.

75   Siddur p. 406.

the remarkable history that underpins their custom and these differences in liturgical practice.

Another acrostic or two may also appear in *Nishmat. Sefer Abudraham* is a work on the laws and customs of prayer by David b. Joseph Abudraham (13th century). He writes:

A–By the mouth of the upright You are exalted

א–בפי ישרים תתרומם

B–And by the words of the righteous You are blessed,

ב–ובדברי צדיקים תתברך

C–And by the tongue of the pious You are sanctified,

ג–ובלשון חסידים תתקדש

D–And in the innards of the holy ones You are praised.

ד–ובקרב קדושים תתהלל.

E–You will find the abbreviations *Yitshak* (Isaac), *Rivkah* (Rebecca)

ה–תמצא בראשי תיבות יצחק רבקה.

F–The upright (*Yisharim*), the righteous (*Tsadikim*), the pious (*Hasidim*), the holy ones (*Kedoshim*) – *Yitshak*

ו–ישרים צדיקים חסידים קדושים, יצחק.

G–You are exalted (*titromam*), You are blessed (*titbarakh*), You are sanctified (*titkadash*), You are praised (*tithallal*) – *Rivkah*

ז–תתרומם תתברך תתקדש תתהלל, רבקה.

H–And there are those who say that the sage who composed this, his name was Isaac.

ח–וי"א כי החכם שחבר זה היה שמו יצחק

I–And his wife's name was Rebecca.

ט–ושם אשתו רבקה

J–And he composed it in honor of Isaac our Patriarch and Rebecca our Matriarch

י–ועשהו לכבוד יצחק אבינו ורבקה אמנו

K–In order to have their merit be remembered for us.[76]

כ–כדי להזכיר לנו זכותם ...

This takes us all the way back to the question of the roots of this prayer and its original meaning, and it also contradicts the claim of papal authorship. In addition, it returns us to our initial understanding of this liturgy as a soulful song of praise to God recited by all that live, and here, particularly by various cohorts of the most spiritual of individuals.

Songs of the soul evoke images of love and so the love of the author and his

---

76   Sv. *Shaharit shel Shabbat.* Jerusalem: 1963.

wife, which parallels the love of the second patriarch and his wife, is a powerful metaphor for the connection of creation to God. In this regard, it is important to remember that the only one of the patriarchs who was monogamous was Isaac. Both Abraham and Jacob had more than one wife who they needed to focus on – at least occassionally.[77]

These acrostics, therefore, also connect nicely to the bride and groom metaphor shared by *Shabbat*, by the Messianic era and by the rainy season discussed above. In all of these themes, two lovers: the water above and the water below, Israel and the Sabbath Bride, God and Israel, come together as did Isaac and Rebecca, in eternal loving connection, and all may find a place in this prayer.

Further, the Biblical Isaac is seen in rabbinic teaching as the embodiment of *avodah* or prayerful worship and service to God.[78] This is yet another image that fits well with the devotional themes of this liturgy and the strong commitment to God embodied by it. Mentioning *Yitshak*, therefore, emphasizes and enhances *Nishmat*'s meaning and importance.

The one negative in all of this is that the *Rivkah* acrostic is only present in *Ashkenazi* texts on the High Holidays when the prayer reads as described here.[79] During the rest of the year there is a somewhat different version that is recited:

A–By the mouth of the upright You are praised,	א–בְּפִי יְשָׁרִים תִּתְהַלָּל.
B–And by the words of the righteous You are blessed,	ב–וּבְדִבְרֵי צַדִּיקִים תִּתְבָּרַךְ.
C–And by the tongue of the pious You are exalted,	ג–וּבִלְשׁוֹן חֲסִידִים תִּתְרוֹמָם.
D–And in the innards of the holy ones You are sanctified.	ד–וּבְקֶרֶב קְדוֹשִׁים תִּתְקַדָּשׁ:

which retains the Isaac acrostic but not the letters of the Rebecca abbreviation in the order necessary for that name to appear.[80]

Since it is unlikely that the text went from one containing the *Rivkah* acrostic to one that didn't have it, it would seem that the non-High Holiday *Ashkenazi* text is the original reading. Hence the Rebecca acrostic may not be part of the prayer as first composed.

---

77 Cf. Genesis 16:3 and Genesis 35:23–26.

78 Cf. Zohar (*Sitrei Torah*), *va-Yetze* 146b. See also Targum Pseudo-Jonathan: Genesis 22:2.

79 Mazor RH, p. 262; Mahzor YK, p. 322.

80 Siddur p. 404.

In the liturgy of *Rosh Hashanah* and *Yom Kippur* there are many references to Isaac and the hope that his merit will help the Jewish people on these days of judgment.[81] Also, the Torah reading for both days of *Rosh Hashanah* features Isaac as a central character. On the first day, the birth of *Yitshak* and the early years of his life are highlighted.[82] Then, on the second day of the holiday, the story of the binding of Isaac as a sacrifice makes up the largest part of the reading.[83] Therefore, changing the prayer to highlight Rebecca, Isaac's life-partner, during these Days of Awe – when there is a particular desire that God's love descend on the community as He determines its fate for the year to come – would be in keeping with that pattern.

Further, Simhah of Vitry, who cites a number of sources that support the idea of an "Isaac" authorship for the prayer – whether referring to the patriarch or to a later individual of the same name – concludes his analysis by denying any connection at all between any Isaac or Rebecca and this prayer.[84] Instead he sees the non-High Holiday *Ashkenazi* version (which he sees as original) as emerging from a series of verses that relate the various pious groups mentioned here to the type of praises they are described as offering to God. His text does not have the Rivkah acrostic at all, and for him, the Isaac acrostic appears to be nothing more than a coincidence that emerged from the particular verses that were cited in writing this prayer.

Despite all of the questions surrounding these possible acrostics, the suggested imagery of love in *Nishmat* had its drawing power. In this regard, Isaac Tyrnau in his *Sefer Haminhagim* (14th–15th century) speaks of adding a special "*Nishmat* of the bridegroom" (נשמת דחתן) – a *piyut* (liturgical poem) included in *Nishmat* – into the synagogue liturgy on the Sabbath before a wedding.[85] Further, an early responsum tells of bridegrooms meeting in the synagogue on

---

81   Cf. Mahzor RH p. 462, where Isaac's merit is mentioned twice.

82   Genesis ch. 21 is chanted as the main reading on this day. Verses 1–12 of the chapter are directly about Isaac, while verses 13–21 tell of the fate of Ishmael and his mother Hagar after he and they were expelled by Abraham for Isaac's sake.

83   Ibid., ch. 22 is the main reading and all but the last five verses of that chapter tell this story.

84   Mahzor Vitry # 161.

85   Laws of *Yotsrot* and *Haftorot*, Jerusalem, 1979. See Elbogen, Ismar, Jewish Liturgy A Comprehensive History, Philadelphia, 1993, p. 169, who lists and briefly discusses the *piyutim* that were added to *Nishmat* including those mentioned here. Also see Wittenberg, Jonathan, A Reshut to Nishmat by Solomon Ibn Gabirol, Prooftexts 8:3, (1988), p. 340–346.

Friday, before *Shabbat*, to recite the prayer of *Nishmat* together, presumably to ask that love and God grace their coming marriages.[86]

In addition, because this prayer was understood to be a place where one could liturgically touch God's love and hope for the coming of the Messiah, and possibly as part of the association of this prayer with Simon Peter's courage, the liturgy of *Nishmat* became a recourse in times of trouble – though this was controversial. For example, some communities wove dirges and commemorative prayers into *Nishmat* on the three Sabbaths leading up to the Ninth of Av (the most tragic day on the Jewish calendar).[87]

David b. Solomon ibn Avi Zimra (1474–1573, head of the Cairo and Egyptian Jewish communities), records and opposes this practice.[88] He praises Egyptian Jewry for joining him in doing away with this custom. On the other hand, before these liturgies were removed, this community did include these texts within *Nishmat*.

In opposition, Hayim Joseph David Azulai (1724–1806), defended the practice of adding a poem called *Mi Kamokha* (Who is Like Unto You) – authored by the famous poet and philosopher Judah Halevi – into *Nishmat* on *Parshat Zakhor*.[89] On this special Sabbath the Torah reading of the day tells of the tragic murderous attacks perpetrated by *Amalek* against the Jews after the Exodus from Egypt.[90] These *Amalekites* are understood by Jewish tradition to represent the perpetrators of unreasoned anti-Semitic hatred throughout Jewish history.[91] The Torah text then calls for the destruction of this eternal congenital enemy of the Jewish people.

Azulai writes:

---

86   *Teshuvot ha-Geonim ha-Chadashot*. Published by Simcha Emanuel, Jerusalem: 1995, #36.

87   Similar additions were made at other important points in the liturgy.

88   Responsa *Radbaz*: 3:645.

89   One of the four special Sabbaths that lead up to Passover. Each one has a special additional Torah reading, chanted from a second Torah scroll after the regular portion of the week has been completed.

90   Deuteronomy 25:17–19.

91   Cf. Rabbi Judah Aryeh Leib ben R. Avraham Mordechai Alter (late 19th–early 20th centuries), *Sefat Emet, Parshat Zahor*. 1897.

A–I do not know what fault they found in it [the *Mi Kamokha* passage].[92]	א–איני יודע מה מצאו בו עול
B–Newcomers have come from close by[93] to change the custom . . .	ב–חדשים מקרוב באו לשנות המנהג . . .
C–But in the holy community of Amsterdam	ג–ובקהילה קדושה אמשטרדם
D–And other large communities	ד–ושאר קהלות גדולות
E–They would not listen[94] to change their custom.	ה–לא אבו שמוע לשנות מנהגם
F–And they recite it in the middle of "The Soul of all that Lives"	ו–ואומרים תוך נשמת כל חי
G–And more power to them.[95]	ז–ויישר כחם.

Apparently some communities tried to find a compromise position in the face of this debate. They moved *Mi Kamokha* to after the repetition of the *Amidah*, effectively reciting it at the end of the prayer service. This practice was also rejected by Azulai.[96]

For some, the loving environment of *Nishmat* could serve as a refuge from historic Jewish troubles as it was being recited on the Sabbath. For others, *Shabbat* was a day to celebrate; not to mourn, memorialize or focus on anti-Jewish persecution.

Finally, in this context, this comment in Responsa *Mikhtam Le-David* speaks for itself:

You should know that it can be found written that he who is in a difficult situation should take an oath that when God will save him he will recite the order of *Nishmat kol hai*.[97]	תדע שכן נמצא כתוב למי שהוא בעת צרה שידור שכשיצילנו השם יתברך לומר סדר נשמת כל חי

Thus we have seen that *Nishmat* is a lovely song of soulful praise to God

---

92   There are several references here to Biblical verses that are cited in this and the next two footnotes. This line is from Jeremiah 2:5.

93   Deuteronomy 32:17.

94   Isaiah 30:9.

95   This is an idiomatic translation of a frequently used congratulatory greeting that literally means, "Their strength is straight."

96   Responsa *Tov Ayin*, #18.

97   *Orah Hayim* #13.

whose origins are older than its earliest mention in rabbinic literature. Because of its beautiful phraseology Rabbi Johanan suggested that it might serve as the "blessing of song" on Passover night at the *Seder*. He also suggested that a section of it be used in response to the joyous moments when the first strong rain of the season fell in Israel each year.

The prayer was then moved to Sabbath morning where it served as the first *Kabbalat Shabbat* liturgy – the first prayer formally welcoming the Sabbath day. That move found support in the confluence of the "groom going out to meet the bride" imagery that appears in connection both with rainfall and with the Sabbath. Also, almost unnoticed, the prayer began to be said on holidays as well. The act of accepting the mystical "extra soul" of *Shabbat* then found its place in *Nishmat* under the influence of medieval kabbalists and the mention of the "soul" as the first word of the liturgy.

For some, the text of *Nishmat* also supported the claim that Simon Peter, the first Pope, was Jewish, and was sent by the Rabbis to lead Christianity. He was to take that religion on a path toward what the Rabbis saw as even greater and more visible theological error than it intrinsically already possessed by the very nature of its beliefs. This theory has absolutely no historical merit, but it served as a source of comfort for those who accepted it during the period of the Crusades. The current *Ashkenazi* practice of introducing the *Shaharit* prayer leader at שוכן עד may well derive from this remarkable assertion.

In addition, this prayer may contain a hint of the love that existed between Isaac and Rebecca and of Isaac's deep commitment to God through worship and service. That suggestion led it to be used by bridegrooms to celebrate their impending marriages.

Finally, some used it when they needed to find a place of refuge in the prayers from which to speak to God during moments of despair and persecution. Apparently this liturgy provided comfort to those people in their time of distress. It was so powerful in this regard, that when confronted by a very bad situation there were those who would take an oath to recite it if God would save them from their difficulties.

That is a remarkably long list of understandings and uses for one relatively short prayer. Some of these understandings of *Nishmat* are no longer commonly known and the customs associated with them, are no longer practiced. Some remain the custom of only a few individuals or congregations. Nonetheless the power of the prayer, and all the various aspects of the history of how Jews understood it, continue to make their impact on Jewish liturgy to this day.

CHAPTER 3

Birkat ha-Hodesh –
Can't We All Get Along

Blessing of the New Moon (Siddur p. 452)

*The congregation recites silently and
the Cantor repeats out loud :*

May it be Your will from before You, God, our
Lord and Lord of our ancestors, that You renew
this month for us for goodness and for blessing.
And give us long life: a life of peace, a life of
goodness, a life of blessing, a life of material well-
being, a life of bodily health, a life in which there
is fear of heaven and fear of sin, a life in which
there is no shame or humiliation, a life of wealth
and honor, a life in which there will be within us
love of Torah and fear of heaven, a life in which
the requests of our hearts will be fulfilled for
good. Amen, Selah.

*The date and time of the beginning of the coming
lunar cycle is announced to the congregation.[1]
The Cantor takes the Torah in his hands.*

ברכת החדש

הקהל בלחש והש"ץ
חוזר בקול רם

יְהִי רָצוֹן מִלְּפָנֶיךָ ה' אֱ-לֹהֵינוּ
וֵא-לֹהֵי אֲבוֹתֵינוּ שֶׁתְּחַדֵּשׁ עָלֵינוּ
אֶת הַחֹדֶשׁ הַזֶּה לְטוֹבָה וְלִבְרָכָה.
וְתִתֶּן לָנוּ חַיִּים אֲרוּכִּים. חַיִּים שֶׁל
שָׁלוֹם. חַיִּים שֶׁל טוֹבָה. חַיִּים שֶׁל
בְּרָכָה. חַיִּים שֶׁל פַּרְנָסָה. חַיִּים
שֶׁל חִלּוּץ עֲצָמוֹת. חַיִּים שֶׁיֵּשׁ
בָּהֶם יִרְאַת שָׁמַיִם וְיִרְאַת חֵטְא.
חַיִּים שֶׁאֵין בָּהֶם בּוּשָׁה וּכְלִמָּה.
חַיִּים שֶׁל עֹשֶׁר וְכָבוֹד. חַיִּים
שֶׁתְּהֵא בָנוּ אַהֲבַת תּוֹרָה וְיִרְאַת
שָׁמַיִם. חַיִּים שֶׁיִּמָּלְאוּ מִשְׁאֲלוֹת
לִבֵּנוּ לְטוֹבָה אָמֵן סֶלָה:

מודיעים לקהל את
תאריך וזמן המולד.
הש"ץ לוקח הספר תורה בידו.

---

1   Jerusalem Standard Time is used. This is particularly interesting in light of the debate
    involving Saadiah Gaon discussed later in the chapter.

The congregation recites silently and the Cantor repeats out loud:

He Who made miracles for our ancestors and redeemed them from slavery to freedom, He will redeem us soon and gather our dispersed from the four corners of the earth; all Israel are friends. And we shall say, *Amen.*

The Cantor says out loud and the congregation repeats:

Rosh Hodesh [New Moon, the commemoration of the beginning of the new month] [name of month inserted here] will be on the [day or days of the week],[2] which is coming upon us and upon all Israel for good.

The congregation recites silently and the Cantor repeats out loud:

The Holy One, Blessed is He, will renew it for us and for all His people the House of Israel, for life and for peace, for joy and for happiness, for salvation and for consolation. And we say: *Amen.*

הקהל בלחש והש"ץ
חוזר בקול רם:

מִי שֶׁעָשָׂה נִסִּים לַאֲבוֹתֵינוּ וְגָאַל אוֹתָם מֵעַבְדוּת לְחֵרוּת. הוּא יִגְאַל אוֹתָנוּ בְּקָרוֹב וִיקַבֵּץ נִדָּחֵינוּ מֵאַרְבַּע כַּנְפוֹת הָאָרֶץ. חֲבֵרִים כָּל יִשְׂרָאֵל וְנֹאמַר אָמֵן:

הש"ץ בקול רם והקהל חוזר:

רֹאשׁ חֹדֶשׁ פְּלוֹנִי יִהְיֶה בְּיוֹם פְּלוֹנִי הַבָּא עָלֵינוּ וְעַל כָּל יִשְׂרָאֵל לְטוֹבָה.

הקהל בלחש והש"ץ
חוזר בקול רם:

יְחַדְּשֵׁהוּ הַקָּדוֹשׁ בָּרוּךְ הוּא עָלֵינוּ וְעַל כָּל עַמּוֹ בֵּית יִשְׂרָאֵל, לְחַיִּים וּלְשָׁלוֹם, לְשָׂשׂוֹן וּלְשִׂמְחָה, לִישׁוּעָה וּלְנֶחָמָה, וְנֹאמַר אָמֵן:

O N THE SABBATH (*Shabbat*) before the New Moon (*Rosh Hodesh*), an apparently simple and straightforward prayer proclaiming the coming of the month and seeking God's blessings for it, is recited in the synagogue. It consists of four paragraphs and an announcement.

The first paragraph asks God to fill the month ahead with good things, while eliminating or preventing anything negative. Next, an announcement is made as to the precise moment in time when the lunar cycle for the new month will begin.[3] This is based on astronomical calculations of the periodic movements

---

2   See a few pages further in this chapter for a discussion of how and why some *Rosh Hodesh* celebrations are two days, and some only one.

3   For reasons that have to do with natural variations in the lunar cycle and the mathematics and structural assumptions of the Jewish calendrical system, the actual time when the cycle begins is not the same as the time announced; see Maimonides (1138–1204), *Hilkhot Kiddush ha-Hodesh* ch. 7; Latham, Lance, *Standard C Date/*

of the moon around the earth. The announcement is made by the Rabbi or by some other participant at the service, but not by the prayer leader (*Hazan*).

The second paragraph evokes God's historic miracles of redemption and asks that such redemptive acts occur again in the near future. This paragraph then concludes with the dramatic claim חברים כל ישראל – "All Israel are friends" – a remarkable statement in the face of the long and sad history of Jewish fratricidal conflict, and of the painful schisms that exist today within the Jewish community.

This is followed by a paragraph that announces the name[4] of the coming month and the day or days (e.g. Sunday, Monday,)[5] of the following week on which *Rosh Hodesh* will be celebrated. (Depending on the month, the New Moon may be commemorated for one or two days as discussed below.) Finally, the last paragraph again asks for God's blessings in the month ahead.

The choreography of the prayer needs explanation. It is recited while the congregation stands.[6] In many synagogues two people are positioned, one on either side of the prayer leader, during the recitation. For the first paragraph one of these two individuals holds a Torah scroll. He then passes it to the *Hazan* to hold as he chants the last three paragraphs. This is a highly unusual, if not a unique way of doing things in our contemporary liturgical practice. Except for the preamble and conclusion of the Torah reading, we do not see the *Hazan* on the bimah with a Torah scroll in his hands during the services.

Time Library, Lawrence Kansas, 1998, p. 281f; and Elkin, Charles and Schechter, Martin. "The 'Molad' Will Be – When." In *Intercom* 20, 1 (1983) pp. 18–22. See also Mandelbaum, Hugo. "The problem of 'Molad Tohu.'" In *Proceedings* (Association of Orthodox Jewish Scientists) 3–4, 1976, pp. 65–84.

4   In early Biblical history the name of any given month was the ordinal number of that month counting from the one that includes the Passover holiday (see discussion below). Even in that era, at least some of the months also had individual names (cf. Exodus 34:18; I Kings 6:37, 38 and 8:2). Today the names used are those brought back from Babylonia by the Jews returning to build the Second Temple [J. Rosh Hashanah 1:2, (56d)], even though at least some of them are also the names of idolatrous gods (Ezekiel 8:14). See Ramban, Exodus 12:2 and see Tigay, Jeffrey H. "The Calendar and Theology." In ed, Daniel J. Elazar, *Jewish Education and Jewish Statesmanship*, Albert Elazar Memorial Book. Jerusalem: 2000, pp. 17–26.

5   The days of the week have always been known by their ordinal numbers – first day through sixth day – leading up to *Shabbat*, the seventh day, the only one with a specific name. See Ramban, loc. cit.

6   Raab, Menachem. "When Standing is Appropriate in Prayer." In *Journal of Jewish Music and Liturgy*, 19, 1997, p. 9.

Birkat ha-Hodesh also follows an interesting responsive pattern. The congregation recites the first paragraph silently. That paragraph is then repeated out loud by the prayer leader. So, too, the second paragraph follows this same arrangement. Then for the third paragraph, the *Hazan* takes the lead and proclaims the name of the new month and the day(s) when *Rosh Hodesh* will be celebrated. The entire paragraph is then repeated by the community. The congregation continues with the last paragraph and the prayer leader again follows suit.

This brief overview describes a number of elements that are part of making this ritual what it is today. It will be our task in this chapter to explain the historical and theological factors that influenced this liturgy's structure, choreography and variable pattern of recitation. Along the way we will discover that many different factors have made their mark on this, superficially, very simple part of the services.

The first part of our story takes us back to the Bible. As the Jews begin to prepare for the Exodus from Egypt when they will become a people free to serve God as they please,[7] the book of Exodus reports:

A–And God spoke to Moses and Aaron in the land of Egypt, saying,	א–ויאמר ה' אל משה ואל אהרן בארץ מצרים לאמר
B–"This month shall be to you the beginning of months; it shall be the first month of the year to you."[8]	ב–החדש הזה לכם ראש חדשים ראשון הוא לכם לחדשי השנה

Even at its most basic level, identifying a particular month as the first of months and requiring that it maintain that position indicates that it is mandatory for the Jewish people to sustain a functioning and accurate calendar.[9]

Further, because the Bible describes each of the holidays of the year as occurring on a particular day of a specific, numbered month (e.g., the tenth day of the seventh month for *Yom Kippur*), there must be some mechanism in place to record and define the counting of months and days for this to make sense. That mechanism is an accurate and functional calendar that has been maintained across the centuries.

---

7   Cf. Exodus 7:26.

8   Ibid., 12:1–2.

9   Maimonides, *Sefer ha-Mitzvot*, Affirmative Commandment #153. For a lengthy discussion see Rabbi Baruch Epstein, Torah Temimah, Exodus 12:7.

The last Biblical element that impacts on this part of our story is finding that the Torah calls the month in which Passover (*Pesah*) falls by two different names. It is both the "first month" (*Hodesh ha-Rishon*/חדש הראשון),[10] and the "springtime month" (*Hodesh ha-Aviv*/חדש האביב).[11] As we shall see, the lunar cycle is central to the Jewish calendar. The problem is that a system based only on lunar months cannot easily maintain the presence of any specific holiday in any particular season. For example, Passover will not always fall in the spring if the calendar only consists of twelve lunar months.

Lunar months are based on the approximately 29½-day revolution of the moon around the earth – the time it takes for the moon to go through all its phases and return to the same point in its journey around our planet. That is why these months are either twenty-nine or thirty days long. Springtime, on the other hand, comes when the earth reaches a particular point in its revolution around the sun – an event that occurs approximately once every 365¼ days.

The number of days in the solar year (365¼) is not neatly divisible by the number of days in a lunar cycle (29½). Dividing the larger number by the smaller one does give us twelve full months per annum, but there is a remainder of close to four tenths of a month. For this reason, a purely lunar calendar, in which a year always consists of twelve months that average 29½ days each in length – such as the one used by the Muslim community – is shorter than the solar calendar by a significant number of days. As a result, each lunar year begins at an earlier point in the solar year. It is for this reason that the annual celebration of the Muslim holy month, *Ramadan*, moves through the solar year, falling first in spring, then a few years later in winter, subsequently in fall and finally in summer, before returning to the springtime. Islam apparently has no objection to such a system; however, the Biblical requirement that *Pesah* fall both in the first month and in the springtime makes a purely lunar calendar untenable to the Jewish community. That is why Judaism has a combined lunar/solar calendar.

Rabbinic literature describes an elaborate system known as *Kiddush ha-Hodesh* (Sanctification of the Month) for maintaining this combined lunar/solar calendar.[12] First, witnesses who saw the new moon as close to its initial ap-

---

10 Cf. Leviticus 23:5.

11 Cf. Exodus 13:4.

12 This system is discussed in M. Rosh Hashanah 1:3–3:1 and in the Babylonian and Palestinian Talmud's analyses of these *mishnayot*. Other terms such as *Ibur ha-Hodesh* and – in regard to expanding the year – *Ibur ha-Shanah* appear, but *Kiddush*

pearance as possible needed to come to the court (the *Sanhedrin*) in Jerusalem, to give testimony that a new month may have begun.[13] Second, that court – after examining their testimony and determining that it was credible – would then let the public know that a page should be turned on the calendar.[14]

Sometimes, the determination of which day would actually be the beginning of the new month was also based on preventing certain holidays from occurring on specific days of the week. For example, *Yom Kippur* was not allowed to fall on a day that is contiguous with a Sabbath – on a Friday or a Sunday – because that would create the very difficult situation of having two days requiring complete cessation of work and no food preparation in a row.[15] In a hot climate like Israel's, before refrigeration, this would be an almost untenable situation.[16]

The court also needed to examine agricultural growth and development during the twelfth month of the year to determine whether spring was immanent. If so, the next month could begin the yearly cycle anew as the

---

ha-Hodesh is the prototype [cf. J. Sanhedrin 1:2, (18c)]. Also, Maimonides includes discussion of the yearly calendar in ch. 10 of *Hilkhot Kiddush ha-Hodesh*. For a survey of traditional sources on this subject see Raab, Menachem. "Kiddush ha-Hodesh, Kiddush ha-Levanah and Birkat ha-Hodesh." In *Journal of Jewish Music and Liturgy*, 27. 2005–2006, pp. 20–29.

13   Ibid., 1:5–7, 9, 2:1,5.

14   Ibid., 1:7–8, 2:1, 5–8.

15   B. Rosh Hashanah 20a, Rabbi Menahem b. Shlomo (12th century), Midrash Sekhel Tov, Genesis 17:14. For a different reason, see Rabbi Yom Tov Lipman Halevi Heller (16th–17th centuries), Tosafot Yom Tov, M. Sukkah 5:5, citing Rashi, Rosh Hashanah 20a, sv. *mishum matya*. He also cites a view that only the court involved in these calculations knew the real reasons and that everything else is simply conjecture.

16   There is disagreement as to whether this was applicable during the era when the system was based only on witnesses; cf. the debate on B. Sukkah 54b, and see B. Shabbat 113a-114b and B. Rosh Hashanah 20a. According to Heller, loc. cit., and to M. Menahot 11:7, even Maimonides, who, he claims, did not believe that the eyewitness system allowed for such modification, did find this type of consideration acceptable during months where the New Moon was obscured by clouds or other factors and there was no eyewitness testimony so that calculations had to be used (cf. *Hilkhot Kiddush ha-Hodesh* 18:8, 10–11); see further below. As such, even according to this view since the calculations were available it would be very rare indeed that *Shabbat* and *Yom Kippur* would fall on adjoining days as the Rabbis could anticipate the problem and adjust in the months before the holiday.

first or springtime month.[17] If the agricultural evidence indicated that spring had not yet come, then an extra or thirteenth month was added before the calendar year could end.[18] By adding this extra month periodically, the Jewish calendar could have lunar months, but stay in line with the solar year and its seasons.[19]

This elaborate system was quite complex and detailed. It required a great deal of expertise, acumen and care to sustain. Things were made even more difficult because the system was severely challenged several times in ancient Jewish history. It was finally suspended as a result of Christian persecutions in the 4th century C.E.[20] At that point in time Christian control of the Holy Land was virtually complete, and Christian authorities were very aggressive in their persecution of the Jewish people. As a result the *Sanhedrin* could no longer function and Rabbis could not be ordained in the way that Jewish tradition understood to go back to Moses ordaining Joshua, his successor.[21] So, too, the Rabbinic community in Israel was forced to stop working on the Palestinian Talmud, thus leaving it as an important but incomplete text.

In response to the difficulties involved in trying to determine the calendar through the use of witnesses as had been done up until then, Rabbeinu Hillel II[22] developed an extremely complex mathematical formula that took all of the various *halakhic* considerations into account and allowed the Jewish

---

17 B. Sanhedrin 10b-13b.

18 B. Megillah 6b.

19 Under the rules of the present calculated calendar this extra month called *Adar Sheni* or Second *Adar*, occurs seven times in nineteen years.

20 See Stern, Sacha. *Calendar and Community: A History of the Jewish Calendar, 2nd Century BCE-10th Century C.E.* Oxford: 2001. He discusses many calendar controversies and various calendar models that he says were in use by different Jewish communities over the course of Jewish history. I do not accept a number of his conclusions, but his work is quite comprehensive. In opposition, see Talmon, Shemaryahu. "What's in a Calendar?: Calendar Conformity, Calendar Controversy, and Calendar Reform in Ancient and Medieval Judaism." In Ronald Troxel et. al., ed., *Seeking Out the Wisdom of the Ancients.* Winona Lake: 2005, pp. 451–460. This source describes calendar controversies in Jewish history that I do not reference here. For general discussion see, Seaver, James Everett. *The Persecution of the Jews in the Roman Empire (300–428).* Lawrence: 1952.

21 Numbers 27:12–23.

22 See *Teshuvot ha-Geonim ha-Hadashot* (Emanuel). Jerusalem: 1995, #37. This is not the famous Hillel of Hillel and Shammai fame, but a later descendant of his.

calendar to function across the generations for the last 1600 years.[23] Except for a very brief period in Palestine in the ninth century that we will also discuss below, Rabbeinu Hillel's calculations have served world Jewry as the final word on all calendrical matters since then. The contemporary determinations of when *Rosh Hodesh* and the holidays are to be celebrated are all derived from his calculations.[24]

Despite this reality, it is the Biblical structure and rabbinic practices from the fourth century and earlier that established the underpinnings of today's *Birkat ha-Hodesh*. Some of these elements need further explication before we can understand their role in this liturgy.

To begin with, just as ancient Jewish authorities understood the importance of having their communities know that the new month had come, later Rabbis saw the same need. This was particularly necessary in ancient times when the determination of the day of *Rosh Hodesh* needed to await the coming of witnesses and could not be found by looking at a calendar that foretold the day on which the celebration of the New Moon would occur.[25] As a result, in all generations those charged with helping the community function correctly have tried to make sure that the Jews under their care remained connected with their calendar. In this way, the community would know when to prepare for and celebrate its holidays and other special days, including *Rosh Hodesh* itself, appropriately.[26]

In our earliest *Siddur*, Seder Rav Amram Gaon (9th century), a prayer similar to *Birkat ha-Hodesh* appears as part of the services on the actual day of *Rosh Hodesh*.[27] It was to be recited after the special Torah reading for that day and before the *Sefer Torah* was returned to the ark.[28] This is somewhat surprising.

The centerpiece of the prayer reads:

---

23 Spier, Arthur. *The Comprehensive Hebrew Calendar*. New York: 1952.

24 Cf. Lipshutz, Yisroel. *The Mechanics of the Jewish Calendar*. 1998; Raab, Menachem. "The Computation of the New Moon." In *Dor le Dor*, 5, 2 (1976–1977), pp. 56–65; Sar-Shalom, R. *Yesodot ha-Luah ha-Ivri*. Tel Aviv: 1967.

25 M. Rosh Hashanah 1:3–4, 2:2–4, 7.

26 Ibid., 1:3–4.

27 See Rabbi Jacob ben Moses Moellin (1360–1427) Sefer Maharil, *Hilkhot Rosh Hodesh* #3 for a description of the announcements that continued to be made on *Rosh Hodesh* itself in various communities.

28 *Seder Rosh Hodesh*. The Torah reading is Numbers 28:1–15.

| With a good sign we shall have New Moon [such and such, day so and so and day so and so] | בסימן טוב יהא לנו ראש חדש [פלו' יום פלו' ויום פלו']. |

By the time these words were said, *Rosh Hodesh* had already been com-memorated by the recitation of *Hallel*[29] and by the addition of *Ya'aleh ve-Yavoh*[30] to the *Shaharit Amidah*, both of which precede the Torah reading in the services. This line would, therefore, seem to be awkward and redundant where it appears – and even more so on the second day of a two-day celebra-tion of *Rosh Hodesh*

Perhaps for this reason, and perhaps because the largest number of Jews ap-pears in the synagogue on the Sabbath,[31] *Shabbat* became the day to announce the coming of a new month. In the words of Rabbi David, son of Rabbi Yosef Abudraham, who describes early Sephardic practice:

A–On the Sabbath before the New Moon,	א–שבת קודם ראש חודש אחר
after reading the *Haftorah*,[32] before *Ashrei*,[33]	קריאת ההפטרה קודם אשרי
B–The prayer leader announces and	ב–מכריז שליח צבור ומודיע
makes known to the congregation	לקהל
C–On which day the New Moon will fall,	ג–באיזה יום יחול ראש חדש
D–And whether it is to be one day or two days.	ד–או אם יהיה יום אחד או שני ימים
E–And he first says,	ה–ואומר תחלה
F–"May it be the will from before heaven	ו–יהי רצון מלפני השמים
G–To establish the house of our life [the Temple]."	ז–לכונן את בית חיינו

---

29   Psalms 113–118 (on *Rosh Hodesh* and the last six days of Passover, Psalm 115:1–11 and Psalm 116:1–11 are omitted), Siddur p. 632 f.

30   A paragraph added to the *Amidah* and to Grace after Meals on all Biblically man-dated holidays (including *Rosh Hodesh*) except Shabbat, that evokes the particular day being celebrated. Its earliest mention by this name is in Masekhet Soferim 19:8, though it may also be referenced on B. Berakhot 30b as well as in other places in the Talmud. See Siddur p. 110.

31   See Lewin, B.M. *Otzar ha-Geonim*, v. 8, Ketubot, # 785, p. 353.

32   The section from the Prophets chanted after the Torah reading on Shabbat morn-ings. The blessings recited before and after the *Haftorah* appear in the Siddur pp. 446–449.

33   Siddur pp. 456–459.

| H–That is what they say in most places in Spain.[34] | ח–כך אומרים ברוב המקומות בספרד |

Often Seder Rav Amram Gaon is the authority when it comes to Sephardic custom, but in this case Abudraham supplanted him.

So, too, Mahzor Vitry, our earliest *Ashkenazi* siddur, says:

A–And if *Rosh Hodesh* falls during the next week	א–ואם חל ראש חדש בשבת הבאה
B–The Cantor announces to the masses the day on which it is established,	ב–מכריז החזן ומודיע לרבים יום קביעותו
C–In order to correctly keep the holidays,	ג–מפני תקנת המועדות
D–To correctly recite the *Musaf* prayers,[35]	ד–ותקנת תפילת המוספים
E–And *Hallel*,[36]	ה–והלל
F–And to have the women refrain from working.[37]	ו–ולבטל בהם הנשים ממלאכה.
G–And then he says:	ז–ואומר:
H–"He Who made miracles for our ancestors	ח–מי שעשה ניסים לאבותינו
I–And redeemed them from slavery to freedom,	ט–וגאל אותם מעבדות לחירות
J–He will redeem us and gather our dispersed peoples from the four corners of all the earth.	י–יגאלינו ויקבץ נידוחינו מארבע כנפות כל הארץ
K–**All Israel are friends**	כ–**חברים כל ישראל**
L–To Jerusalem the holy city;[38]	ל–לירושלם עיר הקודש
M–And let us say Amen.	מ–ונאמר אמן:
N–New Moon [such-and-such], day [so-and-so]."	נ–ראש חדש פלוני יום פלוני:
O–If it is two days, he says,	ס–אם הוא שני ימים אומר
P–"[Such-and-such a day] according to the counting of [this other day].[39]	ע–ויום פלוני חשבונו של יום פלוני:

---

34 Abudraham. *Seder Rosh Hodesh: Hakhrazat Rosh Hodesh.*

35 Siddur pp. 462, 674

36 See n. 29.

37 See Tosefot (12th–14th centuries), Megillah 22b, sv. *ve-she'ein*, who sees this in the Talmud ad. loc.

38 J. Hagigah 3:6 (79d). The connection between Jerusalem and having all Jews be friends is based on a rabbinic midrashic analysis of Psalms 122:3. For further discussion see below.

39 This may be why many have the custom of saying, for example, *Rosh Hodesh* of month X will be on Sunday *and on its morrow* (ולמחרתו), on Monday.

Q–The Holy One, Blessed is He, will renew it for us
R–For joy, happiness, largess, salvation,
success, life and peace;

S–And we say Amen."[40]

פ–יחדשהו הקב"ה עלינו
צ–לששון ולשמחה לריוח
ולהצלה ולהצלחה ולחיים
ולשלום
ק–ונאמר אמן:

While the Roman rite[41] as recorded in *Mahzor Bnei Roma* reads:

A–This is what our Rabbis have decreed:
B–That we should announce before
this holy congregation
C–So that old and young should know
D–That we have *Rosh Hodesh* such-and-such,
E–Such-and-such a day,
F–According to the calculations of our Rabbis.[42]

א–כך גזרו רבותינו
ב–שנכריז בפני הקהל הקדוש
הזה
ג–שיהיו יודעים גדולים וקטנים
ד–שיש לנו ראש חודש פלוני
ה–יום פלוני
ו–בחשבון רבותינו

The practice of announcing the coming of the New Moon on the Sabbath, has roots that go back to Temple times. The Jerusalem Talmud records:

A–The *Musaf* [additional sacrifice] of
Shabbat[43] and the *Musaf* of the New
Moon:[44] which one comes first?
B–Rabbi Jeremiah thought to say that
on the question of the *Musaf* of *Shabbat*
and the *Musaf* of the New Moon, that
the *Musaf* of the New Moon is first.
C–And Rabbi Jeremiah derived this from here

א–מוספי שבת ומוספי ראש
חדש מי קודם?
ב–רבי ירמיה סבר מימר מוספי
שבת ומוספי ראש חודש מוספי
ראש חודש קודמין
ג–חייליה דרבי ירמיה מן הדא

---

40   Rabbi Simhah of Vitry (12th century), Mahzor Vitry, #190.
41   During the Medieval period Italian practices were given a status essentially equivalent
      with Ashkenazi and Sephardi customs (cf. Mahzor Vitry #265). This has changed as
      that community has declined in size and influence. For a brief history of the rite see
      Reif, Stefan. *Judaism and Hebrew Prayer*. Cambridge: 1993, esp. pp. 164–168.
42   See the commentary *Tikun Tefillah* in Siddur Otsar ha-Tefillot. NY: 1966, v. 1 p. 710;
      and see Elbogen, Ismar. *Jewish Liturgy, A Comprehensive History*. Philadelphia: 1993,
      pp. 103–104.
43   Numbers 28:9–10.
44   Ibid., 11–15.

D–The [Levitical] song of the Sabbath [in the Temple], and the song of *Rosh Hodesh*: the song of *Rosh Hodesh* was first.	ד–שירו של שבת ושירו של ראש חדש שירו של ראש חדש קודם
E–Said Rabbi Yossa , this is different.	ה–אמר רבי יוסה שנייא היא
F–For Rabbi Hiyya (end of 3rd century) said in the name of Rabbi Johanan (d.279),	ו–דאמר רבי חייה בשם רבי יוחנן
G–For the sake of *publicizing it* [*Rosh Hodesh*]	ז–כדי לפרסמו
H–And to make known that it [the day] is *Rosh Hodesh*.	ח–ולהודיע שהוא ראש חדש
I–What does he do?	ט–כיצד הוא עושה?
J–He slaughters the Sabbath *Musaf* sacrifices	י–שוחט מוספי שבת
K–And says over them the song of the New Moon.	כ–ואומר עליהן שירו של ראש חדש
L–Nonetheless,	ל–ברם הכא
M–The *Musaf* of the Sabbath as opposed to the *Musaf* of the New Moon,	מ–מוספי שבת ומוספי ראש חדש
N–The *Musaf* of Sabbath comes first	נ–מוספי שבת קודמין
O–Based on the principle that whichever is more frequent than its friend takes precedence over its friend.[45]	ס–על שם כל התדיר מחבירו קודם את חבירו

So, too, a Palestinian amora, Rabbi Yassa (יסא), tells us:

Such as me: that from my earliest recollection I never prayed *Musaf* without knowing when the month would begin.[46]	כגון אנא דמן יומוי לא צלית מוספא מן דלא ידע אימת ירחא

This source locates announcing – or at least finding out – when *Rosh Hodesh* falls, before *Musaf* on the *Shabbat* before the New Moon. That is precisely the point in the services where *Birkat ha-Hodesh* is now recited.

There is some difficulty in identifying this Rabbi Yassa, since the name is so similar to many others. Aaron Hyman, a classic scholar who worked on identifying the rabbis named in Talmudic literature, says that Rabbi Yassa is Rabbi Yossi b. Zebida who lived during the fourth century and was forced to

---

45   Talmud Yerushalmi, Sukkah 5:6 (55d). The parallel source on B. Sukkah 54b gives a similar reason though the discussion is much less detailed.

46   Talmud Yerushalmi, Sanhedrin 5:3 (22d).

leave Israel for Babylonia as a result of the same persecutions that had a pivotal impact on how the Jewish calendar functioned.[47] He apparently managed to return to his homeland at some point,[48] and most importantly for this identification, he seems to have been generally concerned about holiday practices and about maintaining older traditions in other teachings recorded in his name.[49]

For these reasons, I believe that this identification is correct here. Therefore, this comment – which dates from the transition point when Judaism stopped relying on eyewitnesses and turned to the calculated calendar – also tells us that an important source of origin for *Birkat ha-Hodesh* comes from that very moment in history. Rabbi Yossi b. Zebida's personal practice would have taken on an entirely new meaning once the Christian persecutions of the Jews affected the calendar so that the old system could no longer function.[50] What was once a personal pious custom now served as rallying cry for the people.

As the system changed, the liturgy that memorialized the older practice was given its start by someone affected by the very persecutions that forced that change. That fact adds considerably to the power of the prayer, because the same Rabbi Yossi b. Zebida who lived through the tragedies of fourth-century Palestine, helped pave a liturgical path to subsequent survival of the Jewish community's calendar and holidays. That certainly sheds a new light on *Birkat ha-Hodesh*.

Further, if, in fact, announcing the coming of the New Moon on *Shabbat* to the assembled community has roots that go back to the Temple, and to early in Rabbi Yossi b. Zebida's life when witnesses were still determining on which day *Rosh Hodesh* would be celebrated, this would mean that when the announcement was made in that time period, the date of the New Moon would not yet have been fully determined. That would need to wait until the witnesses actually saw the moon and made their way to Jerusalem to testify as to what they had seen.

Also, even if someone had calculated the date when the New Moon should appear, the eyewitness testimony and its acceptance might not ultimately yield

---

47   Aaron Hyman. *Toldoth Tannaim VeAmoraim*. Jerusalem: 1964, v. 2, p. 713f. He cites and disagrees with several other suggested identifications of this name. All Mss. of the Jerusalem Talmud included in Peter Schaefer's *Sinopsis la-Talmud ha-Yerushalmi* (Tubingen: 1995) read as we describe here.

48   Hyman, p. 716.

49   J. Eiruvin 3:9 (21c); see also B. Shabbat 21b, 35b, and B. Horayot 4a.

50   For a description of how the older system deteriorated under this anti-Jewish tyranny see *Teshuvot ha-Geonim ha-Hadashot*, loc. cit.

the same result as these calculations.[51] The process could potentially be influenced by weather conditions, travel and distance difficulties, or even by false sightings caused by other celestial phenomena.[52] As such the actual date of *Rosh Hodesh* would not be known on the Sabbath before the New Moon.[53]

However, since the length of the month parallels the lunar cycles and is always either twenty-nine or thirty days long, awareness that *Rosh Hodesh* would occur at some point during the coming week was available to the sages.[54] Actually, this awareness would take control if, for example, there were several days of cloudy weather at the beginning of the month. In that case *Rosh Hodesh* would not coincide with the actual first appearance of the moon to human eyes. During the rainy season, for example, that might not occur until day thirty-six or thirty-seven (or perhaps even more days) after the previous month had begun, which would throw the entire system out of balance. *Rosh Hodesh* was, therefore, automatically celebrated on the thirty-first day in those circumstances.

So, too, if there were several months in a row that started with cloudy skies, *Rosh Hodesh* would vary between day thirty and day thirty-one after the previous celebration based on rabbinic calculations. This was designed to prevent the appearance of a "mini-month" of some twenty or twenty-five days that would occur if a number of cycles passed and each *Rosh Hodesh* was commemorated thirty-one days after the previous one. That would have been the case if the rule for the first cloudy month were followed for every month.[55]

Despite all of this, even when witnesses were being used and these variations

---

51 For indications that the calculations were available from early on in Jewish history, meaning from at least Second Temple times and certainly from far earlier than Rabbi Yassa, however he is identified, see *Teshuvot ha-Geonim ha-Hadashot*, loc. cit, and Maimonides, loc. cit., ch. 18, and see below. See also Midrash Sekhel Tov, Exodus 12:20, who says these calculations go back to Adam, while Maimonides says they go back to Moses at Sinai (ibid., 18:8).

52 That is the reason why calculations were always necessary at some points in time in every era, see the sources cited in the previous footnote and the discussion that follows.

53 If the witnesses come at the end of day thirty but the Rabbis do not complete their work until day thirty-one, then day thirty-one is Rosh Hodesh because the calendar ultimately depends on the Rabbis sanctifying the month (see Sifra, Emor, 9:10). This is another way in which the calculations and the calendar may not be in sync. Sifra, ad. loc. suggests several others.

54 Cf. Rabbi Moshe ben Rabbi Jacob (13th century), *Sefer Mitsvot Gadol*, #47.

55 See particularly Maimonides, loc. cit. who calls this possibility the "greatest joke and loss" (אין לך דבר שחוק והפסד יתר מזה).

might occur, the Rabbis apparently determined that giving people advance notice that a change of month was imminent – even if the specific day of that change was as yet unknown – was important for the proper functioning of the Jewish community. In this way, people could better prepare for the prayers and holidays that might be just around the calendrical corner. This practice continues in the contemporary *Birkat ha-Hodesh*.

Another indicator of the significance of the New Moon to the Rabbis is the fact that some *Rosh Hodesh* celebrations are two days long, while some are only one.[56] As indicated, the length of the lunar month is either twenty-nine or thirty days. In other words, if today is *Rosh Hodesh*, the next *Rosh Hodesh* will come on day thirty or day thirty-one from now.

Actually, as we have said, the lunar cycle is 29½ days long, which means that – assuming *Rosh Hodesh* was commemorated correctly – some part of the thirtieth day after the last celebration of the New Moon is, in reality, going to be *Rosh Hodesh*. This despite the fact that the moon might not yet have been seen – perhaps only because it was a cloudy day, or, perhaps the witnesses had not yet been able to complete their journey to the court in Jerusalem.

For this reason the Rabbis decided that thirty days after *Rosh Hodesh* would always be a day of celebration of the New Moon.[57] If the witnesses and the Sanhedrin were able to complete their work on the thirtieth day, then this would be the only day of observance. However, if it took until the next day, then that day, the thirty-first since the last New Moon celebration, would also be *Rosh Hodesh* and the commemoration would last for two days.

That pattern has been retained even after the fourth century, despite the reality that the length of any month is now known in advance. Still the custom and practice of ancient Judaism remains in place.

We can now begin to explain the elements that make up *Birkat ha-Hodesh*. Given the importance that Judaism has always put on knowing precisely when the month begins, announcement of the coming of the New Moon would necessarily be made by an important official of the community. In antiquity the Head of the *Sanhedrin* made that declaration.[58] Today it is done by the

---

56   The practice of two-day celebrations for *Rosh Hodesh* may go back to pre-Temple times; see 1 Samuel 20:27.

57   See B. Berakhot 30b, Rashi, ad. loc, sv. *be-hodesh maleh*. And see Maimonides, loc. cit. 8:4, Rabbi Zedakiah Ben Rabbi Avraham ha-Rofe, Shibbolei ha-Leket (13th–14th century), *Inyan Rosh Hodesh*, #168 and Rabbi Yeshayah ben Rabbi Mali (1180–1260), Responsa *Rid* #32.

58   M. Rosh Hashanah 2:7, B. Rosh Hashanah 24a.

prayer leader or *Hazzan* in the middle of the *Birkat ha-Hodesh* liturgy. It is accomplished in these words from the prayer, which constitute the core element from which the rest of the liturgy grew:

New Moon such and such will occur on	ראש חדש פלוני יהיה ביום
such and such a day [or days] that is coming	פלוני הבא עלינו ועל כל ישראל
upon us and on all Israel for good.	לטובה

This is the contemporary iteration of the announcement described by Abudraham, Mahzor Vitry, Mahzor Bnei Roma and even Amram Gaon detailed above. It also echoes the primacy of the *Rosh Hodesh* song over the Sabbath song in the Temple, and the history of Rabbi Yossi b. Zebida's personal practice that we have discussed at length. Further, the possibility is left open for announcing either a one- or two-day celebration of the New Moon. And all these things go back in one way or another to God's command to Moses and Aaron that the yearly and monthly calendars be maintained. All of these different parts of our story are evoked by this one line.

This declaration is then repeated by the congregation as a statement of its affirmation and acceptance of the proclamation and its implications. this parallels ancient practice, as the Mishnah says:

The Head of the Court [*Bet Din*] says: [The	ראש בית דין אומר מקודש
month is] "sanctified," and all the people	וכל העם עונין אחריו מקודש
respond after him: "Sanctified, sanctified."[58]	מקודש.

The choreography of the prayer also derives from the early *Kiddush ha-Hodesh*. Three people are present at the prayer leader's table. Two of them stand on either side of the Cantor as he chants the liturgy. While the prayer leader functions in place of the Head of the Court, the three of them collectively represent the *Bet Din* of three members of the *Sanhedrin* that was necessary to declare the testimony of the witnesses acceptable and to announce that *Rosh Hodesh* was to be celebrated.[60]

Though we no longer have such testimony, the public reporting of the beginning of the lunar cycle by someone other than the Cantor symbolically serves

---

59   M. Rosh Hashanah 2:7.
60   M. Sanhedrin 1:2

in its place. The Cantor's announcement in response mirrors the way the court would react to the witnesses if their testimony was found to be acceptable.

Finally, the reason that the prayer leader holds the Torah and that all stand as he announces the name and day(s) of commemoration of the beginning of the new month also derives from ancient practices of Jewish courts. First, some claim that the custom was for those in attendance to stand when the month was sanctified by the *Sanhedrin*.[61]

In addition, under certain circumstances an oath would be administered by the *Bet Din* as part of their adjudication of the various cases that came before them. Sometimes the person taking the oath was required to hold a precious object – usually a Torah scroll – while swearing.[62] The current practice of taking an oath on a Bible in court or at an inauguration probably derives from here. Those involved in the proceedings would stand.[63]

As such, the announcement of the New Moon on the Sabbath before *Rosh Hodesh* is effectively an oath that the day or days chosen for the celebration are correct. Similarly, the promise is being made that the holidays – whose dates of observance are dependent on when the community begins the month – are also going to be commemorated when they should.

This adds to the explanation of why the announcement is made first by the prayer leader and then repeated by the congregation in the contemporary synagogue. Statements that are repeated can, by dint of that repetition, constitute an oath in Jewish law.[64]

Taking an oath here may seem to be surprising. However, when we have finished discussing the large number of bitter controversies that have swirled around the calendar over the course of Jewish history, as we shall below, it will become much more understandable why it was decided to strengthen the announcement of the date of *Rosh Hodesh* with the trappings of an oath.[65]

---

61 Cf. Rabbi Avraham ha-Levi Gombiner (17th century), Magen Avraham 417.

62 B. Shavuot 38b. See Maimonides, *Hilkhot Shevuout*, 11:8,11,13. Sometimes this is done in the presence of a Torah scroll; see also *Teshuvot ha-Geonim Sha'arei Tsedek*, 4:5:13. For the source of this practice in the oath that Abraham administered to his servant, see Rashi, Genesis 24:2.

63 B. Shavuot, ad. loc. See also Rabbi Avraham ha-Levi Gombiner (17th century), Magen Avraham, *Orah Hayim* 417:1. He says that in ancient times the people present stood when the New Moon was declared.

64 See Rashi to Genesis 8:21 and B. Shavuot 36a.

65 Oaths and doubled statements were often used to support what one is saying; cf.

On the other hand, it is not at all surprising that this proclamation is followed by a request for God to bless the coming month. All transitions come with both stress and possibility, and Judaism, as many other systems of belief, is filled with rituals that carry its practitioners through moments of change. It would be less than human if people did not ask for God's assistance at such a point in time.

There are a number of versions of this "post-announcement" request for God's blessing that one can find in the different liturgical customs that exist today within the Jewish community. A typical example from Sephardic/Israeli practice, that is considerably more expansive in its supplication than the one cited at the beginning of this chapter and the one quoted from *Mahzor Vitry* above reads:

A–The Holy One, Blessed is He, will renew it for us	א–יְחַדְּשֵׁהוּ הַקָּדוֹשׁ בָּרוּךְ הוּא עָלֵינוּ
B–And for all His people the House of Israel	ב–וְעַל כָּל עַמּוֹ בֵּית יִשְׂרָאֵל
C–In every place that they are.	ג–בְּכָל מָקוֹם שֶׁהֵם.
D–For good and for blessing.	ד–לְטוֹבָה וְלִבְרָכָה.
E–For joy and for happiness.	ה–לְשָׂשׂוֹן וּלְשִׂמְחָה.
F–For salvation and for consolation.	ו–לִישׁוּעָה וּלְנֶחָמָה.
G–For good sustenance and financial well-being.	ז–לְפַרְנָסָה טוֹבָה וּלְכַלְכָּלָה.
H–For good life and for peace.	ח–לְחַיִּים טוֹבִים וּלְשָׁלוֹם.
I–For good tidings.	ט–לִשְׁמוּעוֹת טוֹבוֹת.
J–For good news.	י–וְלִבְשׂוֹרוֹת טוֹבוֹת.
K–[In winter: And for rains in their proper time.]	כ–[בחורף: וְלִגְשָׁמִים בְּעִתָּם].
L–And for a complete healing.	ל–וְלִרְפוּאָה שְׁלֵמָה.
M–And for a speedy Redemption	מ–וְלִגְאוּלָה קְרוֹבָה
N–And we say, *Amen*.[66]	נ–וְנֹאמַר אָמֵן:

Similarly, the paragraph that precedes the Cantor's announcement of *Rosh Hodesh* also seems to fit easily within the liturgy – at least at first glance – but

Radak 1 Samuel 20:42; Rabbi Shlomo Ben Rabbi Simeon Duran (1400–1467), *Responsa ha-Rashbash* #512; Rabbi David Ben Solomon Ibn Avi Zimra (1479–1573), *Responsa Radbaz* 2:613. See Rabbi Abraham Hayyim Ben R. Naftali Tzvi Hirsch Schor (16th–17th century), *Torat Hayyim* to B. Shavuot 39a, that an oath was used to strengthen the experience at Sinai for the Jewish people.

66   Nusach Sefard Siddur, p. 492.

there are some surprises and some things to comment on here. The paragraph reads:

A–He, Who made miracles for our ancestors,	א–מִי שֶׁעָשָׂה נִסִּים לַאֲבוֹתֵינוּ
B–And redeemed them from slavery to freedom,	ב–וְגָאַל אוֹתָם מֵעַבְדוּת לְחֵרוּת.
C–He will redeem us soon	ג–הוּא יִגְאַל אוֹתָנוּ בְּקָרוֹב
D–And gather our dispersed from the four corners of the earth;	ד–וִיקַבֵּץ נִדָּחֵינוּ מֵאַרְבַּע כַּנְפוֹת הָאָרֶץ.
E–**All Israel are friends**.	ה–חֲבֵרִים כָּל יִשְׂרָאֵל
F–And we say, *Amen*.	ו–וְנֹאמַר אָמֵן:

As we have said, for traditional Jews the way that the calendar should function, even today, is by using the elaborate system of witnesses and testimony described above. The *Sanhedrin*, based on these witnesses and relying on astronomical, agricultural, calendrical and climatic expertise should then determine whether and when the month has begun and whether and when spring had come to the land of Israel.

The anti-Semitic persecutions that forced the Jewish community to abandon this system and use a calculated calendar are symbolic of the losses and tragedies of the entire diaspora experience. It makes sense, therefore, that before making the public announcement of the calculated New Moon, a prayer is offered for God to redeem the Jewish people from the persecutions that have brought about the need for this announcement. Jewish tradition teaches that with Redemption will come a renewed *Sanhedrin* functioning in a rebuilt Jerusalem that would resume the ancient system of witnesses and testimony.[67] Therefore, as each new month is announced, a prayer is offered expressing the hope that this will be the last time there will be a need to use the system that is currently in place.[68]

Making reference to the Exodus from Egypt in this paragraph of the prayer

---

67   Rabbi Levi ben Chaviv (1483–1545), *Responsa Maharalbakh, Kuntros ha-Semikhah*. This text is part of the historic debate about whether the Sanhedrin can be reestablished before the coming of the Messiah and the rebuilding of Jerusalem, see Maimon, Abraham, Hidush ha-Sanhedrin, Jerusalem, 1957, and Maimon, Judah Leib, Hidush ha-Sanhedrin bi-medinatenu ha-mehudeshet, Jerusalem, 1967.

68   Since the Rabbinic calendar system has been under siege so often in history as we will discuss, I suspect there was some hesitation at saying this explicitly because such a declaration might be used to undermine the legitimacy of the calendar that is being used.

is also appropriate. In addition to that event serving as the prototype redemptive experience for the Jewish community, it is in Egypt that the command to maintain the calendar was first given to Moses and Aaron. Note that the very first source cited at the beginning of this chapter tells of God speaking to them, specifically, in the *land of Egypt*.

It is also the holiday of Passover that commemorates the Exodus, and the need for that holiday to occur both in the first month and in springtime establishes many of the parameters that define the rules of the Jewish calendar. As the Cantor is about to announce the name and date of the new month that is in keeping with the calculated system, he evokes all of these elements that relate to, or that will bring back, the ancient calendar, simply by referring to the Jewish experience in Egypt and its miraculous redemptive conclusion.

We have explained almost all of the historical influences that shaped the last three paragraphs of *Birkat ha-Hodesh*. The one sentence that remains for us to comment on is the one that we highlighted whenever it appeared throughout this chapter – "חברים כל ישראל" (All Israel are friends) – recited by the congregation and then by the prayer leader as the last part of the lead-in to announcing the name of the new month and when it will be celebrated.

This sentence is written as a declarative statement. However, given the many schisms and fractious conflicts that have plagued Judaism over the course of an often troubled history, these three words seem more like a plea for intercommunal tolerance rather than a statement of the state of things within the Jewish community.

The appearance of these words here is both intriguing and appropriate. Conflicts about the calendar within the Jewish community have been among the most acrimonious in Judaism's very contentious recorded history. These controversies ranged from different groups or individuals using dramatically divergent approaches as to the basic rules of how the calendar is to function, to specific disagreements about the date of a particular celebration of *Rosh Hodesh* and, therefore, about the day on which the holidays – which are dependent on the determination of when the month begins – are to fall. A survey of at least some of these conflicts will give us a sense of how widespread and painful these calendrical contretemps have been.

Our earliest record[69] of calendar-based acrimony in the Jewish commu-

---

69   The issues touched on in our discussion of the conflict between the Rabbis and the Sectarians, both in regard to the calendar and in more general terms, are the subject

nity takes us back at least as far as the second century BCE, to the era of the Maccabees[70] and perhaps even earlier.[71] The Hassidim and Pharisees of that era found themselves in broad opposition to several groups of sectarians. Among these sectarians were the Sadducees, the Essenes, the Boethusians, the sect that wrote the Dead Sea Scrolls and whoever authored at least some of the Apocrypha (scholars debate the precise identity of these different groups as such there is almost certainly some overlap on this list).[72] The Apocrypha are books written in Biblical style that were excluded from the Biblical canon by the sages for a number of reasons. Many of these books date from this era.[73]

Rabbinic literature preserves some of the acrimonious elements of this broad ideological debate, including some details concerning specific conflicts about the calendar. For example, we are told that, originally, signal fires were lit when the New Moon was announced. These fires would be started on one

---

of voluminous literature and great debate, far beyond our capacity to detail here. We can do no more than scratch the surface in these footnotes.

70   The Maccabean revolt that led to the rededication of the Temple celebrated on Hanukkah occurred in the 160s BCE.

71   *The Apocrypha and Pseudepigrapha of the Old Testament* by R. H. Charles (Oxford, 1913) dates the book of Jubilees to the early second century BCE and this book uses the Sectarian calendar exclusively. Since it does not invent the calendar, it certainly is somewhat older. Similarly, the Qumran community begins sometime between 200 and 150 BCE according to many scholars, and it, too, uses this calendar, which seems to be an already known quantity. On the other hand, the evidence from the Dead Sea Scrolls themselves, which we discuss below, is that Jerusalem is using a different calendar; presumably the rabbinic calendar (see Schiffman, next note). An important rabbinic text in this regard is B. Ta'anit 17b, which appears to describe a time when the two competing calendars and their advocates struggled for supremacy in the Temple. Eventually the Pharisees won. This may well coincide with the founding of Qumran, or with some other point in time when a group of dissident Priests left Jerusalem for that community. In my opinion this source has been given insufficient attention by scholars who study this period and these events.

72   The literature on this issue is particularly large; I will simply cite some relevant works by my teacher, friend and partner in building the Great Neck, NY eruv, Larry Schiffman, namely, *From Text to Tradition* (Hoboken, 1991), *Reclaiming the Dead Sea Scrolls* (Philadelphia, 1994) and *Understanding Second Temple and Rabbinic Judaism* (Hoboken, 2003); and for balance, I will also cite Hillel Newman's *Proximity to Power* and *Jewish Sectarian Groups of the Ancient Period* (Leiden, 2006), and S. Kent Brown's *Between the Testaments: From Malachi to Matthew* (Salt Lake City, 2002).

73   Along with Charles, see Nickelsburg, George W. E. *Jewish Literature Between the Bible and the Mishnah*. Minneapolis: 2005.

mountain top and then on the next and so on, until the entire Jewish world would quickly come to know that the new month had begun.[74]

Unfortunately, some of the sectarians who were opposed to the rabbinic calendar took to lighting fires when it was not *Rosh Hodesh*. They did so in order to create confusion in the community as to when to celebrate the holidays.[75] In response, the system of signal fires was replaced with a new method of informing people about the coming of the new month. The *Sanhedrin* would send official messengers to let distant communities know when *Rosh Hodesh* had been celebrated.[76]

These messengers could only cover so much ground between the New Moon and, for example, the fifteenth of the month of *Tishrei* when the holiday of *Sukkot* (Tabernacles) is celebrated. As a result, those beyond the reach of the messengers were in doubt as to when to begin the holiday. Since, as we have said, *Rosh Hodesh* can only come either twenty-nine or thirty days after the previous *Rosh Hodesh*, *Sukkot* could fall on one of two days, i.e., either fifteen days after day twenty-nine, or fifteen days after day thirty. Given this "doubtful" day, diaspora communities developed the custom of keeping both days as a holiday, while in Israel only one day, the actual day of the holiday, was commemorated.[77] This custom continues today in Orthodox and many Conservative communities despite the fact that our present system of mathematical calculation removes any question as to which day is actually *Rosh Hodesh*.[78]

Similarly, Rabbinic literature tells us that witnesses to the New Moon were thoroughly cross-examined when they came to court. At least in part this was because of similar sectarian attempts to employ false witnesses who, if accepted by the court, would create error and uncertainty in the system.[79]

So, too, the Talmud tells us of a great debate between the sectarians and the Rabbis concerning how the date of the holiday of *Shavuot* (Pentecost) is to be calculated. The Bible says:

---

74 M. Rosh Hashanah 2:2–4.

75 Ad. loc. 2:2. And see the classic commentaries to this text, e.g., Maimonides and Bartenura.

76 Ibid., 1:3–4 and 2:1. This last Mishnah tells us that there was concern that the sectarians would attempt to pervert this system as well; see below.

77 Cf. Maimonides, Hilkhot Kiddush ha-Hodesh 3:11.

78 Cf. Maimonides ibid. 5:6.

79 M. Rosh Hashanah 2:1.

A–[80] These are the feasts of the Lord,
holy gatherings, which you shall
proclaim in their seasons.

א–אלה מועדי ה' מקראי קדש
אשר תקראו אתם במועדם:

B–In the fourteenth day of the first month
at evening is the Lord's Passover.

ב–בחדש הראשון בארבעה
עשר לחדש בין הערבים פסח
ה':

C–And on the fifteenth day of the same month
is the Feast of Unleavened Bread to the Lord;

ג–ובחמשה עשר יום לחדש
הזה חג המצות לה'

D–Seven days you must eat unleavened bread.

ד–שבעת ימים מצות תאכלו:

E–On the first day you shall have a holy
gathering; you shall do no labor on it.

ה–ביום הראשון מקרא קדש
יהיה לכם כל מלאכת עבדה לא
תעשו:

F–But you shall offer an offering made by fire
to the Lord seven days; on the seventh day is a
holy gathering; you shall do no labor on it.

ו–והקרבתם אשה לה' שבעת
ימים ביום השביעי מקרא קדש
כל מלאכת עבדה לא תעשו:

G–And the Lord spoke to Moses, saying,

ז–וידבר ה' אל משה לאמר:

H–"Speak to the people of Israel, and say to them,

ח–דבר אל בני ישראל ואמרת
אלהם

I–'When you come to the land which I give to you,

ט–כי תבאו אל הארץ אשר אני
נתן לכם

J–And shall reap its harvest,

י–וקצרתם את קצירה

K–Then you shall bring a sheaf of the first
fruits of your harvest to the priest;

כ–והבאתם את עמר ראשית
קצירכם אל הכהן:

L–And he shall wave the sheaf before
the Lord, to be accepted for you;

ל–והניף את העמר לפני ה'
לרצנכם

M–On the next day *after the Sabbath*
the priest shall wave it.

מ–ממחרת השבת יניפנו הכהן:

N–And you shall offer that day
when you wave the sheaf

נ–ועשיתם ביום הניפכם את
העמר

O–A male lamb without blemish of the first
year for a burnt offering to the Lord.

ס–כבש תמים בן שנתו לעלה
לה':

---

80   These are not the numbers of the verses as they appear in printed Bibles, nor does
the breakdown of the lines follow the verses. This text is formatted this way here,
as in all cited texts in this volume that are more than a few lines long, for ease of
comprehension, with the numbers serving as reference points.

P–And the meal offering of it shall be two
tenth deals of fine flour mixed with oil,
Q–An offering made by fire to
the Lord for a sweet savor;
R–And the drink offering of it shall be
of wine, the fourth part of a hin.
S–And you shall eat no bread, nor parched
grain, nor green ears, until the same day
T–That you have brought an offering to your God;

U–It shall be a statute forever throughout
your generations in all your dwellings.
V–And you shall count from the
next *day after the Sabbath,*
W–From the day that you brought
the sheaf of the wave offering;
X–Seven Sabbaths shall be complete;

Y–To the next day after the seventh
Sabbath shall you count fifty days;
Z–And you shall offer a new
meal offering to the Lord.
AA–You shall bring out of your
habitations wave loaves
BB–Two
CC–Of two tenth deals; they shall be of fine flour;
DD–They shall be baked with leaven;
EE–They are the first fruits to the Lord.
FF–And you shall offer with the bread
GG–Seven lambs without blemish of the first year,

HH–And one young bull,
II–And two rams;
JJ–They shall be for a burnt offering to the Lord,
KK–With their meal offering,
and their drink offerings,

ע–ומנחתו שני עשרנים סלת
בלולה בשמן
פ–אשה לה' ריח ניחח

צ–ונסכה יין רביעת ההין:

ק–ולחם וקלי וכרמל לא תאכלו
עד עצם היום הזה
ר–עד הביאכם את קרבן
א־להיכם

ש–חקת עולם לדרתיכם בכל
משבתיכם:
ת–וספרתם לכם ממחרת
השבת
אא–מיום הביאכם את עמר
התנופה
בב–שבע שבתות תמימת
תהיינה:

גג–עד ממחרת השבת השביעת
תספרו חמשים יום
דד–והקרבתם מנחה חדשה
לה':
הה–ממושבתיכם תביאו לחם
תנופה
וו–שתים
זז–שני עשרנים סלת תהיינה
חח–חמץ תאפינה
טט–בכורים לה':
יי–והקרבתם על הלחם
כך–שבעת כבשים תמימם בני
שנה

לל–ופר בן בקר אחד
ממ–ואילם שנים
נן–יהיו עלה לה'
סס–ומנחתם ונסכיהם

LL–An offering made by fire, of sweet savor to the Lord.	עע–אשה ריח ניחח לה':
MM–Then you shall sacrifice one kid of the goats for a sin offering,	פפ–ועשיתם שעיר עזים אחד לחטאת
NN–And two lambs of the first year for a sacrifice of peace offerings.	צצ–ושני כבשים בני שנה לזבח שלמים:
OO–And the priest shall wave them	קק–והניף הכהן אתם
PP–With the bread of the first fruits	רר–על לחם הבכורים
QQ–For a wave offering before the Lord	שש–תנופה לפני ה'
RR–With the two lambs;	תת–על שני כבשים
SS–They shall be holy to the Lord	אאא–קדש יהיו לה'
TT–For the priest.	בבב–לכהן:
UU–And you shall proclaim on the same day,	גגג–וקראתם בעצם היום הזה
VV–That it may be a holy gathering to you;	דדד–מקרא קדש יהיה לכם
WW–You shall do no labor on it;	ההה–כל מלאכת עבדה לא תעשו
XX–It shall be a statute forever	ווו–חקת עולם
YY–In all your dwellings	זזז–בכל מושבתיכם
ZZ–Throughout your generations."[81]	חחח–לדרתיכם:

Rabbinic tradition interpreted the word *Shabbat* (Sabbath) – which can also mean "time of rest"[82] – where it is italicized in this section, to refer to the first day of Passover and not to the seventh day of the week.[83] Since this day is a *Yom Tov* (a sanctified Biblical holiday) most of the prohibitions against work that apply to *Shabbat* are also applicable to the first day of *Pesah*.[84]

Starting to count the fifty days as the Rabbis did leads to *Shavuot* falling at the end of the first week of the month of *Sivan*. In the current Jewish calendar – which relies on prior calculations and not on witnesses – it will always be celebrated on the sixth of that month. That is because the intervening months between *Pesah* and *Shavuot* always have the same number of days each year. When eyewitness testimony was required and the months could have been

---

81   Leviticus 23:4–22.

82   Cf. Ibn Ezra, Leviticus 23:11.

83   M. Hagigah 2:4; B. Menahot 65a; and see Rashi to B. Ta'anit 17b, sv. *"itokam temida."*

84   Rabbi Jacob ben Asher (13th–14th century), Tur *Orah Hayim*, #495.

either twenty-nine or thirty days long, the holiday could have fallen on either the fifth, sixth or seventh of *Sivan* when using the rabbinic system.[85]

In opposition to this tradition, at least some of the sectarians took the word *Shabbat* literally and required that the count of fifty days begin on the day after a Saturday. As a result, on their calendar, *Shavuot*, the fiftieth day, would also always fall on a Sunday seven weeks after the count began. It is not clear from rabbinic literature which Sunday served as the start date for this count and therefore on which Sunday *Shavuot* would be celebrated.[86]

Our first clue to answering this question comes from *Sefer ha-Yovlot* (the Book of Jubilees), a text that is part of the Apocrypha.[87] As we have said, the Apocrypha are books written in Biblical style that for one reason or another (in some cases because they were authored after the close of Biblical prophecy according to the Rabbis' understanding of history) were denied entry into the canon of the Jewish Bible – though, some Christian Bibles do include some of these works.[88]

The Book of Jubilees is a particularly interesting example of this literature. It divides the history of the Jewish people into the fifty-year Jubilee cycles (hence the name).[89] It also describes Jewish life in *halakhic* (Jewish legal) terms, often in ways that would be generally recognizable to traditional Jews today.[90]

However, this is not true when the book describes the calendar or the holidays. For example, in discussing the commemoration of the giving of the Torah (which rabbinic Judaism celebrates on *Shavuot*), the date given for that celebration is the *fifteenth* of *Sivan*, days later than the traditional understanding of when this should occur.[91] This would point to a fifty-day count that began some time *after* Passover.

---

85 B. Rosh Hashanah 6b, Rabbi Baruch Epstein (1860–1942), Torah Temimah, Exodus 24:16 n. 36.

86 The lack of clarity as to which *Shabbat* is meant is given in rabbinic literature as one reason why the sectarians were wrong, B. Menahot 66a.

87 VanderKam, James C. *The Book of Jubilees.* Sheffield: 2001; Segal, Michael. *The Book of Jubilees: Rewritten Bible, Redaction, Ideology and Theology.* Leiden, 2007.

88 Tosefta Yadayim 2:4; J. Sanhedin 10:1, (28a). See especially Seder Olam Rabbah 30:5, that the reign of Alexander the Great, which began the Greek period in Judea, marked the end of prophecy.

89 Leviticus 25:8–13.

90 For example, chapter six of the *Book of Jubilees* discusses the prohibition of eating blood with one's meat at great length.

91 Jubilees 16:13; and see Jubilees 1:1, that Moses descended from Mt. Sinai on the

Confirmation of this suggestion and complete understanding of the sectarian calendar has come with the publication of the entire library of the Dead Sea Scrolls.[92] These scrolls tell us that the sectarians had a calendar that was very different from the one used by the Rabbis. It was not based on witnesses and, to a considerable extent, it was not based on the cycles of the moon. Instead it featured a repetitive three-month cycle of ninety-one days consisting of two months of thirty days and one month of thirty-one. Four such cycles created a year of exactly fifty-two weeks and 364 days.[93] Evidence for this structure appears in a number of places within the scrolls including the Psalm scroll that speaks of 364 daily Psalms and fifty-two weekly Psalms.[94]

Further, in such a structure, all holidays (and the calendar had several that are different from those that the Rabbis celebrated) fall on the same day of the week every year.[95] Hence the calendar we find in Qumran, where the Dead Sea Scrolls were discovered, takes us week by week and month by month through the year informing us that, for example, on Sunday the fifteenth of *Sivan*, *Shavuot* is to be commemorated every time the annual cycle is repeated. This date falls fifty days after the Sunday *that follows Pesah* on their calendar. Hence we now fully understand the debate about the counting of the days mentioned by the Rabbis.

The Dead Sea Scrolls tell us even more. In disagreeing with the rabbinic calendar, the sectarians raised an intriguing philosophical challenge to the sages.

---

sixteenth of Sivan (and, therefore, he received the Torah on the fifteenth). This date for *Shavuot* also appears in the Dead Sea Scrolls calendar that we are about to discuss.

92 In fact, *Jubilees* makes this all clear, particularly in chapter six, but many scholars did not reach that conclusion until all of the Dead Sea Scrolls material became available. The *Book of Jubilees* was available across the centuries; the Dead Sea Scrolls were only discovered in 1946 or 1947, and were only made fully available for general scholarly use in the 1990s.

93 See Ben-Dov, Jonathan. *Head of All Years: Astronomy and Calendars at Qumran in their Ancient Context*. Leiden: 2008. Also see Sacha Stern's "Qumran Calendars: Theory and Practice" in Timothy H. Lim, et. al., ed. *The Dead Sea Scrolls in their Historical Context* (London: 2004, pp. 179–186) for the claim that more than one calendar existed at Qumran as well as discussion of what calendar was used in that community. I do not agree with his conclusions. See also Beckwith, Roger. *Calendar Chronology and Worship*. Leiden: 2005.

94 See especially 4Q320 and 4Q321.

95 For example, Wednesday the first day of the fourth month is "Memorial Day" and Sunday the twenty-second day of the sixth month is the "Feast of Oil."

God put the celestial lights in place and determined their paths. The periodicity of their movements and our experience of them is part of God's glory. Calculating these repetitive cycles presents us with the magnificence of God's creation. Why then would the Sages abandon these calculations (which, as a historical matter, were known to the Babylonians when the Jews were in exile there (586–516 BCE)[96] and may have been known to the ancient Egyptians when the Israelites were slaves there[97]), in order to embrace a system fraught with the possibility, and even the likelihood, of error?[98]

The end of chapter six of the *Book of Jubilees* makes similar claims. It condemns those who follow the gentiles and observe the Moon; who abandon the 364-day Solar year and make it ten days too short; and who, therefore, sanctify profane days and violate the sanctity of the holiest moments on the calendar.

Leaving aside the conflict over the length of the year that seems to derive from an irreducible debate as to whether the solar or lunar cycles are more important, these sectarians are asking a powerful question. What happens if it is a cloudy day and no one sees the moon when it first appears? What happens if the witnesses see a celestial phenomenon that they mistake for the Moon?

As we shall see such errors may have played a role in the controversy between Rabban Gamaliel and Rabbi Joshua about the date of *Yom Kippur* that we will discuss shortly, and that nearly tore the Jewish community apart in the second century C.E. Why would the rabbis subject themselves to the possibility of error and conflict in relation to a matter of such importance? After all, a mistake here might mean that the entire community would fast on a day that was not *Yom Kippur* and eat on a day that was, or eat *Matzah* on the day before Passover or *Hametz* on a day when leavened bread was actually forbidden.[99]

As discussed above, the Rabbis were cognizant of this problem and did make some provisions to keep the errors within bounds. But the point is that they could have eliminated the errors completely and chose not to. From a

---

96   Parker, Richard A. and Dubberstein, Waldo H. *Babylonian Chronology 626 BC-AD 75*. Providence: 1956.

97   Parker, Richard A. *The Calendars of Ancient Egypt*. Chicago: 1950.

98   Talmon, Shemaryahu. "Anti-lunar-calendar Polemics in Covenanters' Writings." In Michael Becker and Wolfgang Fenske, ed. *Das Ende der Tage*. Leiden: 1999, pp. 29–40. We find examples of this criticism in, for example, the Damascus Document, Pesher Hosheah, the Community Rule and in one version of Miktsat Ma'aseh Torah; see Stern, pp. 184–185, who downplays the evidence.

99   For the seriousness of these violations see Exodus 12:15, 19 and Leviticus 23:29.

theological point of view the question of "Why choose to serve God in error when you can serve Him in truth?" would seem to be overwhelming.

The Rabbinic response was almost to take pride in these possible errors. As an example we find this text:

A–If the witnesses came and testified [about the Moon].	א–באו העדים והעידו
B–And they were found to be false witnesses.	ב–ונמצא זוממים
C–How do we know that it is sanctified?	ג–מנין שהיה מקודש
D–It therefore says, "That *you* shall call them in My seasons."[100]	ד–תלמוד לומר אשר תקראו אותם במועדי,
E–If you call them, they are "My seasons"	ה–אם קריתם אתם מועדי
F–And if not, they are not "My seasons."	ו–ואם לאו אינם מועדי.
G–If they were sanctified by people under compulsion or those who were negligent or who were in error,	ז–קידשוהו אנוסים או שוגגין או מוטעים
H–How do we know that it is sanctified?	ח–מנין שהוא מקודש
I–It therefore says, "That *you* shall call them in My seasons."	ט–תלמוד לומר אשר תקראו אותם מועדי,
J–"Them" even if in error.	י–אתם אפילו מוטעים
K–"Them" even compelled.	כ–אתם אפילו אנוסים
L–If you call them – they are "My seasons."	ל–אם קריתם אתם מועדי
M–If not – they are not "My seasons."[101]	מ–ואם לאו אינן מועדי.

This finds remarkable expansion in the following source:

A–It is the way of the world:	א–בנוהג שבעולם
B–The ruler says: "Today is the judgement"	ב–השלטון אומר הדין היום
C–And the thieves say: "Tomorrow is the judgement"	ג–והליסטים אומר למחר הדין
D–Who is responded to?	ד–למי שומעין
E–Certainly, the ruler.	ה–לא לשלטון
F–But the Holy One Blessed be He is not like this.	ו–אבל הק"ה אינו כן
G–The [human] court says:	ז–אמרו בית דין

---

100 Leviticus 23:2
101 Sifra, loc. cit.

H–Today is *Rosh Hashanah* [Judgement Day].   ח–היום ראש השנה

I–The Holy One Blessed be He says   ט–הקב״ה אומר למלאכי

to the ministering angels: השרת

J–"Erect a podium."   י–העמידו בימה

K–"Let the defenders rise."   כ–יעמדו סניגורין

L–"Let the accusers rise."   ל–יעמדו קטיגורין

M–For my children have said,   מ–שאמרו בני היום ראש השנה

"Today is *Rosh Hashanah*."

N–If the court then decided to   נ–נמלכו בית דין לעברה למחר

pass it on to the next day.

O–The Holy One Blessed be He   ס–הקב״ה אומר למלאכי השרת

says to the ministering angels:

P–"Remove the podium."   ע–העבירו בימה

Q–"Let the defenders pass by."   פ–יעברו סניגורין

R–"Let the accusers pass by."   צ–יעברו קטיגורין

S–For my children decided to   ק–שנמלכו בני לעברה למחר

pass it on to the next day.

T–What is the reason?   ר–מה טעמא

U–It is a statute for Israel, a law   ש–כי חוק לישראל הוא משפט

for the Lord of Jacob.[102]   לא-להי יעקב

V–If it is not a statute for Israel, as it were,   ת–אם אינו חוק לישראל כביכול

it is not a law for the God of Jacob.   אינו משפט לא-להי יעקב

W–Rabbi Krispa in the name of Rabbi Johanan   אא–רבי קריספא בשם ר' יוחנן

X–In the past it was, "These are   בב–לשעבר אלה מועדי ה'

the seasons of God."[103]

Y–From now on it's, "That *you* shall call them."[104]   גג–מיכן ואילך אשר תקראו

אותם

Z–Said Rabbi Ilai: דד–אמר רבי אילא

AA–"If you call them, they are 'My seasons,'   הה–אם קריתם אותם הם

מועדי

BB–And if not, they are not 'My seasons.'"[105]   וו–ואם לאו אינן מועדי

---

102 Psalms 81:5.

103 Leviticus 23:2.

104 The continuation of the same verse.

105 J. Rosh Hashanah 1:3 (57b).

For the Rabbis, maintaining the calendar was seen as a partnership between God and the Jews. As opposed to the Sabbath, which is entirely God-originated through the creation chronology of six periods of time when God "worked," and a seventh such period when He rested,[106] holidays are moments to be sanctified by both God and mankind.

This next text tells us that Jewish liturgy was designed to express just this understanding:

A–Sabbath, which is determined and established,	א–שבת דקביעא וקיימא,
B–Whether in prayer or in *Kiddush* [the prayer	ב–בין בצלותא ובין בקידושא
of sanctification over wine], [the blessing	מקדש השבת,
is:] "He, Who sanctifies the Sabbath."[107]	
C–Holidays,	ג–יומא טבא,
D–Here, Israel is the one who determines it.	ד–דישראל הוא דקבעי ליה
E–For they expand the months and establish	ה–דקמעברי ירחי וקבעי לשני
the years – [the blessing is:][108] "He, Who	–מקדש ישראל והזמנים.
sanctifies *Israel* and the times."[109]	

On Sabbath, the sanctification process is from God alone.[110] On holidays, Israel must be involved for the system to work, even if the price of that involvement is occasional error.

This interesting philosophical discussion[111] was unfortunately part of a truly acrimonious schism between the Rabbis and these sectarians. We have already encountered the sectarian practice of lighting ersatz signal fires, and of employing false witnesses to wreak havoc with the rabbinic calendar. The Dead Sea Scrolls tell us that this interference with the calendar was not one-sided.

The Scrolls record an incident in which the "Wicked Priest" in Jerusalem

---

106 Genesis ch. 1.
107 Siddur, pp. 340, 360.
108 Ibid., pp. 658, 666.
109 B. Pesahim 117b. See also B. Menahot 65b.
110 The Rabbis believed that Shabbat existed in this world even without Jews. This was reflected by manifestations of the Sabbath in nature. The most famous is the river Sambatyon that rages and is impassible during the week, but becomes calm on Shabbat; see Genesis Rabbah 11:5 for this, and for other examples, and for an interesting philosophical discussion of the question.
111 See B. Menahot b 65a-b.

dispatched a group of people – a group in which he, himself, may have been included – to harass the High Priest in Qumran on *Yom Kippur*.[112] Presumably that was the Day of Atonement according to the *sectarian calendar* that we find in the Dead Sea Scrolls, but it was not considered *Yom Kippur* in Jerusalem, where it appears that the Rabbis' way of determining the holidays held sway.[113]

It was not just between the sages and the sectarians that calendrical issues served as angry and painful flash-points. Even within the rabbinic community, debates about the calendar created friction and sometimes consequences that were far worse.

A small skirmish in which the Patriarch of the Sanhedrin, Rabban Gamaliel,[114] imposed his will on the community is found in this text:

A–Our Rabbis taught:	א–תנו רבנן:
B–Once the heavens were covered with clouds.[115]	ב–פעם אחת נתקשרו שמים בעבים
C–And the likeness of the moon was seen on the twenty-ninth of the month.	ג–ונראית דמות לבנה בעשרים ותשעה לחדש,
D–The public were minded to declare "New Moon,"	ד–כסבורים העם לומר: ראש חדש,
E–And the court wanted to sanctify it,	ה–ובקשו בית דין לקדשו.
F–But Rabban Gamaliel said to them:	ו–אמר להם רבן גמליאל:
G–"I have it on the authority of the house of my father's father[116]	ז–כך מקובלני מבית אבי אבא:

---

112 See the scroll known as Pesher Habakuk (1QpHab) 2:15. Pesher is a form of commentary found in the Dead Sea scrolls that takes Biblical verses and explains them as referring to contemporary events that affected the life of the Qumran community and its leadership. Each comment begins with the word "pesher"; see Vriezen, Th. C. *Ancient Israelite and Early Jewish literature*. Leiden: 2005, p. 667.

113 See Hanson, Kenneth. *Dead Sea Scrolls: the Untold Story*. Tulsa: 1997, p. 78. He sees this as occurring in Damascus rather than in Qumran. I disagree.

114 I have identified him as the second Rabban Gamaliel, who was Patriarch of the Sanhedrin in Yavneh immediately after the destruction of the second Temple in 70 C.E., and not his grandfather of the same name. First, because he references his grandfather in this source, and second because conflicts and assertive actions like this were very much part of the second Rabban Gamaliel's history as told in rabbinic literature. This is not true of the older individual who bore this name.

115 As discussed, this was a potential problem in the eyewitness system. Apparently the Rabbis were aware of the issue from firsthand experience.

116 An indication that calendar calculations were known to the Rabbis.

H–That the renewal of the Moon takes place after not less than twenty-nine days and a half, and two-thirds of an hour and seventy-three parts."[117]

ח–אין חדושה של לבנה פחותה מעשרים ותשעה יום ומחצה ושני שלישי שעה ושבעים ושלשה חלקים.

I–On that day the mother of Ben Zaza died,

ט–ואותו היום מתה אמו של בן זזא,

J–And Rabban Gamaliel made a great funeral oration over her [to show that the day was not the New Moon, since eulogies are not allowed on *Rosh Hodesh* due to its celebratory nature].[118]

י–והספידה רבן גמליאל הספד גדול.

K–Not because she had merited it,

כ–לא מפני שראויה לכך,

L–But so that the public should know

ל–אלא כדי שידעו העם

M–That the court had not sanctified the month.[119]

מ–שלא קידשו בית דין את החדש.

Rabban Gamaliel also figures in a much more significant dispute about the calendar that brings him into open conflict with Rabbi Joshua another leading sage of his era:[120]

A–On one occasion two witnesses came and said,

א–מעשה שבאו שנים, ואמרו:

B–"We saw it in the morning in the east and in the evening in the west."

ב–ראינוהו שחרית במזרח וערבית במערב.

C–Rabbi Johanan b. Nuri said,

ג–אמר רבי יוחנן בן נורי:

D–"They are false witnesses."[121]

ד–עדי שקר הם.

---

117 Parts of an hour. Rabbinic chronography divided each hour into 1080 parts. This system is still used today when calculating the *molad*.

118 Cf. Rabbi Menachem ben Shlomo Meiri (1249–1315), Beit ha–Behirah, commentary to this source.

119 B. Rosh Hashanah 25a.

120 The second Rabban Gamaliel lived at the same time as Rabbi Joshua.

121 The New Moon always appears close to the sun either preceding it across the sky, or following it across the sky. If the moon is first, it rises before the sun and can be seen in the morning in the east, but at night it sets before the sun and cannot be seen in the west because the sun is too bright. If it follows the Sun, it cannot be seen in the morning because the sun rises first and is too strong. After the sun sets it can be seen in the west for a time. Thus both can't be true for the same New Moon.

E–When they came to Yavneh, Rabban Gamaliel accepted them.

ה–כשבאו ליבנה קיבלן רבן גמליאל.

F–On another occasion, two witnesses came and said, "We saw it at its proper time,"[122]

ו–ועוד באו שנים ואמרו: ראינוהו בזמנו,

G–But on the night which should have been New Moon it was not seen,[123]

ז–ובליל עיבורו לא נראה.

H–And Rabban Gamaliel accepted their evidence.[124]

ח–וקיבלן רבן גמליאל.

I–Rabbi Dosa b. Harkinas said:

ט–אמר רבי דוסא בן הורכינס:

J–"They are false witnesses.[125]

י–עדי שקר הן;

K–How can men testify that a woman has born a child

כ–היאך מעידים על האשה שילדה,

L–When on the next day we see her belly still swollen?"[126]

ל–ולמחר כריסה בין שיניה?

M–Said Rabbi Joshua to him:

מ–אמר לו רבי יהושע:

N–"I see [the force of] your argument."

נ–רואה אני את דבריך.

O–Thereupon Rabban Gamaliel sent to him,

ס–שלח לו רבן גמליאל:

P–"I require you

ע–גוזרני עליך

Q–To appear before me with your staff and your money

פ–שתבא אצלי במקלך ובמעותיך

R–On the day which, according to your reckoning, should be the Day of Atonement."[127]

ק–ביום הכפורים שחל להיות בחשבונך.

S–Rabbi Akiva went and found him [Rabbi Joshua] in great distress.

ר–הלך ומצאו רבי עקיבא מיצר.

T–He said to him: "I can bring proof that whatever Rabban Gamaliel has done is valid,

ש–אמר לו: יש לי ללמוד שכל מה שעשה רבן גמליאל עשוי,

U–Because it says, 'These are the appointed seasons of God, holy convocations, which you shall proclaim in their appointed seasons,'

ת–שנאמר אלה מועדי ה' מקראי קדש אשר תקראו אתם

---

122 Day thirty.

123 Day thirty-one.

124 And declared day thirty *Rosh Hodesh*.

125 Again he is correct for the reason he is about to give.

126 She has not yet given birth.

127 This must have been the New Moon of *Tishrei*. The parallel to the incident in Pesher Habakuk is remarkable, but it is extremely unlikely that there is any connection between them.

V–Whether they are proclaimed at their proper time or not at their proper time,

אא–בין בזמנן בין שלא בזמנן,

W–I have no seasons except these."[128]

בב–אין לי מועדות אלא אלו.

X–He went to Rabbi Dosa b. Harkinas;

גג–בא לו אצל רבי דוסא בן הורכינס,

Y–He said to him: "If we judge the court of Rabban Gamaliel,

דד–אמר לו: אם באין אנו לדון אחר בית דינו של רבן גמליאל

Z–We must judge every court that has existed from the days of Moses until the present time.

הה–צריכין אנו לדון אחר כל בית דין ובית דין שעמד מימות משה ועד עכשיו,

AA–For it says, 'Then went up Moses and Aaron, Nadab and Abihu and seventy of the elders of Israel,'[129]

וו–שנאמר ויעל משה ואהרן נדב ואביהוא ושבעים מזקני ישראל,

BB–Why were the names of the elders not mentioned?

זז–ולמה לא נתפרשו שמותן של זקנים

CC–To show that every group of three which has acted as a court over Israel.

חח–אלא ללמד שכל שלשה ושלשה שעמדו בית דין על ישראל

DD–Is on a level with the court of Moses."

טט–הרי הוא כבית דינו של משה.

EE–He took his staff and his money in his hand,

יי–נטל מקלו ומעותיו בידו,

FF–And went to Yavneh to Rabban Gamaliel,

כך–והלך ליבנה אצל רבן גמליאל

GG–On the day on which the Day of Atonement fell according to his reckoning.

לל–ביום שחל יום הכפורים להיות בחשבונו.

HH–Rabban Gamaliel rose and kissed him on his head,

ממ–עמד רבן גמליאל ונשקו על ראשו,

II–And said to him:

ננ–אמר לו:

JJ–"Come in peace, my teacher and my disciple.

בוא בשלום רבי ותלמידי!

KK–My teacher in wisdom.[130]

סס–רבי בחכמה,

---

128 We have already seen this argument in two previous sources. This is an indication that the question of truth versus error also had its impact among the Rabbis and they felt a need to respond to it.

129 Exodus 24:9.

130 This may imply that he now agreed that Rabbi Joshua was factually correct, but that truth was not the essential element as we discussed above.

| LL–And my disciple because you have accepted my decision."[131] | עע–ותלמידי שקבלת את דברי. |

We take note of two important aspects of this source: First, it is one of three times that Rabban Gamaliel publicly embarrassed Rabbi Joshua.[132] After the third time, he was temporarily removed as *Nasi* (Patriarch of the Sanhedrin). In other words, once again a dispute about the calendar was part of a major rupture in the Jewish community.

Second, the statements of Rabbi Akiva and of Rabbi Dosa b. Hyrkanos again make the point that even if there is an error in the deliberations that lead to the declaration of the new month, once that mistake has been accepted as correct, the calendar is to function in keeping with that error. So, too, Rabban Gamaliel, in his last comment in this text, appears to accept that Rabbi Joshua was factually correct. Nonetheless, procedurally his own opinion was the one that held sway. As the leader of the Sanhedrin, he, and only he, had the power to determine when the court should sanctify the month – even if he was wrong in that determination.

Another even more acrimonious calendar debate occurs some years later among other scholars of the rabbinic period. The tale told in rabbinic literature about this event involves a purposeful act of deceit used to discredit one Rabbi and the tolerance of *kashrut* violations for the same reason. The source reads:

A–Rabbi Safra said [that] Rabbi Abbahu used to relate	א–אמר רב ספרא, רבי אבהו הוה משתעי:
B–[That] when Hananiah the son of Rabbi Joshua's brother went down to the diaspora,[133]	ב–כשירד חנינא בן אחי רבי יהושע לגולה
C–He began to intercalate the years [add leap years as necessary] and fix New Moons outside Palestine.[134]	ג–היה מעבר שנים וקובע חדשים בחוצה לארץ.

---

131 M. Rosh Hashanah 2:9.

132 In the Babylonian Talmud the other two incidents appear on B. Bekhorot 36a and B. Berakhot 27b.

133 To Babylonia.

134 Probably at a time when persecutions prevented doing so in Israel. Normally only the court in Israel, and preferably in Jerusalem, can do this.

D–So they sent after him two scholars,

ד–שגרו אחריו שני תלמידי חכמים

E–Rabbi Jose b. Kippar and the grandson of Rabbi Zechariah b. Kebutal.

ה–רבי יוסי בן כיפר ובן בנו של זכריה בן קבוטל.

F–When he saw them, he said to them, "Why have you come?"

ו–כיון שראה אותם, אמר להם: למה באתם?

G–They replied, "We have come to learn Torah [from you]." [This was designed to build him up in the people's eyes.]

ז–אמרו ליה: ללמוד תורה באנו.

H–He thereupon proclaimed:

ח–הכריז [עליהם]:

I–"These men are the greatest of the generation.

ט–אנשים הללו גדולי הדור הם,

J–And their ancestors served in the Sanctuary"

י–ואבותיהם שמשו בבית המקדש,

K–As we have learned:

כ–כאותה ששנינו:

L–"Zechariah b. Kebutal said:

ל–זכריה בן קבוטל אומר:

M–'Several times I read to him [the High Priest] out of the book of Daniel [to keep him awake on the night of Yom Kippur[135]

מ–הרבה פעמים קריתי לפניו בספר דניאל.

N–Soon they began to declare clean what he declared unclean.

נ–התחיל הוא מטמא והם מטהרים,

O–And to permit what he forbade. [In order to tear him down in the people's eyes.]

ס–הוא אוסר והם מתירים.

P–Thereupon he proclaimed, "These men are worthless, they are good for nothing."

ע–הכריז עליהם: אנשים הללו של שוא הם, של תהו הם.

Q–They said to him, "You have already built and you cannot overthrow,

פ–אמרו לו: כבר בנית ואי אתה יכול לסתור,

R–You have made a fence and you cannot break it down."

צ–כבר גדרת ואי אתה יכול לפרוץ.

S–He said to them, "Why do you declare clean when I declare unclean,

ק–אמר להם: מפני מה אני מטמא ואתם מטהרים,

T–Permit when I forbid?"

ר–אני אוסר ואתם מתירים?

U–They replied, "Because you intercalate years and fix New Moons outside of Palestine."

ש–אמרו לו: מפני שאתה מעבר שנים וקובע חדשים בחוץ לארץ.

---

135 M. Yoma 1:6.

V–He said to them, "Did not Akiva son of Joseph intercalate years and fix New Moons outside of Palestine?"[136]

W–They replied, "Leave Rabbi Akiva alone, who did not leave his equal in the Land of Israel."

X–He said to them, "I also left not my equal in the Land of Israel."

Y–They said to him, "The kids which you left behind have become goats with horns,

Z–And they have sent us to you,

AA–Bidding us,

BB–Go and tell him in our name.

CC–If he listens, well and good; if not, he will be excommunicated.

DD–Tell also our brethren in the diaspora.

EE–If they listen to you, well and good; if not, let them go up to the mountain,

FF–Let Ahia build an altar.[137]

GG–And let Hananiah play the harp,[138]

HH–And let them all become heretics and say that they have no portion in the God of Israel."[139]

II–Immediately, all the people broke out in weeping and cried,

JJ–"Heaven forbid; we have a portion in the God of Israel."

KK–Why do all this?

LL–Because it says, "For out of Zion shall go forth the law, and the word of the Lord from Jerusalem."[140]

ת–אמר להם: והלא עקיבא בן
יוסף היה מעבר שנים וקובע
חדשים בחוץ לארץ?

אא–אמרו לו: הנח רבי עקיבא,
שלא הניח כמותו בארץ ישראל.

בב–אמר להם: אף אני לא
הנחתי כמותי בארץ ישראל.

גג–אמרו לו: גדיים שהנחת
נעשו תישים בעלי קרנים,

דד–והם שגרונו אצלך,

הה–וכן אמרו לנו:

וו–לכו ואמרו לו בשמנו:

זז–אם שומע מוטב, ואם לאו
יהא בנדוי.

חח–ואמרו לאחינו שבגולה:

טט–אם שומעין מוטב, ואם לאו
יעלו להר,

יי–אחיה יבנה מזבח,

כך–חנניה ינגן בכנור,

לל–ויכפרו כולם ויאמרו: אין
להם חלק באלהי ישראל.

ממ–מיד געו כל העם בבכיה
ואמרו:

ננ–חם ושלום! יש לנו חלק
באלהי ישראל.

סס–וכל כך למה?

עע–משום שנאמר: כי מציון
תצא תורה ודבר ה' מירושלים.

---

136 Also during a time of persecution; M. Yevamot 16:7.

137 Presumably a member of this community in Babylon who was a builder.

138 Presumably the villain in this story, who was a Levite, as was his father's brother Rabbi Joshua; see B. Arkhin 11b.

139 This is said about Ahab the evil King of Israel, B. Sanhedrin 102b. See also Joshua 22:27.

140 Isaiah 2:3.

MM–We can understand that if he declared clean they should declare unclean, because this would be more stringent.	פפ–בשלמא הוא מטהר והם מטמאין לחומרא,
NN–But how was it possible that they should declare clean what he declared unclean [leading to the people eating unfit food]?	צצ–אלא הוא מטמא והם מטהרין, היכי הוי?
OO–And has it not been taught, "If a sage has declared unclean, his colleague is not permitted to declare clean;	קק–והא תניא: חכם שטמא אין חברו רשאי לטהר,
PP–If he prohibited, his friend is not allowed to permit"?	רר–אסר אין חברו רשאי להתיר!
QQ–They thought proper to act thus so that the people should not be drawn after him.[141]	שש–קסברי: כי היכי דלא נגררו בתריה.

Once again, any deviation from the normal procedures required by Jewish law for maintaining the calendar was considered to be quite a serious matter. If the Rabbis would go this far against one of their own to prevent any change in the rules from taking place, then we must repeat our conclusion that working to keep the calendar functioning as they believed it should was a fundamental core issue for the rabbinic community in talmudic times.

Remarkably, after the close of the Talmud, in the Geonic era (approximately 800–1000 C.E.), precisely the same issue that led to the surprising rabbinic deception described in the source just discussed, again divided the Jewish community. This time, however, the struggle ultimately ended with the opposite conclusion. As before, this debate became quite nasty and, in this case, it took some time for it to be fully resolved.

Saadiah Gaon (882 or 892–942 C.E.) was arguably the most important scholarly figure who lived in this era.[142] He was born in Egypt, then moved to Israel and finally, to Babylonia.

We have already mentioned that the system of relying on witnesses to determine when to celebrate *Rosh Hodesh* came to an end in the fourth century as a result of Christian persecutions in Palestine. From that point in time until Saadiah's generation there had not been a community in the land of Israel

---

141   B. Berakhot 63a-b.

142   See Steven T. Katz, ed. *Saadiah Gaon*. New York: 1980; Malter, Henry. *Saadia Gaon: His Life and Works*. New York: 1969.

strong enough to try to reassert itself and decide how to apply the calendrical calculations of Rabbeinu Hillel to the daily calendar. Instead, when it came to the calendar, as with all halakhic matters, the Sages in Babylonia held sway. When witnesses were used to determine the new moon, as we saw in the source just discussed, the calendar was to be controlled in Israel. That is except for circumstances such as those that confronted Rabbi Akiva, who under extreme conditions did what was necessary in Babylonia to preserve the calendar for all Jewry – and then for only a brief period of time.

By the early tenth century, because persecution of the Jews in Palestine had eased, a Gaonite (an academy for Torah study led by a powerful chief sage called a Gaon) emerged in the Holy Land. This Gaonite headed by Aaron b. Meir attempted to determine how the calendar should function. In the year 922, based on an opinion that was not accepted in Babylonia, Aaron b. Meir declared that *Pesah* should begin on a particular Sunday. Apparently many in Palestine followed his direction. The Babylonian Gaonite, and the rest of the Jewish world that looked to it for *halakhic* guidance, maintained their understanding of the calendar and began the holiday on the subsequent Tuesday. This was an untenable situation for the Jewish community.

Saadiah led the opposition to this effort.[143] In his opinion, not only was the Gaonite in Babylonia correct on the calendar question itself, but it was accepted as the central *halakhic* authority for the entire Jewish world. Therefore, the sages in Palestine did not have the authority to take this step.

He wrote several forceful letters and a book called *Sefer ha-Mo'adim* (Book of the Festivals), concerning the issues and individuals involved. These eventually helped influence the Jewish community in Palestine to return to the calendar as it was calculated in Babylonia. Nonetheless, for perhaps as much as a year, the holidays were celebrated on different days in Israel as opposed to in Babylonia and the rest of the world.

Given this lengthy and difficult history of conflict within the Jewish community on these issues, it is not surprising that any decision regarding the calendar comes with some sensitivity and concern. Even Rabban Gamaliel who was part of two of these battles, at one point in his career, approached the issue of adding a thirteenth month to the calendar very gingerly in his later years.

Extending the year by one month comes with important economic effects that are not necessarily positive for everyone. For example, anything that comes due on the first of *Nisan* (the first month of the year) such as a loan, would

---

143 Bornstein, Hayyim Jehiel. *Mahloket Rav Seadyah*. 1904.

be delayed twenty nine or thirty days if this step is taken. This will make the debtor happy and the creditor anxious. Therefore not everyone will fully support this decision even though it may be necessary to keep the solar and lunar years in sync.

It is against this background that we read:

A–It has been taught:	א–דתניא:
B–It once happened that Rabban Gamaliel was sitting on a step on the Temple-hill	ב–מעשה ברבן גמליאל שהיה יושב על גב מעלה בהר הבית,
C–And the well-known Scribe, Johanan was standing before him	ג–והיה יוחנן סופר הלז עומד לפניו,
D–While three cut sheets were lying before him.	ד–ושלש איגרות חתוכות לפניו מונחות.
E–He said to him,	ה–אמר לו: ...
F–"... And take the third and write:	ו–וטול איגרתא חדא וכתוב:
G–To our brethren the exiles in Babylon [as we have seen the Patriarch did not need to consult with anyone before making calendrical decisions, and certainly not with people outside of Israel],	ז–לאחנא בני גלוותא בבבל,
H–And to those in Media,	ח–ולאחנא דבמדי,
I–And to all the other exiled of Israel,	ט–ולשאר כל גלוותא דישראל,
J–May your peace be great for ever!	י–שלומכון יסגא לעלם
K–We wish to inform you	כ–מהודעין אנחנא לכון
L–That the doves are still tender	ל–דגוזליא רכיכין,
M–And the lambs still too young	מ–ואימריא ערקין,
N–And that the spring has not come.	נ–וזמנא דאביבא לא מטא,
O–It seems advisable to me and to my colleagues	ס–ושפרא מילתא באנפאי ובאנפי חבריי
P–To add thirty days to this year."	ע–ואוסיפית על שתא דא יומין תלתין
Q–It is possible that this event occurred[144] after he had been deposed.[145]	פ–דילמא בתר דעברוהו.

As indicated above, the incident in which Rabban Gamaliel demanded that Rabbi Joshua appear before him on the date that the latter thought was

144 See Rashi's commentary here.
145 B. Sanhedrin 11b. See also Tosefta Sanhedrin 2:6.

Yom Kippur was one of three conflicts of this type between these two sages. After the third time that Rabban Gamaliel publicly embarrassed his colleague, Rabban Gamaliel was removed from the office of Patriarch. He was reinstated only after making amends.[146]

The source we are discussing here tells us that the kinder and gentler Rabban Gamaliel – who authorized this very gentle letter about the proposed leap year – was Rabban Gamaliel as he had changed after the trauma of losing his position and then being reinstated. Apparently, he was profoundly moved by the conflicts that he had engendered and was being very careful not to repeat his mistakes, particularly on a subject of such great sensitivity.

Armed with this historical background, and probably as a specific response to the painful disagreement in the time of Saadiah Gaon, the phrase חברים כל ישראל was added to *Birkat ha-Hodesh*.[147] In some ways the wish expressed by these words parallels, perhaps unconsciously, the gentleness that Rabban Gamaliel displayed to his colleagues after he learned his painful lesson. One can understand the pathos that underlies this phrase recited as the coming New Moon is announced. These three words are a declaration and perhaps also a statement of hope that everyone in the Jewish community will agree to accept the announcement that is about to be made. It is also a powerful appeal that the schisms of the past that developed over the calendar not appear again.

The phrase itself has an interesting history that fits well with this prayer. Rabbinic Midrash, based on this verse from Psalms 122:3

Jerusalem is built as a city which	ירושלם הבנויה כעיר שחברה
is bound firmly together	לה יחדו

says of Jerusalem:

---

146 B. Berakhot 27b–28a.

147 The phrase does not appear in Seder Rav Amram Gaon, which predates Saadiah's calendar controversy, but it does in Mahzor Vitry, which post-dates these events. Mahzor Vitry follows the words חברים כל ישראל with the phrase: לירושלם עיר הקודש (to Jerusalem the holy city), that evokes the Midrash we are about to discuss. This phrase may also be here to serve as a reminder that despite Saadiah's victory, Jewish belief is that the Temple, the Sanhedrin and the determination of the calendar will ultimately return to Jerusalem. In Masekhet Soferim's description of the sanctification of the New Moon (19:8) mention is made of celebrating before twelve *haveirim*, (twelve sages) who represent the twelve tribes of Israel. Again this is a vision of unity that may have influenced inclusion of this sentence.

[It is] a city that makes all Jews friends[148]	עיר שהיא עושה כל ישראל חברים

The Psalm and the Midrash make reference to a functioning Jerusalem that would presumably be home to a restored calendar system operating as it did in ancient times. Included in that vision is this picture of a people united rather than divided. The hope that this all will become a reality is then expressed in *Birkat ha-Hodesh*.

חברים כל ישראל also has *halakhik* implications, at least on holidays. There are a number of situations in which the Rabbis were lenient in their rulings because of the presumed good will between Jews – particularly on festive days. For example, *amei ha-aretz* (the common people who were not part of the rabbinic community) are normally not fully trusted in regard to whether they have removed the Biblically mandated priestly gifts from produce that they own.[150] For that reason one cannot normally eat fruit and vegetables found in their possession. But around holidays they are thought to be punctilious in fulfilling these requirements, because it is assumed that they are concerned that those from the rabbinic community not inadvertently consume food that would be objectionable to them.[151]

This sends a message to those who are about to hear the announcement of when *Rosh Hodesh* will occur – which also defines the dates of any holidays that fall in the next month – that communal comity is very important. Hopefully, that will prevent any repeat of the conflicts that we have detailed here.

There is a third source of origin for this phrase, and it is an intriguing and painful text to examine. Judges 20:11 reads:

And all the men of Israel were gathered	ויאסף כל איש ישראל אל העיר
to the city as one, friends.	כאיש אחד חברים.

Out of context this sounds like more of the same type of kind and gentle sentiments that we saw associated with the similar-sounding phrases just discussed. In fact the halakhic principle

---

148 J. Hagigah 3:6, 79(d); this is based on the similarity between the word שחברה (bound firmly) and חברים (friends).

149 B. Nidah 33b–34a and J. Hagigah 3:6 79(d), in addition to the source we are about to discuss.

150 Numbers 15:17–21, 18:24; cf. B. Ketuvot 24a.

151 B. Hagigah 26a.

All Jews are friends on festivals.   כל ישראל חברים ברגל

that allows the Rabbis to trust *amei ha-aretz* on holidays is derived from this sentence.[152]

In context, however, this verse is very different. It comes at the end of the story called *Pilegesh be-Giv'ah* that is certainly among the most morally offensive tales in the entire Bible.[153]

We will tell this story briefly, leaving out many of the details. A Jewish man and his concubine (a second-class wife[154]) are travelling on the road as the sun begins to set. They come to the city of Giv'ah where no one will take them in for food or rest. Finally one old man offers them hospitality.

Then in a scene reminiscent of Sodom and Gemorah, this man's home is surrounded by the men of the city demanding that the man who was visiting be sent out to them for immoral purposes.[155] Instead the visitor to Giv'ah sends out the concubine who is then brutally raped repeatedly, and eventually murdered. The man cuts her body into pieces and sends one piece to each of the twelve tribes of Israel as an indication of the terrible tragedy that has occurred.

This man's act and his story galvanize the people of Israel to move against the city of Giv'ah. They demand from the tribe of Benjamin, in whose territory this occurred, that the perpetrators be turned over to them for justice. The singularity of purpose with which this demand was presented is described in the Bible with the words:

And all the men of Israel gathered against   ויאסף כל איש ישראל אל העיר
the city as one man, friends.[156]   כאיש אחד חברים

This is the verse we are discussing.

The tribe of Benjamin refuses to comply, and in the war that ensues it is nearly wiped out – although the Benjamites also inflict serious casualties on the armies of the other eleven tribes. In addition, these eleven tribes ban all

---

152 B. Hagigah 26a, B. Nidah 33b-34a.

153 Judges 19–21.

154 B. Sanhedrin 21a.

155 Genesis 19:4–9.

156 Judges 20:11. See Rashi, ad. loc., who explains חברים here as שוים בעצה אחת (equal, with one opinion), which is precisely the reaction that the community wants to evoke when the determination of when to celebrate Rosh Hodesh is announced.

marriages between their daughters and the men of Benjamin, and it is only with some effort that a way is found to circumvent this ban so that this tribe is able to survive as a part of the Jewish people.

This terrible story, arguably the worst intra-Jewish conflict in history, nonetheless, produced the verse that serves as the proof text for the halakhic principle כל ישראל חברים ברגל, and is the earliest source for the line חברים כל ישראל in *Birkat ha-Hodesh,* which we are discussing. It is remarkable, and perhaps a bit consoling, that out of the unmitigated disaster called *Pilegesh be-Giv'ah* these noble ideas emerged. Again the hope that terrible fratricidal conflict of any type can be avoided makes its way into the liturgy as the month changes, precisely because of the difficult history associated with the calendar and its implementation over the centuries.

We are left, finally, with explaining the origin of the first paragraph of the *Birkat ha-Hodesh* prayer. Here we begin far from the calendar and the New Moon.

After the destruction of the Temple, the same Rabban Gamaliel, the Patriarch whose name we have mentioned several times in this chapter, took a major step toward formalizing Jewish daily worship. Based on other research that I have done, I can say that Rabban Gamaliel took a known communal prayer, the "eighteen" or *Shmoneh Esrei,* and did two important things with it.[157] First, he made it mandatory for every individual to recite the *Shmoneh Esrei* every day as his personal prayer.[158] Second, working with an otherwise unknown individual named Shimon ha-Pekuli and a rarely cited sage, Shmuel ha-Katan, he attempted to create a final authoritative text for that liturgy.[159]

The reaction to these innovations was predictable. While some embraced and accepted his work,[160] others followed the approach of his contemporary, Rabbi Eliezer who said:

---

157 See my dissertation, "The Formalization of Daily Individual Prayer Utilizing the Shmoneh Esrei in the Talmudic Period: Patterns of Acceptance, Rejection, and Modification."

158 M. Berakhot 4:3.

159 B. Berakhot 28b, B. Megillah 17b-18a.

160 Since his work here is the basis of today's practice there are many sources that are supportive. Among the earliest are Tosefta Berakhot 3:6–7, Menahot 6:12 and some of the post-prayer prayers that we are about to discuss, such as the one used by Rabbi Judah ha-Nassi.

One who makes his prayer a fixed text, his prayer is not a supplication.[161]	העושה תפלתו קבע אין תפלתו תחנונים.

In truth, Rabban Gamaliel was attempting to remove spontaneous expression from people's prayer lives. Prior to his formalization of the daily liturgy, people were unrestrained in offering whatever they wished to say to God as their daily supplication.[162]

For the believer, taking away his ability to speak to the Almighty as he chose, would have been a very difficult change to accept. Therefore, as Rabban Gamaliel's decrees gained acceptance, other outlets for spontaneity or individuality appeared. Among these new ways of doing things was the composition of what I like to call 'post-prayer prayers.' These were different individualized texts used by various Rabbis that they appended to their private recitation of the *Shmoneh Esrei* as personal supplications.

Both the Palestinian and Babylonian Talmuds preserve a list of such prayers. The Palestinian Talmud reads:[163]

A–Rabbi Eleazar used to pray three prayers [every day].	א–רבי אלעזר היה מתפלל שלש תפילות
B–After his prayers, what did he say?	ב–לאחר תפילתו מהו אומר
C–"May it be the will from before You, God our Lord and Lord of our ancestors	ג–יהי רצון מלפניך ה' א־להי וא־להי אבותי
D–That hatred of us shall not rise in the hearts of any human being.	ד–שלא תעלה שנאתינו על לב אדם
E–And the hatred of any human being shall not rise in our hearts.	ה–ולא שנאת אדם תעלה על לבינו
F–And may jealousy of us not rise in the hearts of any human being.	ו–ולא תעלה קנאתינו על לב אדם
G–And may no jealousy of any human being rise in our hearts.	ז–ולא קנאת אדם תעלה על לבינו

---

161 M. Berakhot 4:4.

162 All of the personal prayers that predate Rabban Gamaliel described in rabbinic literature are idiosyncratic to the individual and to the moment, B. Yoma 53b; B. Yoma 68b, 70a; B. Ta'anit 24b; B. Sotah 40b, 41a; J. Yoma 7:1 (42a-42b); J. Sotah 7:6 (22a).

163 J. Berakhot 4:4 (8a).

H–And may our Torah be our
profession all the days of our lives.

ח–ותהא תורתך מלאכתינו כל
ימי חיינו

I–And may our words be supplications before You."

ט–ויהיו דברינו תחנונים לפניך

J–Rabbi Hiyya bar Abba added:

י–רבי חייא בר אבא מוסיף

K–"And unify our hearts to fear Your Name.

כ–ותייחד לבבינו ליראה את
שמך

L–And keep us far away from all that You
hate and bring us close to all that You love.

ל–ותרחקינו מכל מה ששנאת
ותקרבינו לכל מה שאהבת

M–And do righteousness with us
for Your Name's sake . . .

מ–ותעשה עמנו צדקה למען
שמך . . .

N–Rabbi Hiyya bar Va prayed:

נ–רבי חייא בר ווא מצלי

O–"May it be the will from before You,
God our Lord and Lord of our ancestors

ס–יהי רצון מלפניך ה' א-להינו
וא-להי אבתינו

P–That You shall put in our hearts to do
complete repentance before You

ע–שתתן בלבינו לעשות
תשובה שלימה לפניך

Q–So that we not be ashamed before
our ancestors in the world to come."

פ–שלא נבוש מאבותינו לעולם
הבא

R–Rabbi Yudin b. Rabbi Ishmael

צ–רבי יודן בירבי ישמעאל

S–Established it for those who say
it to say it after their study.

ק–קבע לה לאמוריה דיימר בתר
פרשתיה כן

T–Rabbi Tanhum bar Iskulistika prayed:

ר–רבי תנחום בר איסכולסטיקא
מצלי

U–"May it be the will from before You,
God our Lord and Lord of our ancestors

ש–יהי רצון מלפניך ה' א-להי
וא-להי אבותי

V–That You break and give us rest from the
yoke of the evil inclination in our hearts,

ת–שתשבור ותשבית עולו של
יצר הרע מלבינו

W–For thus have You created us to do Your will.

אא–שכך בראתנו לעשות רצונך

X–And we are required to do Your will.

בב–ואנו חייבים לעשות רצונך

Y–You want and we want to.

גג–את חפץ ואנו חפיצין

Z–And who prevents this? The yeast in
the dough [the evil inclination].

דד–ומי מעכב שאור שבעיסה

AA–It is revealed and known before You that
we do not have the strength to stand against it.

הה–גלוי וידוע לפניך שאין בנו
כח לעמוד בו

BB–Instead may it be the will before You,
God our Lord and Lord of our ancestors,

וו–אלא יהי רצון מלפניך ה'
א-להי וא-להי אבותי

159

CC–That you remove him from
us and subdue him.

זז–שתשביתהו מעלינו
ותכניעהו

DD–And may You make Your will as
our will with a complete heart."

חח–ונעשה רצונך כרצונינו
בלבב שלם

EE–Rabbi Johanan used to pray:

טט–רבי יוחנן הוה מצלי

FF–"May it be the will from before You,
God our Lord and Lord of my ancestors

יי–יהי רצון מלפניך ה' א־להי
וא־להי אבותי

GG–That You should cause to dwell in our lot
love, brotherhood, peace and friendship.

כך–שתשכן בפורינו אהבה
ואחוה שלום וריעות

HH–And make our end succeed
with good prospects and hope

לל–ותצליח סופינו אחרית
ותקוה

II–And may our borders grow in
the number of students.

ממ–ותרבה גבולינו בתלמידים

JJ–And may we rejoice in our lot
in the Garden of Eden.

נ–ונשיש בחלקינו בגן עדן

KK–And repair for us a good heart.

סס–ותקנינו לב טוב

LL–And a good friend.

עע–וחבר טוב

MM–And may we rise early and
find the desire of our hearts.

פפ–ונשכים ונמצא ייחול לבבינו

NN–And may the cooling of our souls
come before You for good."[164]

צצ–ותבוא לפניך קורת נפשינו
לטובה

The parallel text in the Babylonian Talmud records:[165]

A–Rabbi Eleazar, after concluding his
prayer, used to say the following:

א–רבי אלעזר בתר דמסיים
צלותיה אמר הכי:

B–"May it be Thy will, God our Lord,

ב–יהי רצון מלפניך ה' א־להינו

C–To cause to dwell in our lot love,
brotherhood, peace and friendship,

ג–שתשכן בפורינו אהבה ואחוה
ושלום וריעות,

D–And multiply students in our borders,

ד–ותרבה גבולנו בתלמידים,

E–And make our end succeed with
good prospects and hope,

ה–ותצליח סופנו אחרית ותקוה,

F–And put our portion in the Garden of Eden,

ו–ותשים חלקנו בגן עדן,

---

164 Probably meaning that the self-control of passions should be considered meritorious.
165 B. Berakhot 16b-17a.

G–And repair us with a good friend
and a good impulse in Your world,

H–And may we rise early and find
the yearning of our heart

I–To fear Your Name,

J–And may the cooling of our soul
come before You for good."

K–Rabbi Johanan, on concluding his
prayer, added the following:

L–"May it be Your will, God our Lord,

M–To look upon our shame, and
behold our evil plight,

N–And clothe Yourself in Your mercies,
and cover Yourself in Your strength, and
wrap Yourself in Your loving-kindness, and
gird Yourself with Your graciousness,

O–And may the attribute of Your kindness
and gentleness come before You."

P–Rabbi Zera, on concluding his
prayer, said the following:

Q–"May it be Your will, God our Lord,

R–That we sin not, nor bring upon ourselves
shame or disgrace before our ancestors."

S–Rabbi Hiyya, after praying, said the following:

T–"May it be Your will, God our Lord,

U–That our Torah shall be our craft,

V–And our hearts may not be sick
and our eyes not be darkened."

W–Rav, after his praying, said the following:

X–**"May it be Your will, God our Lord,**

Y–**To give us long life.**

Z–**A Life of peace.**

AA–**A life of goodness.**

BB–**A life of blessing.**

CC–**A life of material well-being.**

ז–ותקננו בחבר טוב ויצר טוב
בעולמך,

ח–ונשכים ונמצא יחול לבבנו

ט–ליראה את שמך,

י–ותבא לפניך קורת נפשנו
לטובה.

כ–רבי יוחנן בתר דמסיים
צלותיה אמר הכי:

ל–יהי רצון מלפניך ה' א-להינו

מ–שתציץ בבשתנו ותביט
ברעתנו

נ–ותתלבש ברחמיך ותתכסה
בעזך ותתעטף בחסידותך
ותתאזר בחנינותך

ס–ותבא לפניך מדת טובך
וענותנותך.

ע–רבי זירא בתר דמסיים
צלותיה אמר הכי:

פ–יהי רצון מלפניך ה' א-להינו

צ–שלא נחטא ולא נבוש ולא
נכלם מאבותינו.

ק–רבי חייא בתר דמצלי אמר
הכי:

ר–יהי רצון מלפניך ה' א-להינו

ש–שתהא תורתך אומנותנו,

ת–ואל ידוה לבנו ואל יחשכו
עינינו.

אא–רב בתר צלותיה אמר הכי:

בב–יהי רצון מלפניך ה' א-להינו

גג–שתתן לנו חיים ארוכים,

דד–חיים של שלום,

הה–חיים של טובה,

וו–חיים של ברכה,

זז–חיים של פרנסה,

DD–A life of bodily health.

חח–חיים של חלוץ עצמות,

EE–A life in which there is fear of sin.

טט–חיים שיש בהם יראת חטא,

FF–A life free from shame or humiliation.

יי–חיים שאין בהם בושה וכלימה,

GG–A life of wealth and honor.

ככ–חיים של עושר וכבוד,

HH–A life in which there will be within us love of Torah and the fear of Heaven.

לל–חיים שתהא בנו אהבת תורה ויראת שמים,

II–A life in which the requests of our hearts will be fulfilled for good."

ממ–חיים שתמלא לנו את כל משאלות לבנו לטובה.

JJ–Rabbi [Rabbi Judah ha-Nassi], after his prayer, said the following:

נן–רבי בתר צלותיה אמר הכי:

KK–"May it be Your will, God our Lord, and Lord of our fathers,

סס–יהי רצון מלפניך ה' א־להינו וא־להי אבותינו

LL–To deliver us from the impudent and from impudence,

עע–שתצילנו מעזי פנים ומעזות פנים,

MM–From an evil man, from evil happenstance, from the evil impulse,

פפ–מאדם רע ומפגע רע, מיצר רע,

NN–From an evil companion, from an evil neighbor,

צצ–מחבר רע, משכן רע,

OO–And from the destructive Accuser;

קק–ומשטן המשחית,

PP–From a hard lawsuit and from a hard opponent,

רר–ומדין קשה ומבעל דין קשה,

QQ–Whether he is a son of the covenant or not a son of the covenant . . ."

שש–בין שהוא בן ברית בין שאינו בן ברית . . .

RR–Rav Safra, after his prayer, said the following:

תת–רב ספרא בתר צלותיה אמר הכי:

SS–"May it be Your will, God our Lord,

אאא–יהי רצון מלפניך ה' א־להינו

TT–To establish peace among the celestial family,

בבב–שתשים שלום בפמליא של מעלה

UU–And among the earthly family,

גגג–ובפמליא של מטה,

VV–And among the students who occupy themselves with Your Torah,

דדד–ובין התלמידים העוסקים בתורתך,

WW–Whether they study Torah for its own sake or for other motives;

ההה–בין עוסקין לשמה בין עוסקין שלא לשמה.

XX–And all who do so for other
motives, may it be Your will that they
come to study it for its own sake."
YY–Rabbi Alexandri, after he
prayed, said the following:
ZZ–"May it be Your will, God our Lord,

AAA–To establish us in a lighted corner and
do not establish us in a darkened corner,
BBB–And let not our hearts be
sick nor our eyes darkened."
CCC–Others say [that] this [was
what] Rav Hamnuna prayed,
DDD–And Rabbi Alexandri, after
he prayed, said the following:
EEE–"Master of the Universe,
FFF–It is revealed and known before You
that our will is to perform Your will,
GGG–And who prevents us?
HHH–The yeast in the dough [the evil
inclination], and subjugation by foreign powers.
III–May it be the will from before You
to deliver us from their hand,
JJJ–And we will return to perform the statutes
of Your will with a complete heart."
KKK–Rava, after his worship, said the following:

LLL–"My Lord, before I was
formed I was not worthy,
MMM–And now that I have been formed,
I am as if I had not been formed.
NNN–I am dust in my lifetime,
all the more so in my death.
OOO–Behold, I am before You as a
vessel full of shame and humiliation.

ווו–וכל העוסקין שלא לשמה,
יהי רצון שיהו עוסקין לשמה.

זזז–רבי אלכסנדרי בתר צלותיה
אמר הכי:
חחח–יהי רצון מלפניך ה'
א־להינו

טטט–שתעמידנו בקרן אורה
ואל תעמידנו בקרן חשכה,
ייי–ואל ידוה לבנו ואל יחשכו
עינינו.
כככ–איכא דאמרי: הא רב
המנונא מצלי לה,
ללל–ורבי אלכסנדרי בתר
דמצלי אמר הכי:
ממם–רבון העולמים,
ננן–גלוי וידוע לפניך שרצוננו
לעשות רצונך,
ססס–ומי מעכב?
עעע–שאור שבעיסה ושעבוד
מלכיות;
פפפ–יהי רצון מלפניך שתצילנו
מידם,
צצצ–ונשוב לעשות חוקי רצונך
בלבב שלם.
קקק–רבא בתר צלותיה אמר
הכי:

ררר–א־להי, עד שלא נוצרתי
איני כדאי
ששש–ועכשיו שנוצרתי כאלו
לא נוצרתי,
תתת–עפר אני בחיי, קל וחומר
במיתתי,
אאאא–הרי אני לפניך ככלי
מלא בושה וכלימה,

PPP–May it be Your will, God our
Lord, that I sin no more,
QQQ–And what I have sinned before
You, wipe out in Your great mercies,
RRR–But not through afflictions and evil diseases."

SSS–This was the confession of Rav
Hamnuna Zuti on the Day of Atonement.
TTT–Mar, the son of Ravina, when he
finished his prayer, said the following:
UUU–"My Lord, guard my tongue from
evil and my lips from speaking falsehood.
VVV–To those that curse me, may my soul be
silent, and may my soul be as the dust to all.
WWW–Open my heart in Your Torah, and
may my soul pursue Your commandments,
XXX–And deliver me from evil happenstance,
YYY–From the evil impulse,
ZZZ–And from an evil woman,
AAAA–And from all evils that
threaten to come upon the world.
BBBB–As for all that plan evil against me, speedily
annul their counsel and frustrate their thoughts.

CCCC–May the speech of my mouth and the
thoughts of my heart be acceptable before You,
DDDD–God, my Rock and my Redeemer."

בבבב–יהי רצון מלפניך ה'
א-להי שלא אחטא עוד,
גגגג–ומה שחטאתי לפניך מרק
ברחמיך הרבים
דדדד–אבל לא על ידי יסורין
וחלאים רעים.

ההההה–והיינו וידוי דרב המנונא
זוטי ביומא דכפורי.
וווו–מר בריה דרבינא כי הוה
מסיים צלותיה אמר הכי:
זזזז–א-להי, נצור לשוני מרע
ושפתותי מדבר מרמה
חחחח–ולמקללי נפשי תדום
ונפשי כעפר לכל תהיה,
טטטט–פתח לבי בתורתך
ובמצותיך תרדוף נפשי,
יייי–ותצילני מפגע רע
ככככ–מיצר הרע
לללל–ומאשה רעה
מממם–ומכל רעות המתרגשות
לבא בעולם,
נננג–וכל החושבים עלי רעה
מהרה הפר עצתם וקלקל
מחשבותם,

סססס–יהיו לרצון אמרי פי
והגיון לבי לפניך
עעעע–ה' צורי וגואלי.

A number of these prayers were found to be meaningful enough to be used by later generations as part of communal Jewish worship. For example, Rava's post-prayer supplication that became Rav Hamnuna Zuti's confessional on the Day of Atonement is now recited by everyone as part of the *Yom Kippur* liturgy.[166] Similarly Rabbi's text now appears at the beginning of the morning

---

166 Mahzor YK p. 98.

service every day of the year,[167] and the prayer of Mar the son of Ravina is *the* post-*Amidah* prayer in the contemporary liturgy.[168]

Most importantly for us here, Rav's post-prayer supplication, with the addition of the words שתחדש עלינו את החדש הזה לטובה ולברכה (renew for us this month for good and for blessing), became the first paragraph of *Birkat ha-Hodesh*. In other words, the decision was made to preserve this text – with minor variations – in the liturgy; but in a place and with a usage quite different from the original intent of its author.

We can find a similar process in the moving of *Nishmat* from Passover night to Sabbath morning described in the previous chapter in this volume. The use of the same prayer text in different ways, at different points in the liturgy, with different meanings, can be found in a number of places in Jewish liturgy.[169] That phenomenon deserves further study.

Finally, this borrowing of the first paragraph of *Birkat ha-Hodesh* from Rav's post-prayer prayer led to an interesting and even amusing error.[170] Some early texts added a marginal note to this section that read ברכת תפלת רב (the blessing of the prayer of Rav). In some later works this line was accidentally incorporated into the text of this liturgy at the very end of the paragraph just before the concluding formula ונאמר אמן (and let us say Amen).

However the words ברכת תפלת רב do not make sense appearing in the prayer at this point. Instead the text was emended slightly to read בזכות תפלת רב (in the merit of the prayer of Rav), meaning that through the merit of Rav's prayer the things that are asked for in this paragraph should come true. This wording is also somewhat strange. Nowhere else in the liturgy do we explicitly call upon the merit of a prayer's author for help in making that supplication effective before God.

In addition, later readers of this text may not even have been aware of Rav's prayer as recorded in the Babylonian Talmud and its relationship to this paragraph. As a result this sentence was further emended in some texts to read בזכות תפלת רבים (in the merit of the prayers of the many), an interesting idea with parallels elsewhere in rabbinic literature and Jewish liturgy, but one that is

---

167 Siddur p.20.
168 Ibid., p. 118.
169 See discussion in the Nishmat chapter in this volume.
170 *Tikun Tefillah*, p. 709.

not native to the prayer.[171] Nonetheless we can find communities today where these versions of the prayer are recited.

This then is the story of *Birkat ha-Hodesh*. As we find it in the prayer book it appears to be a very placid and fairly integrated text. Despite that appearance, much turmoil and many influences have gone into its wording and its choreography: the Biblical command to maintain a fairly complicated calendar based on witnesses; the loss of the Jewish people's ability to do so due to Christian persecutions; the symbolic maintenance of as much of the old way of doing things as possible; praying for Redemption that will bring the community back to the old system; the history of the many ideological struggles in Jewish annals that were fought over the calendar; the felt need to pray for God's blessing and guidance as a page is turned on the calendar; the desire to maintain spontaneity and individuality as we move into an era of formalized prayer; the borrowing of liturgical material from its original context and inserting it in places where it may serve a very different but equally significant role; and a multi-faceted scribal error that began with the desire to identify where part of *Birkat ha-Hodesh* originally came from – all of these things, and more, have gone into making this prayer what it is today. As such, this simple prayer has one of the richest histories of any liturgy that we find in the *Siddur*. It also provides a fascinating example of the multi-faceted influences that make their mark on almost every page of the Jewish prayer book.

---

171 B. Berakhot 8a; Mekhilta: Mishpatim: Masekhta de-Nezikin: 18; *Sifrei*, Numbers: 135.

CHAPTER 4

Reaching for the Face of God – Anim Zemirot, The Song of Glory/שיר הכבוד

Anim Zmirot / Song of Glory (Siddur p. 484)

The Ark is opened

1) Hazzan: I shall create pleasant songs and weave poems, because my soul yearns for You.

2) Congregation: My soul desires the shadow of Your hand in order to know all of Your hidden secrets.

3) Hazzan: Even as I speak of Your glory, my heart yearns for Your love.

4) Congregation: Therefore, I shall speak glories of You, and I shall glorify Your Name with loving songs.

5) Hazzan: I will tell of Your glory, though I have not seen You; I shall describe You, I shall compare You, though I do not know You.

6) Congregation: By the hand of Your prophets, through the secret knowledge of Your servants, You offered an intimation of the beautiful glory of Your splendor.

שיר הכבוד

פותחין הארון:

1) חזן – אַנְעִים זְמִירוֹת וְשִׁירִים אֶאֱרוֹג. כִּי אֵלֶיךָ נַפְשִׁי תַעֲרוֹג:

2) קהל–נַפְשִׁי חָמְדָה בְּצֵל יָדֶךָ. לָדַעַת כָּל רָז סוֹדֶךָ:

3) חזן - מִדֵּי דַבְּרִי בִּכְבוֹדֶךָ. הוֹמֶה לִבִּי אֶל דּוֹדֶיךָ:

4) קהל - עַל כֵּן אֲדַבֵּר בְּךָ נִכְבָּדוֹת. וְשִׁמְךָ אֲכַבֵּד בְּשִׁירֵי יְדִידוֹת:

5) חזן - אֲסַפְּרָה כְבוֹדְךָ וְלֹא רְאִיתִיךָ. אֲדַמְּךָ אֲכַנְּךָ וְלֹא יְדַעְתִּיךָ:

6) קהל - בְּיַד נְבִיאֶיךָ בְּסוֹד עֲבָדֶיךָ. דִּמִּיתָ הֲדַר כְּבוֹד הוֹדֶךָ:

167

7) Hazzan: Your greatness and Your power, they intimated from the might of Your works.

8) Congregation: They described You, but not according to Your reality, they portrayed You according to Your deeds.

9) Hazzan: They allegorized You in multiple varied visions, but behold You are One throughout all the comparisons.

10) Congregation: They saw in You old age and youth, and the hair of Your head both white and dark.

11) Hazzan: Appearing as aged on Judgment Day and as young at a time of battle, as a man of war His arm is all-encompassing.

12) Congregation: He put the hat of salvation on His head, His right hand and His sacred arm will redeem Him.

13) Hazzan: His head is covered with the dew of light, His locks with the drops of the night.

14) Congregation: He will take pride in me for He desires me, and He will be to me a crown of highest status.

15) Hazzan: His head is to be compared to a precious round object of pure gold, and carved on his forehead is the glory of His sacred Name.

16) Congregation: For grace and for glory the highest status of His splendor, His own nation has made a crown for Him.

17) Hazzan: The locks of His head are as in the days of youth, His curls are black ringlets.

18) Congregation: May the Abode of righteousness, the pinnacle of His splendor, please be elevated above His greatest joy.

19) Hazzan: May His treasured nation please be a crown in His hand and a royal diadem the pinnacle of His splendor.

(7 חזן - גְּדֻלָּתְךָ וּגְבוּרָתֶךָ. כִּנּוּ לְתוֹקֶף פְּעֻלָּתֶךָ:

(8 קהל - דִּמּוּ אוֹתְךָ וְלֹא כְּפִי יֶשְׁךָ. וַיְשַׁוּוּךָ לְפִי מַעֲשֶׂיךָ:

(9 חזן - הִמְשִׁילוּךָ בְּרֹב חֶזְיוֹנוֹת. הִנְּךָ אֶחָד בְּכָל דִּמְיוֹנוֹת:

(10 קהל - וַיֶּחֱזוּ בְךָ זִקְנָה וּבַחֲרוּת. וּשְׂעַר רֹאשְׁךָ בְּשֵׂיבָה וְשַׁחֲרוּת:

(11 חזן - זִקְנָה בְּיוֹם דִּין וּבַחֲרוּת בְּיוֹם קְרָב. כְּאִישׁ מִלְחָמוֹת יָדָיו לוֹ רָב:

(12 קהל - חָבַשׁ כּוֹבַע יְשׁוּעָה בְּרֹאשׁוֹ. הוֹשִׁיעָה לוֹ יְמִינוֹ וּזְרוֹעַ קָדְשׁוֹ:

(13 חזן - טַלְלֵי אוֹרוֹת רֹאשׁוֹ נִמְלָא. קְוֻצּוֹתָיו רְסִיסֵי לָיְלָה:

(14 קהל - יִתְפָּאֵר בִּי כִּי חָפֵץ בִּי. וְהוּא יִהְיֶה לִי לַעֲטֶרֶת צְבִי:

(15 חזן - כֶּתֶם טָהוֹר פָּז דְּמוּת רֹאשׁוֹ. וְחַק עַל מֵצַח כְּבוֹד שֵׁם קָדְשׁוֹ:

(16 קהל - לְחֵן וּלְכָבוֹד צְבִי תִפְאָרָה. אֻמָּתוֹ לוֹ עִטְּרָה עֲטָרָה:

(17 חזן - מַחְלְפוֹת רֹאשׁוֹ כְּבִימֵי בְחֻרוֹת. קְוֻצּוֹתָיו תַּלְתַּלִּים שְׁחוֹרוֹת:

(18 קהל - נְוֵה הַצֶּדֶק צְבִי תִפְאַרְתּוֹ. יַעֲלֶה נָּא עַל רֹאשׁ שִׂמְחָתוֹ:

(19 חזן - סְגֻלָּתוֹ תְּהִי נָא בְיָדוֹ עֲטֶרֶת. וּצְנִיף מְלוּכָה צְבִי תִפְאָרֶת:

20) Congregation: When they were weighed down He carried them, He tied a crown to them; Beyond what they were valued, in His eyes He glorified them.

‏20) קהל - עֲמוּסִים נְשָׂאָם עֲטֶרֶת עִנְּדָם. מֵאֲשֶׁר יָקְרוּ בְּעֵינָיו כִּבְּדָם:

21) Hazzan: His pride is upon me, and my pride is on Him and He is near to me when I call to Him.

‏21) חזן - פְּאֵרוֹ עָלַי וּפְאֵרִי עָלָיו. וְקָרוֹב אֵלַי בְּקָרְאִי אֵלָיו:

22) Congregation: He is pure white and crimson, His clothes red, He treads the winepress as He comes from Edom.

‏22) קהל - צַח וְאָדוֹם לִלְבוּשׁוֹ אָדוֹם. פּוּרָה בְּדָרְכוֹ בְּבוֹאוֹ מֵאֱדוֹם:

23) Hazzan: When the knot of the *tefillin* was displayed to the modest one [Moses], a vision of God was revealed before his eyes.

‏23) חזן - קֶשֶׁר תְּפִלִּין הֶרְאָה לֶעָנָיו. תְּמוּנַת ה' לְנֶגֶד עֵינָיו:

24) Congregation: Desiring His people, He gives pride to the humble; Enthroned upon praises, He takes pride in them.

‏24) קהל - רוֹצֶה בְּעַמּוֹ עֲנָוִים יְפָאֵר. יוֹשֵׁב תְּהִלּוֹת בָּם לְהִתְפָּאֵר:

25) Hazzan: The beginning of Your words is truth; You call from the beginning each generation of the nation that seeks deeply after You.

‏25) חזן - רֹאשׁ דְּבָרְךָ אֱמֶת קוֹרֵא מֵרֹאשׁ. דּוֹר וָדוֹר עַם דּוֹרֶשְׁךָ דְּרוֹשׁ:

26) Congregation: Please set the multitude of my poems before You, and may my song come near to You.

‏26) קהל - שִׁית הֲמוֹן שִׁירַי נָא עָלֶיךָ. וְרִנָּתִי תִקְרַב אֵלֶיךָ:

27) Hazzan: May my praise please be a crown for Your head, and may my prayer be prepared like the incense.

‏27) חזן - תְּהִלָּתִי תְּהִי נָא לְרֹאשְׁךָ עֲטֶרֶת. וּתְפִלָּתִי תִּכּוֹן קְטוֹרֶת:

28) Congregation: Let the poor man's song be precious in Your eyes as the poem that is sung over Your sacrifices.

‏28) קהל - תִּיקַר שִׁירַת רָשׁ בְּעֵינֶיךָ. כַּשִּׁיר יוּשַׁר עַל קָרְבָּנֶיךָ:

29) Hazzan: May my blessing rise up upon the head of the Sustainer; He brings death and aids with birth, He is a powerful righteous Being.

‏29) חזן - בִּרְכָתִי תַעֲלֶה לְרֹאשׁ מַשְׁבִּיר. מְחוֹלֵל וּמוֹלִיד צַדִּיק כַּבִּיר:

30) Congregation: And with my blessing [of You] please nod Your head toward me and may You take it for Yourself as the best of spices.

‏30) קהל - וּבְבִרְכָתִי תְנַעֲנַע לִי רֹאשׁ. וְאוֹתָהּ קַח לְךָ כִּבְשָׂמִים רֹאשׁ:

31) Chazzan: Please may my communication with You be sweet, for my soul yearns for You.

‏31) חזן - יֶעֱרַב נָא שִׂיחִי עָלֶיךָ. כִּי נַפְשִׁי תַעֲרוֹג אֵלֶיךָ:

The Ark is Closed

[**Hazzan** and Congregation: Yours, God, is the greatness, the strength, the splendor, the victory and the majesty; for all is in heaven and on earth. Yours, God, is the kingdom, and You are supreme as Head over all. Who can describe the mighty deeds of the Lord, or make known all His praises?]

סוגרין הארון:

[חו"ק - לְךָ ה' הַגְּדֻלָּה וְהַגְּבוּרָה וְהַתִּפְאֶרֶת וְהַנֵּצַח וְהַהוֹד. כִּי כֹל בַּשָּׁמַיִם וּבָאָרֶץ. לְךָ ה' הַמַּמְלָכָה וְהַמִּתְנַשֵּׂא לְכֹל לְרֹאשׁ. מִי יְמַלֵּל גְּבוּרוֹת ה'. יַשְׁמִיעַ כָּל תְּהִלָּתוֹ]

VEN A CURSORY glance at the poem known either by its first words, *Anim Zemirot* or by its proper title, the Song of Glory (שיר הכבוד), indicates that we are looking at a text that is unique within formal synagogue liturgy. For me the first thing that jumps off the page is that the text is written in the singular ("*I* shall create pleasant songs . . ." etc.). This is highly unusual. It flies in the face of a talmudic rule that prayers should be pluralized.[1] Speaking in the plural indicates that one is approaching God on behalf of the community and not only for oneself – which would make the supplicant appear selfish.

Second, the prayer is full of graphic anthropomorphisms that include descriptions of God's age, His hair, His garments and the movement of His head as he makes Himself known to His prophets,[2] His Servants and the supplicant, in response to his offering this prayer. There is a long tradition among rationalist Jewish philosophers that eschews such depictions of God and considers them virtually idolatrous.[3] While it is true that one can find portrayals of this

---

1   See n. 50 in the chapter on *Aleinu* for sources and discussion. The alternate explanation suggested there, that these sources require praying with the community and not wording all prayers in the plural, would not fit here. However, by the time that Rabbi Yehudah he-Hasid wrote this poem, the prohibition against praying in the singular, and the understanding that these sources are to be read as prohibiting such individual expressions in the liturgy, was well established.

2   See Dan, Joseph – *Jewish Mysticism* v. II: "The Middle Ages." Northvale: pp. lxviii–lxix (introduction) – who explains that Saadiah Gaon (882–942) identified both the *Kavod* and the *Shekhinah* as the supreme angel created in order to be revealed to the prophets. This approach was adopted and expanded by *Hasidei Ashkenaz*. See n. 10, that the founding leader of the group was called הנביא.

3   Cf, Maimonides. *Commentary to the Mishnah*: Sanhedrin 10:1. Third of his thirteen principles of the faith.

type in more esoteric texts,[4] the general approach of the mystical community has been to keep these kinds of descriptions of the Deity hidden from the general public because they are considered theologically and even physically dangerous to someone not properly schooled in how to use and understand them.[5]

Third, the structure of this prayer is also unique. It is formulated as a poem divided into two-line stanzas. However, there are only thirty-one lines in this Song, leaving an "orphaned" thirty-first sentence that appears in the text in poetic dissonance, seemingly unresolved and incomplete.

An addendum consisting of two Biblical verses has been added to the Song of Glory (it appears above in square brackets).[6] Its content does not parallel the themes of the liturgy except in the general sense of praising God. Nonetheless, when the poem is chanted in many synagogues, the second of these appended verses is also sung. The first verse is either recited silently or omitted.

Finally, as we conclude our brief overview of the more obvious oddities present in this prayer, we take notice of the fact that it is structured as an alphabetical acrostic – but not from the beginning of the poem. Starting with the fifth sentence each line begins with a letter of the Hebrew alphabet in sequence. This is an unusual arrangement in that alphabetical acrostics usually begin with the first line of the text, and if the prayer or poem is longer than twenty-two lines (the number of letters in the Hebrew alphabet) then whatever other system is used by the author to define the rest of the structure takes over. To have four lines that seem to be completely random as to the letter with which they begin that introduce the song, and another similar group of four at the end, sandwiched around an alphabetical acrostic is unique in our contemporary liturgical lexicon. Also, even the alphabetical acrostic is somewhat inconsistent

---

4   Cf. *Shiur Komah,* one of the *Heikhalot* texts that speaks at length of the dimensions of the different parts of God's "body." See Kuyt, Annelies. "Traces of a Mutual Influence of the *Haside Ashkenaz* and the *Hekhalot* Literature." In N. A. Van Uchelen and I. E. Zwiep ed., *From Narbonne to Regensburg; Studies in Medieval Hebrew Texts,* Amsterdam: 1993. Also see Dan, p. 36, that *Hasidei Ashkenaz* knew the *heikhalot* material but it is not clear how much of it, or how well they understood it. See Scholem, Gershom. *Jewish Gnosticism, Merkabah Mysticism, and Talmudic Tradition.* New York: Jewish Theological Seminary of America, 1960, pp. 26–29 for the relationship between *Aleinu* (which, as stated in the chapter that discusses that prayer, is a *Heikhalot*-influenced liturgical practice) and *Shiur Komah.*

5   Cf. Tosefta, Hagigah 2:1.

6   The verses are I Chronicles 29:11 and Psalms 106:2.

in that the letter reish (ר) actually heads two consecutive lines, while the rest of the letters each begin a sentence only once.[7]

All of these anomalies raise interesting questions. So, too, does the very name of the prayer. What exactly is the כבוד or "glory" that we are singing about and why are we singing about it?

To resolve all of these problems and more, we need to go back to the origin of the poem. Unlike many of the texts that make up the broad expanse of Jewish liturgy, we actually know, specifically, who wrote this song. In fact, an early manuscript that contains שיר הכבוד includes an introductory heading describing it as coming from the poems of Rabbi Yehudah he-Hasid of Regensburg.[8]

Yehudah he-Hasid was the leader of a 13th-century pietistic movement called *Hasidei Ashkenaz* that was centered in Germany.[9] This movement emerged in an era when martyrdom (both voluntary and involuntary), and strong public expressions of Christian and Jewish religiosity were part of the *zeitgeist* and societal landscape. He and his followers struggled to deal with the effects of the Crusades and other acts of persecution that wreaked havoc on the Jewish community. After hundreds of years of relative peace and security, these events shattered the physical structure of the German Jewish landscape in ways that were unimaginable before they occurred – but then became all too real. They also raised the most challenging theological questions, as these Jews, who saw themselves as truly following the path of God, were defeated, disgraced and shamed by people whose religion they saw as totally false, and whose behavior fell far short of their assumptions of what God demanded.

---

7   See Dan, p. 229, that Rabbi Yehudah he-Hasid, the author of *Anim Zemirot*, evolved a mystical theory according to which the words and letters of the prayers are not accidental nor are they in the text only as vehicles to convey the explicit meaning of the liturgy. The literal meaning of the words and letters, their order and especially their numerical values reflect a mystical harmony that was introduced by the Rabbis into the liturgy during the second commonwealth to convey deeper meanings in the text. In some very real ways, the Song of Glory represents an attempt by him to implement that theory in his own work.

8   See Jacobson, Isaachar. *Netiv Binah*, v. 2. Tel Aviv: 1987, p. 261. The heading reads: שיר הכבוד שיסד רבינו יהודה החסיד מריגענשבורג (the Song of Glory that our Rabbi, Yehudah he-Hasid of Regensburg, established).

9   There has been a great deal of scholarly research done on this group. Rather than provide a long bibliography I will simply mention that Joseph Dan, Moshe Idel, Ephraim Kanarfogel and Haym Soloveichik, are among the prominent authors who have written about them.

This was also a movement that produced many important liturgical texts. The original leaders of these pietists were members of the Kalonymus family,[10] who were the authors of many *Piyutim* (liturgical poems) – some of which are recited to this day on, for example, the High Holidays.[11] They also composed a significant number of the *Kinot* or dirges recited on the Ninth of Av, the Hebrew calendar's most serious and significant annual day of mourning for the historic tragedies of the Jewish people.[12]

Hasidei Ashkenaz in general, and Yehudah specifically, produced two other kinds of literature. The first consisted of moral and ethical teachings.[13] In a time when pietism was a mode of life for many people, providing guidance as to how to be pious was an important undertaking for the leaders of this movement.

Second, this pietistic community, through its spiritual leaders and teachers, produced mystical and esoteric compositions. In explaining why they took this bold step (esoteric ideas, almost by definition, are meant to be kept secret),[14] they claimed that they were heirs to a hidden oral tradition. This tradition had been passed down to them over many centuries, perhaps even from Moses himself, who received it at Sinai along with the Torah.[15] They then chose to commit this material to writing. Their precedent for doing so was Rabbi Judah Hanasi's decision in the second century to redact the Mishnah, which took the

---

10   Dan, introduction, pp. lx-lxv briefly describes the history of *Hasidei Ashkenaz* and of their leaders the Kalonymus family. The first leader was Rabbi Samuel b. Kalonymus (d 1180) who was called הקדוש, החסיד and הנביא. His son was Rabbi Judah the pious (החסיד) of Regensberg, author of this prayer and of *Sefer Hasidim* (some believe that other hands from this group took part in composing this book), the group's most important work. He was also a close relative of Rabbi Eleazar b. Judah b. Kalonymus of Worms, author of *Sefer Rokeah*, which includes discussions of liturgical practices and commentary on the liturgy. That work is frequently cited in this volume.

11   Cf. the *Reshut* that begins with the word יראתי that is recited at the beginning of the *Shakharit Amidah* on the first day of *Rosh Hashanah* (Mahzor RH p. 306).

12   Cf. the *Kinah,* מי יתן ראשי מים, that commemorates the tragedies of the Crusades (Kinot p. 270).

13   For example, the signature work of this community, *Sefer Hasidim*, contains considerable material of this type. See Dan, p. 59, for a discussion of the emergence of this ethical literature.

14   Cf. M. Hagigah 2:1.

15   Dan, p. 31 (especially n. 37) says that for this group these teachings were revelations of ancient esoteric lore sometimes described as having been revealed by God to Moses on Mount Sinai. For an alternate theory that was accepted by some *Hasidei Ashkenaz* see Dan, intro p. lxii.

essence of the Oral Law and committed it to writing.[16] In both cases, destruction of critical Jewish institutions, persecution, fear that the material would be forgotten and communal need were enough to overcome whatever concerns existed about changing the status of the material from oral to textual.[17]

The Song of Glory, while certainly liturgical in function, is also part of that mystical and esoteric literature. The poem self-consciously tells us so. In the second line, Yehudah he-Hasid declares:

2) My soul desires the shadow of Your hand in order to know all of Your hidden secrets.	2) נפשי חמדה בצל ידך לדעת כל רז סודך

It then moves on to embody this mystical quest in a way that is more or less unique in formal Jewish liturgy.

Before continuing with our discussion of where the prayer and its search take us, a brief explanation of the nature of this quest is in order. Religion, in simplest terms, is the study of what God wants us to do. Mysticism, on the other hand, is essentially the pursuit of God, Himself; of what God is, of how He looks, of how to connect with Him. By its very nature this is an individual search, because only an individual with special qualities may take such a journey successfully,[18] and because each person will achieve different results and differing understandings that come with whatever connection to the Divine he or she manages to achieve.

For the Jewish mystic this search is profoundly problematic because Judaism generally thinks of God as lacking a body or other physical attributes. It,

---

16   In this regard it is interesting that Rabbi Samuel b. Kalonymus, their founding leader, was called הקדוש (see n. 10 above). In classic rabbinic literature only Rabbi Judah the Prince is allowed to be given this stellar designation, see B. Shabbat 118b.

17   For these concerns in regard to the oral law see B. Gittin 60b, and for the decision to compose written texts that contained this material, an act that had been previously prohibited, see B. Gittin 60a, and B. Temurah 14b. When it comes to *Hasidei Ashkenaz*, Dan, p. 28, cites Rabbi Eleazar from his introduction to *Sefer ha-Hakhma* who posits that after the death of our Rabbi Yehudah he-Hasid and also of Rabbi Eleazar's own son he must write down this esoteric material so that the traditions will not be lost. It is these unusual circumstances that make it imperative that what under normal conditions may not be transcribed, must now be consigned to writing. Dan then comments that Rabbi Yehudah he-Hasid had previously written esoteric works. I am suggesting that he was motivated to do so for similar reasons.

18   See n. 5.

therefore, becomes difficult even to begin to pursue this fundamental mystical endeavor. Over the centuries, different schools of Jewish esoteric teaching have provided a number of alternative approaches in attempting to overcome this basic problem.

The Song of Glory presents a remarkable and truly bold way to resolve this conundrum. Borrowing from various Biblical prophetic visions and from descriptions found in a number of rabbinic midrashim, the poem presents God as He is anthropomorphized[19] through various physical depictions in these texts.[20]

For example the poem contains this sentence:

23) When the knot of the *tefillin* was displayed to the modest one [Moses], a vision of God was revealed before his eyes.	23) קשר תפלין הראה לעניו תמנת ה' לנגד עיניו

This line builds on the rabbinic claim that in some mystical way God wears *tefillin* (phylacteries)[21] and on a midrashic explanation of the following Biblical verses:

And he [Moses] said, "I beg you, show me Your *glory*." And He said, "I will make all My goodness pass before you, and I will proclaim the Name of the Lord before you; and will be gracious to whom I will be gracious, and will show mercy on whom I will show mercy." And He said, "You cannot see My face; for no man shall see Me and live."	ויאמר הראני נא את כבדך ויאמר אני אעביר כל טובי על פניך וקראתי בשם ה' לפניך וחנתי את אשר אחן ורחמתי את אשר ארחם ויאמר לא תוכל לראת את פני כי לא יראני האדם וחי

---

19   Dan, intro, p. lxviii-lxix tells us that this term (*Kavod*) is closely integrated with the problem of divine revelation and the explanation of the anthropomorphic verses in the Bible. See also p. 233–234. See Kuyt, p.65, that the *Kavod* is the only aspect of God which can be the subject of the description of God's limbs.

20   See Grozinger K. E. and Dan J., Mysticism, Magic and *Kabbalah* in *Ashkenazi Judaism*, Berlin, 1995, p. 58 that *Shir ha-Kavod* is based on description of the lover in Song of Songs 5:10–16. Though there are some strong points of contact, I do not agree because these verses do not focus on the head in the same way that we find in the song.

21   B. Berakhot 6a, 7a.

And the Lord said, "Behold, there is a place	ויאמר ה' הנה מקום אתי ונצבת
by Me, and you shall stand upon a rock;	על הצור
And it shall come to pass, while My *glory* passes	והיה בעבר כבדי ושמתיך
by, that I will put you in a cleft of the rock, and	בנקרת הצור ושכתי כפי עליך
will cover you with My hand while I pass by;	עד עברי
And I will take away My hand, and you shall	והסרתי את כפי וראית את
see My back; but My face shall not be seen."[22]	אחרי ופני לא יראו

Before moving to the Midrash, we note that Moses asks to see God's "*Kavod*" (Glory) in this text, and that God makes reference to His *Kavod* in His response. It is no wonder that the author of the Song of Glory (*Shir ha-Kavod*) is drawn to these verses.

A mystical Midrash interprets the "seeing of God's back" to mean that God showed Moses the knot of His *tefillin*.[23] When human beings put on the boxes and straps that are part of the physical structure of this ritual object, the knot of the head *tefillin* is worn on the back of the neck.[24] Hence when God shows Moses His "back," that is what Moses sees.

How all of this is to be understood is something for a profoundly knowledgeable mystic to explain, and this writer does not qualify for that role. Nonetheless, whatever these esoteric images mean, they are the sources from which this line in the Song of Glory is drawn. They also help advance the mystical quest because we now know something about God's "physical" reality – He wears "*tefillin*" that include a "knot" on His "back."

Similarly we find this stanza in the Hymn of Glory:

10) They [the prophets] saw in You	10) ויחזו בך זקנה ובחרות ושער
old age and youth and the hair of	ראשך בשיבה ושחרות.
Your head both white and dark.	
11) Appearing as aged on Judgment Day	11) זקנה ביום דין ובחרות ביום
and as young at a time of battle, as a man	קרב כאיש מלחמות ידיו לו רב
of war His arm is all-encompassing.	

This part of the poem is drawn from rabbinic commentary that God, when

---

22   Exodus 33:18–23.

23   B. Berakhot 7a.

24   *Shulhan Arukh: Orah Hayim*: 27:10.

He presents Himself to human beings in prophetic revelations, takes on different appearances as appropriate to the moment and the vision.[25] Again this teaches us something about how God makes Himself known in this world. Contemplating God's "youth," His "old age," the color of His "hair" and the different "days" on which the these different divine manifestations appear also helps the mystic get to know God.

There is of course theological danger in all of this. An anthropomorphic depiction of God can lead people to what Judaism would see as inappropriate pagan beliefs.[26] I know someone who, while in college, was thinking seriously of joining a cult. This cult was led by an individual who claimed to be the physical embodiment of all gods. This young woman was actually encouraged in the direction of pursuing this cult, when, on attending services in the synagogue on the High Holidays, she read the translation of the Song of Glory and encountered a poetic vision of an embodied deity.

Not only is pagan ideology potentially made more tenable by the imagery of this prayer, so too, supporters of fundamentalist Christianity, with its teaching of God – or a son of God – incarnated in human form, may also find some support in the words of this song. It goes almost without saying that giving aid and comfort to paganism, cult theology or Christianity was as far from the intent of Yehudah he-Hasid as one might imagine. Why then open the door to such possible misunderstandings by writing and publicizing this text?

We will try to understand the answer to this question in terms that made sense to these 13th-century pietists and then in terms that are bit more universal. The name or attribute כבוד, translated here as Glory, was used by *Hasidei Ashkenaz* in two general ways. It was, in their understanding of the Deity, the only aspect of God to which one could ascribe anthropomorphism, because it was from this aspect alone that God would allow physical manifestations of Himself to appear in this world. In this way God's incorporeality could be protected, while allowing those who wanted it, to have some understanding of who the Deity is – at least in this one aspect of His existence.

The *Kavod* was also the address in the Godhead to which all prayers were directed.[27] Even if the supplicant was unaware of this metaphysical reality, his

---

25   Cf. Mekhilta de-Rashbi 15:3; Pesikta de-Rav Kahana #12; Midrash Tanhuma: Yitro: #16.

26   The sources cited in the previous note express this concern as well.

27   See n. 2 and n. 19. For a general discussion of the meaning of *Kavod* for *Hasidei Ashkenaz* and that meaning's antecedents in other texts see Dan, intro, pp. lxviii-lxix,

or her prayers would still pass through the aspect of *Kavod* as they climbed heavenward. The prayer called the "Song of Glory" (*Shir ha-Kavod*) and its anthropomorphic portrayals of God brought those two elements together. That, in and of itself, would be quite significant for those people who were part of Yehudah he-Hasid's inner circle.

Kavod then plays two specific roles in *Anim Zemirot*. We will leave one of these roles for later discussion and begin instead with the fact that the word in different grammatical forms appears five times in lines 3–6 of the poem, and then once again in each of lines 15, 16 and 20, as indicated:[28]

3) Even as I speak of Your **glory**, my heart yearns for Your love.	3) מִדֵּי דַבְּרִי **בִּכְבוֹדֶךָ**. הוֹמֶה לִבִּי אֶל דּוֹדֶיךָ:
4) Therefore, I shall speak **glories** of You, and I shall **glorify** Your Name with loving songs.	4) עַל כֵּן אֲדַבֵּר בְּךָ **נִכְבָּדוֹת**. וְשִׁמְךָ **אֲכַבֵּד** בְּשִׁירֵי יְדִידוֹת:
5) I will tell of Your **glory**, though I have not seen You; I shall describe You, I shall compare You, though I do not know You.	5) אֲסַפְּרָה **כְבוֹדְךָ** וְלֹא רְאִיתִיךָ. אֲדַמְּךָ אֲכַנְּךָ וְלֹא יְדַעְתִּיךָ:
6) By the hand of Your prophets, through the secret knowledge of Your servants, You offered an intimation of the beautiful **glory** of Your splendor.	6) בְּיַד נְבִיאֶיךָ בְּסוֹד עֲבָדֶיךָ. דִּמִּיתָ הֲדַר **כְּבוֹד** הוֹדֶךָ:
15) His head is to be compared to a precious round object of pure gold, and carved on his forehead is the **glory** of His sacred Name.	15) כֶּתֶם טָהוֹר פָּז דְּמוּת רֹאשׁוֹ. וְחָק עַל מֵצַח **כְּבוֹד** שֵׁם קָדְשׁוֹ:
16) For grace and for **glory** the highest status of His splendor, His own nation has made a crown for Him.	16) לְחֵן וּלְ**כָבוֹד** צְבִי תִפְאָרָה. אֻמָּתוֹ לוֹ עִטְּרָה עֲטָרָה:

p. 44 and pp. 233–235. Most significantly, see p. 233 that mystical prayers should be directed to the *Kavod*, and p. 49 that in Rabbi Yehudah he-Hasid's opinion the job of the *Kavod* was accepting the prayers of Israel. As a result, and as he says on p. lxxi, "the Divine Glory . . . became in Ashkenazi Hasidism the main target of prayers."

28　See Dan, p. 84 that *Hasidei Ashkenaz* were concerned with the number of times that any particular linguistic element appears in a Biblical verse or passage. For example Rabbi Yehudah comments on the forty verses that include the word *hasid* in the book of Psalms. See also Dan, intro, p. lxviii, that *Hasidei Ashkenaz* were described by contemporary and subsequent generations as those who "counted the words and

20) When they were weighed down He carried them, He tied a crown to them; Beyond what they were valued, in His eyes He **glorified** them

20) עֲמוּסִים נְשָׂאָם עֲטֶרֶת עִנְּדָם.
מֵאֲשֶׁר יָקְרוּ בְעֵינָיו **כִּבְּדָם**

There is a parallel here to Psalm 24, which reads:

1. A Psalm of David. The earth is the Lord's, and all that fills it; the world, and those who dwell in it.

1) לְדָוִד מִזְמוֹר לה' הָאָרֶץ
וּמְלוֹאָהּ תֵּבֵל וְישְׁבֵי בָהּ:

2. For He has founded it upon the seas, and established it upon the rivers.

2) כִּי הוּא עַל יַמִּים יְסָדָהּ וְעַל
נְהָרוֹת יְכוֹנְנֶהָ:

3. Who shall ascend into the mountain of the Lord? Who shall stand in His holy place?

3) מִי יַעֲלֶה בְהַר ה' וּמִי יָקוּם
בִּמְקוֹם קָדְשׁוֹ:

4. He who has clean hands, and a pure heart; who has not taken My Name in vain, nor sworn deceitfully.

4) נְקִי כַפַּיִם וּבַר לֵבָב אֲשֶׁר לֹא
נָשָׂא לַשָּׁוְא נַפְשִׁי וְלֹא נִשְׁבַּע
לְמִרְמָה:

5. He shall receive a blessing from the Lord, and righteousness from the God of his salvation.

5) יִשָּׂא בְרָכָה מֵאֵת ה' וּצְדָקָה
מֵאֱלֹקֵי יִשְׁעוֹ:

6. This is the generation of those who seek Him, who seek Your face, Jacob. Selah.

6) זֶה דּוֹר דֹּרְשָׁיו מְבַקְשֵׁי פָנֶיךָ
יַעֲקֹב סֶלָה:

7. Lift up your heads, gates! And be lifted up, everlasting doors! And the King of **glory** shall come in.

7) שְׂאוּ שְׁעָרִים רָאשֵׁיכֶם
וְהִנָּשְׂאוּ פִּתְחֵי עוֹלָם וְיָבוֹא מֶלֶךְ
הַכָּבוֹד:

8. Who is this King of **glory**? The Lord, strong and mighty, the Lord mighty in battle.

8) מִי זֶה מֶלֶךְ **הַכָּבוֹד** ה' עִזּוּז
וְגִבּוֹר יְקוק גִּבּוֹר מִלְחָמָה:

9. Lift up your heads, gates! Lift them up, everlasting doors! And the King of **glory** shall come in.

9) שְׂאוּ שְׁעָרִים רָאשֵׁיכֶם וּשְׂאוּ
פִּתְחֵי עוֹלָם וְיָבֹא מֶלֶךְ **הַכָּבוֹד**:

10. Who is this King of **glory**? The Lord of hosts, He is the King of **glory**. Selah.

10) מִי הוּא זֶה מֶלֶךְ **הַכָּבוֹד** ה'
צְבָאוֹת הוּא מֶלֶךְ **הַכָּבוֹד** סֶלָה:

The five-fold appearance of the word *Kavod* at the beginning of *Anim Zemirot* parallels its five-fold appearance at the end of Psalm 24 shown here. Yehudah he-Hasid's use of *Kavod* in this way draws the meaning of this Psalm into the Song of Glory.

---

letters." So, too, Kuyt, p. 65, who says that number of letters and their numerical values are a clue to hidden meanings for this community.

In contemporary Jewish liturgy this chapter is recited on Sundays as the Psalm of the day.[29] So, too, it is said when returning the Torah to the ark after it is read at all times other than on *Shabbat* morning, when Psalm 29 is used for this purpose.[30] Psalm 24 is also recited responsively in dramatic fashion at the end of the nighttime (*Maariv*) service on *Rosh Hashanah* and *Yom Kippur*.[31]

This Psalm calls on God, the King of Glory, (מלך הכבוד) to come through the opening of the "gate of the world" in order to make Himself manifest – particularly as the God of War (verse 8). This is a call for the realization of the eschatological promise that at the end of days all that exists will be seen to function under God's visible power and direct control.[32]

In this regard, מלך הכבוד or the Glorious King is understood by Jewish tradition not as an actual physical manifestation of the Deity, but rather as an emanation or as a symbolic revelation from God. It is a vision of the Creator dressed, as it were, in all of the trappings of His glorious majesty coming to redeem the world as its manifest king.[33]

Central to that vision is the promise that He will use His war powers to judge and punish those who have perpetrated evil in this world. Particularly for pietistic Jews living in a mystically oriented community, who were suffering from the terrible acts of the Crusaders, the desire for this particular vision to become a reality was something that they must have felt deeply each and every day.

It is, also, the first fully expressed picture of the anthropomorphized God that appears in *Anim Zemirot*. Lines 11–12 of the poem read:

11) Appearing as aged on Judgment Day and as young at the time of battle, as a man of war His arm is all-encompassing.	11) זקנה ביום דין ובחרות ביום קרב כאיש מלחמות ידיו לו רב
12) He put the hat of salvation on His head, His right hand and His sacred arm will redeem Him	12) חבש כובע ישועה בראשו הושיעה לו ימינו וזרוע קדשן

---

29   Siddur p. 162.

30   Siddur pp. 148, 458, 460, 512.

31   Mahzor RH p. 78, Mahzor YK 148.

32   Cf. the second paragraph of *Aleinu* as discussed in the chapter that describes the history of that prayer in this volume.

33   This is the meaning of the Psalm; also see Exodus Rabbah: 8:1, Numbers Rabbah 15:13.

These words carry the God of War imagery as their dominant theme, while reminding us that God acts from judgment and not from baser instincts when He appears in this way.

This doublet opens the door to all the other anthropomorphic portrayals of God that appear in the Hymn of Glory, thus providing us with an initial sense of what this poem is coming to say. At the very least it was a response to the desire and need felt by the survivors of the Crusades to have God make an appearance in order to set things right. This poem tells them that God is fully capable of doing just that and embodies a vision of exactly how that can occur. Given the emotionally shattering experience of the Crusades, Yehudah he-Hasid must have believed that the need for a song like this, that would offer some comfort, outweighed the concerns that it raised.

Nonetheless, despite the resonance between the community's need, the vision included in these lines and the Psalm, composing a liturgical text with this open a depiction of a physically manifest Deity was very bold move. We can sense Yehudah he-Hasid's hesitation in taking this step in many ways.

For example, Yehudah he-Hasid does not begin his anthropomorphic descriptions until line ten of the song.[34] It takes him a quorum (a *minyan*) of lines to get to the point where he will allow himself to take that step.[35] Then in line ten we have a generic overview without specifics:

---

34   In line 2 we do find the words בצל ידך (the shadow of Your hand), which may foreshadow the anthropomorphisms to come. However, since this refers to the poet's desire for the "shadow" of God's hand and not for the hand itself, this does not seem to rise to the level of the images that appear later in the song. Further, the "shadow of Your hand" is explained in this line as a metaphor for the place to learn God's secrets. Later in the poem the anthropomorphisms seem to be valuable unto themselves. Finally, the "shadow of Your hand" imagery appears in Isaiah 49:2 and 51:16, where the prophet is described as a weapon to be used by God in remaking the world and in bringing on the Messianic era (see next note). This image is perfect for Yehudah he-Hasid's introduction to this Song of Glory given its meaning and purpose that we explain in this chapter. It also portrays him in the role of the prophet revealing God's word and image (see n. 2 and n. 10).

35   I wonder if this structure was inspired by M. Avot 5:1, which reads, בעשרה מאמרות נברא העולם ("With ten statements was the world created"). Since this poem was ultimately designed to bring on the "new world order" that will come with the arrival of the Messiah, having ten statements that lead to the first manifestation of God as He ushers in that era would serve to create a parallel between the original creation and the eschatological re-creation of the world.

10) They [the prophets] saw in You	10) ויחזו בך זקנה ובחרות ושער
old age and youth and the hair of	ראשך בשיבה ושחרות.
Your head both white and dark.	

Only after this perceptible hesitation does Yehudah he-Hasid get to the particulars of the "God of War, Who brings judgment" imagery.

Further, the first nine lines – the ones that appear before we get to any of these physical portrayals – are quite intriguing. The poet seems to start the poem twice. Line one begins with an *aleph*, the first letter of the Hebrew alphabet. We would therefore expect the next line to begin with a *bet*, the second letter. Instead the second line starts with a *nun*, the third with a *mem*, and the fourth with an *ayin*. It is only in line five that the alphabet begins again with another *aleph* and it is only this time that the song does follow the alphabet all the way through.

To reinforce that this is in fact the pattern, the same number of non-alphabetical lines (four), appear after the conclusion of the alphabetical acrostic. In addition, just as the non-alphabetic lines at the beginning of the poem begin with an *aleph*, so that there is a repeat of the first letter of the alphabet, similarly the non-alphabetic segments at the end of the song start with a *tav*, the last letter of the alphabet. This brackets the acrostic and signals the reader as to the intent of the author. All of this leads us to conclude that the poet is hesitant to begin the alphabetical lines that structure the song and, therefore, to get to the anthropomorphic substance of the poem.

In addition, the letters *nun*, *mem* and *ayin*, that begin the other three introductory lines – the ones following the initial aleph – when arranged as *mem*, *nun*, *ayin* form a Hebrew word that means to "withhold" or to "hold back."[36] This is further indication of the poet's hesitation. He starts with the *aleph* and then, rather than proceed through the alphabet, he veers off and tells us he is "holding back." As we shall see, there is an important parallel to this in the non-alphabetical lines that we find at the end of the poem.

Finally, the words themselves indicate this underlying hesitancy. In lines 1–4, before reaching the actual alphabetical acrostic, Yehudah he-Hasid sings

36 See Dan, p. 80 that according to this group's understanding of sacred texts, in the Bible one can find meaning from reading letters in a different order than the way in which they appear, In this way one can can create non-existent words that offer additional understanding. As previously stated Yehudah he-Hasid seems to have brought all of these esoteric exegetical techniques to the writing of *Anim Zemirot*.

of his desire to be close to God and to know His secrets. He tells us that he will, therefore, write songs and sing of God's Glory. There is nothing in these four lines that speaks directly of the challenging anthropomorphisms to come.[37]

Then, starting from line five through line nine with the coming of the alphabetical acrostic, we find repeated statements indicating the poet's intent to anthropomorphize God and providing justification as to why this is theologically acceptable. He explains that he is not really claiming to have seen God or to actually know Him. Rather, he is following the model of God's prophets and servants. Just as they did, he is using God's own actions to anthropomorphize Him in ways that appropriately depict what He has done. Further, despite the varied visions that the prophets had in which they saw the Deity in different ways, the author believes in the underlying and indivisible unity and singleness of God.

In sum, Yehudah he-Hasid advances at least four rationales or apologetics, in only five lines, for the dramatic step he is about to take. In fact, some of these justifications appear more than once. We can only conclude that these five lines offer the theological defense that allows him to compose this text, while further expressing his hesitation about what he is doing. It also further explains why the poem is written in the singular and not in the plural. It is Yehudah he-Hasid's quest, his burden and his decision to write this prayer as he does.

Most of the rest of the song presents the various anthropomorphic images he chooses to highlight. These depictions slowly become mixed with Yehudah he-Hasid's hope that the poem itself will mystically become part of these descriptions of the Creator, thus adding to God's glory.

For example the last of the alphabetical lines reads:

27) May my praise please be a crown for Your head, and may my prayer be prepared like the incense [of the Temple].[38]	27) תהלתי תהי לראשך עטרת ותפלתי תכון קטרת

and the poem continues two lines later with:

---

37 See n. 34.

38 The imagery of crowns being created from words – particularly from words of prayer – can be found quite frequently in rabbinic and Heikhalot literature. Cf. Pesikta Rabbati: Piska 10, Exodus Rabbah 21:4, Sefer Heikhalot: ch. 28, and see the chapter on *Kaddish* in this volume.

29) May my blessing rise up upon the head of
the Sustainer; He brings death and aids with
birth, He is a powerful righteous Being.

(29 בִּרְכָתִי תַעֲלֶה לְרֹאשׁ
מַשְׁבִּיר. מְחוֹלֵל וּמוֹלִיד צַדִּיק
כַּבִּיר:

Finally Yehudah he-Hasid asks for this anthropomorphic response:

30) And with my blessing [of You] please
nod Your head toward me and may You
take it for Yourself as the best of spices.

(30 ובברכתי תנענע לי ראש
ואותה קח לך כבשמים ראש

And he concludes by paralleling the song's first sentence:

1) I shall create pleasant songs and weave
poems, because my soul yearns for You.

(1 אנעים זמרות ושירים אארוג
כי אלך נשפי תערוג

with this line:

31) Please may my communication be sweet
to You, for my soul yearns for You.

(13 יערב נא שיחי עליך כי נפשי
תערוג אלך

As indicated, the last four lines of the song are not part of the acrostic, although the first of these four repeats the *tav*, the final letter of the alphabet. In this way, the four non-alphabetical lines at the beginning parallel the four non-alphabetical lines at the end, and the repeated *aleph* that introduces the acrostic parallels the repeated *tav* that concludes it, creating a marvelous symmetry.

In addition to the reason suggested above for this arrangement, this structure also serves as a reminder that God's reality extends beyond the limits of the letters of the alphabet. Simply put, the Almighty cannot be captured in any verbal, pictorial or physical description. Thus the very structure that Yehudah he-Hasid chose for the Song of Glory provides yet another theological defense for the composition itself and for its composer.

We can now take the final step in articulating the meaning of this prayer in order to understand the purpose of this liturgy in more practical terms than the mystical, philosophical and literary conceptualizations that have been presented thus far. The Song of Glory consists of the four non-alphabetical lines introducing the poem and the four non-alphabetical sentences that conclude it, with the lines in between following the Hebrew alphabet of twenty-two letters. That should give us thirty sentences. Except that if you count, you will find that there are thirty-one.

The key to fully understanding the Song of Glory lies in that thirty-first line; but we must realize that there are actually two sentences that fit that designation. There is the actual thirty-first line

| 31) Please may my communication with You be sweet, for my soul yearns for You | 31) יֶעֱרַב נָא שִׂיחִי עָלֶיךָ כִּי נַפְשִׁי תַעֲרוֹג אֵלֶיךָ |

and the thirty-first line in a literary sense:

| 25) The beginning of Your words is truth; You call from the beginning each generation of the nation that seeks deeply after You. | 25) ראש דברך אמת קורא מראש דור ודור עם דורשיך דרוש |

Both of these are critically important to the meaning of this prayer.

To understand what I mean by the "literary thirty-first line," we must recall that there are two sentences beginning with the letter *resh* in the poem. That is why there are thirty-one and not thirty sentences here. Given the intricacies of all that we have seen so far we can be sure that Yehudah he-Hasid worked very hard to get this song to be precisely thirty-one lines long. Further, the doubling of the letter *resh* must have some particularly important meaning for this poem that is specific to that letter and to no other. It is, therefore, the second or extra *resh* sentence that we are calling the literary thirty-first line.

The word "*resh*" means beginning or head.[39] Concomitantly a large majority of the anthropomorphic images that appear in the song are images of God's "head." These include the head *tefillin*, the hair color, the head nod, and the crown. This is also true of virtually all of the other anthropomorphic portrayals in *Anim Zemirot*. In fact, the word ראש (rosh) appears more frequently than any other in the poem. It is there at least twelve times,[40] while the word *kavod*, found so frequently at the beginning of the song, has, as we have seen,

---

39 Kuyt, p.69, claims that the letter *resh* is associated with the head in this type of mystical literature and Dan, p. 77, says that in the *Ashkenazi Hasidic* concept of language, the name of the letter is significant, so that the true way to read a word includes the full name of the letters. This system of exegesis is called מילוי.

40 In addition, the word רש meaning a "poor man," used here to refer to the author, but which sounds like ראש, also appears once, as do other words such as מצח (forehead)

"only" eight appearances. This, too, points us to the extra *resh* line as being particularly important.

This sentence that we see as so essential reads as follows:

25) The beginning of Your words is truth; You call from the beginning each generation of the nation that seeks deeply after You.

25) ראש דברך אמת קורא

מראש דור ודור עם דורשיך

דרוש

This line, along with the word ראש that appears twice, also contains the similar sounding word, דרוש (drosh). The only other sentence where we find two appearances of ראש is the penultimate line. That is the point in the text where Yehudah he-Hasid requests of God that He indicate that He has received and accepted this prayer positively by nodding His head. This parallel dual use of the word ראש that draws these two lines together provides us with yet another indication of the importance of this second *Resh* sentence within this work. It suggests that God's acceptance of the song is dependent on His viewing this literary thirty-first line in a positive light.

How, then, to understand the meaning of this sentence? Much of Medieval *Piyut* (liturgical poetry) is composed around oblique references to earlier texts that draw the meaning of those texts into the liturgy. That is what happens here.

This literary thirty-first line is a complex hybrid sentence joining two Biblical verses, an acrostic hinted at in a *Midrash*, a *midrashic* tale and a plea for Divine response. It also needs to be read three different ways depending on which of these antecedent sources is being referenced. That is an awful lot to pack into one relatively short sentence.

The first verse that is referred to here is Psalms 119:160, which reads:

The beginning [or "pinnacle"] of Your word is truth, and all of Your righteous judgments endure forever.

ראש דברך אמת ולעולם כל

משפט צדקך

It proclaims that God's words and His judgments are both true and righteous at all times – including in the aftermath of the Crusades and their ter-

---

and קוצותיו (locks of hair). We are also about to discuss the word דרוש another soundalike for ראש.

rible consequences for the Jews. They are also particularly true at their first appearance.[41]

The Midrash logically joins this verse from Psalms with the beginning of the Torah, the first manifestation of God's words:

From the very commencement of the world's creation, "The beginning of Your word is truth." Thus, "In the beginning God created" [is corroborated by and also corroborates this statement].[42]	מתחלת ברייתו של עולם ראש דברך אמת, בראשית ברא א־להים

The first words of the Torah have been affirmed as true by this verse in Psalms. So, too, the claim made by this sentence in Psalms that these initial words of Genesis are true, is supported by the appearance of אמת (truth) that can be found as an anagram by examining the last letter of each of the first three words of the Bible בראשית ברא א־להים.[43] As such, the first part of the line in *Anim Zemirot* that we are discussing might better be translated, "The beginning of Your words is truth, as can be read from the beginning."

The midrashic tale evoked here appears in many places throughout rabbinic literature including in two parallel sources in the Babylonian Talmud (Sanhedrin 38b and Avodah Zarah 5a).

A–Did not Resh Lakish say,	א–והאמר ריש לקיש
B–"What is the meaning of the verse This is the book of the generations of Adam?[44]	ב–מאי דכתיב: זה ספר תולדות אדם וגו'?
C–Did Adam have a book?"	ג–וכי ספר היה לו לאדם הראשון?
D–What it teaches is that the Holy One, blessed be He, showed to Adam	ד–מלמד שהראה לו הקב"ה לאדם הראשון

---

41 There may also be a polemic against the New Testament in the use of this verse at this time in history. If God's first words are true and they last forever, then there is no room for a "New Testament" to replace the Old Testament.

42 Genesis Rabbah 1:7.

43 See n. 36.

44 Genesis 5:1.

45 The words in parentheses appear in the Avodah Zarah source but not in the Sanhedrin text.

E–Each generation with its expositors [*Dorshav*, which can also be translated as "seekers"],	ה–דור דור ודורשיו,
F–Each generation with its sages,	ו–דור דור וחכמיו,
G–[Each generation with its leaders];[45]	ז–[דור דור ופרנסיו],
H–When he reached the generation of Rabbi Akiva,	ח–כיון שהגיע לדורו של רבי עקיבא,
I–He rejoiced at his teaching, but was grieved about his death,[46]	ט–שמח בתורתו ונתעצב במיתתו,
J–And said, "How precious are Your friends[47] unto me, O God!"[48]	י–אמר ולי מה יקרו רעיך א"ל.

This Midrash supports the translation of the line we are discussing as originally presented above:

The beginning of Your words is truth; You call from the beginning each generation of the nation that seeks deeply after You.

This rabbinic text indicates that the scholars, seekers and leaders of every generation were called to their respective roles from the beginning of time. As such Yehudah he-Hasid, the scholar and leader of his community, must have received God's imprimatur for searching out and publicizing the anthropomorphisms that appear in the Song of Glory from the moment of creation. Also, since the "beginning of God's words is truth," then his presence as leader of the community and his decision to take this step must be part of that original divine verity, since his place was determined from the "beginning of God's words." This type of intricate interweaving of themes from earlier Jewish literature is typical of medieval *piyut*, though rarely are the implications quite as dramatic as they are here.

Further, this *midrashic* text references the martyrdom of Rabbi Akiva that occurred during the Hadrianic persecutions in the second century C.E. The Midrash then cites an anthropomorphic verse that speaks of Rabbi Akiva – a leader and seeker of his generation – as "God's friend" in reference to

---

46 Rabbi Akiva died a terrible and torturous martyr's death, cf. B. Berakhot 61b; also see the chapter on *Keriyat Shema* in this volume.

47 Most commentators to Psalms translate this word as "thoughts." The translation here follows Rashi and fits with the way this Midrash is using this verse in this context, since the focus is on people (particularly on Rabbi Akiva's dedication to the Creator) and not on God's thoughts.

48 Psalms 139:17.

his martyrdom. This draws the contemporaneous experiences that *Hasidei Ashkenaz* had with the Crusades through the prism of the earlier Midrash into the poem. In light of the terrible deaths of so many Jews and Jewish leaders during this era, God now has many more "friends" that have joined Him in heaven.

There is again much justification here for describing God in the "friendly" and personal terms that we find in *Anim Zemirot*. So many of God's intimates – the "seekers" of the generations of the Crusades – were connected with *Hasidei Ashkenaz*, and have suffered martyrdom. It is the least that God can do to allow some of His own intimate details to be revealed at this time. After all, as we shall see in the next two paragraphs, it was this revelation that these martyrs were seeking during their lives. This reference to martyrdom also opens the door to an even more profound meaning of the Song of Glory for Yehudah he-Hasid that we will discuss below.

The second verse referenced here is Psalms 24:6, from the very Biblical chapter that is so important to the Song of Glory. That verse reads

This is the generation of those who seek	זה דור דרשיו מבקשי
Him, who seek Your face, Jacob. Selah.	פניך יעקב סלה

and is the verse that appears immediately before the Psalm starts using the word כבוד (kavod) over and over again. It is, therefore, the sentence that serves as the gateway into the Psalm's call for the revelation of God's *Kavod* in the form of the King of Glory.

Its import for our poem is that the scholars of each generation, who were called to their tasks from the beginning of time as part of God's eternal truth, are engaged in seeking the revelation of God's face (an obviously anthropomorphic quest) on behalf of Jacob (Israel). So, too, those who were searching for this revelation during the era of the Crusades and who were martyred were also part of this quest. Yehudah he-Hasid, who was called to his task – in God's truth – from the beginning of time, has simply continued on this same road. When woven together in this way, these verses, these Midrashim and this sentence in *Anim Zemirot* turn the appearance of anthropomorphisms in שיר הכבוד into successful landmarks on the road to completing the author's and his generation's sacred search for the revelation of God, Himself, through His *Kavod*. These anthropomorphisms are also positive steps in completing the task of the seekers of every generation.

The last three words of this line in the poem can then be read as a dramatic plea that God seek after the nation that not only has come searching for Him; but that has also succeeded in revealing at least some elements of His anthropomorphic nature. The words עם דורשיך דרוש can be translated as "seek after the people who seek after You." The desired response is, presumably, that God, in turn, fully reveal Himself to them.

This is reflected in the penultimate verse of the song when God is asked to nod His head as an indication of His full and complete acceptance of the poet's words and actions.[49] If God accepts the intricate meaning, rationales and plea of the literary thirty-first line, then, as we approach the end of the prayer, He is asked to indicate that this is so. In the aftermath of the Crusades the felt need for this final validation from God was particularly poignant. The tragedy was overwhelming, and the need for consolation and Divine approval of the "despised" Jews and their search was equally profound.[50]

In sum, then, the extra ר' line provides a defense for the poem, a validation of Yehudah he-Hasid's role as leader, support for revealing anthropomorphisms and a call for God to seek after the well-being of the Jewish people in response to what is being revealed in the song. It also parallels the next to last line of the poem and evokes that line's call for God's validation. No other line in *Anim Zemirot* is as profound and multifaceted in its meaning and import, and no other line gives more of an indication of the purpose for which this poem was written.

Turning now to the actual thirty-first sentence, we find a remarkable artistic device that leads to an understanding of the song that is even more dramatic than what we have already seen. Poems, especially those recited responsively like *Anim Zemirot*, normally require an even number of phrases so that the song is balanced and that there be no unresolved melodic tension when its recitation is complete. Since there are an odd number of lines here, we find an unusual "orphaned" sentence needing resolution at the end of the poem.

In other words, this supplication –

31) Please may my communication with You be sweet, for my soul yearns for You.	יֶעֱרַב נָא שִׂיחִי עָלֶיךָ כִּי נַפְשִׁי (31 תַּעֲרוֹג אֵלֶיךָ

---

49   See the chapter on *Kaddish* in this volume for another example of this anthropomorphic response.

50   See n. 65 in the chapter on *Nishmat* in this volume.

– stands out in unresolved dissonance because in the original composition there is nothing to balance it. Further, the fact that the second half of this line evokes the very first sentence of *Anim Zemirot* sends a message to us that the entire song is out of sync. It says that from the very beginning of the poem through to the very end, the poet has not received his desired response, because after everything is said and done even the sentiments expressed in the first line remain unrequited.[51]

The current practice of singing the verse

Who can tell the powerful actions of God, make known all His praises.[52]	מי ימלל גבורות ה' ישמיע כל תהלתו

at the end of *Anim Zemirot*, which will be discussed further below, adds an element that is not native to the song.[53] This line is one of two "add on" verses that were not part of the original composition.[54] It also provides a melodic resolution to the "hanging" line that Yehudah he-Hasid purposefully did not want to have resolved – at least not in this way.

To understand what Yehudah he-Hasid was trying to accomplish with this "orphaned" sentence we must return to the term כבוד (Glory) and discuss its second impact on this prayer. In doing so is necessary to recognize that

---

51   See Liebreich, Leon J. "The Benediction Immediately Preceding and the One Following the Recital of the Shema" in *Revue des Etudes Juives* 125, 1966, pp. 151–165. He calls this literary device an "Envelope Figure" and describes its use in a number of Biblical and liturgical sources, particularly in *Keriyat Shema* and the blessings that proceed and follow it. This device sets off and defines a single idea within a larger text just as it does here.

52   Psalm 106:2

53   See David ben Baruch Kalonymus Sperber (late 19th–20th centuries). Responsa *Afarkasta De-Anya*, 2, *Yoreh Deah*, #118, New York: 2002. He presents a conceptual reason for reciting this verse after שיר הכבוד. He bases his support for this verse on a practice of Mordecai Yoffe (1530–1612,) author of *Ha-Levush* (a commentary to the Code of Jewish law), that is recorded in David HaLevi (1586–1667), Taz: Orah Hayim 51:2. Yoffe recited מי ימלל at a different point in the services and Sperber sees a parallel to offering it after *Anim Zemirot*. He shows no awareness of the history and literary creativity that went into this prayer. Further, the late date of this responsum and the use of a proof text that makes no mention of the Song of Glory indicate that this is a recent practice.

54   The other one is I Chronicles 29:11.

numerology plays an important role in Jewish mysticism.[55] The Gematria or numerological value of the word כבוד is thirty-two, one more than the (current) thirty-one verses of the Song.[56] This, as we shall see, gives us the final piece of the puzzle.

Let us briefly take a look back into history. As we have said, these German pietists, the *Hasidei Ashkenaz*, suffered through the period of the Crusades and particularly the first Crusade. The first Crusade was a shattering event for western European Jewry.[57] Having lived in relative peace and security for perhaps a thousand years in that part of the world, living as they did in pious pursuit of God's will, they could not understand why the Almighty would allow their community to be ravaged, their *Yeshivot* to be destroyed, their spiritual leaders to be horribly tortured and so many of their co-religionists to be murdered.

These tragedies created a theodicy crisis, the depth and pain of which is palpable in, among other things, the dirges or *Kinot* written for the Ninth of Av (*Tishah B'Av*) that commemorate the Crusades and other events of this era. For example, these words from a *Kinah* by Meir of Rotenberg (1215–1293) – perhaps the leading Rabbi of his generation[58] – that mourns the burning of twenty-four cartloads of Jewish books in the streets of Paris in 1242, give us a sense of how difficult the times were for Jewish believers.[59]

A–Sinai, in place of a cloak, cover your clothing with sackcloth,	א–תחת מעיל תתכם סיני לבושך בשק

---

55 See Dan, p. 84, that analyzing the numeric value of words and letters is inherent in Jewish culture, and, therefore, that one of the levels of meaning that *Hasidei Ashkenaz* saw in sacred texts is conveyed by the numerical value of the words.

56 See Dan intro, pp. lvi-lvii, who cites *Sefer ha-Bahir* from the end of the 12th century where in par. 61 and par. 63, the text mentions that the heart (לב lev) of God equals thirty-two, which is the same as the number of esoteric paths of wisdom. These paths were used by God to create the world.

57 There are a great number of books and articles published on this subject – far too many to cite here. One can get a sense of the impact in Shlomo Eidelberg, ed., *The Jews and the Crusaders: the Hebrew chronicles of the first and second Crusades.* Hoboken, NJ: 1996.

58 Cf. Kanarfogel, Ephraim. *Preservation, Creativity, and Courage: The life and works of R. Meir of Rothenburg.* Jewish Book Annual, 50: 1992, pp. 249–259.

59 See Temko, Allan. "The Burning of the Talmud in Paris." In *Alan Corre: Understanding the Talmud.* New York: 1975, pp. 124–140.

B–Garb yourself in widow's clothing, change your blouse.	ב–תעטה לבוש אלמנות תחליף שמליך
C–I will shed tears until they become a river,	ג–אוריד דמעות עדי יהיו כנחל
D–And they will reach the graves of Your two most noble officers,	ד–ויגיעו לקברות שני שרי אציליך
E–Moses and Aaron on Mount Hor.	ה–משה ואהרן בהר ההר
F–And I will ask them if there is a new Torah, and therefore that is why Your scrolls were burnt.[60]	ו–ואשאל היש תורה חדשה בכן נשרפו גליליך

To find a Rabbi of the stature of Meir of Rotenberg effectively wondering whether the New Testament had replaced the "old" is truly shocking. How deep was the pain that he was trying to express? How open was the Jewish people's wound that he saw it necessary to speak in this way to God?

So, too, these words from the Sabbath morning prayer *Av ha-Rahamim* that also comes from this time period, are powerfully poignant when one remembers that they were written in response to the tragic events we are discussing:[61]

A–Father of Mercy Who dwells in the high places,	א–אַב הָרַחֲמִים שׁוֹכֵן מְרוֹמִים.
B–In His great mercy He will remember with compassion the pious, the upright and the pure.	ב–בְּרַחֲמָיו הָעֲצוּמִים הוּא יִפְקֹד בְּרַחֲמִים הַחֲסִידִים וְהַיְשָׁרִים וְהַתְּמִימִים.
C–The holy communities, who gave their lives for the sanctification of His Name.	ג–קְהִלּוֹת הַקֹּדֶשׁ שֶׁמָּסְרוּ נַפְשָׁם עַל קְדֻשַּׁת הַשֵּׁם.
D–They were loved and pleasant in their lives and in their deaths they were not separated.	ד–הַנֶּאֱהָבִים וְהַנְּעִימִים בְּחַיֵּיהֶם וּבְמוֹתָם לֹא נִפְרָדוּ.
E–They were swifter than eagles and stronger than lions to do the will of their Maker, and the desire of their Rock.	ה–מִנְּשָׁרִים קַלּוּ מֵאֲרָיוֹת גָּבֵרוּ לַעֲשׂוֹת רְצוֹן קוֹנָם וְחֵפֶץ צוּרָם.
F–May our Lord remember them for good together with the other righteous of the world.[62]	ו–יִזְכְּרֵם אֱ-לֹהֵינוּ לְטוֹבָה עִם שְׁאָר צַדִּיקֵי עוֹלָם.

It is significant that those who survived the Crusades chose to make *Tishah B'Av* (the ninth of Av) the focus of their commemoration of these tragedies even

---

60   Kinot, p. 360f.
61   Cf. Nulman, Macy. *The Encyclopedia of Jewish Prayer*. Northvale, NJ: 1993, p. 54.
62   Siddur p. 454.

though the high point of the violence of the first Crusade in Franco-Germany occurred between Passover and *Shavuot*.[63] The ninth of Av, the most tragic day in all of Jewish history, commemorates many terrible events, but most specifically it evokes the destruction of both the first and second Temples. By commemorating the Crusades in this way, those who lived through them effectively equated the tragedy that befell their communities with the destruction of the Temple.

In fact, the words of one of the *Kinot* say just that:

A–Take this to your hearts and construct a bitter eulogy	א–שימו נא על לבבכם מספד מר לקשרה
B–Because their [the victims of the Crusade] murder – in terms of mourning and rolling in the dust – is equivalent	ב–כי שקולה הריגתם להתאבל ולהתעפרה
C–To the burning of our God's House, the hall and the porch.[64]	ג–כשרפת בית א׳להינו האולם והבירה

To the survivors, uniting their pain with the loss of the Temple was the strongest statement they could make about the depths of their suffering.

But connecting *Tisha B'av* with the Crusades also brings with it a very different aspect of Jewish tradition. An often-cited rabbinic text predicts that the ninth of *Av* will be the birth day of the Messiah.[65] Part of the contemporaneous reaction evoked by the Crusades – in at least some circles – was the belief that

---

63   See n. 57; also see Magen Avraham, Orah Haim 248:8, and a work called *The Mainz Anonymous: A Jewish Crusade Chronicle*. See discussion of this work in Chazan, Robert. "The First Crusade as Reflected in the Earliest Hebrew Narrative." *Viator*, 29, 1998, pp. 25–38. See also the *Kinah* discussed in the next note.

64   This *Kinah* was written by Kalonymus b. Judah. It begins with the words,מי יתן ראשי מים, *Kinot* p. 270f. These lines appear on p. 274. This *Kinah* also makes the claim that it is impermissible to add new days of mourning to the calendar, but that claim can be challenged. See for example *Taz: Orah Haim* 566:3; Mishnah Berurah: ad. loc. 10; and *Magen Avraham: Orah Haim:* 568:10, who mention the 20th of Sivan as being a Fast Day that commemorates the terrible Chmelniki massacres that brought great suffering to the Jewish community in parts of Eastern Europe starting in 1648. See also, Wolowelsky, Joel B. "Observing Yom HaSho'a," *Tradition* 24, 4 (1989), pp. 46–58.

65   J. Talmud 2:4 (5a).

that generation had suffered the terrible "birth pangs of the Messiah,"[66] and that, therefore, they would come to experience God's complete redemption of the Jewish people as well.[67] Specifically commemorating these events on the Ninth of Av was an indication that this generation was to be included in the dynamics of both the destruction and the final redemption that are part of the totality of the *Tisha B'av* ambience.

The Song of Glory shared this approach – in fact, it represents the cutting edge of this approach. The Glorious King (מלך הכבוד), is called by Psalm 24 to appear and bring proper order to the world. The Song of Glory (שיר הכבוד), with suitable hesitation, presents visions of God in manifestations of *Kavod* that serve to begin that desired revelation of the Almighty starting with the Warlord image of the Deity that also appears in Psalm 24. The extra *resh* line validates the quest for uncovering these aspects of God's *Kavod* and asks God to fully reveal Himself at this time of martyrdom. *Anim Zemirot* uses thirty-one sentences to fulfill its role in this cosmic drama, bringing the world to the verge of *Kavod*, which numbers thirty-two. Musically it leaves us hanging, waiting for that thirty-second sentence when the full *Kavod* will be realized.

In this way Yehudah he-Hasid's poem pushes God to the verge of His final ultimate messianic revelation. The poet just needs Him to take that last step, to complete the song, to resolve the musical dissonance, to fully reveal Himself and redeem the world. Yehudah he-Hasid has been seeking that response from the first line of the poem through to its last sentence and just needs God to do His part. *Anim Zemirot* has prepared the way, God just needs to "walk the walk."

Further, the literary thirty-first line, the extra *resh* sentence, reminds God, as it were, that His words – including by implication His promises of redemption – are true and, therefore, that He should make them manifest. In addition, this sentence tells us that God calls each generation to its destiny. Yehudah he-Hasid's generation's destiny had been unimaginable suffering. Since those who lived through the Crusades were pious seekers of God, it was not their sins that caused their suffering. They must therefore be experiencing the "birth pangs of the Messiah." For all of these reasons and more, it was time for God to make Himself manifest and bring the redemption to these poor holy people. In

---

66 Cf. B. Sanhedrin 98b.
67 Cf. Cohn-Sherbok, Dan. *Judaism: history, belief, and practice.* London: 2003, p. 451.

this way Yehudah he-Hasid's decision to write the song – along with the song itself – serve both as a demand and as a mystical challenge to God.

In addition, the last four lines of the song – the sentences that are not part of the alphabetical acrostic – are headed by the following letters: תבו־י. This can easily mean "You, God, come!"[68] though this phrase is missing the silent letter א at the end of the word תבוא (come). The letter *aleph*, the first letter of the Hebrew alphabet, is often used to represent God,[69] and its absence here reflects the missing 32nd verse and concomitantly reinforces the call to God to make Himself manifest *now*! And since the last line of the song is so similar to the first line – and that first line begins with the missing א – the entire prayer comes full circle, tied into a very neat and complete package.

This literary symmetry is also on display if we look at the acrostic found in the first four lines of the song – before the alphabetical structure begins – and compare it to the acrostic that appears in the last four lines, after the alphabet is concluded. The initial acrostic reads א־מנע , which was explained above as relating to the poet's hesitation in writing *Anim Zemirot* and sharing it with the community. The א was understood as his making a false start on going through the alphabet, which is then followed by מנע meaning to "hold back."[70] It is only after these four lines that the poet does begin the alphabet again and carries it through to completion.

This is certainly a correct understanding of the structure of these lines, but we have seen that Yehudah he-Hasid did not hesitate to build more than one meaning into at least some parts of this text. There is also a second meaning to this acrostic that emerges as we discover the acrostic that appears in the last four lines of the song.

In reading the two acrostics together, א־מנע can mean "God held back," which is followed by the various depictions of God in His anthropomorphic manifestations that Yehudah he-Hasid has now made public by writing this song. As a result of this text God has been brought much closer to this world. The poem then concludes with the call יבו־י , "God, come." The Almighty

---

68 Cf. *Peirush Siddur ha-Tefillah la-Rokeah, "Ashrei."* Jerusalem: 1994, p. 159 (see n. 10). The letter י is used to represent God even more frequently than the letter א, which is discussed in the next sentence.

69 Cf. *Peirush Siddur ha-Tefillah la-Rokeah,* ad. loc. and *Sefer Rokeah, Hilkhot Yom ha-Kippurim,* #217.

70 As indicated above the letters are out of order, but rearranging letters was an acceptable form of exegesis for *Hasidei Ashkenaz* (see n. 36).

is called by Yehudah he-Hasid, so that He can complete the work of the Song of Glory, write the 32nd line and bring the full measure of His *Kavod* to His people. In other words, the Almighty may be hesitant to reveal Himself, but Yehudah he-Hasid, in the aftermath of the Crusades, is going to force the issue anyway. The audacity, desperation and raw exposed spiritual yearning encompassed by *Anim Zemirot* generally, and by these acrostics specifically is positively breathtaking.

The extraordinary circumstances in which Yehudah he-Hasid found himself and his generation, allowed him – one might even say demanded of him – to write this dramatically bold and unconventional prayer. The more one understands Jewish existential pain in the era of the Crusades, and the more one unravels the structure of this song in light of that pain, the more one can penetrate the poignancy, pathos and piety that underlies this remarkable text. Further study of *Anim Zemirot* does not add significantly to our understanding of the history of the prayer, which is our primary quest here, so we will not pursue that study in this venue. But further analysis of this text does indicate how hard Yehudah he-Hasid labored to bring his theme into virtually every word of the poem, in keeping with the structure and methodology that we have described here.

Today's post-Holocaust era raises many of the same theodicy questions and theological challenges as the era of the Crusades. The religiously courageous stance embodied in *Anim Zemirot* provides an intriguing response to these questions and challenges. Those who were part of Rabbi Yehudah he-Hasid's world and who embraced this poem that he composed, rather than leave the faith as some might under these circumstances, used their encounter with tragedy to deepen their connection to God. They did so, in part, because Yehudah he-Hasid was willing to evoke Judaism's mystical anthropomorphic conceptions of the Almighty in order to demand that God respond by making Himself manifest through complete and final redemption of His people.

This was a bold move, taken at a time of communal desperation. Nonetheless, it helped get *Hasidei Ashkenaz* through those terrible times, and it left a legacy of one very significant and powerful prayer that we find in in contemporary Siddurim (prayer books).

As indicated, many communities today sing מי ימלל גבורות ה' ישמיע כל תהלתו ("Who can describe the mighty deeds of the Lord, or make known all His praises?") after concluding the Hymn of Glory. This practice does not fit with the history and meaning of *Anim Zemirot* as presented here. It is done to musically resolve the "hanging" thirty-first verse. Unfortunately it also resolves the messianic and mystical tension of the poem without God making an appearance as the prayer demands. This modern-day practice also responds to the anthropomorphisms in the text by saying that no human can ever adequately describe God.[71]

Though all of this may be theologically more palatable, easier on our ears and more compatible with our sense of rhythm and melodic balance, it, unfortunately, takes away the sting of the poem and removes some of the harsh edge of its demands. Gone is the musical and numerological challenge of ending after thirty-one verses. Communities that follow this practice no longer leave God to complete the poem and console the Jewish people for the sadness of their history by revealing His glory. Instead they resolve the issues themselves, however inadequately. We will have more to say about this below.

For some time after it was composed, *Anim Zemirot* was recited only in mystical circles and in esoterically oriented communities that were influenced by the practices of *Hasidei Ashkenaz*. In the 14th and 15th centuries, it came to be used on *Yom Kippur* in many synagogues.[72] This was a natural transition, because the liturgy of the Day of Atonement is filled with a large number of prayers that originate in esoteric texts or that were composed by mystically oriented poets (*Paytanim*).[73]

Initially, after this transition to more general use of the prayer, the recitation of the Song of Glory was limited to *Yom Kippur* eve.[74] However, in many contemporary congregations it is said early in the morning on both *Rosh Hashanah* and *Yom Kippur*, or only on *Yom Kippur*, as an entré into the services of the day.[75] One of the themes of the Days of Awe is that God's presence as King and ruler of the world is more manifest at that time of the year than at any

---

71 See David ben Baruch Kalonymus Sperber, Responsa *Afarkasta De-Anya*, 2, *Yoreh Deah*, #118, who offers this explanation as the reason for the recitation of this verse after *Anim Zemirot*. He also suggests a second and somewhat forced explanation for the presence of this verse.

72 Rabbi Isaac Tyrnau. *Sefer ha-Minhagim* (Tyrnau), "Yom Kippur." Jerusalem: 1979; Rabbi Jacob Ben Moses Moellin. *Sefer Maharil, Hilkhot Leil Yom Kippur*. Jerusalem: 1989 (both of these works were composed in the 14th–15th centuries).

73 We have seen in both the *Shema* and *Aleinu* chapters in this volume that mystical material was more readily acceptable for general communal use on *Yom Kippur* than on other days.

74 See n. 71 and Mahzor YK p. 188.

75 Mahzor RH p. 164.

other time.[76] Including this prayer in the liturgy is certainly in keeping with that theme.

Then in the sixteenth century it began to be used more frequently. At that point in time esoteric teachings were increasingly introduced into the general Jewish community and a number of liturgies with mystical origins such as *Kabbalat Shabbat* (the service that welcomes the Sabbath, recited on Friday evenings) were widely accepted as part of Jewish prayer practice.[77] The desire to recite the Song of Glory more regularly was supported by this trend, though the significant presence of anthropomorphism and mystical imagery continued to evoke considerable opposition (some partial and some total) from important sages. Among those debating whether and when to recite *Anim Zemirot* were Joel Sirkis (1561–1640), Solomon Luria (1510–1574), Moses Isserless (d. 1572), Mordecai Yaffe (1535–1612), and Elijah of Vilna (d. 1808).

Initially, in this era, *Anim Zemirot* was recited every day, a practice supported by Joel Sirkis.[78] But Mordecai Yaffe considered this liturgy to be too sublime for such frequent and mundane use.[79] He sought to limit its recitation to Sabbaths and holidays. Moses Isserless, in one of his responsa,[80] cites Solomon Luria as rejecting any use of this prayer since "it should not be written down."[81] Isserless then defends its recitation. Elijah of Vilna offered yet another opinion. He argued that if it is to be recited at all, it should be said only on *Yom Tov* (holidays) when the joy of the day gives one's soul enough space to understand the true meaning and purpose of the prayer.[82]

Eventually the opinion of Mordecai Yaffe became the practice of most *Ashkenazi* congregations and so the Song of Glory is sung in these synagogues

---

76   B. Berakhot 12b, B. Rosh Hashanah 18a, B. Yevamot 49b, 105a.

77   See Elbogen, Ismar (1993). *Jewish Liturgy: A comprehensive history*. Philadelphia: 1993, p. 292, and Idelsohn, A. Z. *Jewish Liturgy and Its Development*. New York: 1932, pp. 51, 128.

78   *Bach, Orah Hayim*, #132.

79   *Levushei Tekhelet*, #133. Jerusalem: 1965.

80   Responsa #126. He here calls the poem *Shir ha-Yihud*, which is actually the name of a set of seven prayers that consist of different texts designed to be recited individually, one for each day of the week in succession (cf. Mahzor YK p.164). From the context, however, it appears that he is referring to *Anim Zemirot*; and Elbogen, p. 64, says that *Anim Zemirot* was viewed as the conclusion of *Shir ha-Yihud* by some sages.

81   This takes us back to the beginning of our discussion of the history of this prayer and of *Hasidei Ashkenaz* and their use of mystical traditions (see nn. 15–17).

82   *Maaseh Rav* #53.

only on Sabbaths and festivals.[83] Nonetheless we find *Siddurim* (prayer books) from the end of the nineteenth and early twentieth centuries that still retain this song as a daily prayer.[84]

There are two Biblical verses found in the Siddur after *Anim Zemirot*. Only the second (*mi yemallel*) is sung out loud. These lines were added to the prayer book for reasons having nothing to do with the original purpose of the Song of Glory.[85]

In many congregations mourner's *Kaddish* is recited after concluding *Anim Zemirot*.[86] There is a *halakhic* (Jewish legal) opinion that this form of *Kaddish* may only be said following the recitation of Biblical verses.[87] Hence the inclusion of these two passages between the Hymn of Glory and *Kaddish* to enable the mourner to say the prayer.[88] We find a similar set of verses after *Aleinu*, another prayer which is traditionally followed by the mourner's *Kaddish*.[89]

The themes of the verses chosen are as follows: for the first verse, the many wonderful attributes of God, such as His greatness and power; and, for the second verse, the fact that no one can adequately offer God's praises. In a general sense these texts reflect the message of this song, but without its anthropomorphic or mystical imagery and without its demand for God to act.

The singing of the מי ימלל sentence, again, appears to be motivated only by the lack of musical resolution created by the thirty-one lines of the poem, and

---

83 Siddur p. 484.

84 Cf. Hertz, J. H. *The Authorized Daily Daily Prayer Book*. New York: 1948, pp. 214–218.

85 Ya'akov of Emden, *Siddur Yaavetz:* (also called) *Siddur Beis Ya'akov*: the encyclopedia of Jewish prayer. Jerusalem: 2002, lacks these verses. Emden lived from 1698–1776.

86 Siddur p. 486. See the chapter that discusses the history of *Kaddish* in this volume.

87 See the discussion in the chapter on *Kaddish* in this volume, and see Rabbi Shalom ben Rabbi Yitzchak of Neustadt, *Minhagei Maharash*, #89. This work was composed in the late 14th or early 15th century. It is from the same era in which *Anim Zemirot* came into general use.

88 See *Bach: Orah Hayim:* #132 based on B. Sotah 49a, that *Kaddish* can be recited after *Anim Zemirot* because it contains the *Aggadah* that tells of God wearing *tefillin*. As such these verses would be unnecessary. In opposition see Yissachar Dov ben Yisrael Lezer Parnass Eilenburg, *Be'er Sheva:* Sotah 49a, that the mourner's *Kaddish* is customarily said only after Biblical verses. That is also true after the Song of Glory. This author was a student of Mordechai Yaffe.

89 See Siddur p. 160 and see Neustadt, loc. cit., #90, that there are places in the Rhineland that did not recite Mourner's *Kaddish* after *Aleinu* on weekdays because they did not recite any Biblical verses at that point in the service.

not by an understanding of the real meaning of the prayer. Those communities that do not sing מי ימלל would seem to be in much closer accord with what Rabbi Judah he-Hasid wanted to accomplish with this poem, than the communities who do raise their voices in song at this point in the liturgy.

The custom in many communities is to have a pre-*Bar Mitzvah* boy lead the recitation of this poem, either as a free-standing liturgy or while serving as prayer leader for the concluding part of the services. Generally, children of that age may not serve as Cantor until they reach maturity. On the other hand, adults in mourning normally do serve as prayer leader as part of their mourning practices.[90] Particularly in the Middle Ages, an era when life expectancy was considerably lower than it is today, and where anti-semitic acts were also taking their tragic toll, the presence of young boys in the synagogue with recently deceased parents or other relatives would be a frequent occurrence. Since *Anim Zemirot* was not yet a regular and fully accepted part of the services at that point in history,[91] the rules were relaxed so that young boys were allowed to officiate for the chanting of this song during a time when they were in mourning for someone they had loved and lost.[92] Then, once this was offered – under tragic circumstances – to those who were pre-*Bar Mitzvah*, even those young men not in mourning were given an opportunity to lead the singing of this song. So, too, as the prayer became a regular part of services the custom of having children lead continued.[93]

The mystical element reappears here as well. The contents of this song is sublime and touches on noble aspects of Judaism's most secret esoteric lore. Since children are pure by their very nature, some say that the poem should

---

90   See Ramoh: *Yoreh Deah*: 376:4.

91   Reif, Stefan C. *Judaism and Hebrew Prayer: New perspectives on Jewish liturgical history*. Cambridge: 1993, p. 213. This source says that the custom of having a child recite this prayer reflects the fact that this recitation was controversial (his description is that there was an "intrinsic difficulty" with reciting the Song of Glory). He claims that use of a child in cases like this "mitigates any serious objection on the part of the congregation."

92   See Moses Feinstein: Responsa *Igrot Moshe*: *Yoreh Deah*: 4:61 that when *Anim Zemirot* became an established custom it began to be considered part of prayer (מאחר שנהגו שייך זה להתפילה).

93   I heard this explanation from Dr. Irving Agus (ob"m), who was a Professor of Jewish History at Yeshiva University when I was a student there.

be recited in its purity by one who is, himself, pure and that this is the reason why young boys serve as Cantor for its recitation.[94]

Though this prayer, unlike many others, comes from one author and one place, many historical forces have had their impact on it. The Crusades, theodicy questions raised by those historic tragedies, anthropomorphic visions of God in the Bible and Midrash, Psalm 24, Jewish mysticism, numerology, literary creativity, a remarkable and unusual use of acrostics, the addition of Biblical verses for purposes of reciting *Kaddish*, musical dissonance and the pursuit of its resolution, the meaning and use of the term כבוד (kavod), thirteenth-century German pietists and their concerns, debate about when a prayer of such mystical power should be recited and finally, the use of a young boy as prayer leader, all have played a role here. In the end, the Song of Glory – our thirty-one line poem – though written by one person, seems to have been influenced by almost as many factors as there are lines in the song.

---

94   See Jacobson, p. 260, based on Leviticus Rabbah: 7:3, and see Song of Songs Rabbah 4:1 [6].

CHAPTER 5

Aleinu – Climbing the Stairway to Heaven

It is our task to praise the Master of all, to ascribe greatness to the Creator of all Who has not made us as the nations of the lands and did not place us as the families of the Earth. Who has not made our share as them and our lot as all their multitude. For they bow down to nothingness and emptiness and pray to a god who cannot save. But we kneel, bow down and give thanks before the King Who is King of Kings, the Holy One, Blessed be He. For He stretches out Heaven and founds the Earth, and His precious throne is in the Heavens above and His powerful presence is in the loftiest heights. He is our Lord and there is no other. True is our King, there is nothing beside Him, as it is written in His Torah: Know this day and take to your heart, that God is the Lord, in Heaven above and on the Earth below, there is none other.

Therefore we hope in You, God our Lord, that we may quickly see the splendor of Your might,

עָלֵינוּ לְשַׁבֵּחַ לַאֲדוֹן הַכֹּל. לָתֵת גְּדֻלָּה לְיוֹצֵר בְּרֵאשִׁית. שֶׁלֹּא עָשָׂנוּ כְּגוֹיֵי הָאֲרָצוֹת. וְלֹא שָׂמָנוּ כְּמִשְׁפְּחוֹת הָאֲדָמָה. שֶׁלֹּא שָׂם חֶלְקֵנוּ כָּהֶם וְגוֹרָלֵנוּ כְּכָל הֲמוֹנָם. שֶׁהֵם מִשְׁתַּחֲוִים לְהֶבֶל וָרִיק וּמִתְפַּלְלִים אֶל אֵל לֹא יוֹשִׁיעַ: וַאֲנַחְנוּ כּוֹרְעִים וּמִשְׁתַּחֲוִים וּמוֹדִים לִפְנֵי מֶלֶךְ מַלְכֵי הַמְּלָכִים הַקָּדוֹשׁ בָּרוּךְ הוּא: שֶׁהוּא נוֹטֶה שָׁמַיִם וְיוֹסֵד אָרֶץ. וּמוֹשַׁב יְקָרוֹ בַּשָּׁמַיִם מִמַּעַל. וּשְׁכִינַת עֻזּוֹ בְּגָבְהֵי מְרוֹמִים: הוּא אֱ-לֹהֵינוּ אֵין עוֹד. אֱמֶת מַלְכֵּנוּ. אֶפֶס זוּלָתוֹ. כַּכָּתוּב בְּתוֹרָתוֹ. וְיָדַעְתָּ הַיּוֹם וַהֲשֵׁבֹתָ אֶל לְבָבֶךָ. כִּי ה' הוּא הָאֱ-לֹהִים בַּשָּׁמַיִם מִמַּעַל וְעַל הָאָרֶץ מִתָּחַת. אֵין עוֹד:

עַל כֵּן נְקַוֶּה לְךָ ה' אֱ-לֹהֵינוּ לִרְאוֹת מְהֵרָה בְּתִפְאֶרֶת עֻזֶּךָ.

to remove idolatry from the Earth, and idols will be utterly cut off, to repair the world through the Almighty's sovereignty. And all humanity will call in Your Name, to turn all the Earth's wicked toward You. All the world's inhabitants will recognize and know that to You every knee should bend, every tongue should swear. Before You, God, our Lord, they will bend every knee and prostrate themselves, and to the glory of Your Name they will give ultimate value, and they will all accept the yoke of Your rule, that You will reign over them soon for all eternity. For the kingdom is Yours and for all eternity You will reign in glory as it is written in your Torah: God shall reign for all eternity. And it is said: God will be King over all the world; on that day God will be one and His Name will be One.

לְהַעֲבִיר גִּלּוּלִים מִן הָאָרֶץ. וְהָאֱלִילִים כָּרוֹת יִכָּרֵתוּן. לְתַקֵּן עוֹלָם בְּמַלְכוּת שַׁדַּי. וְכָל בְּנֵי בָשָׂר יִקְרְאוּ בִשְׁמֶךָ לְהַפְנוֹת אֵלֶיךָ כָּל רִשְׁעֵי אָרֶץ. יַכִּירוּ וְיֵדְעוּ כָּל יוֹשְׁבֵי תֵבֵל. כִּי לְךָ תִּכְרַע כָּל בֶּרֶךְ. תִּשָּׁבַע כָּל לָשׁוֹן. לְפָנֶיךָ ה' אֱ-לֹהֵינוּ יִכְרְעוּ וְיִפֹּלוּ. וְלִכְבוֹד שִׁמְךָ יְקָר יִתֵּנוּ. וִיקַבְּלוּ כֻלָּם אֶת עֹל מַלְכוּתֶךָ. וְתִמְלֹךְ עֲלֵיהֶם מְהֵרָה לְעוֹלָם וָעֶד. כִּי הַמַּלְכוּת שֶׁלְּךָ הִיא וּלְעוֹלְמֵי עַד תִּמְלֹךְ בְּכָבוֹד. כַּכָּתוּב בְּתוֹרָתֶךָ. ה' יִמְלֹךְ לְעֹלָם וָעֶד: וְנֶאֱמַר. וְהָיָה ה' לְמֶלֶךְ עַל כָּל הָאָרֶץ. בַּיּוֹם הַהוּא יִהְיֶה ה' אֶחָד וּשְׁמוֹ אֶחָד:

OTHER THAN *KADDISH,* which we discuss in the next chapter, the most frequently recited prayer in the liturgy of the contemporary synagogue is *Aleinu.* It usually appears as a text containing two paragraphs. The first asks Jews to recognize their obligation to praise God because of the special and unique nature of their place in His universe and their relationship with Him, the one true God. The second presents a far more universal picture of a healed world under His rule.[1] In this vision of a better future, all will come to recognize and worship God out of knowledge of Him and appreciation of what He has given to His creations.

Aleinu appears in this format at the end of essentially every service in

---

1   I am referring to the words לתקן עולם במלכות שדי (to repair the world through the Almighty's sovereignty) that appear in the prayer. *Tikun Olam,* as it is referred to here, is found most often in mystical sources (cf. Zohar: Bereishit 35a). It is also the way that it is used colloquially today. However, in Rabbinic literature, it means something very different. It is used to describe pragmatic decrees or enactments designed to solve problems that negatively affect the proper functioning of society (cf. M. Gittin ch. 4–5).

the *Siddur*.[2] This includes not only the three daily prayer services, but also special liturgical events such as a circumcision ceremony,[3] *Kiddush Levanah* (Sanctification of the Moon – a prayer recited in the presence of a visible Moon during a point in its monthly revolution around the Earth when it is both waxing and visible),[4] and *Birkat ha-Hamah* (the Blessing of the Sun).[5] The latter is recited at daybreak once every twenty-eight years at the point in time when Jewish tradition says that the sun returns to the exact location where it was at the moment it was created.

One can also find the prayer in the *Musaf Amidah* (the central liturgy of the additional service), of the High Holidays (also called the ימים נוראים – the Days of Awe). On the first of the High Holidays, *Rosh Hashanah*, the two paragraphs are said in both the silent personal *Amidah* and in the prayer leader's public repetition of *Musaf*. These two sections are recited sequentially when said by the individual supplicant, but several other prayers intervene between the two paragraphs when they are offered during the Cantor's repetition.[6] On *Yom Kippur*, the second of the High holidays, *Aleinu* is completely absent from the personal silent *Amidah* and only the first paragraph appears in the *Musaf* communal repetition of that day.[7] All of this needs explanation.

The origin of *Aleinu* is unclear. Rabbinic texts differ on where to look to find the roots of this liturgy. One claim is that Joshua, Moses's successor, wrote *Aleinu* after his miraculous conquest of the city of Jericho as he brought the

---

2   Cf. Siddur pp. 158–161.

3   See the explanatory note, Siddur p. 214. See also Weisberg, Yosef David. *Otzar ha-Bris: Encyclopedia of the Laws and Customs of the Bris Milah and Pidyon Haben*. Brooklyn: 2002.

4   See the explanatory note, Siddur p. 616. There are different opinions as to on exactly which days *Kiddush Levanah* may be recited, see Caro, J. *Shulhan Arukh: Orah Ha'im*, 426, and the standard commentaries ad. loc. Also see Lipschitz, Chaim U. *Kiddush Levono: The Monthly Blessing of the Moon*. Brooklyn: 1987; and Raab, Menachem. "Kiddush ha-Hodesh, Kiddush ha-Levanah and Birkat ha-Hodesh." In *Journal of Jewish Music and Liturgy*, 27, 2005–2006, pp. 20–29.

5   Shulhan Arukh, Ibid., 229:2; and see Rabbi Israel Meir Ha-Kohen, Mishnah Berurah, ad. loc. 8. Polen, Nehemia and Wolff-Polen, Lauri. *A Blessing for the Sun: a Study of the Birkat ha-Hammah from Early Times to the Present* (together with a new edition of the Birkat ha-Hammah liturgy). Everett, MA: 1980.

6   Mahzor RH pp. 454, 500, 506.

7   Mahzor YK p. 550.

Jewish people into the promised land.[8] The Bible tells us that this city was captured after its walls collapsed while the Jews were circling around it.[9]

On examination, however, there is nothing in the themes or wording of this prayer that relates in any obvious way to the story of Joshua and Jericho, or to the Jewish people first entering the land of Israel. Nonetheless some Sages do defend this opinion.

One intriguing example of such a defense appears in Rabbi Nathan b. Rabbi Yehuda's *Sefer ha-Mahkim* (13th century).[10] The Bible says that Joshua (יהושע) was originally called Hosea (הושע), and that Moses added the letter yod (י) as a prefix to his name.[11] In all likelihood he did this to include a reference to God in the name by which his eventual successor would be known.[12]

Nathan b. Yehuda refers to Joshua's original name as שם קטנותו (his childhood name) and finds it in *Aleinu*. However, to accomplish this Nathan tells us to travel *backward* through the text. If one does so, then the "heh" (ה) of הוא א־להינו (He is our God) found at the end of the first paragraph, the "vav" (ו) of ואנחנו כורעים (and we bow) in the middle of the prayer, the "shin" (ש) of שלא עשנו (He has not made us) further up in the liturgy and the "ayin" (ע) of עלינו (it is incumbent on us), the first word of the prayer, spell out Joshua's birth name.

In addition, for this to work, Nathan must insist that those who have the reading אבל אנחנו כורעים and not ואנחנו כורעים (both mean "but we kneel" and either version works equally well in the text) are wrong, and must stop using this alternative. The problem is that replacing the "vav" (ו) of ואנחנו with the "aleph" (א) of אבל, ruins the reverse acrostic. Today the custom is to use ואנחנו כורעים. But even if this is the original reading, I will leave it to you, the reader, to decide what you think of this proof that Joshua was the author of *Aleinu*.[13]

---

8 *Teshuvot ha-Geonim Sha'arei Teshuva*, #43, Leverno: 1869. The claim of Joshua's authorship appears in the question; in the answer, Hai Gaon (939–1038) is cited as accepting that claim as correct.

9 Joshua ch. 6.

10 End of the section on *Shaharit*.

11 Numbers 13:16.

12 Midrash Aggadah: Numbers 13:16, and see Rabbi Samuel Eliezer ben Rabbi Judah HaLevi Edels (16th–17th century). *Hiddushei Aggadot*, Sotah 24b, sv. *Davar zeh.* Even secular Biblical scholars see the presence of "yah" or "yahu" in a Biblical era name as an indication that the individual was connected in some way to the God of the Bible. See Rendsburg, Gary A. *The Hebrew Bible: New Insights and Scholarship.* New York: 2008, p. 8.

13 A second supportive argument is that one part of the prayer has 152 words which

I will just add that Rabbi Elazar of Worms (1160–1230) supports this claim and sees a sign of Joshua's modesty in this hidden, backwards signature.[14] He also explains that Joshua learned his modesty and this practice of hiding one's name in one's prayer compositions from Moses, the most modest of all men.[15] Moses (משה) is said to have written the psalm for the Sabbath day.[16] This text begins with the words מזמור שיר ליום השבת (a song, a poem for the Sabbath day) and Moses's name is hidden as: מזמור שיר ליום השבת. It is from here that Joshua learned to do what he did in *Aleinu*.

There is a second tradition that attributes authorship of the prayer to the Men of the Great Assembly (*Anshei Knesset ha-Gedolah*).[17] This institution is said to have guided the Jewish people during the major part of the Persian period.[18] That era began with the return of the Jews to Zion from Babylonia to build the second Temple in 516 BCE, and lasted until the Greek conquest of the Middle East at the hands of Alexander the Great in 324 BCE. It is not absolutely certain exactly when in that time frame *Anshei Knesset ha-Gedolah* began its work, though many associate its origin with the gathering of the

---

is the numerical equivalent of בן נ (the son of Nun). Others point to another section of the prayer that has 158 words, the same as the value of בן נון (the son of Nun spelled somewhat differently). Nun was Joshua's father. See the introduction to ch. 3 of Abraham ben Azriel, (13th century) *Arugat ha-Bosem*, 1939, p. 98.

14   Commentary to the Siddur of the *Rokeah*, "Malkhiyot," p. 657. Jerusalem: 1994.

15   Numbers 12:3.

16   Psalm 92. See Genesis Rabbah 22:13. One problem with this is that the Midrash claims that Adam actually wrote it, that it was forgotten and that Moses restored it. How then was he showing off his modesty in the first verse if he didn't compose it? This question does not seem to have troubled Elazar of Worms. But see Rabbi Yehudah ben Rabbi Shmuel He-Chasid (Rabbi Elazar's teacher), *Sefer Hasidim* #355 and #356, who mentions only Moses as the author. On the other hand, paragraph 356 sees the acrostic created from the first 4 words of Psalm 92 as spelling למשה (to Moses), hardly a sign of modesty. (See the chapter on Anim Zemirot for a discussion of scrambled acrostics such as this.)

17   Manasseh ben Israel (1604–1657). *Vindiciae Judaeorum*. London: 1743, p. 2, v. 4.

18   Maimon, Yehudah Leib ha-Cohen. "מי היו אנשי כנסת הגדולה." In מזכרת 565, 1963; Schiffer, Ira Jeffrey. "The Men of the Great Assembly." In William Scott Green ed. *Persons and Institutions in Early Rabbinic Judaism*, 237–276, Missoula, MT: Scholars Press, 1977; Bin Nun, Yoel. אנשי כנסת הגדולה הם חותמי האמנה במעמד עזרא ונחמיה, in משלב 36 : 5–20, 2001.

people and its leaders, and the signing of a charter to govern the Jews who had returned from Babylonia, described in Nehemia 8–10.[19] One individual, Simeon the righteous (Shimon ha-Tsadik), who lived when Alexander came to Israel, is described as being "of the remnants of the Great Assembly."[20]

Traditional sources claim that the group numbered 120 strong at any given time,[21] which means that several thousand individuals would have served in this institution as it held sway for much of the Persian Period. Nonetheless, Shimon ha-Tsadik is the only person ever expressly described as being part of the Men of the Great Assembly in either the Bible or in any ancient rabbinic text.

Maimonides (Rambam, 1138–1204), in the introduction to his law code, draws from names that appear in Biblical and rabbinic texts that tell of this era, and lists all of the individuals who he believes served as part of this body. Several of them are not obvious candidates for membership. For example he includes Mordecai, one of the heroes of the Book of Esther. Mordecai would seem to have lived in Persia for most, if not all of his life, while the Men of the Great Assembly served in Israel. Nonetheless, Rambam makes him part of this institution. Further, even if we accept all of Maimonides' suggestions as correct, he still finds only thirteen names that he can describe as having been members of this group.[22]

The point of all of this is that despite the remarkably anonymous nature of

---

19   Many traditional sources such as Maimonides, whom we are about to cite, treat the period of the Men of the Great Assembly as if it lasted for only one generation of some 34 years in duration (see Genesis Rabbah 35:2, Midrash Tehillim 36:8, Seder Olam Rabbah ch. 30). However, if the origin of the institution is found in Nehemia ch. 8–10, from the beginning of the Persian period, while Shimon ha-Tsadik dates from the end of that era, their period of rule was significantly longer than that. For discussion of the problem from very different perspectives, see First, Mitchell. *Jewish History in Conflict*. Northvale: 1997.

20   M. Avot 1:2. Also see B. Yoma 69a.

21   There is no rabbinic source that specifically gives this number for the members of this institution. However, the combination of the claim cited below that the Men of the Great Assembly instituted prayers (B. Berakhot 33a) and the claim that 120 elders instituted the *Shmoneh Esrei* (B. Megillah 17b, J. Berakhot 2:4 (4d) yields this number. Other possibilities exist; for example, J. Megillah 1:5 (70d) and Ruth Rabbah 2:4 speak of eighty-five elders, which is in keeping with what we find in Nehemiah ch. 10. Whatever the number, there were certainly far more than thirteen individuals involved.

22   Even if we were to accept the view that this institution lasted for one generation, and assuming no changes in personnel during that time, we would still only know thirteen

the Men of the Great Assembly, they are credited by the Rabbis with initiating or developing some of the most important elements of Judaism. For example, rabbinic sources tell us that it was *Anshei Knesset ha-Gedolah* who decided at least some of the critical questions concerning which books were or were not to be included in the Biblical canon.[23] In fact, according to these sources, they are to be given credit for writing or editing some of the books of the Bible, themselves.[24]

Anshei Knesset ha-Gedolah are also said to have initiated many important communal rules and regulations such as not blowing the *Shofar* (the ram's horn) on the first day of *Rosh Hashanah* when it falls on the Sabbath, despite the lack of any Biblical indication that this is the practice to follow.[25] They did so to protect against someone inadvertently carrying the ram's horn in a public area on *Shabbat*, which would violate a Biblical prohibition.

For our purposes, the most important part of their activity was their involvement in developing the liturgy. As the Rabbis tell us:

A–Rav Shaman b. Abba said to Rabbi Johanan:	א–אמר ליה רב שמן בר אבא לרבי יוחנן
B–... It was the Men of the Great Assembly who instituted for Israel	ב–...אנשי כנסת הגדולה תקנו להם לישראל
C–Blessings, prayers, sanctifications and separation liturgies.[26]	ג–ברכות ותפלות קדושות והבדלות,

It would, therefore, not be surprising for them to have composed *Aleinu* as part of their work in shaping early Jewish liturgy.

Aleinu does include a number of elements that would tend to associate this liturgy with the Persian period. First, there is explicit mention of kneeling and bowing before God, an activity strongly associated with the Temple[27] – and the Temple was rebuilt at the beginning of this era. Second the phrase מלך מלכי המלכים (King Who is King of Kings) that appears in *Aleinu*, is a designation

---

names of the 120 members, assuming all of Maimonides' suggested participants are correct.

23 Cf. Avot de-Rabbi Nathan 1.
24 B. Baba Bathra 15a.
25 Midrash Sehel Tov: Genesis 22:18.
26 B. Berakhot 33a.
27 M. Yoma 6:2.

for God often used in the Persian period, but not in other eras. For example, we find this phrase in the Biblical book of Daniel, which dates from the time when Persia ruled the Middle East.[28] We also have evidence that, along with the Jews, the Persians used this title for their chief deity at this point in history.[29]

Third, there is no reference to rebuilding the Temple in the text. In a prayer that speaks of the eventual coming together of all humankind to worship God, it is likely – if the Temple did not stand – that there would be some way in which the promise of its eventual reconstruction would make an appearance. Particularly because there are Biblical prophecies that the rebuilt Temple will serve as the place where all peoples will come to worship, we would expect that theme to be included here.[30] Mentioning this promise would be unnecessary only if the Temple were standing – as it was during the period of the Men of the Great Assembly. Though this is an argument from silence, which is generally a weaker way to prove a point, it does add some support to the opinion that this liturgy originated in the Persian period – or at least at some point during the era of the second Temple.

Finally, much of the prayer is written in Biblical poetic form and the Men of the Great Assembly were around when the last texts of the Bible were being composed. This poetic form is called parallelism.[31]

This literary device has very specific characteristics. Most of the lines of the poem are divided into two parts. The first half of each sentence can then be divided into three segments. These three segments are mirrored in the second half of the sentence, usually using words or phrases that are synonymous with what appears in the first half of the line. These segments may appear in the same, or in a different order in the two parts of the sentence. Occasionally, one of the segments may be abbreviated or not appear at all in one half of the line.

This type of parallelism runs through virtually the entire first paragraph of *Aleinu*. Taking the beginning of the prayer as an example we find:

---

28   Daniel 2:37.

29   Cheyne, Thomas Kelly, and Black, John Sutherland. *Encyclopedia Biblica*, sv. "Persia," column 3661, New York: 1899.

30   Cf. Zechariah 14:16.

31   Kugel, James L. *The Idea of Biblical Poetry: Parallelism and its History*. Baltimore: Johns Hopkins University Press, 1998.

C	B	A
לאדון הכל	לשבח	עלינו
ליוצר בראשית	גדולה	לתת
כגויי הארצות	עשנו	שלא
כמשפחות האדמה	שמנו	ולא

A	B	C
It is our obligation	to praise	the Master of all
to give	honor to	the Creator of Genesis
Who has not	made us	as the nations of the lands
and has not	put us	as the families of the Earth

Therefore, it would seem likely that *Aleinu* was composed before the close of the Biblical canon. Putting this all together suggests that the Persian period is the correct place to look for the origin of this prayer.

Some suggest a third possible origin for *Aleinu*. Rav was one of the leaders of the Babylonian Jewish community in the early part of the third century C.E. There are those who credit him with composing *Aleinu*. Rabbinic literature speaks of *Teki'ata De-be Rav* (the shofar blowing of the school of Rav) in referring to the *Musaf* service of *Rosh Hashanah*.[32] Since *Aleinu* is part of that service, and has apparently been there from its earliest days, that would make Rav the author of this liturgy.

As with Joshua, there is little to associate him with the themes or wording of the prayer; although in regard to other parts of the liturgy, Rav was an innovator. For example, it is he who first suggested using the blessings of *Shmoneh Esrei* for personal requests. At his suggestion, one may add additional supplications to any of the *Amidah*'s benedictions as long as these supplications are similar to the theme of the blessing to which they are added.

To take two specific examples, the blessing of רופא חולי עמו ישראל (*rofeh holei amo Yisrael* – He Who heals the sick of His people Israel) would provide an opportunity to pray for the recovery of a sick friend or relative. Similarly, the benediction מברך השנים (*me-varekh ha-shanim* – Who blesses the years), which asks God for proper rainfall and abundant crops, could be used to ask God to improve someone's financial situation.[33] While this allows for some

---

32   J. Avodah Zarah 1:2 (39c).

33   B. Avodah Zarah 8a.

spontaneity to enter into the formalized text of the *Amidah*,[34] it does not offer any support for the specific claim that Rav is the father of *Aleinu*.

Further, we are shortly going to encounter an association between Rabbi Akiva and a version of *Aleinu*. Rabbi Akiva lived at least half a century before Rav, which would make the theory of Rav as author of *Aleinu* untenable. The most we would be able to say is that Rav included an already extant *Aleinu* prayer into the *Rosh Hashanah* liturgy.

Whichever of these three theories we accept – and even if one wishes to propose an entirely different origin for the prayer – none of this helps us explain the purpose and function of *Aleinu* as we find it in the contemporary *Siddur*. To do that, we need to turn to one early appearance of this liturgy, found in a very different type of literature than we have presented thus far.

As discussed in detail in the *Keriyat Shema* chapter, Jewish prayers are often strongly influenced by the esoteric teachings of the rabbinic period known as *Heikhalot* or *Merkavah* mysticism.[35] One of the prominent themes of the literature that preserves this mysticism is a description of the mystic as he climbs through the seven Heavens to stand before God's throne of glory. There he joins the celestial choir and sings the Almighty's praises along with the angelic hosts.[36]

A section of this literature called *Ma'aseh Merkavah* (The Work of the Chariot)[37] preserves a discussion between Rabbi Ishmael and Rabbi Akiva

---

34   For discussion of this issue see the chapter on *Birkat ha-Hodesh* in this volume.

35   For a partial bibliography of studies of Heikhalot literature see Boustan, Ra'Anan S. "The Study of Heikhalot Literature: Between Mystical Experience and Textual Artifact," In *Currents in Biblical Research*, Vol. 6, (2007) No. 1, 130–160. There is a more complete bibliography online at http://faculty.biu.ac.il/~barilm/bibmyshk. html. For the place of *Aleinu* in *Heikhalot* literature and whether it originates in this mystical literature or in the *Musaf Amidah* of *Rosh Hashanah* see Meir Bar-Ilan. "Mekorah Shel Tefilat Aleinu le-Shabei'akh." In *Da'at*, 43, 1999, pp. 5–24. In my opinion, both sources draw on an older prayer, which is why it is not an easy fit in either place, but the *Heikhalot* usage is older for the reasons discussed in this chapter.

36   See Scholem, Gershon. *Jewish Gnosticism, Merkabah Mysticism, and Talmudic Tradition*. New York: 1960; but for a different view, see Schaefer, Peter. *The Hidden and Manifest God: Some Major Themes in Early Jewish Mysticism*, Albany: 1992. In actuality, both opinions may be correct.

37   See Swartz, Michael. "Alay le-Shabbeah: a Liturgical Prayer in Ma'aseh Merkabah." In *Jewish Quarterly Review*. 78:2–3, p. 180, n. 4.

about the latter's journey into the Heavens.[38] Scattered through this text are a number of questions that Rabbi Ishmael asks of Rabbi Akiva.

Focusing on the first few paragraphs of this material, Rabbi Ishmael's initial request is to be taught the proper prayer to recite as one enters the "chariot" (the heavenly journey).[39] At the same time he asks to be told (or be shown) the appropriate praises with which to approach a particular celestial being, who, by its name, appears to be in charge of Heaven's esoteric knowledge (רוזיי ה' א־להי ישראל – the Secret One, God the Lord of Israel).[40] Somewhat later in the section he asks what this being does and how it is possible to observe him in safety.[41] In between, he asks about some of the magnificent celestial architectural structures that one sees in Heaven.[42]

Even this brief description gives us an intimation of the literary style of this literature. These questions do not follow an order that exhibits any obvious logical pattern. They seem to move from subject to subject and back again, pursuing an internal logic not available to the uninitiated reader, or following the author's or editor's very personal stream of consciousness. When we add in the responses of Rabbi Akiva to these questions, the text simply becomes even more confusing. The style of his answers follows a similar stream of consciousness to that of the questions and their presence brings additional levels of complexity.

In particular, the prayers cited by Rabbi Akiva in this dialogue often contain words that do not match the task that these liturgies supposedly accomplish.[43] As such, when a result is ascribed to prayer and that result appears between two different liturgies, it is not always clear which of the two prayers is the one that actually accomplishes the task.

Further, while some scholars have tried to determine what belongs where in

---

38   See Scholem (henceforth GS), Appendix C, and Schaefer, *Synopse zur Heikhalot Literatur*. Tubingen, 1981 (henceforth Sy) par. 544–559, the entire *Ma'aseh Merkabah* section goes from par. 544–596. For discussion see Swartz, Michael. *Mystical Prayer in Ancient Judaism: An Analysis of Ma'aseh Merkavah*. Tubingen: 1992

39   GS par. 1, Sy par. 544.

40   In GS par. 4 and Sy par. 547, Rabbi Akiva teaches that anyone who keeps the praises of this being in his heart has a secret purification prayer revealed to him by this being, who also then gives him various spiritual gifts as part of a personal relationship that is created between this angel and the supplicant.

41   Ad. loc.

42   GS par. 3, Sy par. 546.

43   See Swartz p. 181.

terms of the text's original meaning, that is no guarantee that over the course of history other readers didn't come to different conclusions.[44] Particularly if the individual studying this material was a believer with a mystical bent trying to draw as much meaning from these complex and obscure texts as possible, he would be likely to read this material far more expansively than contemporary scholars. Of course, it is these believers who would impact on the way these prayers were understood and used, and not current-day professors of Jewish studies.

We are about to examine some of this material more closely using the considerations we have just described, but we will do so slowly because of the complexities that we have mentioned. Our starting point will be the building blocks of the text and some general observations. This will be followed by a detailed description of a section of this material that is critically important to the history of *Aleinu*.

We turn now to Rabbi Akiva's answers to Rabbi Ishmael's initial questions: From within the somewhat bewildering statements that he makes in his answers, several comments stand out. First, he cites several prayers that helped him as he began his journey, and at one point he says:

I prayed a prayer of mercy and through it I was saved.[45]	תפלת רחמים התפללתי ועל ידי כן הוצלתי

At another point Rabbi Akiva recalls:

Once I prayed this prayer I saw 6,400,000,000 angels of glory.[46]	כיון שהתפללתי התפילה הזו ראיתי שש מאות וארבעים אלף רבוא מלאכי כבוד

From the context, these appear to be celestial beings who will provide protection for him on his journey.

Most importantly for our purposes, Rabbi Akiva reports:

---

44   Cf. Swartz and Bar-Ilan.
45   GS par. 4, Sy par. 547.
46   GS par. 5, Sy par. 550.

At the time that I went up and observed	בשעה שעליתי וצפיתי בגבורה
the Power, I saw all of the creations that are	ראיתי כל הבריות שיש בתוך
in the midst of the paths of Heaven.[47]	שבילי שמים

Finally, among the small group of prayers that Rabbi Akiva recites as he begins his journey is one that is very familiar. It reads:

A–It is *my* duty to praise the Master of All,	א–עלי לשבח לאדון הכל
B–To grant greatness to the One	ב–לתת גדולה ליוצר בראשית
Who formed creation.	
C–For He has not made us like	ג–שלא עשאנו כגויי הארצות
the nations of the lands	
D–And has not given us the same	ד–ולא שמנו כגויי האדמה
position as the nations of the Earth.	
E–For He has not assigned *my*	ה–שלא שם חלקי בהם
portion among them,	
F–Nor *my* lot like all their multitudes . . .[48]	ו–וגורלי ככל המונם . . .

In other words, he offered the first paragraph of the *Aleinu* prayer in the singular, rather than in the plural, as it is known from the *Siddur*.[49] On the other hand, the second paragraph – which, because of how it is worded, offers very few opportunities to vary between plural and singular – remains in the plural even in the *Ma'aseh Merkavah* text.

Reciting prayers in the singular in this way is generally thought to be prohibited;[50] but in the universe of *Heikhalot* mysticism, many things that are

---

47 GS par. 2, Sy par. 545.

48 GS par. 5, Sy par. 551.

49 Siddur p. 158; Rabbi Jacob ben Asher, Tur (13th–14th centuries), *Orah Hayim*, #133 mentions the presence of *Aleinu* in *Heikhalot* literature, and determines the correct reading of the prayer based on how the liturgy appears in this literature. So, too, Nahmanides (1194–1270), Exodus 15:26, mentions the esoteric nature of *Aleinu*. See also Rabbi Menachem Recanati (13th–14th centuries), ad. loc. See Weider, Naftali, "Be'etyah shel Gematria Anti-Notsrit Ve-Anti-Islamist," in his *Hitgabshut Nusah ha-Tefillah*, v. 2, Jerusalem: 1998, pp. 457–460 for other early references to *Aleinu* as a liturgy that can be found in *Heikhalot* texts.

50 B. Berakhot 29b-30a. Seder Rav Amram Gaon, *Berakhot u-Vakashot*; Rabbi David HaLevi (16th–17th centuries), Taz *Orah Hayim* 565; Rabbi Israel Meir Ha-Kohen (19th–20th centuries); Mishnah Berurah, ad. loc. My own previously published

not allowed outside of that world are permitted. For example, Rabbi Akiva – who is a major figure in this literature – is portrayed as kneeling and bowing an uncountable number of times in his private prayer,[51] despite the usual limit of four such genuflections established by rabbinic literature.[52] Similarly, normative halakhah forbids praying to angels, while in *Heikhalot* literature this is a common practice.[53]

I have written elsewhere that the efforts of the Patriarch Rabban Gamaliel to formalize personal prayer by requiring daily individual recitation of the *Shmoneh Esrei* and by mandating an authoritative text for that liturgy were motivated, at least in part, by his desire to control mystical excesses in the Jewish community.[54] As we have seen here, much of the practice of the mysticism of the rabbinic period was accomplished through prayer.[55] Only true adepts like Rabbi Akiva were allowed to follow these esoteric practices, because they could be dangerous to the physical or spiritual well-being of those not truly skilled

---

understanding of the B. Berakhot passage is that it recommends using the same text as the community (i.e., the *Shmoneh Esrei*) and does not speak to singular versus plural wording (see my dissertation, *The Formalization of Daily Individual Prayer Utilizing the Shmoneh Esrei in the Talmudic Period: Patterns of Acceptance, Rejection, and Modification*). This appears to be the reading of She'iltot de-Rav Ahai: *Lekh Lekha*, 8, and of Maimonides: Mishneh Torah: *Hilkhot Tefillah* 8:1.

51 Tosefta Berakhot 3:5, B. Berakhot 31a.

52 B. Berakhot 34a-b.

53 Maimonides' fifth of his thirteen principles of the faith. See his commentary to the Mishnah, Sanhedrin, ch 10, introduction. Rabbi Yosef Albo (14th–15th century), Sefer ha-Ikkarim 2:28, 3:18 makes this an act of heresy as does Rabbi Shlomo ben Rabbi Simeon Duran (1400–1467), *Responsa Harashbash*, #189. On the other hand, at least six times in the first four paragraphs of *Ma'aseh Merkavah*, mention is made of prayer to celestial beings other than God. See *Responsa ha-Geonim, Musafiyah* (Lyck), #116, Jerusalem, 1966, for a disagreement on this issue. See also Rabbi Avraham ben David (ibn Daud) Ha-Levi (Ra`avad) (1110–1180), Ha-Emunah ha-Ramah 2:6. For a modern discussion, which includes the issue of parts of the contemporary liturgy that seem to be directed at angels, see Feinstein, Moses (20th century), Responsa *Igrot Moshe, Orah Hayim*, 5:43.

54 See my dissertation.

55 See Scholem and Schaefer, and the sources we have cited and are about to cite from *Heikhalot* literature, as well as the discussions in the chapters on *Shema* and *Anim Zemirot* in this volume.

in using them.[56] For the rest of the Jewish world the normal, rationalist rules were to be followed.

The requirement that prayers speak to the needs of the many, and not to the pursuit of an individual agenda, may have been part of Rabban Gamaliel's or his students' efforts in this arena.[57] In *Heikhalot* literature, the mystic either walks his path alone, or with a few companions who have their own individual experiences as they travel through the Heavens.[58] Requiring that the prayers be recited in the plural prevents using them as part of a personal quest of this type. For this reason, prayers used by the general public would be worded as requests for the many, while Rabbi Akiva's personal supplication – as he travelled his mystical path – was in the singular.

The paragraph that includes Rabbi Akiva's "singular" version of *Aleinu* in *Ma'aseh Merkavah* begins with these words:

A–Rabbi Akiva said, "Once I prayed this prayer	א–אמר רבי עקיבא כיון שהתפללתי התפילה הזו
B–I saw 6,400,000,000 angels of glory	ב–ראיתי שש מאות וארבעים אלף רבוא מלאכי כבוד

---

56   Tosefta: Hagigah 2:3; J. Hagigah 2:1 (77b); B. Hagigah 14b. See also B. Hagigah 13a and B. Shabbat 80a, and for significant restrictions as to how one is to teach this mystical material in public, see M. Hagigah 2:1, Tosefta Hagigah 2:1, B. Hagigah 14b. See *Responsa Rashbash,* loc. cit, for criticism of those who publicized medieval Jewish mysticism (*Kabbalah*) for similar reasons.

57   Even if we accept my alternate explanation (see n. 50), that the text in the Bavli that is purported to require plural formulations of the prayers, actually means that one should pray the same text as the community, the effect on mystical practices would be the same. Absent the use of the appropriate liturgical tools, the mystical journey would be over before it began (see GS par. 1, Sy par. 544). The Bavli in the source we are discussing, Berakhot 29b-30a, is telling a story about *Tefillat ha-Derekh* (Prayer for a Journey). Its appearance in the Babylonian Talmud includes mystical elements. In this text it is the prophet Elijah who teaches the importance of reciting this prayer. Another story about praying on a journey appears on Berakhot 3a. That source includes another appearance by Elijah and a *Bat Kol*. The requirement to involve the many is said as a corrective to the practice first suggested in the text. The comment means either that the supplicant should recite the Prayer for a Journey in the plural, or that he should join with the congregation and use *Shmoneh Esrei*. In either case, one would not be reciting a prayer that was part of a personal mystical quest.

58   Tosefta: Hagigah 2:3, J. Hagigah 2:1 (77b), B. Hagigah 14b,

C–Who were standing next to the throne of glory . . .	ג–שעומדין כנגד כסא הכבוד
D–And I gave praise over all my limbs:	. . .
E–'It is my duty to praise . . .'"[59]	ד–ונתתי שבח על כל אברייי
	ה–עלי לשבח . . .

If we follow the paragraph structure of *Ma'aseh Merkavah*, and the simplest understanding of lines A-C, the appearance of these angels would seem to come as a result of Rabbi Akiva's recitation of *Aleinu* (*Ali*). On the other hand, since the words of this liturgy speak of giving praise, perhaps the angels appear after the prayer that is preserved in the previous paragraph,[60] and then this prayer of praise is recited in response to their appearance.[61] Conversely, as we have said, the words of the prayers in *Heikhalot* literature often do not have anything to do with the task they perform. Therefore, *Aleinu* (*Ali*) may have nothing at all to do with line D.[62] It is also possible that the *Ali* supplication and the appearance of so many angels are simultaneous actions, thus causing Rabbi Akiva to respond by praying ever more intensely as he goes through the words of this liturgy.

Also, the paragraph before this one begins with the question:

| Rabbi Ishmael said, "How can one look at them and see what the Secret One, God the Lord of Israel is doing [and survive safely]?" | אמר רבי ישמעאל: היך יכול לצפות בהן ולחזות מה עושה רוזיי ה' א-להי ישראל? |

to which Rabbi Akiva responds:

---

59   GS par. 5; In Sy, lines A-D of this section are par. 550, and line E begins par. 551. For simplicity's sake we will follow GS's numbering. Sy's breakdown does not materially affect what we say here. Similarly, Sy presents different manuscript readings of this material. In some cases the readings are quite different from one another. However none of these differences affect the core of the argument being made here, though some small details of the description might change if we rely on a different manuscript. For simplicity, I have therefore chosen to follow GS's reading throughout.

60   This prayer that appears in GS par. 4, and Sy par. 548–549, is too mystical for inclusion in the *Siddur*. It includes angelic names and prayers directed at the angels mentioned (see n. 53), among other things that do not comfortably fit within the usual daily liturgy.

61   Swartz p. 181–182. But Swartz also points out that the words of these prayers may have nothing to do with their impact.

62   See previous note.

"I prayed a prayer of mercy and
through it I was saved."[63]

תפלת רחמים התפללתי ועל ידי
כן הוצלתי

There then follows a lengthy prayer.

Immediately after that we find Rabbi Akiva's claim that the prayer he recited brought about the appearance of myriads of angels and his recitation of *Ali le-Shabeï'ah* that we just discussed. If all of this is read in the expansive, stream of consciousness style of the *Heikhalot* literature itself, then this version of *Aleinu* can now be described as a prayer associated with God's merciful protection, and with the appearance of multitudes of angels who are the agents that provide this Divine protection, for the one who recites it.

In addition, and most importantly for our study, the statement by Rabbi Akiva at the very beginning of the *Ma'aseh Merkavah* material, that

"At the time that I went up and observed
the Power, I saw all of the creations that are
in the midst of the paths of Heaven,"[64]

בשעה שעליתי וצפיתי בגבורה
ראיתי כל הבריות שיש בתוך
שבילי שמים

reaches fruition immediately after Rabbi Akiva concludes his recitation of *Ali le-Shabeï'ah*.

The very next words – that, in fact, begin the next paragraph of the text[65] – have Rabbi Ishmael citing Rabbi Akiva on how difficult it is to comprehend the seven *Heikhalot* (Heavens). This is followed by Rabbi Akiva's description of the enormous number of celestial beings that each *Heikhal* contains – from one through seven – and then a second run-through of the seven Heavens with a depiction of the prayers recited at each level and how they manage to rise to the next highest *Heikhal*. It is the very enormity of what is presented here that makes it so difficult to examine and understand the celestial universe. Nonetheless, this entire universe was laid open before Rabbi Akiva as he began his journey after reciting *Ali le-Shabeï'ah*.

For our purposes, this adds a dimension to *Aleinu* that is key to how the liturgy is used today. *Aleinu* is a prayer that opens up vistas of unexplored heavenly worlds to the supplicant. It helps him realize the possibility of climbing

---

63   GS par. 4, Sy par. 547.
64   GS par. 2, Sy par. 545.
65   GS par. 6, Sy par. 554.

to new and unimagined celestial heights, while, at the same time, providing the merciful protection of myriads of God's angels on this journey. In other words, it provides very powerful spiritual provisions for anyone using it on a religious quest.

As previously mentioned, *Aleinu* found its place in the High Holiday liturgy at a significantly earlier moment in history than the point in time when it began to be used as a prayer that concludes almost all of the services.[66] There is a direct parallel between Rabbi Akiva's recitation of *Aleinu* at the beginning of his journey into Heaven and how it is used on the Days of Awe.

On *Rosh Hashanah* both the private personal recitation of *Musaf* and the subsequent public communal repetition of it, begin in the same way as they would on any other holiday.[67] But as the prayer proceeds, the text moves to a unique second stage.

On every other holiday, the *Musaf Amidah* contains seven blessings. Only on *Rosh Hashanah* do we find nine benedictions. This liturgy begins with the same set of three blessings that begin every *Amidah* recited in Jewish prayer every day of the year. Another set of three concludes the liturgy. These, too, are part of Jewish daily practice. On all other holidays there is then one middle blessing that speaks to the special time that is being celebrated.

Only on *Rosh Hashanah* do we find three unique benedictions called *Malkhiyot*, *Zikhronot* and *Shofarot* occupying the middle of the *Amidah*.[68] These blessings evoke the themes of God's rule over the world, His remembrance of all things, and His revelation to His creations. These sections of the liturgy begin with a claim that God rules or that He remembers or that He reveals Himself, which sets the agenda for the benediction.[69] This is followed by ten Biblical verses that prove the claim, and then by a plea that God act on

---

66　The relevant evidence will be mentioned as we proceed with our discussion.

67　Mahzor RH pp. 448–450, 470–496, 536–552 (though there are some added lines and a significant number of *piyutim* inserted into the liturgy at this point, the basic structure of the first three blessings remains the same); Siddur pp. 674–676

68　Mahzor RH pp. 454–464, 500–520, 554–570. Discussion of these sections appear at least as early as the Mishnah, M. Rosh Hashanah 4:5–6. For use of *Zikhronot* and *Shofarot* on Fast Days convened because of lack of rainfall see M. Ta'anit 2:3.

69　In *Malkhiyot* this is implicit in *Aleinu*, particularly from the middle of the first paragraph through the second paragraph, while in *Zikhronot* and *Shofarot* it is stated outright as the section begins. See Nahmanides, loc. cit., who discusses the "kingship" and rule aspects of this prayer.

these three attributes to the benefit of the Jewish people and the world. Each section is then followed by the sounding of the *shofar*.[70]

This part of the *Musaf Amidah* is the dramatic peak of the *Rosh Hashanah* prayer service. Many comments in rabbinic literature speak of the spiritual power of these three blessings[71] and of the sounding of the *shofar*.[72] The community, here, has entered a new liturgical universe of interaction with God, beyond what is experienced at other times.

The first paragraph of *Aleinu* is the transitional paragraph in both the silent and public prayer of *Rosh Hashanah*. It serves to begin the *Malkhiyot* or Kingship section and just as for Rabbi Akiva, it opens the door to a higher level of liturgical interaction with God in realms beyond the physical universe. Presumably it also helps protect the supplicant as he makes his journey through this part of the prayer with its intricate series of verses.[73]

Particularly in an era before printing was invented, these verses would all have had to be reproduced without error from the supplicant's memory of Biblical texts. *Rosh Hashanah* is Judgment Day. An error that occurs when speaking to God as He is making life and death decisions about those praying to Him is certainly a frightening prospect.[74] Hence the need for a protective prayer like *Aleinu*.

The high drama of the Days of Awe that we have just touched on may also explain why the restrictions against mystical practices were loosened here. The need to connect even more closely with the Deity at the moment of judgment would naturally tend to allow elements of the *Heikhalot* literature – which

---

70   Some communities sound the *shofar* both in the silent and the communal *Amidah*, while others do so only during the communal recitation. For sources see Rabbi Ovadiah Yosef (contemporary), Responsa *Yehave Da'at*, 6:37.

71   Cf. Tosefta Rosh Hashanah 1:12, B. Rosh Hashanah 16a, 32a.

72   Cf. Leviticus Rabbah 29:3.

73   Today's practice assumes that ten verses are mandatory for each section. That is not necessarily true in earlier sources, see M. Rosh Hashanah 4:6, Tosefta Rosh Hashanah 2:12, Rosh Hashanah 32a-b, Shulhan Arukh: *Orah Hayim* 591:4.

74   Many of the special prayers of the High Holiday liturgy speak of the fear of error in offering the required supplications, cf. the *Hineni* paragraph recited by the Cantor before beginning *Musaf* on the High holidays (Mahzor RH pp.444–447). Interestingly, and strongly supportive of our position here, *Aleinu* as currently recited in the repetition of the *Musaf Amidah* is interrupted between its two paragraphs by several additional *piyutim* asking God's help in finding the right words to say at this critical point in the liturgy (Mahzor RH pp. 502–505).

are all about connecting with God – to emerge in places where they might otherwise be suppressed.

A similar dynamic was at play in the way *Shema* is included and recited in the *Yom Kippur* liturgy, as we discussed in the chapter on *Keriyat Shema* in this volume. It is also true that many of the extra *piyutim* (liturgical poems) incorporated into the High Holiday liturgy are directly related to *Heikhalot* passages.[75] However, these prayers come from authors who did not reject use of this material in the liturgy, and they did engender some opposition.[76] Finding *Heikhalot* material in the middle of the *Musaf Amidah* of the Days of Awe without any known opposition is dramatically different. It tells us that even some who were otherwise opposed to inclusion of *Merkavah* material could not deny the need to seek closer contact with God at this sacred point in the Jewish year.

On *Yom Kippur* there is no such second level in the silent private *Amidah* of *Musaf*, so there is no *Aleinu*.[77] However in the public, communal *Amidah* there certainly is such a higher level. The repetition of the *Amidah* during *Musaf* on *Yom Kippur* includes the section known as the *Avodah*.[78] Here the prayer leader takes on the role of the *Kohen Gadol* (High Priest) in the Temple as he carried the fate of the Jewish people with him while performing the sacrificial

---

75   For example the *piyut Ha-Aderet ve-ha-Emunah* that is recited on Yom Kippur (Mahzor YK p. 402), can be found in Eisenstein, Judah, *Otsar ha-Midrashim*, NY: 1915; *Sefer Heikhalot* ch 26:7; and again in Wertheimer, Solomon, *Batei Midrashot*, Jerusalem: 1952, "Pirkei Heikhalot," ch. 28:1. See Sy par. 275, 322.

76   Cf. Rabbi Yaakov ben Yehuda Landa (15th century), *Sefer ha-Agur*, Berakhot #117, Rabbi Eleazar Ben David Fleckeles (18th–19th century) *Teshuvah Me-Ahavah*, 1:1. See Langer, Ruth, "Kalir was a Tanna: Rabbenu Tam's Invocation of Antiquity in Defense of The Ashkenazi Payyetanic Tradition," in *Hebrew Union College Annual* 67 (1996) pp. 95–106 and Yahalom, Joseph, "The Poetics of Spanish Piyyut in Light of Abraham Ibn Ezra's Critique of its pre-Spanish Precedents" in *Abraham Ibn Ezra y su tiempo* (1990), pp. 387–392.

77   Mahzor YK pp. 486–495.

78   Mahzor YK. pp. 554–585. The section is called by this name as early as the Geonic period and several different liturgical versions of the High Priest's service were written by different authors from as early as that era (Cf. *Teshuvot ha-Geonim ha-Hadashot* (Emanuel), #115.

service of that day.[79] The liturgy describes in great detail precisely what the High Priest did on *Yom Kippur* in the Temple.[80]

This service is best known for the fact that it included the one moment of the year when the *Kohen Gadol* would enter the Holy of Holies.[81] In *Heikhalot* literature the *Heikhal* or main sanctuary of the Temple is often considered to be the lowest level of Heaven.[82] Entering the Holy of Holies would therefore constitute a deeper penetration into the mysteries of the celestial universe and an opening up of the higher realities of the Heavens.[83]

Again *Aleinu* marks the transition point appearing as it does just before the beginning of the *Avodah* section.[84] It opens the door for the Cantor to enter this extra level of the prayer service where he functions through his recitation as the High Priest. It also offers the hope of Divine or angelic protection as the prayer leader travels this difficult liturgical journey with the lives of the community resting on his shoulders.[85]

On *Yom Kippur* the second paragraph of *Aleinu* does not appear. This second paragraph, as it is understood in its liturgical context on *Rosh Hashanah*, is there to present the premise of the *Malkhiyot* section and the first three of the ten "proof-text" verses for that blessing mentioned above. Since there is no *Malkhiyot* section in the liturgy on the Day of Atonement, this paragraph does not belong in *Musaf* on *Yom Kippur*.

Also, since the High Priest's service on this day is described in the Bible as a ritual focused on atoning for the sins of the Jewish people,[86] there may not have been a thematic and theological opening for the second paragraph to enter the liturgy at this point.

---

79   See Leviticus 16.

80   It is based primarily on Mishnah Yoma 3–7; there is also some *Heikhalot*-related material incorporated in this section as well.

81   M. Yoma 5:1.

82   Cf. Isaiah 6:1 and Rashi ad. loc.; Exodus Rabbah 2:2; Masekhta Semahot: *Sefer Hibut ha-Kever* 1:1; Rabbi Isaac ben Rabbi Joseph Caro (15th–16th century), *Toledot Yitshak*, Exodus 38:21.

83   Davies W.D., et. al., *The Cambridge History of Judaism*, Cambridge: Cambridge University Press, 2006, pp.758–759. See Rabbi Tsadok ha-Kohen Rabinowitz (19th century), Pri Tsadik: *Devarim le' Erev Yom ha-Kippurim*.

84   Mahzor YK pp. 550.

85   See the words of *Hineni*, the Cantor's introduction to Musaf an the High holidays, Mahzor RH p. 444, Mahzor YK p. 482.

86   Leviticus 16:5, 15–17, 21–22, 30–34.

This second paragraph includes the imperative:

to fix the *entire world* under the rule of Almighty.   לתקן עולם במלכות שדי

It also envisions a time when all people will see and appreciate the wisdom and morality of the Creator.

While those may be fine sentiments, they do not fit easily into a service that focuses on the ritual performance of the Jewish High Priest in the Jewish Temple as he attempted to achieve atonement for a year's worth of Jewish sins. Nonetheless, the current Ashkenazi *piyut* that is used by the Cantor to describe the service in the Temple begins with God's creation of the entire world. It then details human history through Abraham's birth, and then Jewish history until the choice of the Levites to serve in the Temple. Perhaps the universalistic theme, in a more understated way, finds its place in the liturgy here, just as it begins: right after recitation of the first paragraph of *Aleinu* and some other sections added at a later date that we will discuss shortly.[87] Initially this *Avodah piyut* was said immediately after *Aleinu*, and may have taken the place of *Aleinu*'s second paragraph in providing something of a universalistic theme.

In contrast, *Rosh Hashanah* is God's Judgment Day for the entire world.[88] As such, a paragraph with a more universalistic theme would be better suited for the liturgy of that holiday. In fact, as we have said, this second paragraph of *Aleinu* appears in the silent personal *Musaf Amidah* on *Rosh Hashanah* and in the communal repetition of it – on both days of the holiday. Nonetheless, the first paragraph of *Aleinu* does appear in the repetition of the *Musaf* service on *Yom Kippur* to help make the transition to the most spiritually significant moment of the liturgical year.

It is important to note that originally the second paragraph came immediately after *Aleinu* on *Rosh Hashanah*.[89] However, over time, many communities have allowed other paragraphs to be inserted between the two parts of the prayer during the repetition of the *Amidah*.[90] These paragraphs, which also

---

87   Mahzor RH pp. 502–505 and 556–559, Mahzor YK pp. 552–555.

88   Tosefta Rosh Hashanah 1:11, B. Rosh Hashanah 16a.

89   See Seder Rav Amram Gaon: Seder Rosh Hashanah.

90   Rabbi Moshe Ben Rabbi Shmuel, Minhag Marseilles, Tefillat Rosh Hashanah, from the late 12th or early 13th century, already has another paragraph intervening between the two *Aleinu* sections. This despite the fact that his work relies heavily on Seder Rav Amram Gaon that was some 300 years older.

appear after *Aleinu* on *Yom Kippur* and before the *Avodah*, ask for God's help in guiding the Cantor to choose the proper words, and to display appropriate expertise in what he says.

This supports our contention that an important transition point in the liturgy occurs here. If that were not true, why have this series of supplications asking for divine guidance in choosing the words of the prayers in the middle of things, rather than at the beginning? Because new spiritual vistas open up after the recitation of *Aleinu* on the High Holidays, these prayers for help and guidance make sense here.

The second paragraph does come along with the first when this liturgy becomes the prayer that concludes the services. Before discussing that next step in *Aleinu*'s history in general terms, we turn to two specific examples of *Aleinu* as a concluding prayer that are particularly interesting to us.

The use of *Aleinu* as the liturgy that provides entry into Heaven may help explain why it appears at the end of the *Kiddush Levana* and *Birkat ha-Hamah* services. Though part of why it makes its appearance in these places in the way that it does has to do with its use as the usual concluding prayer, there is also a direct textual connection between Rabbi Akiva's *Aleinu* and these liturgies.

Genesis Rabbah 6:6 reads as follows:

1–Where are the spheres of the sun and the moon put?	א–היכן גלגל החמה ולבנה נתונים?
2–In the second Heaven (*raki'a*),	ב–ברקיע השני,
3–As it says, "And God set them in the *raki'a* of the Heaven."[91]	ג–שנאמר: ויתן אותם א־להים ברקיע השמים,
4–Rabbi Phinehas said in Rabbi Abbahu's name,	ד–רבי פנחס בשם רבי אבהו אמר:
5–"This verse is explicit,"	ה–מקרא מלא הוא,
6–And the Men of the Great Assembly explained it [further]:	ו–ואנשי כנסת הגדולה פירשו אותו
7–"You are God alone; You have made the Heaven and the Heaven of Heavens, with all their host."[92]	ז–אתה הוא ה' לבדך אתה עשית את השמים שמי השמים

91   Genesis 1:17.

92   Nehemiah 9:6. The Men of the Great Assembly are here credited with writing the book of Nehemiah, particularly because Nehemiah was probably part of that group–see discussion above. In B. Baba Bathra 15a, Ezra is credited with beginning, and

וכל צבאם וגו',

8–Thus where are all their hosts put? ח–היכן הוא כל צבאם נתונים?

9–In the [second] *'raki'a'* that is above the Heaven. ט–ברקיע שהוא למעלה מן

השמים,

10–From the Earth to the *'raki'a'* is י–ומן הארץ ועד הרקיע מהלך

a five hundred years' journey, ה' מאות שנה,

11–And the thickness of the *'raki'a'* is כ–ועוביו של רקיע מהלך ת"ק

a five hundred years' journey, שנה,

12–And from the first *'raki'a'* to the next ל–ומרקיע עד הרקיע מהלך

'raki'a' is a five hundred years' journey. ת"ק שנה,

13–See how high it is! מ–ראה כמה הוא גבוה,

In other words, it is in the second level of Heaven that the sun and the moon – the thematic focus of these liturgies – are encountered. As the mystic travels above the visible Heaven to the celestial levels not normally accessible to human beings, he encounters the Sun, the Moon and the hosts of Heaven (presumably the stars and the angels), in all their glory, unlike the pale reflection of their power that we experience in this world. And the key that opens the door to this second level, and to the myriads of angelic beings that live there, is *Aleinu*.

Again this parallels the revelation of the celestial *heikhalot* that comes to Rabbi Akiva after he recites this prayer as described in *Ma'aseh Merkavah,* and may explain why *Aleinu* became part of *Kiddush Levana* and *Birkat ha-Hamah.* At the moment when these heavenly inhabitants are being celebrated, reciting a prayer that gives someone access to them certainly makes sense.

We do not find the presence of *Aleinu* in these special services in written texts until the nineteenth century. Yet there are indications that some communities included this liturgy in *Kiddush Levana* and *Birkat ha-Hamah* much earlier.[93] The discussion of whether to include *Aleinu* at the end of these special services – found in Jewish legal literature in the nineteenth and twentieth centuries – is quite intriguing. The discussants indicate that this is a long-standing custom in some communities, but that the reason for its recitation has been

---

Nehemiah with concluding, the writing of this book. Again if both were members of the Great Assembly there is no contradiction between these sources.

93 See Rabbi Yekutiel Yehuda Halberstam, Resposa Divrei Yetziv, #96, Rabbi Ovadia Yossef, Responsa *Yabbia Omer*: 5:36, and Responsa *Yechavveh Da'at* 4:18, Rabbi Israel Meir Ha-Kohen, *Bei'ur Halakha* 426, sv. *umevarekh*.

lost. As a result, some scholars offer their own reasons for its inclusion. The silence of earlier sources as to the practice and origin of this custom suggests an esoteric origin such as the one described here. As discussed, esoteric ideas are often held to a limited circle and not written down.

The general use of *Aleinu* as the concluding prayer of the services first appears in *Siddurim* in the 12th century.[94] *Aleinu* is a prayer of transition. Its appearance in *Heikhalot* literature involved moving to a higher spiritual and celestial experience. Using it at the end of services would seem to retain the transition element, though in this context it means moving back into the mundane world and not to the exalted precincts of Heaven.

But *Aleinu* is also a prayer that offered angelic protection for the one taking the journey. If reciting this liturgy provides the possibility of safety to one transitioning back into the physical universe from the spiritual experience of prayer, it would make sense for it to appear at the end of services. This would have been particularly true in the twelfth century, the era of the Crusades, which was one of the more dangerous periods for Jews in the history of the world.[95]

When *Aleinu* began to be used as the concluding prayer for services, the second paragraph was included. It sends a message that after the recitation of

---

94 Rabbi Simhah of Vitry (12th century), Mahzor Vitry, #99, 193, 232. See *Ta-Shma, Israel: Ha-Tefillah ha-Ashkenazit ha-Kedumah*, Jerusalem: 2003, ch. 10, who sees the origin of *Aleinu* as a concluding prayer as coming from the individual custom of some in this era to recite the *Ma'amadot* at the end of services. He does not explain how the more general usage developed. Many scholars cite Rabbi Elazar of Worms (1160–1230), *Sefer Rokeah*, Hilkhot Tefillah # 324, as the first source to indicate this practice. Elazar of Worms was associated with the mystical community known as *Hasidei Ashkenazi*, which would bring him close to those who were familiar with *Heikhalot* literature (see the chapter on *Anim Zemirot* in this volume) and to the dynamic cited here. He also calls *Aleinu* שיר מפואר ומהודר ומעוטר ומקודש ומרומם (a beautiful, glorious, regal, holy and exalted song) that should be sung with all of one's strength (יתכוין האדם בכל מאודו – Peirush Siddur ha-Tefillah le-Rokeah #132), which evokes Rabbi Akiva's introduction to the prayer in *Heikhalot* literature. However, the custom also appears in Rabbi Moshe ben Rabbi Shmuel, *Minhag Marseilles* (1150–1220), "Tefillah le-Yemot ha-Hol," p.100, which is slightly earlier. In addition, my reading of Mahzor Vitry #99 sees it there as well. Nonetheless, the presence of *Aleinu* in *Heikhalot* literature as described, had an early and significant impact on its usage as the concluding prayer. See also Weider (loc. cit, p. 453), who describes various early mystical practices and associations with Aleinu without indicating that they are esoteric in nature.

95 See discussion in the chapter on *Anim Zemirot* on this volume.

the prayers, when Jews go back into this world to do their work and God's, they should understand that they must include all of humanity in that effort and not just their fellow Jews. Even though much of "humanity" is treating them very badly, all of God's children are still of serious concern to Him and His people.

Further, as discussed in the chapter on *Keriyat Shema*, *Heikhalot* literature repeatedly makes the point that human beings are superior to angels. In this literature, prayer is an activity shared by human beings and angels. Perhaps there is, then, a bit of a sense of rising to a higher level as the supplicant returns to the world of people and again begins his efforts לתקן עולם במלכות שדי (to fix the *entire world* under the rule of Almighty), something which angels cannot do.

We should also take note of the fact that if we look again at the three claimed origins for the prayer, at least two of them represent moments of significant positive spiritual transition. Joshua brought the Jewish people from their wanderings in the desert into Israel, and Jericho marked the first acquisition of territory in the promised land by that generation. The Men of the Great Assembly were the institutional and governmental structure that gave a sense of permanence to the second entry of the Jews into the land of their ancestors. These certainly represent moments of significant spiritual advance for the Jewish people.

It is not clear how much the transitional nature of these proposed authors figured into the suggestion, or the actuality, that they composed *Aleinu*. However, we would have been remiss if we had not taken note of the conceptual parallel between their lives and the way this prayer is used in *Heikhalot* mysticism and in the liturgy. Certainly, either Joshua or the Men of the Great Assembly fit, in a conceptual sense, with what we have described to this point.

The use of *Aleinu* at the end of the prayer service beginning in the twelfth century – the era of the Crusades – opens up another chapter in its history.[96] That is its role in the Christian-Jewish conflict of that time period. In 1171, in the city of Blois, thirty-four Jewish men and seventeen Jewish women were burned at the stake because they refused to accept baptism. The contemporaneous records of this act of martyrdom tell of these Jews singing *Aleinu* with a "soul-stirring" melody as they gave their lives to sanctify God's Name.[97] This

---

96   See Mahzor Vitry #193, that it is to be used in this way on holidays, and #232, that this is also true on Rosh Hodesh. Also see Siddur Rashi #419, that it is said at the end of all prayers.

97   Posner, Raphael, et. al., ed, *Jewish Liturgy: Prayer and Synagogue Service through the Ages*. Jerusalem: 1975, p. 110.

song accompanied their souls' "transition" into Heaven. Also, since martyrs occupy a special exalted place in the World to Come, it was believed that this song became part of their transition to that special place as well.[98]

Though it is extremely doubtful that these martyrs were aware of Rabbi Akiva's use of *Aleinu* at the beginning of his celestial journey, the parallel here is still intriguing and might well have drawn contemporary mystical thinkers to endorse the expanded use of this liturgy in Jewish worship. For them, and for those people whom they taught, *Aleinu* would now become a prayer expressing the supplicant's willingness to make the ultimate sacrifice. Having worshippers promise their complete fealty to God, at the point in time when they were about to return from the spiritual experience of prayer to the dangerous mundane world in which they lived, would be a very powerful liturgical climax to daily prayer.

Given this history, it is remarkable that the second paragraph was retained as part of this prayer at the conclusion of services. The first paragraph speaks of the special connection that only the Jewish people have to the one true God – a theme that would be comforting in this era. Nonetheless, in the face of the terrible persecutions that the Jews suffered in the period of the Crusades, they did not leave the first paragraph of the prayer to stand alone as a statement of Jewish superiority, nor did they add a second paragraph that would serve as a diatribe against "inferior" gentiles.

While it is true that the persecutions would end should the vision presented by the second paragraph become reality, nonetheless this is the most noble and inclusive conclusion to the tragedies that the Jews were suffering that might be envisioned. A prediction that all non-Jews will be destroyed would also bring about the end of Jewish suffering and death, but in a very different and far less morally uplifting way. The fact that the more ethical and spiritual choice was put in place in the liturgy is deserving of respect, and should serve as a model for those who understand how profound an act this was.

In short, in the same historical time frame in which *Aleinu* first became the concluding prayer at services and the Crusades were wreaking their havoc, the paragraph with the more "universal" theme found and retained its place in Jewish worship. This text sees all of humanity – including Christians and

---

98   This is a theme already found in rabbinic midrash, cf. *Pesikta DeRav Kahana*, Piskah 11:14. It can be found even earlier in Josephus (cf. *Wars* I:33:2). It also appears in the Book of Enoch (cf. 22:12), a Heikhalot text.

Crusaders – as sharing in, and contributing to, the ultimate end point of history when the world will be repaired under God's rule and all will willingly call in the Name of the one true God.

While this certainly represents an act of moral and liturgical courage and transcendence, the prayer does embody an ideological polemic. Not only does *Aleinu* posit a special connection between Jews and the one true God in its first paragraph, it also, in its second paragraph, saw everyone else as coming to believe in that God in the fullness of time. This paragraph also teaches that it will be the sovereignty of that God that will bring about the redeemed world. By implication this means that it will not come from an already revealed Messiah, a new prophet or even the claimed son of God. And all of this is implied in the prayer without denigrating either the Moslem or Christian faith in explicit terms.

The claim that this liturgy was insulting to non-Jews became a public issue in the 14th century, though not because of the second paragraph. The challenge was joined in regards to a sentence that was removed from the first paragraph in many *Siddurim*, though it does appear in one form or another in some more recent publications of the prayer book.

Let us look at the censored versions of *Aleinu* so that we can fully appreciate the fact that there is a sentence missing. The prayer reads:

It is our task to praise the Master of all,	עלינו לשבח לאדון הכל
to ascribe greatness to the Creator of all	לתת גדולה ליוצר בראשית
Who has not made us as the nations of the lands	שלא עשנו כגויי הארצות
and did not place us as the families of the Earth	ולא שמנו כמשפחות האדמה
Who has not made our share as them	שלא שם חלקנו כהם
and our lot as all their multitude.	וגורלנו ככל המונם

Thematically, we are in a section that compares the Jewish people and its position in the world to that of the Gentiles.

The prayer then proceeds, in most printed editions, to say:

But we kneel, bow down and give thanks	ואנחנו כורעים ומשתחוים
before the King Who is King of Kings,	ומודים לפני מלך מלכי המלכים
the Holy One, Blessed be He.	הקדוש ברוך הוא

It appears that a comparative statement describing what the Gentiles are doing is missing.

That comparison is provided in this sentence recently restored to some prayer books.

For they bow down to nothingness and emptiness and pray to a god who cannot save.	שהם משתחוים להבל וריק ומתפללים אל אל לא יושיע

While this certainly does denigrate "the others" – which has led at least one Rabbi that I know to refuse to reintroduce it into the services in his synagogue – we must remember that this sentence appears in the first and not the second paragraph of *Aleinu*.

In that context, it can be understood as part of the rationale that explains why Rabbi Akiva's prayer served to unlock the door of Heaven and provide him with a vision of the celestial magnificence as he praised the one true God. Since he is in possession of specialized knowledge and of a unique connection to that God that others lack, he carries with him the possibility of this privileged entry to the heavenly precincts.

Similarly, on *Rosh Hashanah* the Jewish people are able to evoke an understanding of the structure of God's kingship, remembrances and revelations because of their privileged position with God. This also serves as part of the rationale for the prayer leader's ability to emulate the High Priest on *Yom Kippur*, a role that does not exist outside of Judaism.[99] Simply put, others – Gentiles – would not be appropriate in these roles, as they don't pray to, or believe in, the God Who is at the center of these important theological events. Instead they worship deities with no divine power at all.

It is, again, remarkable that both in the *Heikhalot* and *Rosh Hashanah* contexts, the texts continue with a vision that ultimately sees non-Jews as eventually taking part in the greater revelation of God's rule and His glory that will come with the dawning of the Messianic era. *Yom Kippur* is the one exception here, and we discussed some possible reasons for its unique liturgical structure above.

---

99   In Jewish thought it is dangerous for someone other than the *Kohen Gadol* to approach the Holy of Holies and, under some circumstances, even the Temple itself, see Numbers 1:51, 3:10, 3:38 and 18:7 and the famous sage Hillel's response to the prospective convert who wanted to become High Priest, B. Shabbat 31a.

Nonetheless, the presence of *Aleinu* in Jewish worship three times every day of the year, with additional recitations at the heart of the High Holiday liturgy and on other special occasions, and particularly the claim that gentile gods do not offer any possibility of salvation, directs a fatal dagger at the central teachings of Christianity. After all, belief in the saving power of Jesus is arguably the most important tenet of Christianity. It is no wonder that this sentence became a significant point of controversy.

In the 14th century an apostate named Pesah Peter, who had left Judaism for the Church, pointed out that the numerological value of the word וריק (nothingness), which equals 316, is the same as the numerical value of ישו (Jesus).[100] In point of fact, this calculation is correct, though, as we shall see, it is unlikely in the extreme that this was the original intent of the prayer.

Nonetheless, this charge was taken seriously and it – or variations of it – can be found from that point in time through the end of 18th century. In fact, its impact on Jewish liturgy can be felt even later.

The Jews found many ways to challenge this claim, some of which emerge naturally from what we have already discussed. First, the prayer may well predate Christianity as both Joshua and the Men of the Great Assembly lived centuries earlier than the birth of that religion. Therefore, *Aleinu* could not possibly include an anti-Christian polemic if either of these suggested authors composed it. Second, even Rav, who postdates the beginnings of Christianity, lived in Babylonia at a time when Christianity had no presence there.[101] There would have been no reason for him to include an attack on Jesus in a prayer that he composed.

Third, the phrase "nothingness and emptiness" first appears in this verse from Isaiah

For the Egyptians shall help [and in reality offer] nothingness and emptiness.[102]	ומצרים הבל וריק יעזרו

The object of Isaiah's condemnation is Egypt, and this prophet lived three

---

100 See Yaakov Elbaum, "Al Shnei Tikunei Nusakh be-Tefilat Aleinu." In *Tarbits*, 42, 1973, pp. 204–208; Elbogen, Ismar. *Jewish Liturgy: a Comprehensive History*. Philadelphia: 1993, p. 72. Also see Weider, loc. cit.

101 Rav lived in the 2nd and 3rd centuries C.E.

102 Isaiah 30:7.

quarters of a millennium before Christianity made its appearance on the world stage.

So, too, the description of people praying to "a god who does not save" also appears in Isaiah in a verse that describes all of the pagan nations of his time.

A–Assemble yourselves and come;	א-הקבצו ובאו
B–Draw near together, you of the nations who have escaped;	ב-התנגשו יחדו פליטי הגוים
C–They have no knowledge those who carry the wood of their carved idols,	ג-לא ידעו הנשאים את עץ פסלם
D–And pray to a god who cannot save.[103]	ד-ומתפללים אל אל לא יושיע:

All of this would, therefore, make this numerological challenge to the intent of this prayer seem quite farfetched and unsustainable. Nonetheless, to be complete in our historical review, we must note that there was at least one Jewish text that provided support, and may even have been the source, for the claim made by Pesah Peter. In the 13th century, in the era of the Crusades, the author of a work – which included commentary on *piyut* – called *Arugat ha-Bosem*, gave vent to some of the anger that had developed in the Jewish community in the wake of these murderous persecutions.[104] He wrote that the Hebrew words להבל וריק were numerologically equivalent to ישו ומחמט (Jesus and Mohammed). However, in order to create this numerological equivalency it was necessary to misspell Mohammed as Mahmat.[105]

The controversy surrounding this sentence led to the Italian community changing the wording of the offending phrase to:

---

103 Isaiah 45:20.

104 See n. 13 above. Elbaum claims (p. 206), that Rabbi Aharon ben Rabbi Jacob Ha-Cohen (13th–14th century), Sefer Kolbo #122, also hints at this. That text is completely obscure and it is not at all clear what it means. He also cites other possible supporters of this numerological polemic and various defenders against that idea. See Weider, who cites manuscripts that have it in Mahzor Vitry. He also cites others who hint at it.

105 Elbaum, loc. cit., says that many medieval Ashkenazi sources called Mohammed by this name. I find that claim somewhat questionable. See Weider, p. 456, who cites at least one source that does not read the name this way. Elbaum, as Weider, also points out that the numerology only works with a slight change in the wording that is not the usual reading of the prayer.

| They, formerly [in the past], bowed down to nothingness and emptiness.[106] | שהיו משתחוים להבל וריק |

instead of saying שהם משתחוים ("they bow down . . ." *now* – in the present tense).

However, since this did not remove the words that were claimed to carry the "offensive" numerological content and given that this wording could be read as granting divine status to contemporary gentile gods, this suggestion met only limited success, as both Jews and Christians had reason not to like it. Some communities, therefore, chose to remove the verse entirely, while others maintained their traditional practice and continued to recite it. Eventually the gentile authorities used their power to settle the matter.

Before describing what the gentile authorities did, we need to mention one more piece of the story. Some Jews tried to reintroduce a reference to the missing verse in a remarkable way. The word ריק (rik) is very similar to the Hebrew word רוק, meaning saliva or spitting. For this reason, when some would reach the missing sentence, they would spit. This would evoke the missing line. It would also express their feelings about the removal of the verse and, to be honest, would denigrate the other gods referenced in the missing text. This practice is mentioned by Rabbi Jacob b. Moses Moellin in his *Sefer Maharil* that he wrote in the early 15th century.[107]

On August 28, 1703, an edict was passed and confirmed by the Prussian government. The title of this edict was "Edict Concerning the Jewish *Aleinu* Prayer and that they Should Omit Certain Words and Not Spit or Jump Away." This lengthy title introduces a law requiring, among other things, that *Aleinu* be recited out loud at public services and that Prussian soldiers be posted in the synagogue to insure compliance with the suppression of this verse (please see copy of the first and last page of the original decree at the end of this chapter).[108]

This edict was reaffirmed in 1716 and again in 1750. Nonetheless, the custom of spitting made its mark in another way.

There is a Yiddish expression rarely if ever used today, but I do remember it from my childhood. The expression is "Er kummt tsum oysshpayen," meaning "He comes at the spitting." It refers to someone who arrives at the synagogue

---

106 Elbaum, loc. cit. p. 207; Idelsohn, A. Z. *Jewish Liturgy*. New York: 1995, Appendix 3.

107 Rabbi Jacob ben Moses Moellin, Sefer Maharil, *Minhagei Tefillah*, 3, and *Seder Musaf shel Rosh Hashanah* 5.

108 See Elbogen, loc. cit, and Idelsohn. See also *Encyclopedia Judaica*, Jerusalem: 1972 sv. *Aleinu*.

very late in the services, and it preserves the national memory of spitting during the closing prayer of *Aleinu*. (In fact, *Aleinu* is no longer always the very last thing recited. Other prayers have been added over time in some communities, at least on some days in some of the services.[109] But once *Aleinu* has been recited, there is very little time left in the proceedings and the most significant elements of the liturgy have long since come and gone for that day.)

In today's more religiously tolerant atmosphere, where one religion's censorship of another religion's liturgy has become less and less acceptable, at least in western countries, this sentence has made something of a comeback. In the early 20th century, Dutch congregations were reciting this verse. So, too, the religious Zionist youth group *B'nei Akiva* brought the verse back to its services as did the Chabad–Lubavitch community. In other communities or synagogues there are different customs. Some recite it, some don't and some continue to debate what to do. I am not familiar with anyone who spits during Aleinu, but I have been told that some Chassidic synagogues do.

Aleinu is one of Jewish liturgy's more ubiquitous prayers. Questions remain whether it was composed by Joshua, the Men of the Great Assembly, Rav or by someone else. The strongest direct evidence suggests that it comes from the Persian period, but a claimed reverse acrostic is said to reveal both Joshua the author and Joshua the loyal modest pupil of Moses.

Nonetheless, the key to understanding the prayer's purpose in Jewish liturgical practice is not to be found in a discussion of its origins, but rather in its appearance in *Heikhalot* literature and its use in the era of the Crusades.

Rabbi Akiva used a personal version of this prayer to gain entry and angelic protection as he moved from the mundane to the metaphysical world on his mystical journey. Immediately after he recited this prayer the seven Heavens and what they contain were revealed to him.

As a liturgy of transition to a higher spiritual plane that helps provide security for someone trying to travel through the rarified reality of God's celestial domain, *Aleinu* is recited by Jews as they enter into the unique spiritual structure of the *Rosh Hashanah Musaf Amidah*. Similarly, the Cantor takes on the liturgical role of High Priest on *Yom Kippur* having just been armed with these words as well.

---

109 For sources and analyses of some aspects of this issue see the discussion of the "Song of the Day" in the chapter on *Kaddish* in this volume. See also Bar-Ilan and Tah-Shmah, loc. cit.

In the 12th century, the prayer became a transitional recitation for Jews as they returned from their daily devotions to the mundane world. This may have been done to commemorate the victims of the Crusades, some of whom had used *Aleinu* as a martyrdom song. At the moment of their deaths, their souls were understood to have gone through a transition from the fires of persecution to the light of the highest reaches of the World to Come. In reciting *Aleinu* the Jews of that era may have been committing themselves to lay down their own lives for their God if it became necessary.

It may also have been seen as a prayer that offered celestial protection for the supplicant in this world, in those particularly dangerous times. Some may also have perceived it as aiding the worshipper in his transition from the angelic realm of prayer to the realm of human endeavor, which *Heikhalot* texts actually see as superior in some ways. Or perhaps for some combination of these reasons the recitation of *Aleinu* came to be the closing act of all daily services.

The second paragraph of *Aleinu*, with its more universal vision, and which first appears in the *Heikhalot* text and in the *Rosh Hashanah Musaf Amidah*, was retained when *Aleinu* became the concluding liturgy. This, despite the fact that the Jews were suffering terribly from Christian persecution at that time. It served to mitigate statements of existential superiority that appear in the first paragraph of *Aleinu* with a vision of a united mankind, a healed world and a voluntary universal acceptance of the one true God.

Using *Aleinu* to end the liturgy got an extra boost when it came to *Kiddush Levanah* and *Birkat ha-Hamah*. *Aleinu* helped Rabbi Akiva begin his celestial journey. According to *Heikhalot* texts, one of the first things he would encounter on this journey – as he came to the second Heaven – is the fact that this level of Heaven is the home of the sun and the moon, which are celebrated in these prayers. This would make *Aleinu* an obvious choice for these special liturgical events

Aleinu became a martyr's prayer in Blois in 1171 and then became part of Jewish–Christian polemics a century or so later. This led to modification and censorship of the text, soldiers in the synagogue and spitting at the end of services. Recently some have tried to bring back the original wording of the prayer.

This is a remarkably varied series of influences coming together to shape one fairly short liturgy. Nonetheless, in many ways *Aleinu*'s rich history is prototypical of Jewish worship. It should remind us of the many factors – historical, theological, mystical and pragmatic – that have influenced Judaism's sacred prayer texts.

Wir Friderich von Gottes Gnaden/ König in Preussen/ Marggraf zu Brandenburg/ des Heil. Römischen Reichs Ertz-Cämmerer und Churfürst/ Souverainer Printz von Oranien/ zu Magdeburg/ Cleve/ Jülich/ Berge/ Stettin/ Pommern/ der Cassuben und Wenden/ auch in Schlesien/ zu Crossen Hertzog/ Burggraf zu Nürnberg/ Fürst zu Halberstadt/ Minden und Camin/ Graf zu Hohenzollern/ der Marck/ Ravensberg/ Lingen/ Moers/ Bühren und Lehrdam/ Marquis zu der Vehre und Vlißingen/ Herr zu Ravenstein/ der Lande Lauenburg und Bütow/ auch Arlay und Breda. Geben hiermit allen und jeden Prälaten/ Grafen/ Herren/ denen von der Ritterschafft/ Verwesern/ Haupt-und Amtleuten/ Magistraten in Städten und Flecken/ Gerichts-Obrigkeiten/ Befehlshabern/ Verwaltern/ Schultzen in Dörffern/ wie auch insgemein allen Unsern Unterthanen/ Gläubigen und Ungläubigen/ über welche der allerhöchste GOtt Uns in Unserm Königreich/ Churfürstenthum/ Fürstenthümern/ Graf und Herrschafften/ nach seinem allerhöchsten Rath und Willen gesetzet/ nebst Entbietung Unsers gnädigen Grusses/ zu vernehmen/ daß Uns gebühre/ Lob/ Preiß/ Ehr und Danck zu geben/ dem/ der Uns Königreich/ Macht/ Stärcke/ Ehre und Herrligkeit verliehen hat/ und daß mit Uns alle/ so auf Erden seine Stadthalter/ und seines Reichs Amt-Leute seyn/ nebst der Verherrlichung des grossen Namens GOttes/ auch diesen Haupt-Zweck haben müssen/ daß sie nicht allein die zeitliche Wollfarth Ihrer anvertrauten Unterthanen befördern/ sondern/ weil dieselbe nicht für diese Welt allein geschaffen/ und in dem sterblichen Leibe eine unsterbliche Seele tragen/ auch dafür nöthig zu sorgen haben/ daß/ wo sie nicht alle zu GOtt bekehret/ wenigstens doch ihr Gericht ihnen einsten nicht schwerer werde.

Wann dann/ in solcher Erwegung/ Wir mit erbarmenden Augen das arme Juden-Volck/ so Uns GOtt in Unsern Landen unterwürffig gemachet/ ansehen/ so wünschen Wir woll hertzlich/ daß dis Volck/ welches der HErr ehemals so hoch geliebet/ und vor allen andern Völckern zu seinem Eigenthum erwehlet hatte/ endlich von seiner Blindheit möchte befreyet/ und mit Uns zu einer Gemeinschafft in dem Glauben an den aus ihnen selbst gebornen Meßiam und Heyland der Welt gebracht werden: Weil aber das grosse Werck der Bekehrung zu dem geistlichen Reich Christi gehöret/ und Unsere weltliche Macht keinen Platz darinn findet/ Wir auch die Herrschafft über die Gewissen der Menschen dem HErrn aller Herren einig überlassen/ so müssen Wir Zeit und Stunde abwarten/ welche der barmhertzige GOtt/ sie zu erleuchten/ seinem allein gnädigen Willen vorbehalten hat/ indessen sie mit Gedult ertragen/ und die Mittel zu ihrer Bekehrung mit aller Liebe und Sanfftmuth anwenden lassen: Wie Wir dann hiermit insonderheit die Geistlichen und Seelensorger ermahnet haben wollen/ so offt sie Gelegenheit dazu ersehen/ sich zu bemühen/ wie sie dis ungläubige Volck mit Sanfftmuth gründlich überzeugen/ und dem Meßia/ Unserm HErrn/ zu führen mögen/ und alle und jede/ so den Namen Christi unter Uns bekennen/ ernstlich dahin anweisen/ ihnen

First page of Prussian decree.

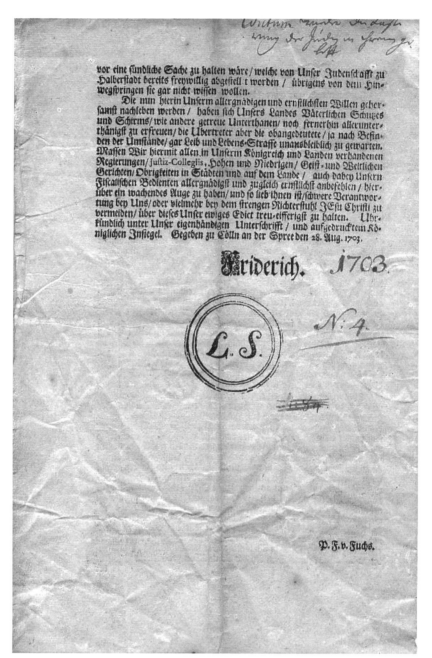

vor eine sündliche Sache zu halten wäre / welche von Unser Judenschafft zu
Halberstadt bereits freywillig abgestellt worden / übrigens von dem Hin-
wegspringen sie gar nicht wissen wollen.

Die nun hierin Unserm allergnädigen und ernstlichsten Willen gehor-
samst nachleben werden / haben sich Unsers Landes Väterlichen Schutzes
und Schirms / wie andere getreue Unterthanen / noch fernerhin allerunter-
thänigst zu erfreuen / die Ubertreter aber die obangedeutete / ja nach Befin-
den der Umstände / gar Leib und Lebens-Straffe unausbleiblich zu gewarten.
Massen Wir hiermit allen in Unserm Königreich und Landen verhandenen
Regierungen / justiz-Collegiis, Hohen und Niedrigen / Geist- und Weltlichen
Gerichten / Obrigkeiten in Städten und auf dem Lande / auch dabey Unsern
Fiscalischen Bedienten allergnädigst und zugleich ernstlichst anbefehlen / hier-
über ein wachendes Auge zu haben / und so lieb ihnen ist / schwere Verantwor-
tung bey Uns / oder vielmehr bey dem strengen Richterstuhl JEsu Christi zu
vermeiden / über dieses Unser ewiges Edict treu-eifferigst zu halten.   Uhr-
kundlich unter Unser eigenhändigen Unterschrifft / und aufgedrucktem Kö-
niglichen Insiegel.   Gegeben zu Cölln an der Spree den 28. Aug. 1703.

Friderich.   1703.

L. S.

N. 4.

P. F. v. Fuchs.

From the collection of Linda and Joel Berkowitz.

Last page of Prussian decree with signature.

CHAPTER 6

Kaddish: The Response
that Keeps on Giving

This chapter is dedicated in memory of
Abraham and **Zina Gontownik**,
proud Jews of Vilna and Memphis, TN, Holocaust
survivors, and guiding lights of hope, faith and
optimism in the face of monumental odds,
and their daughter **Chaye**, who perished in the Shoah,
and their son **Sidney**, who died on Nissan 24, 5770.

Lovingly dedicated by
Anne and **Jerry Gontownik**; **Ari** and **Shira**, **Zev**,
Daniela and **Ruth Zina**, **Yoni**, **Ranan**, **Hillel** and **Ezra**.

Abbreviated Kaddish (cf. Siddur p. 82)	חצי קדיש
May His great Name be magnified and sanctified, Amen.	יִתְגַּדַּל וְיִתְקַדַּשׁ שְׁמֵהּ רַבָּא. אָמֵן:
In the world, which He created according to His will.	בְּעָלְמָא דִּי בְרָא כִרְעוּתֵהּ
May He empower His rule in your lifetime, in your days, and in the lifetimes of the entire house	וְיַמְלִיךְ מַלְכוּתֵהּ בְּחַיֵּיכוֹן וּבְיוֹמֵיכוֹן וּבְחַיֵּי דְכָל בֵּית יִשְׂרָאֵל

of Israel,[1] swiftly and in the near future; and say, Amen.

May His great Name be blessed, forever and ever.

בְּעֲגָלָא וּבִזְמַן קָרִיב. וְאִמְרוּ אָמֵן:

יְהֵא שְׁמֵהּ רַבָּא מְבָרַךְ לְעָלַם וּלְעָלְמֵי עָלְמַיָּא.

Blessed, praised, beautified, exalted, elevated, glorified, raised high and lauded be the Name of the Holy One, Blessed is He

Above (during the Ten Days of Penitence, include here: "and beyond") any blessings and hymns, praises and consolations, which are uttered in the world; and say, Amen.

יִתְבָּרַךְ וְיִשְׁתַּבַּח וְיִתְפָּאַר וְיִתְרוֹמַם וְיִתְנַשֵּׂא וְיִתְהַדָּר וְיִתְעַלֶּה וְיִתְהַלָּל שְׁמֵהּ דְּקֻדְשָׁא בְּרִיךְ הוּא.

לְעֵלָּא מִן כָּל (בעשי"ת לְעֵלָּא לְעֵלָּא מִכָּל) בִּרְכָתָא וְשִׁירָתָא תֻּשְׁבְּחָתָא וְנֶחֱמָתָא דַּאֲמִירָן בְּעָלְמָא. וְאִמְרוּ אָמֵן:

Mourner's Kaddish and Full Kaddish without the Titkabel ("accept [our prayers]") paragraph
(Cf. Siddur, p. 56 and pp. 598-601)

קדיש יתום, קדיש
שלם בלי תתקבל

May His great Name be magnified and sanctified, Amen.

יִתְגַּדַּל וְיִתְקַדַּשׁ שְׁמֵהּ רַבָּא. אָמֵן:

In the world, which He created according to His will.

בְּעָלְמָא דִּי בְרָא כִרְעוּתֵהּ

May He empower His rule in your lifetime, in your days, and in the lifetimes of the entire house of Israel, swiftly and in the near future; and say, Amen.

וְיַמְלִיךְ מַלְכוּתֵהּ בְּחַיֵּיכוֹן וּבְיוֹמֵיכוֹן וּבְחַיֵּי דְכָל בֵּית יִשְׂרָאֵל בְּעֲגָלָא וּבִזְמַן קָרִיב, וְאִמְרוּ אָמֵן:

May His great Name be blessed, forever and ever.

יְהֵא שְׁמֵהּ רַבָּא מְבָרַךְ לְעָלַם וּלְעָלְמֵי עָלְמַיָּא:

Blessed, praised, beautified, exalted, elevated, glorified, raised high and lauded be the Name of the Holy One, Blessed is He

יִתְבָּרַךְ וְיִשְׁתַּבַּח וְיִתְפָּאַר וְיִתְרוֹמַם וְיִתְנַשֵּׂא וְיִתְהַדָּר וְיִתְעַלֶּה וְיִתְהַלָּל שְׁמֵהּ דְּקֻדְשָׁא. בְּרִיךְ הוּא.

---

1   Elbogen, Ismar. *Jewish Liturgy: A Comprehensive History.* NY: 1993, pp. 83–84. This source records the custom of adding the words, "in the life of . . ." which was followed by naming important people such as the Babylonian Exilarch, the heads of the

Above (during the Ten Days of Penitence, include here: "and beyond") any blessings and hymns, praises and consolations that are uttered in the world; and say, Amen.

לְעֵלָּא מִן כָּל (בעשי"ת לְעֵלָּא לְעֵלָּא מִכָּל) בִּרְכָתָא וְשִׁירָתָא תֻּשְׁבְּחָתָא וְנֶחֱמָתָא דַּאֲמִירָן בְּעָלְמָא. וְאִמְרוּ אָמֵן:

May abundant peace descend from Heaven, and life, upon us and upon all Israel; and say, Amen.

יְהֵא שְׁלָמָא רַבָּא מִן שְׁמַיָּא וְחַיִּים עָלֵינוּ וְעַל כָּל יִשְׂרָאֵל. וְאִמְרוּ אָמֵן:

He Who establishes peace (during the Ten Days of Penitence, say: "The peace") in His high places, may He create peace upon us, and upon all Israel; and say, Amen.

עוֹשֶׂה שָׁלוֹם (בעשי"ת הַשָּׁלוֹם) בִּמְרוֹמָיו הוּא יַעֲשֶׂה שָׁלוֹם עָלֵינוּ וְעַל כָּל יִשְׂרָאֵל וְאִמְרוּ אָמֵן:

Kaddish with the Titkabel paragraph
(Cf. Siddur, p. 156)

קדיש תתקבל

May His great Name be magnified and sanctified, Amen.

יִתְגַּדַּל וְיִתְקַדַּשׁ שְׁמֵהּ רַבָּא. אמן:

In the world, which He created according to His will.

בְּעָלְמָא דִּי בְרָא כִרְעוּתֵהּ

May He empower His rule in your lifetime, in your days, and in the lifetimes of the entire house of Israel, swiftly and in the near future; and say, Amen.

וְיַמְלִיךְ מַלְכוּתֵהּ בְּחַיֵּיכוֹן וּבְיוֹמֵיכוֹן וּבְחַיֵּי דְכָל בֵּית יִשְׂרָאֵל בַּעֲגָלָא וּבִזְמַן קָרִיב, וְאִמְרוּ אָמֵן:

May His great Name be blessed, forever and ever.

יְהֵא שְׁמֵהּ רַבָּא מְבָרַךְ לְעָלַם וּלְעָלְמֵי עָלְמַיָּא:

Blessed, praised, beautified, exalted, elevated, glorified, raised high and lauded be the Name of the Holy One, Blessed is He

יִתְבָּרַךְ. וְיִשְׁתַּבַּח וְיִתְפָּאַר וְיִתְרוֹמַם וְיִתְנַשֵּׂא וְיִתְהַדָּר וְיִתְעַלֶּה וְיִתְהַלָּל שְׁמֵהּ דְּקֻדְשָׁא. בְּרִיךְ הוּא.

academies and – in the case of Yemenite Jewry – Maimonides, to *Kaddish*, at this point in the prayer. For more on this, see Danzig, Neil. "Two Insights from a Ninth-century Liturgical Handbook: the Origins of 'Yequm Purqan' and 'Qaddish de-Hadata.'" In Stefan C. Reif, ed., *The Cambridge Genizah Collections*. Cambridge: 2002, pp. 74–122.

Above (during the Ten Days of Penitence, include here: "and beyond") any blessings and hymns, praises and consolations that are uttered in the world; and say, Amen.

May the prayers and requests of all of the House of Israel be accepted before their Father, Who is in heaven; and say, Amen.

May abundant peace descend from Heaven, and life, upon us and upon all Israel; and say, Amen.

He Who establishes peace (during the Ten Days of Penitence, say: "The peace") in His high places, may He create peace upon us, and upon all Israel; and say, Amen.

לְעֵלָּא מִן כָּל (בעשי"ת לְעֵלָּא לְעֵלָּא מִכָּל) בִּרְכָתָא וְשִׁירָתָא תֻּשְׁבְּחָתָא וְנֶחֱמָתָא דַּאֲמִירָן בְּעָלְמָא. וְאִמְרוּ אָמֵן:

תִּתְקַבֵּל צְלוֹתְהוֹן וּבָעוּתְהוֹן דְּכָל בֵּית יִשְׂרָאֵל קֳדָם אֲבוּהוֹן דִּי בִשְׁמַיָּא, וְאִמְרוּ אָמֵן:

יְהֵא שְׁלָמָא רַבָּא מִן שְׁמַיָּא וְחַיִּים עָלֵינוּ וְעַל כָּל יִשְׂרָאֵל. וְאִמְרוּ אָמֵן:

עוֹשֶׂה שָׁלוֹם (בעשי"ת הַשָּׁלוֹם) בִּמְרוֹמָיו הוּא יַעֲשֶׂה שָׁלוֹם עָלֵינוּ וְעַל כָּל יִשְׂרָאֵל וְאִמְרוּ אָמֵן:

Kaddish of the Rabbis
(Siddur, pp. 54–56)

קדיש דרבנן

May His great Name be magnified and sanctified, Amen.

In the world, which He created according to His will.

May He empower His rule in your lifetime, in your days, and in the lifetimes of the entire house of Israel, swiftly and in the near future; and say, Amen.

May His great Name be blessed, forever and ever.

Blessed, praised, beautified, exalted, elevated, glorified, raised high and lauded be the Name of the Holy One, Blessed is He

Above (during the Ten Days of Penitence, include here: "and beyond") any blessings and hymns,

יִתְגַּדַּל וְיִתְקַדַּשׁ שְׁמֵהּ רַבָּא. אמן:

בְּעָלְמָא דִּי בְרָא כִרְעוּתֵהּ

וְיַמְלִיךְ מַלְכוּתֵהּ בְּחַיֵּיכוֹן וּבְיוֹמֵיכוֹן וּבְחַיֵּי דְכָל בֵּית יִשְׂרָאֵל בַּעֲגָלָא וּבִזְמַן קָרִיב. וְאִמְרוּ אָמֵן:

יְהֵא שְׁמֵהּ רַבָּא מְבָרַךְ לְעָלַם וּלְעָלְמֵי עָלְמַיָּא:

יִתְבָּרַךְ. וְיִשְׁתַּבַּח וְיִתְפָּאַר וְיִתְרוֹמַם וְיִתְנַשֵּׂא וְיִתְהַדָּר וְיִתְעַלֶּה וְיִתְהַלָּל שְׁמֵהּ דְּקֻדְשָׁא בְּרִיךְ הוּא.

לְעֵלָּא מִן כָּל (בעשי"ת לְעֵלָּא לְעֵלָּא מִכָּל) בִּרְכָתָא וְשִׁירָתָא

praises and consolations that are uttered in the world; and say, Amen.	תֻּשְׁבְּחָתָא וְנֶחֱמָתָא דַּאֲמִירָן בְּעָלְמָא. וְאִמְרוּ אָמֵן:
Regarding Israel	עַל יִשְׂרָאֵל
And regarding our Rabbis	וְעַל רַבָּנָן.
And regarding their students	וְעַל תַּלְמִידֵיהוֹן
And regarding all the students of their students	וְעַל כָּל תַּלְמִידֵי תַלְמִידֵיהוֹן.
And regarding anyone who is occupied with Torah	וְעַל כָּל מַאן דְּעָסְקִין בְּאוֹרַיְתָא
In this place	דִּי בְאַתְרָא הָדֵין
Or in any place	וְדִי בְכָל אֲתַר וַאֲתַר.
They and you should have	יְהֵא לְהוֹן וּלְכוֹן
Abundant peace, grace, kindness, compassion, long life and plentiful sustenance	שְׁלָמָא רַבָּא חִנָּא וְחִסְדָּא וְרַחֲמִין וְחַיִּין אֲרִיכִין וּמְזוֹנֵי רְוִיחֵי
And salvation before their Father in Heaven (and on Earth),	וּפֻרְקָנָא מִן קֳדָם אֲבוּהוֹן דְּבִשְׁמַיָּא (וְאַרְעָא)
And say, Amen.	וְאִמְרוּ אָמֵן:
May abundant peace descend from Heaven, and life, upon us and upon all Israel; and say, Amen.	יְהֵא שְׁלָמָא רַבָּא מִן שְׁמַיָּא וְחַיִּים עָלֵינוּ וְעַל כָּל יִשְׂרָאֵל. וְאִמְרוּ אָמֵן:
He Who establishes peace (during the Ten Days of Penitence, say: "The peace") in His high places, may He create peace upon us, and upon all Israel; and say, Amen.	עוֹשֶׂה שָׁלוֹם (בעשי"ת הַשָּׁלוֹם) בִּמְרוֹמָיו הוּא יַעֲשֶׂה בְרַחֲמָיו שָׁלוֹם עָלֵינוּ וְעַל כָּל יִשְׂרָאֵל וְאִמְרוּ אָמֵן:

Kaddish after Burial or after concluding (siyum) the study of the Bible[2] (Siddur, p. 848)	קדיש לאחר קבורה או לסיום התנ"ך
May His great Name be magnified and sanctified, Amen.	יִתְגַּדַּל וְיִתְקַדַּשׁ שְׁמֵהּ רַבָּא. אָמֵן:
In the world, which He will renew,	בְּעָלְמָא דְּהוּא עָתִיד לְאִתְחַדָּתָא

---

2   I have seen this form of *Kaddish* used in this way at a *siyum* of this type. I can find no clear reference to it, but, if one follows the logic of this chapter and of the sources cited below, it makes sense to use it at such an occasion.

And will resurrect the dead,

וּלְאַחֲאָה מֵיתַיָא,

And raise them to life eternal,

וּלְאַסָקָא לְחַיֵּי עָלְמָא,

And rebuild the city of Jerusalem,

וּלְמִבְנֵי קַרְתָּא דִירוּשְׁלֵָם,

And will establish His sanctuary in it;

וּלְשַׁכְלוּלֵי הֵיכָלֵיהּ בְּגַוֵּיהּ,

And will uproot idol worship from the land,

וּלְמֶעֱקַר פּוּלְחָנָא נוּכְרָאָה מֵאַרְעָנָא,

And put the worship of heaven in place

וּלְאָתָבָא פּוּלְחָנָא דִשְׁמַיָּא לְאַתְרָהּ,

And empower the Holy One, Blessed be He, in His reign and in His majesty.

וְיַמְלִיךְ קוּדְשָׁא בְּרִיךְ הוּא בְּמַלְכוּתֵיהּ וְיקָרֵיהּ

In the world, which He created according to His will.

May He empower His rule in your lifetime, in your days, and in the lifetimes of the entire house of Israel, swiftly and in the near future; and say, Amen.

בְּחַיֵּיכוֹן וּבְיוֹמֵיכוֹן וּבְחַיֵּי דְכָל בֵּית יִשְׂרָאֵל בַּעֲגָלָא וּבִזְמַן קָרִיב. וְאִמְרוּ אָמֵן:

May His great Name be blessed, forever and ever.

יְהֵא שְׁמֵהּ רַבָּא מְבָרַךְ לְעָלַם וּלְעָלְמֵי עָלְמַיָּא:

Blessed, praised, beautified, exalted, elevated, glorified, raised high and lauded be the Name of the Holy One, Blessed is He

יִתְבָּרַךְ. וְיִשְׁתַּבַּח וְיִתְפָּאַר וְיִתְרוֹמַם וְיִתְנַשֵּׂא וְיִתְהַדָּר וְיִתְעַלֶּה וְיִתְהַלָּל שְׁמֵהּ דְּקֻדְשָׁא. בְּרִיךְ הוּא.

Above (during the Ten Days of Penitence, include here: "and beyond") any blessings and hymns, praises and consolations that are uttered in the world; and say, Amen.

לְעֵלָּא מִן כָּל (בעשי"ת לְעֵלָּא לְעֵלָּא מִכָּל) בִּרְכָתָא וְשִׁירָתָא תֻּשְׁבְּחָתָא וְנֶחֱמָתָא דַּאֲמִירָן בְּעָלְמָא. וְאִמְרוּ אָמֵן:

May abundant peace descend from Heaven, and life, upon us and upon all Israel; and say, Amen.

יְהֵא שְׁלָמָא רַבָּא מִן שְׁמַיָּא וְחַיִּים עָלֵינוּ וְעַל כָּל יִשְׂרָאֵל. וְאִמְרוּ אָמֵן:

He Who establishes peace (during the Ten Days of Penitence, say: "The peace") in His high places, may He create peace upon us, and upon all Israel; and say, Amen.

עוֹשֶׂה שָׁלוֹם (בעשי"ת הַשָּׁלוֹם) בִּמְרוֹמָיו הוּא יַעֲשֶׂה שָׁלוֹם עָלֵינוּ וְעַל כָּל יִשְׂרָאֵל וְאִמְרוּ אָמֵן:

Kaddish after Concluding the study of a Sacred Text of Significance[3]

(Cf. The end of any Talmudic Tractate)

קדיש לאחר סיום מסכתא

May His great Name be magnified and sanctified, Amen.

יִתְגַּדַּל וְיִתְקַדַּשׁ שְׁמֵהּ רַבָּא. אָמֵן:

In the world, which He will renew,

בְּעָלְמָא דְּהוּא עָתִיד לְאִתְחַדָּתָּא

And will resurrect the dead,

וּלְאַחָאָה מֵיתַיָּא,

And raise them to life eternal,

וּלְאַסָּקָא לְחַיֵּי עָלְמָא,

And rebuild the city of Jerusalem,

וּלְמִבְנֵי קַרְתָּא דִירוּשְׁלֵים,

And will establish His sanctuary in it;

וּלְשַׁכְלוּלֵי הֵיכְלֵיהּ בְּגַוַּיהּ,

And will uproot idol worship from the land,

וּלְמֶעְקַר פּוּלְחָנָא נוּכְרָאָה מֵאַרְעֵנָא,

And put the worship of heaven in place

וּלְאָתָבָא פּוּלְחָנָא דִשְׁמַיָּא לְאַתְרֵהּ,

And empower the Holy One, Blessed be He, in His reign and in His majesty.

וְיַמְלִיךְ קוּדְשָׁא בְּרִיךְ הוּא בְּמַלְכוּתֵיהּ וִיקָרֵיהּ

In the world, which He created according to His will.

May He empower His rule in your lifetime, in your days, and in the lifetimes of the entire house of Israel, swiftly and in the near future; and say, Amen.

בְּחַיֵּיכוֹן וּבְיוֹמֵיכוֹן וּבְחַיֵּי דְכָל בֵּית יִשְׂרָאֵל בַּעֲגָלָא וּבִזְמַן קָרִיב. וְאִמְרוּ אָמֵן:

May His great Name be blessed, forever and ever.

יְהֵא שְׁמֵהּ רַבָּא מְבָרַךְ לְעָלַם וּלְעָלְמֵי עָלְמַיָּא:

Blessed, praised, beautified, exalted, elevated, glorified, raised high and lauded be the Name of the Holy One, Blessed is He

יִתְבָּרַךְ. וְיִשְׁתַּבַּח וְיִתְפָּאַר וְיִתְרוֹמַם וְיִתְנַשֵּׂא וְיִתְהַדָּר וְיִתְעַלֶּה וְיִתְהַלָּל שְׁמֵהּ דְּקֻדְשָׁא. בְּרִיךְ הוּא.

Above (during the Ten Days of Penitence, include here: "and beyond") any blessings and hymns, praises and consolations that are uttered in the world; and say, Amen.

לְעֵלָּא מִן כָּל (בעשי"ת לְעֵלָּא לְעֵלָּא מִכָּל) בִּרְכָתָא וְשִׁירָתָא תֻּשְׁבְּחָתָא וְנֶחֱמָתָא דַּאֲמִירָן בְּעָלְמָא. וְאִמְרוּ אָמֵן:

---

3   Cf. B. Shabbat 118b-119a; *Ramo* (16th century), *Orah Hayim* 551:10; Moses Feinstein (20th century), Responsa *Igrot Moshe: Orah Hayim* 1:157; Mordecahi Fogelman (20th century), Responsa *Beit Mordechai* 1:56.

Concerning Israel and concerning its Rabbis
עַל יִשְׂרָאֵל וְעַל רַבָּנָן.

And concerning their students and concerning all the students of their students
וְעַל תַּלְמִידֵיהוֹן וְעַל כָּל תַּלְמִידֵי תַלְמִידֵיהוֹן.

And concerning anyone who is occupied with Torah
וְעַל כָּל מַאן דְּעָסְקִין בְּאוֹרַיְתָא

In this place or in any place
דִּי בְאַתְרָא הָדֵין וְדִי בְכָל אֲתַר וַאֲתַר.

They and you should have
יְהֵא לְהוֹן וּלְכוֹן

Abundant peace, grace, kindness, compassion, long life and plentiful sustenance
שְׁלָמָא רַבָּא חִנָּא וְחִסְדָּא וְרַחֲמִין וְחַיִּין אֲרִיכִין וּמְזוֹנֵי רְוִיחֵי

And salvation before their Father in Heaven (and on Earth) and say, Amen.
וּפֻרְקָנָא מִן קֳדָם אֲבוּהוֹן דִּבִשְׁמַיָּא (וְאַרְעָא) וְאִמְרוּ אָמֵן:

May abundant peace descend from Heaven, and life, upon us and upon all Israel; and say, Amen.
יְהֵא שְׁלָמָא רַבָּא מִן שְׁמַיָּא וְחַיִּים עָלֵינוּ וְעַל כָּל יִשְׂרָאֵל. וְאִמְרוּ אָמֵן:

He Who establishes peace (during the Ten Days of Penitence, say: "The peace") in His high places, may He create peace upon us, and upon all Israel; and say, Amen.
עוֹשֶׂה שָׁלוֹם (בעשי"ת הַשָּׁלוֹם) בִּמְרוֹמָיו הוּא יַעֲשֶׂה שָׁלוֹם עָלֵינוּ וְעַל כָּל יִשְׂרָאֵל וְאִמְרוּ אָמֵן:

K*ADDISH* IS PERHAPS the most famous prayer in the *Siddur* (prayer book). Its recitation by mourners during their period of bereavement and on the occasion of a *yahrzeit* (the anniversary of the death of a close relative),[4] along with its derivative use as a liturgical response to tragedy often included in, for example, Holocaust memorial services, give it a very significant place in Jewish consciousness.[5] It also appears at least twice in all

---

4   I do not discuss the use of *Kaddish* on a *Yahrzeit* here. That is part of a larger story of how the annual commemoration of a relative's – particularly a parent's – death changed in fundamental ways as a result of Jewish mysticism's understanding of what happens to the soul on that day. In short, it is believed that the soul is born into a newer, higher reality each year, and that *Kaddish* aids in this process. That led to the introduction of the *Yahrzeit Kaddish* recitation in the 16th century, against significant opposition. See Ribner, David. "A Note on the Hassidic Observance of the *Yahrzeit* Custom and its Place in the Mourning Process." *Mortality*, 3:2 (1998), pp. 173–180.

5   For a personal memoir about the recitation of *Kaddish* after the loss of a loved one that incorporates a great deal of profound analysis and many of the historical

formal synagogue prayer services, in contexts that do not have anything at all to do with sadness and loss. In point of fact, *Kaddish* is the single most frequently recited text in traditional Jewish worship.

Several variations of *Kaddish* appear in the contemporary *Siddur*. These alternative forms (which are presented in full at the beginning of this chapter) contain a central core section that is the same in all of the variations. Some forms of *Kaddish* differ from the others in the words that appear at the beginning of the liturgy. Others vary in the paragraphs that come after this central section of the prayer. Nonetheless, in all its forms this central core of the text of *Kaddish* remains the same.

Surveying these prayers from shortest to longest, the list of *Kaddish* forms includes, first, the "*Half Kaddish*" (or, more correctly, the "*Abbreviated Kaddish*"). It is recited at the end of various sections of the prayer service, such as following the early morning songs of praise (*Pesukei de-Zimra*), or after reading from the Torah.[6] It, like all recitations of *Kaddish* requires the presence of a *minyan* (quorum of ten), before it can be offered.[7]

Next in size is the "*Full Kaddish*" – without the *Titkabel* paragraph (תתקבל צלותהון, "receive our prayers"). This form of *Kaddish* is recited on rare occasions by the prayer leader, in association with certain special elements of the liturgy. For example, it is offered after the paragraph that begins with the words ואתה קדוש (*Ve-Atah Kadosh*, "and You are holy") when that liturgy is said on *Purim* night in connection with the reading of the Biblical book of Esther.[8] It is also recited after chanting the Biblical book of Lamentations (*Eikhah*), reciting various *Kinot* (dirges) and again offering *Ve-Atah Kadosh* on the night of *Tishah B'Av* (the Ninth of *Av*), the saddest day on the Jewish calendar.[9]

On the other hand, this is actually the most familiar form of the liturgy, because – although it is said only infrequently by the prayer leader – it is also used as the *Mourner's Kaddish*. The *Mourner's Kaddish* appears at least once, if not more frequently, in every prayer service.[10] This includes services that

---

sources and roots of the prayer, see my friend, congregant and board member Leon Wieseltier's *Kaddish* (New York: 1998).

6 Siddur, pp. 86–88, and the note at the top of p. 152.

7 Joseph Caro (16th century), *Shulhan Arukh: Orah Hayim* 53:3, 234:1.

8 See the explanatory note, Siddur, p. 600.

9 Kinot, p. 68.

10 Cf. Siddur, p. 160.

are not part of the usual synagogue routine such as a circumcision, *Kiddush Levanah* and *Birkat ha-Hamah*.[11]

Next in size is *"Kaddish Titkabel"* (the *Full Kaddish* with the *Titkabel* paragraph). This additional paragraph asks God to accept the prayers of "the entire house of Israel." As a rule, every time an *Amidah* (the central prayer of most formal Jewish liturgical services) is recited, a *Kaddish* of this type follows, though other prayers may intervene.[12] The only exception is that in the face of abject mourning, such as when services convene at the home of someone who has lost a close relative,[13] it is deemed inappropriate for that individual to also bear the burden of having to ask God to accept his prayer.[14] The pain that the mourner has suffered gives that mourner – and those praying with him – a special entree to God. On such an occasion the *Full Kaddish* without *Titkabel* is used instead after the *Amidah*.

Kaddish Titkabel is also used to conclude the early morning *Selihot* (penitential prayer service) of the High Holiday period.[15] These additional prayers constitute their own liturgical entity.[16] At their conclusion, each day of Selihot – after beseeching God to forgive all sins even as He comes to judge the world at this time of the year – this form of *Kaddish* is recited, in order to ask the Almighty to accept these special supplications.[17]

The next largest iteration is *"Kaddish de-Rabbanan"* (the *Rabbis' Kaddish*) offered after studying a section from rabbinic literature – particularly if it is

---

11 For a description of these liturgical events, see the chapter on *Aleinu* in this volume.

12 Cf. Siddur, p. 158.

13 Though this is the usual practice today, it was actually once quite controversial; see Responsa Rabbi Akiva Eiger, *Mahadurah Tinyana* #24 (the author lived from 1761–1837); Stern, Betsalel. Responsa *Betsel ha-Khokhman* 4:68 (he lived from 1911–1989) and Yosef, Ovadiah (contemporary scholar). Responsa *Yabi'a Omer* 4 Yoreh De'ah #32.

14 This is also true at *Shaharit* on the saddest day of the year, *Tishah B'Av*, when this paragraph is skipped as well; Kinot, p. 402. Those who object to this practice in a mourner's house (see previous note) see the non-recitation in that venue as different from following this custom on *Tishah B'Av*.

15 *Shulhan Arukh: Orah Hayim* 581:1.

16 Rabbi Menachem Ben Rabbi Yosef Ben Rabbi Yehuda Chazan (12th–13th centuries), *Seder Troyes* #2. He also cites opinions that this form of *Kaddish* should not be used because *Selihot* has no *Amidah*. The present practice is to say *Kaddish Titkabel*.

17 Selihot, p. 50.

aggadic (non-legal) in nature.[18] This *Kaddish* also appears in daily services, at those points where sections from rabbinic texts are recited as part of the liturgy.[19] It does not include the "*Titkabel*" paragraph, but it does add a passage that seeks God's blessings for those who are involved in the study of Torah.[20] This passage reads:

A–Regarding Israel	א–עַל יִשְׂרָאֵל
B–And regarding our Rabbis	ב–וְעַל רַבָּנָן.
C–And regarding their students	ג–וְעַל תַּלְמִידֵיהוֹן
D–And regarding all the students of their students	ד–וְעַל כָּל תַּלְמִידֵי תַלְמִידֵיהוֹן.
E–And regarding anyone who is occupied with Torah	ה–וְעַל כָּל מָאן דְּעָסְקִין בְּאוֹרַיְתָא
F–In this place	ו–דִּי בְאַתְרָא הָדֵין
G–Or in any place	ז–וְדִי בְכָל אֲתַר וַאֲתַר.
H–They and you should have	ח–יְהֵא לְהוֹן וּלְכוֹן
I–Abundant peace, grace, kindness, compassion, long life and plentiful sustenance	ט–שְׁלָמָא רַבָּא חִנָּא וְחִסְדָּא וְרַחֲמִין וְחַיִּין אֲרִיכִין וּמְזוֹנֵי רְוִיחֵי
J–And salvation before their Father in Heaven (and on Earth),	י–וּפֻרְקָנָא מִן קֳדָם אֲבוּהוֹן דְּבִשְׁמַיָּא (וְאַרְעָא)
K–And say, Amen.	כ–וְאִמְרוּ אָמֵן:

Next in length is the "Burial *Kaddish*" recited at a funeral.[21] The burial Kaddish is unique in what we have seen thus far in that the changes to the liturgy are at the beginning of the Kaddish. In the other Kaddish forms that we have seen so far the changes have been made towards the end of the prayer.

---

18   The question of which *Kaddish* form should be said after precisely which text, or whether a text is needed at all for recitation of, for example, *Mourner's Kaddish*, is a large one, which we touch on only briefly here. There are many sources that discuss these issues: cf. Rabbi Yissachar Dov ben Yisrael Lezer Parnass Eilenburg (1550–1623). *Be'er Sheva*: Sotah 49a; note 114 on page 496 of *Peirush Siddur ha-Tefillah la-Rokeah*: *Mishnat Ba-Meh Madlikin* (Jerusalem, 1994); Rabbi Zedakiah ben Rabbi Avraham ha-Rofe (13th century). *Shibbolei ha-Leket: Inyan Tefillah* #8; Rabbi Judah Ben Isaac Ayash (18th century). *Bet Yehudah: Orah Hayim* #31.

19   Cf. Siddur, pp. 52–54.

20   Rabbi David ben Rabbi Yosef Abudraham (13th century), in the section called *Ha-Kaddish u-Pheirusho*, makes this point.

21   Cf. Rabbi Moses Ben Nachman (Nahmanides, 1194–1270). *Torat ha-Adam: Sha'ar ha-Avel: Inyan ha-Hathalah*.

Kaddish in all its iterations is an eschatological prayer. Its call for God to be "magnified and sanctified," to visibly empower His reign in this world and to do so in the very near future – along with other declarations and requests made in the different parts of its various texts – certainly has overt messianic implications. Nonetheless, the extra words that appear in the first paragraph of the Burial *Kaddish* draw an even more graphic and explicit picture of the end of days than anything we have seen before. Even a superficial reading of the following excerpt makes this abundantly clear:

A–In the world, which He will renew,	א–בְּעָלְמָא דהוא עתיד לאתחדתא
B–And will resurrect the dead,	ב–ולאחאה מיתיא,
C–And raise them to life eternal,	ג–ולאסקא לחיי עלמא,
D–And rebuild the city of Jerusalem,	ד–ולמבני קרתא דירושלים,
E–And will establish His sanctuary in it;	ה–ולשכלולי היכליה בגוויה,
F–And will uproot foreign worship from the land,	ו–ולמעקר פולחנא נוכראה מארענא,
G–And put the worship of heaven in place	ז–ולאתבא פולחנא דשמיא לאתרה,
H–And empower the Holy One, Blessed be He, in His reign and in His majesty.	ח–וימליך קודשא בריך הוא במלכותיה ויקריה.

In fact there are very few, if any, texts in the synagogue liturgy that describe and aspire for the messianic era in such dramatic and clear terms.

This same form of *Kaddish* is also recited at a *siyum* (completion) of the study of the Bible.[22] When one studies through all of Biblical literature from the first verse in Genesis to the last sentence in Chronicles, that is cause for a celebration. At such an event special prayers are recited and this type of *Kaddish* is said.

Similarly, at the celebration that comes with completing a tractate of the Talmud or an order of the Mishnah, a related form of *Kaddish* is recited.[23] It

---

22 See nn. 2–3.

23 For a discussion of the rationale for making the completion of a text into a celebration see Rabbi David ben Rabbi Baruch Kalonymus Sperber. Responsa *Afarkasta De-Anya*, 1:154. There are sources that allow for a *siyum* after completing only a tractate from the Mishnah and not a complete order, but in practice that is not usually treated as joyous enough to merit a celebration. For discussion see Stern, op. cit. 4:99.

is essentially the same as the one just described. However, since rabbinic texts – not Biblical texts – have been studied, the additional material from *Kaddish de-Rabbanan* calling for God's blessings to descend on Rabbis and scholars is added to the prayer.

The liturgical parallel created by using the same form of *Kaddish* after completing the study of a sacred book and also when one marks the end of someone's life is quite powerful. Jewish thought often expresses great respect for learning and that respect has, in turn, earned the Jewish People the appellation, the "People of the Book."[24] When the end of one's sojourn on this earth arrives, the book of his or her life is closed; but the respect for the wisdom contained in that book knows no bounds. The education that might be gathered by others through studying this individual's accomplishments; the knowledge that might be gained from analyzing the deceased's lifetime of experiences; the insight that might emerge from reviewing what values this person taught or lived by – these need to be recognized. And the metaphor that equates the life one lives with a sacred book is, therefore, very powerful.

The famous British poet, John Donne (1572–1631), wrote in his *Meditation 17*:

All mankind is of one Author, and is one volume; when one man dies, one chapter is not torn out of the book, but translated into a better language; and every chapter must be so translated; God employs several translators; some pieces are translated by age, some by sickness, some by war, some by justice; but God's hand is in every translation; and His hand shall bind up all our scattered leaves again, for that library where every book shall lie open to one another.

The Jewish tradition of using the same *Kaddish* form at the end of the study of a book and at the end of a life would seem to be a liturgical expression of these poignant sentiments.

One more point about the use of *Kaddish*. We note that many of our descriptions of when it is recited refer to its being said at the "end" of something: a section of the liturgy, a text, a book, or even a life. This usage as a concluding

---

24   The phrase actually originates in the Koran (29:45–49, *Sura Al-Ankabut*) and refers to both Jews and Christians since both hold the Bible as sacred. But Jews have used the term in speaking about themselves in order to express their general love for learning.

prayer – as a final response – is actually found wherever and whenever *Kaddish* makes an appearance today.[25]

To understand why *Kaddish* is used in contemporary Jewish liturgy as described here, we must go back in time to discover its beginnings and its history. In that regard, as we turn to our oldest sources, we find that what is known today as *Kaddish* (sanctification) was once called by a very different name.[26] Rather than being referred to as a prayer of sanctification, which comes from the second word of this liturgy, יתקדש (*yitkaddash* will be sanctified), it was known instead by the most important sentence of the central or core section of the prayer.

May His great Name be blessed forever.	יהא שמיה רבה מברך לעלם ולעלמי עלמיא

That phrase is said today both by the individual reciting *Kaddish* (the Cantor or the mourner), and by the entire congregation.[27] In rabbinic literature, however, it is always described as a congregational response.[28] The origin of the use of this phrase by the congregation takes us back to the Bible. Psalm 113 reads:

Praise God – the servants of God, praise!	הללו יה הללו עבדי ה'
Praise the Name of God.	הללו את שם ה':

---

25 Cf. Maimonides. *Mishneh Torah: Seder Tefilot: Nusah Birkhot ha-Tefillah* and Moses Feinstein. Responsa *Igrot Moshe: Orah Hayim* 1:101. See also Elbogen, p.80.

26 See the sources cited below. In a late rabbinic text, *Yalkut Shimoni*: Isaiah 429, we find *Kaddish* called *Yitgadal ve-Yitkadash* for the first time. This source borrows heavily from the earlier rabbinic material discussed below.

27 Cf. Siddur, p. 52. For discussion of how the prayer leader and the congregation are to recite this sentence see Rabbi Jacob ben Asher (13th–14th century). *Tur: Orah Hayim* # 56; Rabbi Joseph Ben Moses (15th century). *Sefer Leket Yosher* 1:17:3; Rabbi Jacob ben Asher. *Tur: Orah Hayim* # 56; Rabbi Mordechai Halevi (17th century). Responsa *Darkhei Noam: Orah Hayim* #11.

28 The one possible exception is Sifrei: Deuteronomy 306, which reads: ומנין לאומרים יהא שמו הגדול מבורך שעונים אחריהם לעולם ולעולמי עולמים (How do we know that when they say, "May His great Name be blessed" that they respond after them, "forever and ever"?). There is no further context here and so this may simply indicate a congregational response to the one leading the liturgical response to a study session.

May the Name of God be blessed,	יהי שם ה׳ מברך מעתה ועד
from now and forever.	עולם:
From the dawning of the sun in the east until	ממזרח שמש עד מבואו מהלל
its setting in the west God's Name is praised.	שם ה׳:
God is raised above all nations; His	רם על כל גוים ה׳ על השמים
Glory is above the heavens	כבודו:
Who is like God our Lord, Who rises up to sit	מי כה׳ א-להינו המגביהי לשבת:
[on his throne to rule above all creation];	
Who lowers Himself to observe	המשפילי לראות בשמים
the heavens and the earth;	ובארץ:
Who stands up the destitute individual from the	מקימי מעפר דל מאשפת ירים
dust, raises the poor from the garbage heap,	אביון:
To have them sit with the philanthropists,	להושיבי עם נדיבים עם נדיבי
with the generous ones of his people?	עמו:
He establishes the barren woman of the house as	מושיבי עקרת הבית אם הבנים
the joyous mother of the children, praise God.	שמחה הללו י-ה:

As the chapter begins those who serve God are asked to praise Him and His Name. The second verse then makes this declaration:

May the Name of God be blessed, forever.	יהי שם ה׳ מברך מעתה ועד
	עולם

This appears to be the praise of choice for this Psalm. In fact, it should be read as the affirmative response by those in attendance to the request in the first verse, and was probably recited responsively in this way whenever this chapter was used liturgically.

David – who wrote this text, according to Jewish tradition[29] – then goes on to describe the breadth of God's fame and give some examples of His benevolent powers of salvation from difficult circumstances. Thus salvation has now become associated with this affirmative response.

This verse also makes a second appearance in the Bible as part of an intriguing story. In the second chapter of the book of Daniel, we are told that the Babylonian King, Nebuhadnezzer, has a dream that troubles him. He demands of his wise men and soothsayers that they explain to him what it means. Their response is to ask for details of the dream so that they can interpret it.

---

29   B. Baba Bathra 14b. See also B. Pesahim 117a.

This king is no fool, however. He knows that if he describes the dream there will be no shortage of explanations. On the other hand if he withholds the details a true seer should be able to tell him both the dream and its meaning. Anyone who can't do that is not really blessed with the magical, mystical powers that these people claim that they possess.

Not surprisingly none of these seers can meet the king's challenge. The king decrees death on all wise men for this affront. This includes Daniel, the hero of the book that bears his name, who was not present at this conversation with the King.

Then Daniel receives a vision from God that shows him both the King's dream and its meaning. The Bible presents Daniel's response to this vision as follows (the text is in Aramaic, the language of Babylonia):[30]

Then was the mystery revealed to Daniel in a night vision.	אדין לדניאל בחזוא די ליליא רזה גלי
Then Daniel blessed the God of heaven.	אדין דניאל ברך לא־לה שמיא:
Daniel spoke and said, "*Blessed be the Name of God for ever and ever,*	ענה דניאל ואמר להוא שמה די א־להא מברך מן עלמא ועד עלמא
For wisdom and might are His."[31]	די חכמתא וגבורתא די לה היא:

In keeping with David's usage, Daniel offers the italicized phrase in praise of God. He does so in reaction to a moment of great significance that will provide personal salvation from death for him, since he will now be able to respond as the King demanded. At the same time he will be able to show the power of God to everyone in Babylon.

The translation of this phrase into Aramaic, which is how we find it in the liturgy today, is the first step on the road to the contemporary *Kaddish*. Its appearance in the book of Daniel in this way suggests that people in Babylonia in Daniel's time[32] were accustomed to using this sentence as a response to vindication and salvation.[33]

---

30 It is also the language of *Kaddish* for reasons discussed below.

31 Verses 19–20.

32 6th century BCE.

33 See also *Targum* Pseudo-Jonathan: Exodus 15:3, where this phrase is included in the translation/commentary at the beginning of the Song of the Sea. That song is itself

The dream and its meaning are particularly important here. Excerpting the relevant parts of the Biblical text, we will let the source speak for itself:

You, O king, saw, and behold a great image.	אנת מלכא חזה הוית ואלו צלם חד שגיא
This great image, which was mighty and of surpassing brightness, stood before you; and its form was terrifying.	צלמא דכן רב וזיוה יתיר קאם לקבלך ורוה דחיל
This image's head was of fine gold,	הוא צלמא ראשה די דהב טב
His breast and his arms of silver,	חדוהי ודרעוהי די כסף
His belly and his thighs of bronze,	מעוהי ויככתה די נחש
His legs of iron,	שקוהי די פרזל
His feet partly of iron and partly of clay.	רגלוהי מנהין די פרזל ומנהין די חסף
While you looked, a stone was cut out by no hand,	חזה הוית עד די התגזרת אבן די לא בידין
Which struck the image on its iron and clay feet, and broke them in pieces.[34]	ומחת לצלמא על רגלוהי די פרזלא וחספא והדקת המון
Then was the iron, the clay, the bronze, the silver and the gold broken in pieces together, and became like the chaff of the summer threshing floors;	באדין דקו כחדה פרזלא חספא נחשא כספא ודהבא והוו כעור מן אדרי קיט
And the wind carried them away, so that no place was found for them;	ונשא המון רוחא וכל אתר לא השתכח להון
And the stone that struck the image became a great mountain, and filled the whole earth.	ואבנא די מחת לצלמא הות לטור רב ומלת כל ארעא
This is the dream; and we will declare its meaning to the king.	דנה חלמא ופשרה נאמר קדם מלכא
You, O king, are king of kings;	אנת מלכא מלך מלכיא
To whom the God of heaven has given the kingdom, the power, the strength and the glory.[35]	די א־לה שמיא מלכותא חסנא ותקפא ויקרא יהב לך

---

a response to God's miraculous salvation of the Jewish people from the Egyptians. See also Exodus 15:18 and Deuteronomy 6:4.

34 The English expression "feet of clay" derives from these verses.

35 This is the source of the similar line in the Lord's Prayer, but it doesn't appear in *Kaddish*; see discussion below.

And wherever the children of men live, the beasts וּבְכָל דִּי דָירִין בְּנֵי אֲנָשָׁא חֵיוַת

of the field and the birds of the sky has He given to בָּרָא וְעוֹף שְׁמַיָּא יְהַב בִּידָךְ

your hand, and has made you ruler over them all. וְהַשְׁלְטָךְ בְּכָלְּהוֹן

You are this head of gold. אַנְתְּ הוּא רֵאשָׁה דִּי דַהֲבָא

And after you, shall arise another וּבַתְרָךְ תְּקוּם מַלְכוּ אָחֳרִי אֲרַע

kingdom inferior to you, מִנָּךְ

And another third kingdom of bronze, וּמַלְכוּ תְּלִיתָאָה אָחֳרִי דִּי נְחָשָׁא

which shall bear rule over all the earth. דִּי תִשְׁלַט בְּכָל אַרְעָא

And the fourth kingdom shall be strong as iron; וּמַלְכוּ רְבִיעָאָה תֶּהֱוֵה תַקִּיפָה

כְּפַרְזְלָא

Iron breaks in pieces and subdues all things; כָּל קֳבֵל דִּי פַרְזְלָא מְהַדֵּק וְחָשֵׁל

כֹּלָּא

and like iron that breaks, so shall it וּכְפַרְזְלָא דִּי מְרָעַע כָּל אִלֵּין תַּדִּק

break and crush all things. וְתֵרֹעַ

And as you saw the feet and toes, partly וְדִי חֲזַיְתָה רַגְלַיָּא וְאֶצְבְּעָתָא

of potters' clay, and partly of iron, מִנְּהֵן חֲסַף דִּי פֶחָר וּמִנְּהֵן פַּרְזֶל

the kingdom shall be divided; מַלְכוּ פְלִיגָה תֶּהֱוֵה

But there shall be in it of the strength of the iron, וּמִן נִצְבְּתָא דִּי פַרְזְלָא לֶהֱוֵא בַהּ

just as you saw the iron mixed with miry clay. כָּל קֳבֵל דִּי חֲזַיְתָה פַּרְזְלָא מְעָרַב

בַּחֲסַף טִינָא

And as the toes of the feet were partly of וְאֶצְבְּעָת רַגְלַיָּא מִנְּהֵן פַּרְזֶל

iron, and partly of clay, so the kingdom וּמִנְּהֵן חֲסַף מִן קְצָת מַלְכוּתָא

shall be partly strong, and partly brittle. תֶּהֱוֵה תַקִּיפָה וּמִנַּהּ תֶּהֱוֵה תְבִירָה

And as you saw iron mixed with miry clay, they וְדִי חֲזַיְתָ פַּרְזְלָא מְעָרַב בַּחֲסַף

shall mix themselves with the seed of men; טִינָא מִתְעָרְבִין לֶהֱוֹן בִּזְרַע אֲנָשָׁא

But they shall not cleave one to another, וְלָא לֶהֱוֹן דָּבְקִין דְּנָה עִם דְּנָה

just as iron does not mix with clay. הֵא כְדִי פַרְזְלָא לָא מִתְעָרַב עִם

חַסְפָּא

And in the days of these kings shall וּבְיוֹמֵיהוֹן דִּי מַלְכַיָּא אִנּוּן יְקִים

the God of heaven set up a kingdom, אֱ־לָהּ שְׁמַיָּא מַלְכוּ דִּי לְעָלְמִין לָא

which shall never be destroyed; תִתְחַבַּל

And the kingdom shall not be left to other people, וּמַלְכוּתָה לְעַם אָחֳרָן לָא

but it shall break in pieces all these kingdoms, תִשְׁתְּבִק תַּדִּק וְתָסֵיף כָּל אִלֵּין

and consume them all, and it shall stand forever. מַלְכְוָתָא וְהִיא תְּקוּם לְעָלְמַיָּא

Just as you saw that the stone was cut out of כָּל קֳבֵל דִּי חֲזַיְתָ דִּי מִטּוּרָא

of the mountain by no hands, and that אִתְגְּזֶרֶת אֶבֶן דִּי לָא בִידַיִן וְהַדֶּקֶת

it broke in pieces the iron, the bronze,	פרזלא נחשא חספא כספא
the clay, the silver and the gold;	ודהבא
The great God has made known to the	א־לה רב הודע למלכא מה די
king what shall come to pass hereafter;	להוא אחרי דנה
And the dream is certain, and its meaning is sure.[36]	ויציב חלמא ומהימן פשרה

This vision of four kingdoms followed by the coming of the reign of God that will bring the messianic era is an important text that has led to much eschatological speculation. Discussion and debate has centered around the question of which nations are represented by the four kingdoms and about what hints can be found here as to when that ultimate messianic moment will begin.[37]

Looking at the texts of all of the *Kaddish* prayers, from the shortest to the longest iterations, they, too, describe an era of Divine rule and revelation that will emerge with the salvation brought by the coming of the Messiah. In fact, the *Sephardic* and *Nusach Ari*[38] recensions of the prayer explicitly evoke that era in the words ויצמח פורקניה ויקרב משיחה (may His salvation sprout forth and may He bring His Messiah closer) that appear in the first paragraph of their versions of *Kaddish*.[39] Since the core of the prayer comes from this vision in the book of Daniel with the echo of King David's words in the background, we now know why it is so eschatological in nature.

Further, Daniel's reaction to the vision that God gave him establishes the central line of *Kaddish* as a response that comes *after* something significant has occurred or has been said. Another way of looking at this is that the central line of *Kaddish* is said in thanks for being able to accomplish something significant or on the dawn of a new significant era. God gave Daniel the means

---

36 Verses 31–45.

37 Nahmanides (Ramban) on Genesis 14:1 saw the four kingdoms as Babylonia, Persia, Greece and Rome, while Abraham ibn Ezra (Daniel 2:39) saw Greece and Rome together as one of the kingdoms, and included Islam as the fourth Kingdom. For those who wish to read contemporary history into this chapter of Daniel this is a particularly pointed debate. See Roth, Norman. *Medieval Jewish Civilization*. New York: 2002, p. 529.

38 A prayer rite that follows the teachings of Rabbi Isaac Luria, who lived in the 16th century, best known today from the prayer book used by *Chabad Hasidim*. *Siddur Tehillat Hashem*. Brooklyn: 2001, cf., p. 26.

39 Nusach Sefard Siddur, pp. 54–56. The earliest appearance of a version of this phrase is in Davidson, I. *Siddur Rav Saadiah Gaon*. Jerusalem: 1978, p.35. Saadiah Gaon lived from 882 or 892 to 942 C.E.

to accomplish his own salvation when God told him what the dream was and how it was to be interpreted. Daniel then responded by expressing God's praises using a phrase that is central to Kaddish as we know it. In short, this Biblical story and Daniel's role in it set the tone for the wording and later liturgical usage of *Kaddish*.

The first words of *Kaddish*, יתגדל ויתקדש (magnified and sanctified), also appear in the Bible. *Ezekiel*, chapter thirty-eight, concludes with this statement:

Thus will I magnify Myself, and sanctify Myself; and I will make Myself known in the eyes of many nations, and they shall know that I am the Lord.[40]	והתגדלתי והתקדשתי ונודעתי לעיני גוים רבים וידעו כי אני ה'

Again these words are part of an eschatological text. This chapter describes the final conflict between good and evil, the war of Gog and Magog – the ultimate Armageddon when good will emerge triumphant. This description *ends* with this verse that then takes a very prominent position in *Kaddish* – the prayer that serves as a concluding prayer wherever it appears. So, too, the messianic theme of this Biblical chapter also finds a central place in *Kaddish*.

These texts, taken from Daniel and Ezekiel, speak of dramatic prophetic visions and of great eschatological battles. If we are not yet in the world of mysticism, we are certainly close to it.[41]

We can take the last step into the mystical world by reminding ourselves that

Blessed be the Name of His glorious kingdom for ever and ever,[42]	ברוך שם כבוד מלכותו לעולם ועד

a later development and the rough Hebrew equivalent of:

May his great Name be blessed, forever and ever,	יהא שמיה רבה מברך לעלם ולעלמי עלמיא

---

40   V. 23.

41   See the chapters on Messiah (pp. 98–109) and on Mysticism (pp. 156–163) in my *Contemporary Orthodox Judaism's Response to Modernity*. Jersey City: 2004.

42   Siddur, p. 90.

which itself developed from another similar phrase:[43]

May the Name of God be blessed, now and forever.	יהי שם ה' מברך מעתה ועד עולם

is – as we saw in the chapter on *Shema* – the response of the angels to the earthly congregation's proclamation of:

Hear O Israel Hashem our God Hashem is One.[44]	שמע ישראל ה' א־להנו ה' אחד

Once we are dealing with angelic responses there is no longer any doubt that we are in the universe of the mystical. In keeping with what we have seen thus far, this very similar sentence is used as a response to something significant: the daily proclamation of the Jew's belief in God. It is also, as discussed, the "beautiful tiara" and the "spicy pudding" that was "taken" by Moses from heaven – at some personal risk – and brought to the Jewish people.[45]

Because of this "theft" from on high, it is recited in a whisper on most days of the year. It is only said out loud in the synagogue on *Yom Kippur* (the Day of Atonement). On that day the Jewish people are considered to be like angels, and so they recite this liturgy as it is done in heaven.[46] On the other hand, this phrase was used – in full voice[47] – in the Temple itself in place of *Amen* at all times; but this was true only in the Temple.[48]

This leads to an obvious question. Despite all of the hesitation about offering this response out loud in *Shema*, and in the face of limiting its general use only to the Temple, the parallel Aramaic phrase is proclaimed in full voice over and over again when the various forms of *Kaddish* are said on a daily basis. The number of these recitations changes from day to day. The total depends on whether or not a holiday or other special occasion is being celebrated; but

---

43   Nehemiah 9:5 represents a further development that includes more words from *Kaddish,* but it does not impact our story in any dramatic way so we do not discuss it in the body of this chapter.

44   Deuteronomy 6:4. On the usage of this verse as an angelic response to *Shema*, see Deuteronomy Rabbah: *Parshat Va'ethanan.* Jerusalem: 1940.

45   Deuteronomy Rabbah, ad. loc.; B. Pesahim 56a.

46   See also Deuteronomy Rabbah, ibid., Vilna: 1878.

47   M. Yoma 3:8.

48   See Berakhot 53b and Rashi, ad. loc., sv. *ve'yevarkhu.*

there are never less than thirteen instances within any given twenty-four-hour period of time when this sentence is heard in the synagogue.[49] Why should there be this dramatic difference in liturgical practice when it comes to these two similar sentences?

There appear to be at least three reasons as to why this difference exists – and all three emerge from the world view of early Jewish mysticism. First, the hesitation about reciting ברוך שם (barukh Shem) out loud in *Shema* comes from it having been "stolen" from on high. Presumably the heavenly hosts would be angry if they heard the Jewish people using it at a time when they are not part of the angelic choir as they are on *Yom Kippur*. On the other hand, Daniel's response – even though it is quite similar – came from Daniel himself, who was in this world when he offered it, and, as such, it should be fair game for others to use as well.[50]

Second, and this is an important element in many parts of the liturgy, some rabbinic texts teach that angels do not understand Aramaic.[51] Therefore, they would not be aware that their precious phrase is being used in this way in *Kaddish*.[52] That would not be true when the phrase is recited in Hebrew as it is in *Shema*. Even if, as discussed below, the choice of Aramaic for *Kaddish* was motivated by the fact that this was the language spoken by most Jews at that time,[53] nonetheless the presence of this sentence in Aramaic would allow

---

49 That is the number in contemporary *Ashkenazi* practice.

50 See Haas, Israel. "Kaddish Yatom." In *Morasha* 2, 1972, p. 91. Minor differences are very significant in *Heikhalot* literature. See the discussion of the angels taking three words to enter God's presence as opposed to human beings needing no more than two words to do so in the chapter on *Shema* in this volume.

51 This idea appears in many sources, cf. Sotah 33a. See Haas, p. 96 for discussion and various sources that explain the importance of this for *Kaddish*, and see Yahalom, Joseph. "Angels Do Not Understand Aramaic: on the literary use of Jewish Palestinian Aramaic in late antiquity." *Journal of Jewish Studies* 47:1 (1996): pp. 33–44 for opinions and evidence that challenge this idea.

52 *Mahzor Vitri* #87. For a contemporary restatement of this explanation see Rabbi Eliezer Waldenberg. Responsa *Tsits Eliezer* 14:1. See also Rabbi Aharon ben Jacob Ha-Cohen. *Kol Bo* #7, that in the end of days human beings will be greater than angels. Therefore, if this prayer that asks God to bring that time period into existence were in Hebrew, the angels would understand it and would try to garble it before it got through, to prevent this from happening.

53 Cf. Tosefot: Berakhot 3a, sv. *ve-onin*. This source expressly disagrees with the "angels don't understand Aramaic" theory. See also Rabbi Elazar Of Worms (1130–1260). *Peirush Siddur ha-Tefillah la-Rokeah* #77, p. 441. He also explains why the last line

mystically oriented Jews to embrace the "out loud" proclamation of this text, while hesitating about using the Hebrew translation of this phrase that appears in *Shema* in the same way.[54]

Third, in discussing this prayer we stand squarely in the world of mysticism. Perhaps the answer lies in a more global understanding of the liturgical realities of that universe. We have seen in our discussion of *Aleinu* that the rules of prayer as presented in rabbinic texts do not always apply in the same way when we read about worship in mystical works. Therefore, the dynamic that results in an inaudible recitation of this phrase in *Shema* may lead to a different conclusion when reciting *Kaddish*.

Perhaps we can simply say that as the prayers carry the supplicant heavenward, as recitation and study of rabbinic texts makes the individual more spiritual, as those who have suffered a loss accompany a friend or loved one on their final journey to the next world, they can be seen to enter a mystical realm where they can respond as the angels do. Since *Kaddish* is a prayer of conclusion it always appears after the students or supplicants have already taken their mystical journey through study or worship. On the other hand, *Shema* may only mark the beginning of that spiritual trek.[55]

The more "accomplished" mystical reality of *Kaddish* is reflected in many rabbinic sources that speak of the spiritual power of the יהא שמיה רבה (*yehei Shmei Rabah*) phrase. For example, this source from the Babylonian Talmud tells us:

A–Whenever Israel goes into the synagogues and academies	א–אלא בשעה שישראל נכנסין לבתי כנסיות ולבתי מדרשות
B–And responds, "May His great Name be blessed,"	ב–ועונין יהא שמיה הגדול מבורך

---

   of *Kaddish* is in Hebrew. Also see *Mahzor Vitry* #128 for more general explanations of why some prayers may be said in Aramaic.

54 *Mahzor Vitry,* based on a source that appears on B. Berakhot 3a that we will discuss shortly, claims that if this line is recited in Hebrew so that the angels can understand it, it discomfits them because they do not want to see God respond with anguish as they know He will. They therefore attempt to garble it before it gets to God. Hence the Aramaic recitation.

55 See n. 50 above and the discussion in the *Shema* chapter in this volume. Also see Haas, loc. cit. for a discussion of the superiority of human beings over angels reflected in *Kaddish*.

C–The Holy One, Blessed be He, nods His head and says,	ג–הקדוש ברוך הוא מנענע ראשו ואומר:
D–"Happy is the king who is thus praised in this house.	ד–אשרי המלך שמקלסין אותו בביתו כך,
E–Woe to the father, who had to banish his children,[56]	ה–מה לו לאב שהגלה את בניו,
F–And woe to the children who had to be banished from the table of their father."[57]	ו–ואוי להם לבנים שגלו מעל שולחן אביהם.

We previously discussed the significance of the anthropomorphic image of God nodding His head when responding to human prayers in the *Anim Zemirot* chapter. This action represents a profound statement of divine approbation that is the desired reaction sought by anyone seeking a mystical connection with God.

This mystical connection with God that comes through recitation of יהא שמיה רבה receives even more dramatic expression in the following passage from *Heikhalot* literature:

A–And He created a [celestial] wheel on the Earth	א–ובר אופן אחד בארץ
B–And its top is opposite the holy creatures	ב–וראשו כנגד חיות הקודש
C–And it serves as the translator between Israel and their Father in Heaven[58]	ג–והוא מתורגמן בין ישראל לאביהן שבשמים
D–As it says, "and behold there was a wheel on the Earth next to the creatures"[59]	ד–שנאמר וארא והנה אופן אחד בארץ אצל החיות,
E–And its name is Sandalphon	ה–וסנדלפון שמו
F–Who ties crowns for the Master of Glory	ו–שקושר כתרים לבעל הכבוד
G–Made from the *Kedushot*, the "Blessed is He" and the "*Amen* May His great Name . . ." that the children of Israel respond in the synagogues.[60]	ז–מקדושות וברוך הוא ואמן יהא שמיה רבא שעונין בני ישראל בבתי כנסיות,

---

56 This is the line that indicates God's anguish; see n. 54.

57 B. Berakhot 3a.

58 Apparently Sandalphon does understand Aramaic and translates from that language so that the prayers can be used to construct the crowns described here.

59 Ezekiel 1:15.

60 For a discussion of crowns of this sort see the chapter on the Song of Glory.

H–And He causes the crown to swear	ח–ומשביע את הכתר בשם
by means of the explicit Name.[61]	המפורש
I–And it goes and rises upon	ט–והולך ועולה לו בראש
the head of the Master.	האדון,
J–From here the sages said, "Whoever does away	י–מכאן אמרו חכמים כל
with *Kaddish* and *Barekhu* and '*Amen* May His	המבטל קדיש וברכו ואמן יהא
great Name . . .' causes the tiara to be diminished.	שמיה רבא גורם למעט העטרה
K–And is punished by excommunication	כ–וחייב נדוי
L–Until he repents and brings a sacrifice before	ל–עד שישוב ויביא קרבן לפני
the righteous in the eschatological future."[62]	הצדיקים לעתיד לבוא.

In corresponding fashion recitation of יהא שמיה רבא has a profound positive effect on the supplicant's standing in heaven.

A–Rabbi Joshua b. Levi said:	א–אמר רבי יהושע בן לוי:
B–"He who responds, '*Amen*, May His great	ב–כל העונה אמן יהא שמיה
Name . . .' with all his might,	רבא מברך בכל כחו
C–His decreed sentence is torn up,	ג–קורעין לו גזר דינו,
D–As it is said, 'When retribution was	ד–שנאמר בפרע פרעות
annulled in Israel, for that the people offered	בישראל בהתנדב עם ברכו ה'.
themselves willingly, Bless ye the Lord'[63]	
E–Why 'when retribution was annulled' [i.e.,	ה–מאי טעמא בפרע פרעות
why is there no punishment being meted out]?	
F–Because they blessed the Lord."	ו–משום דברכו ה'.
G–Rabbi Hiyya b. Abba said in	ז–רבי חייא בר אבא אמר רבי
Rabbi Johanan's name:	יוחנן:
H–"Even if he has a taint of idolatry,	ח–אפילו יש בו שמץ של עבודה
	זרה
I–He is forgiven:	ט–מוחלין לו,
J–It is written here, 'When retribution	י–כתיב הכא בפרע פרעות
was annulled [*bifroa pera'oth*]';	

---

61 Causing celestial creatures to swear, which means controlling their behavior, is a major theme in *Heikhalot* literature; see Schaefer, Peter. *The Hidden and Manifest God*. Albany: 1992. For a 12th–13th century discussion of using this mystical technique and the dangers in doing so, see Rabbi Jacob of Marvege's Responsa *Min Hashamayim* #9.

62 Eisenstein, Judah. *Otsar ha-Midrashim*. Tel Aviv: 1969, p. 253.

63 Judges 5:2.

K–Whilst elsewhere [in connection with the idolatrous sin of the golden calf], it is written,[64] '[And Moses saw that the people] were broken loose [*parua*].'"[65]

כ–וכתיב התם כי פרע הוא.

As a result of this source and its call for יהא שמיה רבא to be said "with all one's might," in some synagogues the decibel level achieved during this recitation is significantly louder than at any other time during the services. This is in remarkable contrast to the almost inaudible expression of the similar ברוך שם sentence every day of the year except on *Yom Kippur* when it, too, is often said "with all one's might."

The claim that יהא שמיה רבא can affect God's decrees at any point in time is restated even more forcefully in a Midrash that reads as follows:

A–And not only that,

א–ולא עוד

B–But at the time that they answer '*Amen*, May His great Name be blessed . . .'

ב–אלא בשעה שעונין אמן יהא שמיה רבא מברך,

C–Even if their decree has been sealed,

ג–אפילו נחתם גזר דינם

D–I forgive and atone their sins for them.[66]

ד–אני מוחל ומכפר להם עונותיהם.

This means that even a "final" decision by God can still be changed by using this response.

It is no wonder that the Babylonian Talmud concludes:

If one [in a dream] answers, "May His great Name be blessed," he may be assured that he has a share in the world to come.[67]

העונה יהא שמיה רבא מברך מובטח לו שהוא בן העולם הבא

The impact of יהא שמיה רבא receives perhaps its most dramatic expression in this text, which is again from *Heikhalot* literature:

---

64   Exodus 32:25.
65   B. Shabbat 119b.
66   Midrash Mishlei: Parsha 10.
67   B. Berakhot 57a.

A–In the eschatological future the Holy One Blessed be He will reveal the [esoteric] reasons for [the teachings of] the Torah to Israel

א–לעתיד לבוא מגלה הקדוש ברוך הוא טעמי תורה לישראל
...

B–And David will recite a song before the Holy One Blessed be He

ב–ואומר דוד שירה לפני הקדוש ברוך הוא

C–And the righteous will respond after him,

ג–ועונין אחריו הצדיקים

D–"May His great Name be blessed, forever and ever. Let [Him] be blessed."[68]

ד–אמן יהא שמיה רבה מברך לעלם ולעלמי עלמיא יתברך,

E–From the midst of the Garden of Eden

ה–מתוך גן עדן,

F–And the sinners of Israel respond *Amen* from the midst of Hell.

ו–ופושעי ישראל עונין אמן מתוך גיהנם.

G–Immediately the Holy One Blessed be He says to the angels,

ז–מיד אומר הקדוש ברוך הוא למלאכים

H–"Who are these who respond *Amen* from Hell?"

ח–מי הם אלו שעונין אמן מתוך גיהנם?

I–He said before Him,

ט–אומר לפניו

J–"Master of the Universe,

י–רבונו של עולם

K–These are the sinners of Israel.

כ–הללו פושעי ישראל

L–Even though they are in great distress, they strengthen themselves and say *Amen* before You."

ל–שאף על פי שהם בצרה גדולה מתחזקים ואומרין לפניך אמן.

M–Immediately the Holy One Blessed be He said to the angels,

מ–מיד אומר הקדוש ברוך הוא למלאכים

---

68 I believe this is the earliest source that adds the word *Yitbarakh* to the end of this sentence as is the custom in some circles. This is done as an affirmation and an emphatic counterpoint to this central response, even though it makes no contextual or grammatical sense within the prayer itself. Nonetheless, *Seder Rav Amram Gaon* (9th century), in *Keriyat Shema U-Virkotehah* and *Tsiduk ha-Din*, reads this part of Kaddish as: לעלם ולעלמי עלמיא יתברך אמן וישתבח ... So, too, Maimonides' *Seder Tefilot: Nusah ha-Kaddish* cites the same reading. See also *Shulhan Arukh: Orah Hayim* 56:3 and Rabbi Israel Meir Ha-Kohen Kagan (1839–1933). *Mishnah Berurah*, ad. loc. The latter cites Elijah of Vilna as being opposed to this practice because of the grammatical issues mentioned here. For discussion see Yaakov Gartner. "Ha-Ma'aneh be-Kaddish 'Yehei Shmei Rabbah Mevarakh." *Sidra* 11 (1995): pp. 39–53. Unfortunately, Gartner missed this source.

N–"Open the gates of the Garden of Eden for them and let them come and sing before Me,"	נ–פתחו להם שערי גן עדן
	ויבואו ויזמרו לפני
O–As it says, "Open the gates and let the righteous nation, protector of the faith, enter."[69]	ס–שנאמר פתחו שערים ויבא
	גוי צדיק שומר אמונים,
P–Do not read this as "protector of the faith" [shomer emunim], but rather as "those who recite Amens" [she'omrim Ameinim].[70]	ע–אל תקרי שומר אמונים אלא
	שאומרים אמנים

In a liturgical context, *Amen* is a word offered by a respondent to indicate his agreement and full participation in the prayer that has just been said.[71] One can even effectively recite a prayer or blessing simply by answering *Amen* to someone else's recitation of it.[72] Those in Hell are, therefore, joining with the righteous and saying the central line of *Kaddish* when they are heard from purgatory in this text.[73] That is sufficient to allow them to escape their final punishment.

We will discuss the power of *Kaddish* to affect the fate of one who has already passed from this world at length below. But even here, an understanding that those in purgatory could join the chorus of the righteous, and then be invited to sing before God in this way, is another testimony to the great impact that יהא שמיה רבה can have in heaven according to early Jewish mystics.

Eventually this phrase achieves the ultimate stature that any liturgy can possibly aspire to in rabbinic literature. B. Sotah (49a) says:

| A–How, in that case, can the world endure? | א–ואלא עלמא אמאי קא |
| | מקיים? |

---

69   Isaiah 26:2.

70   Eisenstein, loc. cit., p. 84. Some of this material also appears on B. Shabbat 119b in connection with the source from the same page cited above.

71   This goes back to its first appearances in the Bible: Numbers 5:22, Deuteronomy 27:15–26.

72   Maimonides. *Mishnah Torah: Hilkhot Berakhot* 1:11.

73   One could read this text to mean that the sinners are saying *Amen* to David's song. But Rabbi Moses Ben Joseph Trani (1500–1580), in Responsa *Mabit* #117, reads as suggested here. See also Rabbi Menashe Klein (contemporary). *Mishneh Halakhot* 15:60

74   This is the prayer known today by its first words, *Uva le-Tsion Go'eil* (Siddur,

B–Through the *Kedushah* recited toward
the end of the morning services,[74]

C–And through "May His great Name
…" recited after studying *Aggadah*;[75]

ב–אקדושה דסידרא

ג–ואיהא שמיה רבא דאגדתא

Returning to *Kaddish* itself, and given our previous discussion of the escha-tological meaning and overall importance of this prayer, we – not surprisingly – find this sentence having a direct impact on the Messiah in *Heikhalot* literature:

A–At the moment that the Messiah
goes out and grasps the four rings [of
the Divine throne] and gives voice,

א–בעת שהמשיח יוצא ואוחז
בארבע הטבעות ונותן קולו

B–At that point the entire heaven
that is over the garden trembles

ב–אזי מזדעזע כל הרקיע שעל
הגן

C–And seven angels stand in wait by him

ג–ושבעה מלאכים מזומנים
אצלו

D–And they say to him: "Chosen
one of God, be silent.

ד–ואומרים לו בחיר ה' החרש!

E–For the time when the evil kingdom will
be uprooted from its place has arrived."

ה–כי כבר הגיע זמן מלכות
הרשעה שתעקר ממקומה

F–And the voice is heard from the
synagogues and academies.

ו–והקול נשמע מבתי כנסיות
ובתי מדרשות

G–For they say with all their might: "*Amen*. May
His great Name be blessed, forever and ever."[76]

ז–שאומרין בכל כוחן אמן יהא
שמיה רבה מברך לעלם ולעולמי
עולמים,

H–At that moment the Holy One Blessed be He
causes all the firmaments [heavens] to tremble.

ח–אזי הקדוש ברוך הוא מזעזע
כל הרקיעים

---

pp. 154–156), which describes the prayers of the angels in heaven. The verses that they use are known as *Kedushah* and are also those that appear in the liturgy called *Kedushah* recited during the repetition of the *Amidah* (Cf. *Siddur*, p. 100).

75 This text seems to require or at least to prefer aggadic material before one recites *Kaddish* but see below.

76 Presumably during the recitation of *Kaddish*.

I–And He causes two tears to	ט–ומוריד שתי דמעות לים
fall into the great ocean	הגדול,
J–And the righteous enter	י–והצדיקים נכנסים
K. And the Messiah enters into that Sanctuary	כ–והמשיח נכנס לאותו היכל
[heaven] that is called[77] the "Bird's Nest."[78]	הנקרא קן צפור.

From a mystical perspective this sentence and entire prayer have obviously been granted an exalted place in Jewish liturgy. Further, we have now encountered a second source that gives us another reason why many people have the custom of reciting יהא שמיה רבא as loudly as they can. We certainly have come a long way from the daily whispered recitation of ברוך שם כבוד מלכותו לעולם ועד to proclaiming at the top of one's lungs יהא שמיה רבה מברך לעלם ולעלמי ולעלמי עלמיא (with the possible addition of יתברך).

One final mystical source will bring us back to the earthly history of this prayer.

A–Rabbi Ishmael said:	א–רבי ישמעאל אומר
B–At the time when Israel gathers in the	ב–בשעה שישראל נאספין
academies and they hear *Aggadah* from a Sage,	בבתי מדרשות ושומעין אגדה
	מפי חכם,
C–And after that they respond: "May	ג–ואחר כך עונין אמן יהא שמיה
His great Name be blessed,"	רבא מברך,
D–At that time the Holy One	ד–באותה שעה הקדוש ברוך
Blessed be He rejoices[79]	הוא שמח
E–And is raised in His world.	ה–ומתעלה בעולמו,
F–And He says to the ministering angels,	ו–ואומר למלאכי השרת
G–"Come and see	ז–בואו וראו

---

77 Deuteronomy 22:6–7. The image of the bird's nest, where the mother bird is chased away before the baby birds or eggs are taken, can serve as a promise that no matter what persecutions the "evil kingdom" brings upon the Jewish people there will still be a saving remnant. That would seem to be its meaning here.

78 Eisenstein, loc. cit.

79 This would seem to contradict *Mahzor Vitry*'s understanding that the angels see this response as causing God anguish. See n. 54.

80 The angels do not understand what the Jews have said until God or Sandalphon translates for them since this line is in Aramaic. In truth mystical sources are often inconsistent on details like this and it may not always be necessary to reconcile these

H–This people that I created in My world, how much they praise Me."[80]	ח–עם זו שיצרתי בעולמי כמה הן משבחין אותי,
I–At that moment they clothe Him in magnificence and beauty	ט–באותה שעה מלבישין אותו הוד והדר,
J–For this reason it says:[81] "In the multitudes of the people is the beauty of the King."[82]	י–לכך נאמר ברב עם הדרת מלך.

This text and the one from B. Sotah discussed just above tell us that *Kaddish* began as a prayer said after a study session, and, in particular, after one that includes material that comes from the non-legal texts of Jewish tradition.[83] So, too, the source that describes how the souls of the wicked will be redeemed from purgatory portrays יהא שמיה רבא as a response recited after God teaches the "reasons of the Torah" (טעמי תורה Taamei Torah). None of these early mentions of the prayer ever refers to it as a mourner's liturgy – that will come later in Jewish history and follow a different historical path that we will discuss.

At this point we need to remind ourselves of two other important aspects of *Kaddish*. As indicated by the words of the prayer, and as we have seen in two of the *Heikhalot* texts,[84] *Kaddish* is a prayer that has strong messianic and eschatological associations.

Further, one of the iterations of *Kaddish* is *Kaddish de-Rabbanan*. This is the version recited today after a study session. It includes words that are unique to this form of the prayer. These words ask for various blessings of life, peace, salvation and mercy to come to Rabbis, students and anyone else involved in Torah study, whether in the location where this study has just been concluded or anywhere else.

In addition, the evil kingdom referenced in the source that tells of the Messiah and his powerful voice can refer to Rome or other powers that have persecuted the Jewish people, but it usually refers to the Hadrianic persecutions

---

differences. We have seen several examples of these inconsistencies throughout this volume.

81 Mishlei 14:28.

82 Midrash Mishlei, ad. loc.

83 See n. 18. Also see Rabbi Jacob ben Asher (*Tur: Orah Hayim* # 579), who mentions reciting the *Rabbis' Kaddish* as part of services after the "sermon" is delivered and before the Torah is returned to the Ark on a fast day.

84 Both from Eisenstein, p. 84.

that occurred from 135–138 C.E. in the aftermath of the Bar Kokhba rebellion.[85] A quick review of the history surrounding these events is in order here.

In the decades before Hadrian became emperor in Rome, there had been at least two extremely violent conflicts between the Romans and the Jews. These were, first, the "Great War" – which began in 66 C.E. – that led to the destruction of the Temple four years later. Shortly thereafter, a series of conflicts known as the Kitos Wars broke out around the Middle East between Jews and Romans in the years 115–119 C.E. Then, during his reign he had to suppress the Bar Kokhba rebellion, which took a bloody toll on each side.[86]

Hadrian decided that the reason why the Jews rebelled against the Romans every couple of decades or so, and more importantly why they often met with enough success to at least partially destabilize the Roman empire before ultimately being suppressed, was because of their commitment to their faith. Do away with that faith, Hadrian thought, and the problem would be solved.[87]

As a result, during the three years from the defeat of Bar Kokhba until Hadrian's death, this emperor was responsible for the murder of many Jews. He made important Jewish practices such as Torah study, ordination of Rabbis and circumcision illegal under penalty of death. Nonetheless, we know that many Jews – at great risk and cost – tried to practice their faith anyway.[88]

For example, there is a well known story of ten rabbinic martyrs whose deaths are memorialized in several medieval texts, versions of which find their

---

85 Cf. B. Berakhot 61b, B. Shabbat 130a, B. Baba Bathra 60b. See Michael Weitzman. "Tefillat ha-Kaddish ve-ha-Peshititah le-Divrei ha-Yamim." In *Hikrei ever ve-Arav*, edited by H. Ben-Shamai, Tel Aviv: 1993, pp. 261–291. This source says that the earliest name from rabbinic history cited in a text that includes a phrase from *Kaddish* is Rabbi Jose b. Halafta who lived in this era.

86 There are many books and articles on this subject: cf. Alon, Gedaliah. *The Jews in their Land in the Talmudic Age*. Harvard, 1980; and Cohen, Shaye J. D. "Judaism under Roman Domination: From the Hasmoneans through the Destruction of the Second Temple." In Visotzky. *From Mesopotamia to Modernity*, edited by Burton L. and Fishman, David E. Boulder, CO: 1999, pp. 57–69.

87 Again there is a great deal of literature on this subject; cf. Bowersock, Glen Warren. "A Roman perspective on the Bar Kochba war." In *Approaches to Ancient Judaism*. II, edited by William Scott Green, Chico: 1980, pp. 131–141; Barnard, Leslie William. "Hadrian and Judaism." In *Journal of Religious History* 5 (1969): pp. 285–298.

88 See the sources cited in n. 85. Also, B. Sanhedrin 13b-14 and B. Avodah Zarah 18a, among others.

way into the Ninth of Av and *Yom Kippur* liturgies.[89] There is no historical basis for uniting their deaths into one narrative or for seeing their martyrdoms as part of one story. On the other hand, rabbinic literature ascribes the terrible deaths of at least some of these ten to the Hadrianic period and often to their attempts to defy Hadrian's decrees.[90]

It would not be surprising that a group study session held under these extreme circumstances would conclude with a prayer that yearns for God's re-established holy presence in this world and for the coming of the messianic era. Especially since this liturgy's central response comes from David's call to praise God at times of salvation and from Daniel's words when he was miraculously saved from death by Divine intervention, both of which fit perfectly in this context. The Jews certainly needed miraculous salvation at this point in history. Evoking these sources might well be thought to influence God to act to help his people. It also makes sense that if specific words appear in this liturgy designed to bless the Rabbis and those who are involved in Torah study, that these words would ask for blessings of life, peace, salvation and mercy on their behalf in the face of the then present danger. This makes the *Rabbis' Kaddish* the oldest form of the prayer that we possess.

In addition, in order to maximize the involvement of as many people as possible, this prayer was recited in Aramaic.[91] This is the language that was most familiar to the common people at that time. In this era there was widespread use of the *Meturgamon*, who translated the Torah readings in the synagogue and the Rabbis' teachings into Aramaic.[92] That, too, is an indication that using this language instead of Hebrew opened the door to the largest number of Jews being able to fully understand the liturgy.

Also, given the Rabbinic claim that angels do not understand Aramaic this prayer would have a special cachet. Prayers offered to the Almighty in this language travel directly to God, without angelic intervention or mediation. That would naturally contribute to the association of mystical powers with this prayer as we have seen in the sources cited above.

Reciting this prayer specifically after the study of aggadic material also fits

---

89   Kinot, p. 248; Mahzor YK, p. 586.

90   For a thorough treatment of these martyrs and the literature that grew around them as well as for another source that discusses the history of the period, see Welner, Alter. *Asseret Harugei Malkhut: ba-Midrash uva-Piyut.* Jerusalem: 2005.

91   See nn. 51–54.

92   Cf. M. Megillah 4:4, 10; Tosefta Megillah 3:41; *Masekhet Soferim*, 18:5–6

well here, as much of that material incorporates teachings of consolation, condemnation of gentiles, praise of the Jews and discussions of the messianic era.[93] This would be particularly welcome in Hadrianic times and a natural lead-in to the themes of *Kaddish*.

Again, this appears to be the oldest use of the prayer as a complete liturgy that goes beyond its core responsive line. For the reasons cited and some others discussed below, dating the prayer to use at study sessions in the Hadrianic era makes sense. It is also used in this way even today, though there seems to be a recent return to this practice. Twenty years ago the study sessions that I remember did not usually conclude with *Kaddish*. Today more and more of them do.[94]

Use of *Kaddish* after study can also be found at a *siyum* – when one concludes one's learning of the entire Bible, an order of the Mishnah or a tractate of the Talmud.[95] As opposed to the general practice of reciting *Kaddish* after Torah study, which appears to have gone through a period of some neglect, this use of the prayer seems to have always been in vogue across the generations. Perhaps the fact that there is often a public celebration that includes recitation of *Kaddish* and other special prayers at a *siyum* ensured its continuous liturgical presence in this way.

The *Siyum Kaddish* includes a section that tells us explicitly that at least the words of this section come from a time when Jerusalem was a city in ruins and foreign worship was rampant in the land of Israel. It also looks forward to the resurrection of the dead, and to being reunited with them in a rebuilt Jerusalem. When combined with our analysis of *Kaddish de-Rabbanan* (the unique section of the *Rabbis' Kaddish* is also included at a *siyum* for a rabbinic text), and the sense that it emerged from a world in which persecution and murder of Jews involved in Torah study was rampant, this too fits well with the era of Hadrian. As we shall see, some used the *Rabbis' Kaddish* with the special

---

93   See Eilenburg, loc. cit., who claims, based on Sotah 40a, that significantly more people are drawn to the study of *Aggadah* than are drawn to study of law. That would fit with the agenda of involving as many people as possible in Torah study and in the prayer in this era. See also Rabbi Chaim Yosef David Azulai (1724–1806) *Birkei Yosef: Orah Hayim* #55, that *Aggadah* "draws the heart." See Elbogen, p. 80, who claims that it was mandatory for these lectures to conclude with eschatological words of consolation and that *Kaddish* grew out of that practice. Nonetheless he sees the prayer as significantly older than I do. See Jacobson, loc. cit., pp. 369–370 for other opinions.

94   Rabbi Jacob Ben Moses Moellin (1360–1427). Responsa *Maharil* #64 and Responsa *Maharil Hachadashot* #28 – This author says that reciting the *Rabbis' Kaddish* fell into disuse because people were not familiar with it.

95   See nn. 2, 3 and 23.

section of the *Siyum Kaddish* after any study of a rabbinic text, not just at a *siyum*. That would make it even more identifiable as a Hadrianic era liturgy.

Finally, the sources cited thus far all speak of this prayer as being recited in "synagogues and academies" and never in the Temple, despite the similarity between its central sentence and the general response to prayers that was offered there. This indicates a post-Temple origin for the prayer in a form that is at least similar to the one that we know. We will have a bit more to say about this below when we discuss the parallels between *Kaddish* and the "Lord's Prayer."

From recitation at the end of Torah study, we move to the place that *Kaddish* occupies within formal prayer. In keeping with its connection to learning, *Kaddish* was first used in the synagogue after Torah reading.[96] It also found a place at the end of services as a liturgy of conclusion and response.[97] From there, different forms of *Kaddish* were used to conclude different sections of the *Siddur* as described at the beginning of this chapter. Whether the *Abbreviated Kaddish* or *Full Kaddish* (without תתקבל), this prayer makes its appearance in order to indicate that a section of the service has ended and to evoke the eventual successful response to all prayers – the coming of the Messiah.

Full Kaddish with תתקבל (*Kaddish Titkabel)* deserves special mention here. The extra paragraph, which gives the liturgy its name, asks God to accept the prayers of all Israel. It is recited, therefore, once after every recitation of the *Amidah* (with the exception of during mourning, noted above).[98] The *Amidah* is the quintessential prayer or *tefillah*, and so this form of *Kaddish* is appropriately used in this way.

Often this *Kaddish* does not come immediately after the *Amidah* with which it is associated. Sometimes there may even be another *Kaddish* or two that intervenes.[99] This is true in *Shaharit* (the morning service), where in the usual weekday order of things, *Tahanun* (the post-*Amidah* prayer of supplication) and the *Abbreviated Kaddish* that follows it come between the *Amidah* and *Kaddish Titkabel*.[100] On Monday and Thursday mornings, Torah reading and the *Abbreviated Kaddish* that concludes that part of the service also intervene.[101] Similarly on Saturday night when there is no Biblically mandated holiday in

---

96 *Masekhet Soferim* 21:5–6.

97 Ibid., 10:6 and 18:10.

98 Abudraham, loc. cit.

99 Cf. Siddur, pp. 120–156.

100 Siddur, pp. 124–138.

101 Siddur, pp. 138–148.

the week ahead, *Abbreviated Kaddish* follows the *Amidah* and then *Kaddish Titkabel* comes after the extra verses recited at the close of the Sabbath. When those verses are not recited, which occurs when there is a holiday during the subsequent week, only *Kaddish Titkabel* is said.[102]

In all of these cases *Kaddish Titkabel* marks the end of the central section of the prayers, which includes the *Amidah,* while the other appearances of *Kaddish* conclude various subsections of the service. For example, on the usual Saturday night, *Abbreviated Kaddish* comes after the *Amidah* while *Kaddish Titkabel* marks the end of the essential part of the entire service that includes the *Amidah* and the special verses.

Understanding the history of the prayer in this way flies in the face of the earliest scientific studies of the liturgy. Zunz and Elbogen (who followed him) were both pioneers of modern scholarly liturgical research and used philological methods developed for Biblical study to analyze prayer texts.[103]

One of the assumptions of this methodology is that if two texts are similar, the shorter one is earlier and the longer one is later, as the greater length indicates that sections have been added to the *urtext* (original version).[104]

Whether this assumption is true when it comes to the Bible is not our issue here; but it is most assuredly not true in the *Siddur* where many prayers borrow smaller units from larger prayers.[105] In this case, our analysis shows that some version of *Kaddish de-Rabbanan* that is longer is significantly older than the *Abbreviated Kaddish*. In fact, even the name of the shorter form suggests

---

102 Siddur, pp. 594–600.

103 Elbogen, op. cit.; Zunz, Leopold. *Ha-Derashot Be-Yisrael: Hishtalshelutan ha-Historit.* Ed. Hanokh Albek. Jerusalem: 1954, pp. 163–186, 219–220. For a discussion of the place of liturgical studies in the *Wissenschaft Des Judentums,* see Reif, Stefan C. *Judaism and Hebrew Prayer: new perspectives on Jewish liturgical history.* Cambridge: 1993, pp. 266–270.

104 Cf. Elbogen, p. 80.

105 Cf. In the chapter on *Nishmat* in this volume, the discussion of *Ilu Finu* (a part of *Nishmat*), which was also used as a prayer recited in response to rainfall. Another example is the sentence שמע קולינו ה' א-להינו חוס ורחם עלינו וקבל ברחמים וברצון את תפילתנו Hear our voice, God our Lord, have compassion and mercy on us and receive our prayer with mercy and acceptance), which is part of a larger blessing and a much larger liturgy (the *Shmoneh Esrei* – the daily central prayer; Siddur, p. 108), whose origin is no later than the era of the Mishnah (M. Berakhot 4:3). Yet it appears by itself as part of *Selihot* (the Penitential prayers) from the Geonic period, recited, among other times, on *Yom Kippur*; Mahzor YK, p. 126.

that this latter prayer is an abbreviation of the *Full Kaddish* and not a form that is closer to an *urtext*.

Kaddish was also incorporated into the prayers at a funeral. But contrary to what some might expect, this was not because of any association with mourning or because of any supposed affect that it might have on the dead. Instead, a geonic era (800–1000 C.E.) responsum says:

A–You should know	א–הוי יודע
B–That *Kaddish* that is *Yitgadal* [יתגדל –"May He be magnified"],	ב–כי קדיש שהוא יתגדל
C–We have found nothing at all in it that deals with the deceased;	ג–לא מצאנו לו עיקר על המת
D–Rather, it is said after the eulogy or after the prayer called "Justification of the Judgment" [*Tsiduk ha-Din*, a prayer recited at a funeral that has many Biblical verses incorporated into it].	ד–אלא לאחר המספד או לאחר צידוק הדין
E–For in all places where there are words of Torah, we respond "May His Great Name . . ." after them,	ה–שכל מקום שיש שם דברי תורה עונין אחריהם אמן יהא שמיה רבא,
F–And that is true of a eulogy and that is true of the "Justification of the Judgment."[106]	ו–וכן הספד וכן צידוק הדין

Even at a funeral it is still the *Rabbis' Kaddish* that is said, and this again indicates that responding to Torah study was the original meaning and purpose of the prayer.

So, too, Rabbi Aharon ben Rabbi Jacob Ha-Cohen (13th–14th centuries) says this in his work on prayer customs called *Kol Bo*, and in his later and more comprehensive *Orhot Hayim*:

Kaddish does not come for anything but the verses in the "Justification of the Judgment."[107]	קדיש לא בא אלא בשביל פסוקי צדוק הדין

In fact, he carries this idea to its logical conclusion. On festive days such as

---

106 *Teshuvot ha-Geonim Coronel.* #94. For discussion and parallels in the writings of Saadiah Gaon, see Danzig, op. cit., p. 109f.

107 *Kol Bo* #114; *Orhot Hayim: Hilkhot Avel* #11.

the New Moon or *Hanukah*, when eulogies are prohibited and *Tsiduk ha-Din* is not recited, these works indicate that *Kaddish* is also not to be included at a funeral.[108] Today, long after *Kaddish* has been accepted as a mourner's prayer, a remnant of this practice remains the rule. When, unfortunately, a funeral must be held on an otherwise festive day, the *Burial Kaddish* is not said. In its place the deceased's relatives use the *Mourner's Kaddish*.[109]

Despite the comments of the Medieval authorities cited here – and some that we have yet to encounter – the reference to resurrection of the dead in the *Burial Kaddish* began to have an impact on the understanding of the meaning of this form of *Kaddish,* and of the liturgy in general, within the Jewish community. This change was given additional impetus by something we have already seen. There is a liturgical confluence of *Kaddish* forms that has the text of this prayer that is recited at a *siyum* read the same as the one offered at a burial. At the end of a book that one has studied and at the closing of the book of someone's life in this world, the same *Kaddish* is used. In this way *Kaddish* began to become a prayer associated with death in the popular imagination.

So, too, we can see that the idea of associating this liturgy with the dead had already begun to make inroads in some quarters as early as the geonic period. The responsum from that era cited here is clearly reacting negatively to the suggestion that this prayer might have some impact on the deceased. In that regard, we find mention of "turning one's face away" from the body before reciting *Kaddish* at a funeral in the twelfth century.[110] This, too, is an indication that the prayer should not be seen as being directed at the person who has died. It is more than likely that this practice was instituted because people were making precisely that connection.

Over time, some of the recitations of *Kaddish* were given to those in

---

108 Other books composed in the medieval period take a similar position on this; cf. *Mahzor Vitry* #275. Also, Rabbi Menahem b. Shlomo (12th century), in *Midrash Sekhel Tov* (Genesis, ch. 50), takes the same position that *Kaddish* at a burial is about the biblical verses and not about the dead. This work then cites the text of what we have called the *Burial Kaddish* with its reference to resurrection.

109 Rabbenu Yeruchum (13th–14th century). *Toldot Adam ve-Hava* 28:3. Moellin, in *Sefer Maharil: Hilkhot Hodesh Nissan,* agrees and adds that neither *Tsiduk ha-Din* nor the *Rabbis' Kaddish* is recited at a funeral during the month of *Nissan*; also see Lamm, Maurice. *Jewish Way in Death and Mourning.* New York: 1969, p. 66.

110 Cf. *Midrash Sekhel Tov,* loc. cit. In Addition, *Orhot Hayim* (and *Kol Bo*), loc. cit. actually have the mourners leaving the cemetery before reciting *Kaddish*.

mourning,[111] and this eventually became the universal practice in all Jewish communities. But this did not occur until many hundreds of years after this liturgy was first used to conclude a study session and then recited to mark the end of the various sections of the services.

Before explaining why and how this occurred, it is important to reiterate that *Kaddish* is a part of communal worship that – originally – had nothing to do with mourning, and that, at least conceptually, should therefore be recited whether or not there is a mourner in attendance. Given the history we have described, it should also be said after any study session, as long as a *minyan* is present, without regard to whether a mourner was part of the group that was studying.[112]

Nonetheless, because of the strong associations that grew between mourners and the recitation of *Kaddish*, many in the Jewish community tended to forget the original purpose of the prayer. For example, compare the description of *Kaddish de-Rabbanan* in Maimonides' (Rambam's) code from the late 12th century with a comment about the same form of the liturgy that we find in the writings of Rabbi Abraham Zvi Hirsh Eisenstadt from the 19th century. Maimonides – who lived in the era when *Kaddish* became a mourner's prayer in Europe, but who was not yet experiencing that change in Egypt where he made his home – writes as follows:

A–*Kaddish* of the Rabbis:	א-קדיש דרבנן
B–Whenever ten or more Jews are involved in study of the oral law,	ב-כל עשרה מישראל או יתר שעוסקין בתלמוד תורה שעל פה
C–Even *Midrashim* and *Aggadot*,[113]	ג-ואפילו במדרשות או באגדות
D–When they conclude	ד-כשהן מסיימין
E–One of them recites *Kaddish* using this text:	ה-אומר אחד מהן קדיש בנוסח זה:

---

111 Moellin, loc. cit.; Rabbi Yekhiel Mikhel Ben Rabbi Aaron Halevi Epstein (19th century), *Arukh ha-Shulhan: Orah Hayim* 133:1; Rabbi Benjamin Ben Mattathias (16th century), Responsa *Binyamin Ze'ev* (1829–1908) #202; Sperber, loc. cit. 1:8.

112 See the sources cited in the previous two footnotes.

113 Even though some of the sources we have seen mandate that *Kaddish* be said *only* after study of *Aggadah*, Maimonides here makes such a recitation secondary. See discussion and some sources above, n. 18.

F–"May His great Name be magnified and sanctified.   ו–יתגדל ויתקדש שמיה רבא

G–He will renew the world,   ז–דעתיד לחדתא עלמא

H–And will resurrect the dead,   ח–ולאחייא מתייא

I–And remove life,[114]   ט–ולמיפרק חייא

J–And rebuild the city of Jerusalem,   י–ולמיבני קרתא דירושלם

K–And establish His holy Sanctuary;   כ–ולשכללא היכלא קדישא

L–And will uproot idol worship from the land,   ל–ולמיעקר פולחנא נוכראה מן ארעא

M–And put the worship of heaven in its place in its splendor and in its uniqueness   מ–ולאתבא פולחנא דשמיא לאתריה בזיויה ויהודיה

N–And empower the Holy One, Blessed be He, in His reign," etc.   נ–וימליך מלכותיה וכו'

O–Until "consolations that are uttered in the world; and say, Amen.   ס–עד ונחמתא דאמירן בעלמא ואמרו אמן,

P–Regarding our Rabbis   ע–על רבנן

Q–And regarding their students   פ–ועל תלמידיהון

R–And regarding the students of their students   צ–ועל תלמידי תלמידיהון

S–Who are occupied with Torah   ק–דעסקין באורייתא

T–In this place or in any place   ר–די באתרא הדין ודי בכל אתר ואתר

U–They and you should have grace, kindness, compassion, help and largess   ש–יהא להון ולכון חינא וחסדא ורחמי וסייעתא ורווחא

V–From before their Father in Heaven. And say, Amen.   ת–מקדם אבוהון דבשמיא ואמרו אמן

W–May [great] peace," etc.   אא–יהא שלמא וכו',

X–And this is what is called *Kaddish of the Rabbis* [*Kaddish de-Rabbanan*].[115]   בב–וזהו הנקרא קדיש דרבנן.

We note first that Maimonides uses a version of what we have called the *Siyum* (or *Burial*) *Kaddish* as the *Kaddish* to be recited after every study session for which a *minyan* is present. If this is, in fact, the original form of *Kaddish*

---

114 This should probably read: ולמיפרק עמיה ("and to free His people"). See Jacobson, Isaachar. *Netiv Binah*, v. 1. Tel Aviv: 1964, p. 367. Also see Maimonides' general presentation of *Kaddish* in the same section that contains the phrase we have suggested here.

115 *Mishneh Torah: Seder Tefillot: Nusah ha-Kaddish.*

de-Rabbanan, the extra eschatological lines that do not appear in the *Rabbis'*
Kaddish add support for the idea that this prayer – and its use as a post-script
to Torah study – originate in the horrors of Hadrian's persecutions and the
extreme yearning for salvation that would have been a reality in the Jewish
community at that time.

Second, in this passage Maimonides indicates that recitation of *Kaddish* is
not limited only to the synagogue nor is it connected in any way to situations
in which mourners are present. In fact, Rambam does not even give priority
to mourners in saying this prayer, and he makes no mention of a *Mourner's*
Kaddish anywhere in his code. Anyone present can lead the recitation of
Kaddish when it is said.[116]

Nonetheless, the growing association between the prayer and mourning
had its effect. Abraham Eisenstadt writes about the recitation of the *Rabbis'*
Kaddish:

A–It is clear that if both [parents] are alive, he should not say *Kaddish*.	א–משמע דאם שניהם חיים לא יאמר קדיש
B–And that is specifically in regard to *Mourner's Kaddish*.	ב–וזה דוקא קדיש יתום
C–But *Kaddish de-Rabbanan* he can say.[117]	ג–אבל קדיש דרבנן יכול לומר

Even though *Kaddish* had been entrenched in the liturgy for many centuries without any connection to death, once it was given, in part, to mourners, it became associated with the loss of a relative – particularly of parents.
Therefore Eisenstadt says, if no mourners are present, only one who has once
been in mourning for a parent is considered appropriate to say the prayer. This
is not true with regard to the *Rabbis' Kaddish*, just as Maimonides said. But in
Rambam's time he didn't need to worry about any sensitivities raised by an association between the prayer and mourning. On the other hand, in Eisenstadt's
era he felt compelled to deal with just these sensitivities.

Interestingly, in practice, Eisenstadt may not have succeeded in maintaining
the recitation of the *Rabbis' Kaddish* as a liturgy that anyone with living parents
is comfortable offering. In my experience, it is very hard, if not impossible, to

---

116 He mentions *Kaddish* nearly forty times in his code, and it is always the prayer leader
    or one of the assembled who leads – never a mourner.

117 *Pitkhei Teshuva* 376:4.

get someone who has both father and mother still alive to recite either the *Mourner's Kaddish* or *Kaddish de-Rabbanan* unless they first get explicit permission from their parents.[118]

Mourner's Kaddish is, of course, understood as being for mourners.[119] In the case of the *Rabbis' Kaddish,* since there are places in the formal services where mourners are the ones who offer it, many people assume (apparently incorrectly) that it is therefore a prayer that is also reserved only for them.[120] Most people would choose to forego this important liturgy rather than say it while still enjoying the presence of their mother and father in this world. To their minds saying *Kaddish* would be disrespectful to or unlucky for their parents.[121]

Nonetheless, when called on to serve as *Hazzan,* these same individuals will have no hesitation about reciting this liturgy when it appears in places that were not given to the mourners; in fact, most people don't give it a second thought. This, despite the historical reality that the origin of *Kaddish* as a concluding text is the same for all forms of the prayer, despite the fact that reciting *Kaddish* after study is the oldest use of the liturgy and despite the fact that for most of its history there was no association between this part of the services and the loss of a loved one. The connection between mourning and *Kaddish* certainly has had a profound impact on how people understand and use this prayer.

How then did *Kaddish* come to be seen as the mourner's prayer? There is a philosophical and a mystical answer to this question, each of which deserves thorough discussion, since both – independently – have had a dramatic impact on Jewish consciousness and practice.

We will begin with philosophy. It is well known that people who suffer a loss may tend to question or deny God. Asking people who find themselves in that circumstance to stand in the midst of a congregation of their fellow

---

118 See Rabbi Moses ben Israel Isserless. Responsa *Ramo* # 118 and *Shulhan Arukh: Orah Hayim* 132:2. For discussion and sources on whether one parent can prevent recitation of *Kaddish* after the death of the other one, see Yosef, op. cit. 3 *Yoreh De'ah* 26.

119 When *Mourner's Kaddish* is recited by someone not in mourning because no one who has suffered a loss is present at services (which, as we have seen, is a practice that accurately reflects the early history of the prayer as a response and conclusion), Isserless (*Yoreh De'ah* 376:4) says that it should be said "for all the dead of Israel" (בעד כל מתי ישראל). This is another indication of how far the connection between this prayer and mourning has penetrated into Jewish consciousness.

120 Cf. Siddur, p. 52

121 Cf. Yosef, loc. cit.

Jews to affirm that God's greatness and sanctity will grow in this world, that His great Name should be blessed forever and that He rise above the power of any praise or blessing to describe Him is asking for an act of emotional and theological courage.[122]

It is also an act of healing.[123] Reciting *Kaddish* in this way can begin to repair the mourner's shattered relationship with God. It makes God a real presence in the mourner's life. One who finds his way to the synagogue three times a day to say this prayer may find that this helps him transcend the pain and loss and get in touch with something larger that restores meaning and moral equilibrium to his universe.

Often this restored equilibrium stays with the mourner beyond the mourning period. Many people who come to synagogue just to say *Kaddish* end up much more connected to their Judaism than they were previously. This may manifest itself in continuing attendance at services or in involvement in other religious rituals. It is for these reasons that personal recitation of *Kaddish* by the mourner is much preferred, while hiring someone or otherwise finding a replacement to recite the prayer as some people do, is significantly less desirable.[124]

The beginning of the transition that allowed *Kaddish* to become a mourner's prayer along the lines just described can be found in our earliest source that connects *Kaddish* and mourning – *Masekhet Soferim*. The underlying rationale in this text seems to be the healing dynamic just discussed. The source, which dates from no later than the eighth century and may be from as early as the third century, reads as follows:[125]

---

122 Cf. Lamm, p. 155; also see Haas, pp. 93–94 for others who take this approach.

123 If one compares this rationale for the recitation of *Kaddish* with Elisabeth Kubler-Ross's famous five stages of grief, this seems to parallel "acceptance," the fifth and usually the most difficult stage to achieve. See Kubler-Ross, Elisabeth. *On Death and Dying*. New York: 1969.

124 For sources that strongly prefer that the son or child be the one reciting the prayer, see discussion below.

125 Elbogen (op. cit), p. 81, dates *Masekhet Soferim* to the 6th–7th century, while Hermann Strack, in *Introduction to the Talmud and Midrash* (Minneapolis: 1992, p. 248), says it is from the eighth century. *The Literature of the Sages* by Shmuel Safrai (Philadelphia: 1987–2006) favors something closer to the later date, but all agree that the work contains significantly older material going back to some time after the close of the Mishnah. Certainly this text dates from after the destruction of the Temple and it describes a practice that appears to have been introduced shortly after that tragic event.

A–On Sabbaths [when the Temple stood] the inhabitants of Jerusalem would gather

א–בשבתות היו מתקבצין יושבי ירושלים,

B–And go up to the Temple Mount,

ב–ועולין להר הבית,

C–And they would sit between these two gates

ג–ויושבין בין שני שערים הללו,

D–In order to perform acts of kindness for one another

ד–כדי לגמול חסדים לזה ולזה,

E–But when the Temple was destroyed

ה–משחרב בית המקדש

F–They established that bridegrooms and mourners should come to the synagogue

ו–התקינו שיהיו החתנים והאבלים באים לבית הכנסת,

G–In order to perform acts of kindness for one another

ז–כדי לגמול חסדים לזה ולזה,

H–Bridegrooms in order to praise them and accompany them to their homes;

ח–חתנים לקלסן ולהלוותן לבתיהם,

I–Mourners:

ט–אבילים,

J–After the Cantor completed the *Musaf* prayer

י–לאחר שיגמור החזן תפילה של מוסף,

K–He would go behind the door of the synagogue.

כ–הולך לו אחורי דלת של בית הכנסת,

L–Or to a corner of the synagogue.

ל–או בפינת הכנסת,

M–There he would find the mourners and all their relatives.

מ–ומוצא שם האבילים וכל קרובים,

N–And he would recite a blessing over them

נ–ואומר עליהן ברכה,

O–And after that he would say *Kaddish*

ס–ואחר כך אומר קדיש

P–But he would not say, "In the world that He will renew" [the extra words of the *Burial Kaddish*, the *Siyum Kaddish* and Maimonides' version of *Kaddish de-Rabbanan*].

ע–ואין אומרים בעלמא דעתיד לחדתא,

Q–Except in response to [the words of] a student or in response to one who gives a discourse.[126]

פ–אלא על התלמיד ועל הדרשן.

There is a good deal of material in this source that requires comment. First,

---

126 *Masekhet Soferim 19:9.* (This last line seems to support Maimonides' version of Kaddish de-Rabbanan.) Nahmanides, in *Torat ha-Adam*, loc. cit., reads this last line as: אלא על תלמיד הדרשן (Except in response to the student who gives the discourse), which supports our translation here.

this text again indicates that the *Burial Kaddish*, despite its reference to resurrection of the dead, was originally a prayer associated with study and only derivatively a liturgy that became part of the rituals surrounding mourning. If it were about loss, then it should have been recited by the Cantor whenever mourners were present and the caveat found in line Q would have no place in this text. Nonetheless, the fact that this source finds it necessary to explicitly reject the use of this form of the prayer here, may again suggest that some were beginning to see *Kaddish* as a liturgy associated with death and advocating for use of this form of the prayer as a liturgical response to the loss of a loved one.

Second, this source supports the idea that, despite its central sentence, *Kaddish* is a post-Temple prayer that did not have a place in the ritual of the Temple while it stood. It describes this liturgy as being recited among the mourners only after the Temple was destroyed.

Third, *Kaddish* is again a concluding liturgy said here after the recitation of a blessing. This benediction is likely related to the Mourner's Blessings (*Birkat Aveilim*), mentioned in rabbinic literature.[127] These blessings appear to parallel the seven blessings (*Sheva Berakhot* or *Birkat Hatanim*), recited during the week after a wedding.[128] Just as when one rejoices for seven days following a marriage, these benedictions are part of celebrating the new couple; the analogous custom was to honor the mourners by using a different collection of blessings after the loss of a loved one.[129]

Finally – and most importantly at this point in our analysis – *Kaddish*, in this source, is clearly part of a ritual of consolation, healing and reconciliation that focuses on the mourners and not on the dead. We can read this text to say that after the tragedy and the loss, the hope is expressed through *Kaddish* that God's Name will again become great. This will bring complete consolation to the mourner. That interpretation opens the door to the rest of the philosophical explanation suggested above.

There is one glaring difference between the ritual described in this text and current practice. In *Masekhet Soferim* it is not the mourners, but the prayer

---

127 M. Megillah 4:3; M. Moed Katan 3:7. For the content, see B. Ketuvot 8b. See Nahmanides, loc. cit., and op. cit., *Tokhen ha-Inyanim: Sha'ar ha-Mihush* #48, who reads this source from *Masekhet Soferim* as I do here.

128 M. Megillah 4:3. For the content, see B. Ketuvot 7b-8a. Also see Katz, Menahem. "Birkat Hatanim U-Virkat Aveilim." In *Kenishta* 3 (2007): pp. 155–186.

129 See *Masekhet Semahot* 2:1 that these blessings are for "the honor of the living" (כבוד לחיים). This is echoed by many authorities across the centuries.

leader who recites *Kaddish*. It is not the one who suffers the tragedy who reconciles with God as is done today, but the Cantor who prays that this reconciliation come to those who have suffered a tragic loss – or perhaps he is just offering the concluding prayer that comes after the blessing that he recites and is not referring to the mourners at all when he says *Kaddish*. One could read this source either way.

This text reflects an intermediate stage between *Kaddish* being used exclusively as a prayer offered after Torah study and at the conclusion of various parts of the prayer service, and the point where some of its recitations were given to mourners. It may well embody the beginnings of the now commonplace view that *Kaddish* is a prayer that is primarily about death and mourning. Even if the original intent of the ritual was not to associate *Kaddish* with mourning, it is understandable that the popular imagination would make precisely that connection on seeing or experiencing this practice. In fact it would strain credibility to suggest that this did not occur. In short, while this text may describe and try to protect *Kaddish* as a concluding prayer, practice and popular imagination were busy associating it with death.

As such, this source may be our earliest textual indication of an emerging understanding of *Kaddish* that the geonic responsum, Aharon b. Jacob (both cited above) and, ironically, also this source itself, tried unsuccessfully to combat. Chronologically, this text is older than either of these other two authorities, and if these sources are taken in order of their appearance we see a pattern suggesting that there was a growing belief that *Kaddish* and loss are connected, even as our extant texts tried to fight against just that perception.

Much of the explication of the philosophical explanation offered here emerges after the fact – after mourners begin to recite *Kaddish*.[130] Nonetheless, even as *Kaddish* was being said by the prayer leader as described in *Masekhet Soferim*

---

130 The explanation is found in books and articles written in the 20th and 21st centuries. I do not find this rationale in any earlier traditional text. Where it exists before the last century, it is expressed in two other liturgical practices: reciting the blessing *Dayan ha-Emet* (the true Judge) in association with the loss of a loved one, and in the recitation of *Tsiduk ha-Din* at a funeral. Both of these liturgical elements accept God's judgment as righteous, which does some of the work of healing, though they do not go anywhere near as far as *Kaddish* in reestablishing God's glorious position in the world and in the mind and heart of the mourner. See M. Berakhot 9:2, B. Berakhot 46b; also see *Teshuvot ha-Geonim Geonim Kadmonim* #74 for an interesting use of these liturgical elements in a ritual of communal reconciliation.

for whatever reason we assign to that recitation, one can see the beginnings of what we have called the philosophical explanation start to emerge. Reciting *Kaddish* in this ritual and reading this text in *Masekhet Soferim* simply helped open the door for that understanding to grow. Since the *Burial Kaddish* with its reference to resurrection was being recited at funerals in the medieval period, momentum for this shift in perception simply grew until it became unstoppable.

A second text in *Masekhet Soferim* supports the idea that *Kaddish* is about the state of the relationship between the Jews and God. It discusses the liturgy of *Tishah B'Av*, the saddest day of the Jewish calendar. Again, it comes from an era when mourners were not the ones mandated to recite this prayer. It reads:

A–In the nighttime prayer, no one [causes] another to hear	א–בתפילת ערבית אין אדם שומע לחבירו,
B–Because they pray in a whisper	ב–מפני שהן מתפללין בלחישה,
C–And they do not say either "Bless" [*Barekhu*][131] or "May His Name"[132]	ג–ואין אומרים לא ברכו ולא יהי שם.
D–But in the morning service [*Shaharit*], after these songs and verses,	ד–אבל בתפילת שחרית לאחר המזמורין והפסוקין אילו,
E–They say in the *Yotzer* [the beginning of the *Shema* blessings], *Barekhu* in a low voice	ה–האומרים ביוצר ברכו בקול נמוך,
F–And they do not mention "*Kadosh*"	ו–ואין מזכירין קדוש,
G–And also not *Kaddish*	ז–ואף לא קדיש;
H–But in the afternoon service [*Minhah*] they say "*Kadosh*" and *Kaddish*.[133]	ח–אבל בתפילת המנחה אומרים קדוש וקדיש.

The Ninth of Av commemorates the worst tragedies in Jewish History such as the destruction of both Temples. As such, the relationship between God and the Jewish people is at its lowest ebb on that day. For the first part of the day, according to this tradition, this shattered relationship is reflected in

---

131 Siddur, p. 256.

132 This does not appear to be a contemporary custom, but it is cited in more detail earlier in *Masekhet Soferim* 10:6. It refers to the verse from Psalms 113:2 that is the Hebrew translation and origin of "May His great Name …" (יהא שמיא), that apparently was used in the liturgy in the communities that served as the source for the practices described in *Masekhet Soferim*.

133 *Masekhet Soferim* 18:10.

the non-recital of *Kaddish* and other prominent parts of the liturgy. Only as the day progresses does the healing begin. Particularly at *Minhah* – which is offered after the middle of the day, when the sadness and mourning of *Tishah B'Av* generally begins to diminish – *Kaddish* can again find its usual place in the prayers according to this text.[134]

Even though this source does not accurately portray contemporary practice, which includes recitation of *Kaddish* at each of the services on *Tishah B'Av*, it again tells us that this prayer was originally – and for many centuries – about the relationship between God and the Jews.[135] Given that understanding, it makes sense that some might not recite the prayer on the Ninth of Av. This source does not describe *Kaddish* as a liturgy of reconciliation, but it does help create the foundation for making that claim.

After the mourners began to offer this prayer, the newer understanding of this liturgy began to merge with the way in which it was used originally. A source that was written in the 14th or 15th century shows us that this is so. It embodies an interesting mix in which *Mourner's Kaddish* is portrayed as a liturgy recited in response to loss, while retaining its identity as a conclusion to Torah study. The approach taken by this text has had at least a visual impact on *Mourner's Kaddish* in the contemporary *Siddur* and an unintended musical influence on the Song of Glory.

A–And our teacher Rabbi Shalom of blessed memory said	א–ואמר מורינו הרב שלום ז"ל
B–That those places in the Rhein that don't recite *Mourner's Kaddish* on weekdays,[136]	ב–שאותן מקומות שברינוס שאין אומרין קדיש יתום בחול,

---

134 Cf. *Shulhan Arukh: Orah Hayim* 559:3.

135 Kinot, p. 402. Contemporary practice does remove the *Titkabel* paragraph from the *Shaharit* post-*Amidah Kaddish* on *Tishah B'Av*.

136 Moellin (*Sefer Maharil: Hilkhot Semahot* #23), who lived at approximately the same time, reports: ומנהג במגנצא שאין אומרים קדיש יתום בכל יום רק ג' פעמים בשבת (And the custom in Mainz is that they do not recite *Mourner's Kaddish* every day, only three times on the Sabbath). On the other hand, in his Responsa *Maharil* #36, he says that in Austria it is said every day. Intriguingly, once *Kaddish* began to be understood as a prayer designed to redeem the dead (see below), we find reports of communities that recited it only on weekdays because of a belief that Hell closes down for *Shabbat* and other special days; see Rabbi Abraham Chaim Ben Masud Chai Addadi's Responsa *va-Yikra Avraham* (19th century) #18.

C–That is because they do not say, "As
it is written in Your Torah" [this phrase
introduces two Biblical verses in our current
texts[137]] after *Aleinu le-Shabei'ah*.[138]
D–And then it is not *Kaddish* recited on verses.[139]

ג–היינו משום שאין אומרין
ככתוב בתורתך אחר עלינו
לשבח,
ד–ואז לא הוי קדיש על
פסוקים.

This limits the recitation of even *Mourner's Kaddish* to a practice that can
only occur after Torah study of some type.[140] That would mean that the historically earliest use of this prayer (from the Hadrianic persecutions back in the
2nd century) would still control how it is recited today – or at least it did in
some communities in the 14th to 15th centuries.

Most contemporary congregations do include the section that begins, "As
it is written ..." in *Aleinu*, but some authorities did not consider even this to
be enough. That is because the verses included in this section are part of the
praises that are intrinsic to *Aleinu*, and not real Torah study.[141] As a result, other
texts were included after the prayer so that *Kaddish* could be said.[142]

Nonetheless, most communities today do not recite these extra sentences.[143]
Still, they appear after *Aleinu*, and others can be found in the *Siddur* following
the Song of Glory.[144] That is the visual impact that I mentioned.

---

137 The verses are Exodus 15:18 and Zechariah 14:9.

138 Siddur, p. 160. This phrase is in the body of *Aleinu* today, though it is not in the
version that appears in the *Heikhalot* texts (see the chapter on *Aleinu* in this volume
for discussion of this prayer in those sources).

139 Rabbi Shalom Ben Rabbi Yitzchak of Neustadt. *Minhagei Maharash* #90.

140 See n. 18, and see Azulai loc. cit.; *Kol Bo* # 6; Sperber, loc. cit.

141 Rabbi Yikhya Ben Joseph Tzalakh (18th century). Responsa *Pe'Ulat Tsadik* 3:78. He
sees this opinion reflected in Joseph Caro's *Bet Yosef Orah Hayim* 25:13 (in our texts
55:1) and in *Rokeah*. In opposition, see Rabbi David Halevi (16th–17th centuries).
Turei Zahav: Orah Hayim 55:1, 3.

142 Mishlei 3:25; Isaiah 8:10 and 46:4

143 Whether *Kaddish* can only be said after the prayers and types of texts designated,
or whether – once the mystical understanding that leads to a desire to increase the
number of times this prayer is recited takes hold – it can be offered under other
circumstances, is debated in traditional texts; cf. Tzalach, loc. cit.; Halevi, loc. cit.
and Azulai, loc. cit.

144 Siddur, p. 160 and p. 486. But see Azulai, loc. cit., for sources that say that Kaddish
should *not* be said after verses from the Torah because they "need no strengthening"
(שאין צריכים חזוק).

The practice of singing the second of the verses that appear after *Anim Zemirot*

Who can tell the powerful actions of God; make known all His praises[145]	מִי יְמַלֵּל גְּבוּרוֹת ה' יַשְׁמִיעַ כָּל תְּהִלָּתוֹ

is something we discuss at length in the chapter on the Song of Glory. However, in most of those communities that do not sing this line – as with the sentences that appear in the prayer book after *Aleinu* – these texts are skipped.

The mystical conceptualization of *Kaddish*, which we are about to discuss, controls current practice on this issue and it does not require the recitation of verses in order for *Kaddish* to be recited. Ironically, it is the lack of proper understanding of the esoteric meaning of the Song of Glory that leads to the singing of this verse in those communities where it is sung, and therefore to the *de facto* restoration of the original non-mystical practice of reciting *Kaddish* only after study. This is accomplished when *Kaddish* is said after *Anim Zemirot* and the singing of "Who can tell ..." rather than simply after the Song of Glory alone.

To return to our central theme, the above source indicates that in some communities in the Rhine valley in the Middle Ages, reciting *Mourner's Kaddish* only on Sabbaths and holidays was considered to be enough. If the purpose of the prayer is to publicly reconcile with God before the community there is some logic to attempting such a reconciliation only on *Shabbat* and holidays when many more people attend synagogue than on weekdays.

In addition, this practice is in keeping with the first of the *Masekhet Soferim* sources that we cited – the earliest one to associate mourners and *Kaddish* – that describes the recitation of this prayer in the presence of those who have suffered a loss as exclusively a Sabbath practice. On the other hand, this rationale and this way of doing things will simply not make any sense once the mystical understanding of the *Mourner's Kaddish* takes hold of Jewish popular imagination. We will explain why below.

Turning now to the mystical side of this liturgy, we again ask these questions: How did this prayer come to be recited by mourners, and how did the understanding of this liturgy change as a result? These issues, as they play out in mystical texts, are fundamental to our study of *Kaddish* because the esoteric

---

145 Psalms 106:2; Siddur, p. 486.

side of this prayer, which is never more than just below the surface, plays a pivotal role here as well.

Let us return to this text from Heikhalot literature:

A–In the eschatological future, the Holy One Blessed be He will reveal the [esoteric] reasons for [the teachings of] the Torah to Israel . . .	א–לעתיד לבוא מגלה הקדוש ברוך הוא טעמי תורה לישראל . . .
B–And David will recite a song before the Holy One Blessed be He	ב–ואומר דוד שירה לפני הקדוש ברוך הוא
C–And the righteous will respond after him,	ג–ועונין אחריו הצדיקים
D–"May His great Name be blessed forever and ever. Let [Him] be blessed."	ד–אמן יהא שמיה רבה מברך לעלם ולעלמי עלמיא יתברך,
E–From the Garden of Eden	ה–מתוך גן עדן,
F–And the sinners of Israel respond *Amen* from Hell.	ו–ופושעי ישראל עונין אמן מתוך גיהנם.
G–Immediately the Holy One Blessed be He says to the angels,	ז–מיד אומר הקדוש ברוך הוא למלאכים
H–"Who are these who respond *Amen* from Hell?"	ח–מי הם אלו שעונין אמן מתוך גיהנם?
I–He said before Him,	ט–אומר לפניו
J–"Master of the Universe,	י–רבונו של עולם
K–These are the sinners of Israel.	כ–הללו פושעי ישראל
L–Even though they are in great distress, they strengthen themselves and say *Amen* before You."	ל–שאף על פי שהם בצרה גדולה מתחזקים ואומרין לפניך אמן.
M–Immediately the Holy One Blessed be He said to the angels,	מ–מיד אומר הקדוש ברוך הוא למלאכים
N–"Open the gates of the Garden of Eden for them and let them come and sing before Me,"	נ–פתחו להם שערי גן עדן ויבואו ויזמרו לפני
O–As it says, "Open the gates and let the righteous nation, protector of the faith, enter."	ס–שנאמר פתחו שערים ויבא גוי צדיק שומר אמונים,
P–Do not read this as "protector of the faith" [*shomer emunim*], but rather as "those who recite Amens" [*she'omrim Ameinim*].[146]	ע–אל תקרי שומר אמונים אלא שאומרים אמנים (עי' שבת קי"ט:).

---

146 Eisenstein, loc. cit., p. 84.

As discussed above, this source grants the central response of *Kaddish* the power to save sinners from punishment in the afterlife when those suffering in purgatory react to it appropriately.

This concept takes on an added dimension in this story from a work called *Rokeah*:[147]

A–And the orphan says *Kaddish*: "May [His Name] be magnified... May His [great] Name ... May [His Name] be blessed... May great peace..." and "He Who makes peace..." [these are the first words of the five paragraphs of the *Mourner's Kaddish*] until "And say, *Amen*."	א–והיתום אומר קדיש, יתגדל, יהא שמיה, יתברך, יהא שלמא רבא ועושה שלום במרומיו עד ואמרו אמן.
B–Why does the orphan recite *Kaddish*?	ב–למה היתום אומר קדיש
C–Because of an incident that occurred:	ג–משום מעשה שהיה:
D–An incident occurred involving Rabbi Akiva, who was walking in a cemetery	ד–מעשה ברבי עקיבא שהיה מהלך בבית הקברות
E–And happened upon a person who was naked and charcoal black	ה–ופגע באדם אחד שהיה ערום ושחור פיחם
F–And was carrying on his head what seemed like ten loads	ו–והיה טוען על ראשו כסבור עשרה טעונין,
G–And he was running with them like a galloping horse.	ז–והיה רץ בהם כסום שהוא רץ,
H–Rabbi Akiva commanded him and caused him to stop	ח–גזר עליו רבי עקיבא והעמידו,
I–And he said to that man,	ט–ואמר לאותו האיש
J–"Why are you doing hard work like this?	י–למה אתה עושה עבודה קשה כזאת,
K–If you are a slave and your master is doing this to you, I will redeem you from his hand	כ–אם עבד אתה ואדוניך עושה לך כך אני אפדה אותך מידו,
L–And if you are poor, I will make you rich."	ל–ואם עני אתה אני מעשיר אותך,
M–He said to him, "I ask you not to delay me, lest those who are appointed over me become angry with me."	מ–אמר לו בבקשה ממך אל תעכבני שמא ירגזו עלי אותם הממונים עלי,
N–He said to him, "What is this	נ–אמר לו מה זו ומה מעשיך,

---

and what is your work?"

O–He said to him, "That man [meaning himself] is dead

ס–אמר לו אותו האיש מת הוא

P–And every day they send me to chop wood and they burn me with it."

ע–ובכל יום ויום שולחים אותי לחטוב בעצים ושורפין אותי בהם,

Q–He said to him, "My son, what was your work in the world from which you came?"

פ–אמר לו בני מה היה מלאכתך בעולם שבאת הימנו,

R–He said to him, "I was the tax collector and I was from among the leaders of the people, and I showed favoritism to the wealthy and I killed the poor."

צ–אמר לו גבאי המס הייתי והייתי מראשי העם ונושא פנים לעשירים והורג עניים,

S–He said to him, "Have you not heard anything from those appointed over you as to whether there is a way to fix [your situation]?"

ק–אמר לו כלום שמעת מן הממונים עליך אם יש לך תקנה,

T–He said to him, "I ask you not to delay me, lest those who are masters of punishment become angry with me, for that man has no way to fix [his situation].

ר–אמר לו בבקשה ממך אל תעכבני שמא ירגזו עלי בעלי פורענות שאותו האיש אין לו תקנה,

U–For I have heard from them something which cannot come to be.

ש–אלא שמעתי מהם דבר שאינו יכול להיות,

V–For if this poor man had a son who would stand in the community and say,

ת–שאילמלא היה לעני זה בן שהוא עומד בקהל ואומר

W–'Blessed is God, Who is blessed,' and they respond after him, 'Bless God Who is blessed,'

אא–ברכו את ה' המבורך ועונין אחריו ברוך ה' המבורך,

X–Or he says: 'May [His Name] be magnified' [Kaddish], and they respond after him: 'May His Name be blessed.'

בב–או יאמר יתגדל ועונין אחריו יהא שמיה מברך,

Y–Immediately they would free that man from his punishment;

גג–מיד מתירין אותו האיש מן הפורענות,

Z–But that man did not leave a son in the world

דד–ואותו האיש לא הניח בן בעולם,

AA–But he left his wife pregnant

הה–ועזב אשתו מעוברת

BB–And he does not know, if she gives birth to a male, who will teach him Torah

וו–ואינו יודע אם תלד זכר מי מלמדו תורה

CC–For that man has no one who has affection for him in the entire world."

זז–שאין לאותו האיש אהוב בעולם.

DD–At that moment Rabbi Akiva accepted upon himself to go and search out whether he had given birth to a son so that he could teach him Torah and have him stand before the community.

EE–He said to him, "What is your name?"

FF–He said to him, "Akiva."

GG–"And the name of your wife?"

HH–He said to him, "Shushniba"

II–"And the name of your city?"
He said to him, "Dukia."

JJ–Immediately Rabbi Akiva was filled with great anguish and he went and inquired about him.

KK–Once he came to that place,
he inquired about him.

LL–They said to him, "May the bones of that evil man be ground up."

MM–He asked about his wife.

NN–They said to him, "May her name and her memory be blotted from the world."

OO–He asked about the son.

PP–They said to him, "Behold, he is uncircumcised; even in regard to the commandment of circumcision they did not involve themselves with him."

QQ–Immediately Rabbi Akiva took him and circumcised him and sat him down before himself

RR–And he did not receive Torah until he sat over him for forty days while fasting.[148]

חח–באותו שעה קבל עליו רבי עקיבא לילך ולחפש אם הוליד בן כדי שילמדנו תורה ויעמידו לפני הצבור,

טט–אמר לו מה שמך

יי–אמר לו עקיבא,

כך–ושום אינתתך

לל–אמר לו שושניבא,

ממ–ושום קרתך אמר לו דוקיא,

נן–מיד נצטער רבי עקיבא צער גדול והלך ושאל עליו,

סס–כיון שבא לאותו מקום שאל עליו,

עע–אמרו לו ישתחקו עצמותיו של אותו רשע,

פפ–שאל על אשתו

צצ–אמרו לו ימחה שמה וזכרה מן העולם,

קק–שאל על בן,

רר–אמרו לו הרי הוא ערל אפי' מצות מילה לא עסקו בו,

שש–מיד נטלו רבי עקיבא ומלו והושיבו לפניו,

תת–ולא היה מקבל תורה עד שישב עליו מ' יום בתענית,

---

148 Heikhalot literature includes the idea of gaining knowledge through mystical practices that brings the aid of the angel in charge of wisdom (*Sar Hokhma*). This is part of "making angels swear" see n. 61. Also see Schafer, Peter. *Synopse zur Hekhalot-Literatur*. Tubingen: 1981, p. 11f. For discussion see, Orlov, Andre. *The Enoch-Metatron Tradition*. Tubingen: 2005, p. xii. Also see David Halperin's *The Faces of the Chariot* (Tubingen: 1988, p. 427f) for the tradition that forty days of fasting is effective in this regard beginning with the story of Moses's forty-day fast on Sinai that led to his effortlessly receiving the Torah.

SS–And an echo from heaven emerged and said to him, "Rabbi Akiva, go and teach him."   אאא–ויצאה בת קול ואמרה לו רבי עקיבא לך ולמד לו,

TT–He went and taught him Torah, *Keriyat Shema*, the eighteen blessings and grace after meals.   בבב–הלך ולמדו תורה וקרית שמע וי"ח ברכות וברכת המזון,

UU–And he stood him before the community and he said . . . [the reason for the ellipsis here is explained below].   גגג–והעמידו לפני הקהל ואמר . . .

VV–At that moment they immediately freed the dead [man] from punishment.   דדד–באותה שעה מיד התירו המת מן הפורענות,

WW–Immediately he came to Rabbi Akiva in a dream and said,   ההה–מיד בא לרבי עקיבא בחלום ואמר

XX–"May it be the will from before God that your mind find rest in the Garden of Eden   ווו–יהי רצון מלפני הקב"ה שתנוח דעתך בגן עדן

YY–For you saved me from the judgment of Hell."   זזז–שהצלת אותי מדינה של גיהנם,

ZZ–Immediately Rabbi Akiva began and said,   חחח–מיד פתח רבי עקיבא ואמר

AAA–"God, may Your Name exist forever; God, Your memory is for all generations."[149]   טטט–יהי שמך ה' לעולם ה' זכרך לדור ודור.

BBB–And so, too, I found in *Tanna Debei Eliyahu Rabbah*:[150]   ייי–וכן מצאתי בתנא דבי אליהו רבא

CCC–A minor who says, "May [His Name] be magnified" saves his father from punishment.[151]   כככ–קטן האומר יתגדל מציל אביו מן הפורענות.

This source allows a son to positively and unequivocally affect the existential state of his father in the World to Come through recitation of *Kaddish* in this world. The connection between *Kaddish*, mourning practices and the dead is now established and secure.[152]

---

149   Paraphrasing Psalms 135:13.

150   This text does not appear in our versions of *Tanna Debei Eliyahu Rabbah*.

151   #107 *Ve-Yiten Lekha* p. 602. For an an analysis of the text see Krygier, Rivon. *The Multiple Meanings of the Mourner's Kaddish*.

152   Cf. *Orhot Hayim: Hilkhot Avel* and Rabbi Solomon Ben Jechiel Luria (16th century). *Yam Shel Shlomo*: Kiddushin, ch. 1. Originally, *Mourner's Kaddish* was said by boys below the age of majority because they were too young to lead services, which is the usual practice of adult mourners. Since this *Kaddish* – as opposed to the other prayers mentioned in this source that are part of daily services – was a late addition to the

But before we decide that we have come to the end of this part of the story of *Kaddish*, there are still some important questions to ask and points to make. Two that stand out immediately are these: Does the ability of the son to change the lot of the dead extend to other relatives reciting this liturgy in response to a loss? Further, can this mystical redemption also include non-relatives, or even complete strangers, if one says *Kaddish* for them?[153]

Answers to these questions will emerge as we discuss this text, but first we must deal with some more basic issues concerning this source. This story, in one way or another, is repeated in the works of a significant number of other sages. For example, Rabbi Yitshak ben Rabbi Moshe (1180–1250) writes as follows:

A–And so, too, my teacher Rabbi Elazar of Worms [the author of *Rokeah*] found	א–וכן מצא מורי ה"ר אלעזר מוורמשא
B–In *Tanna Debei Eliyahu Rabbah*	ב–דתנא דבי אליהו רבא
C–That a minor who says, "May [His Name] be magnified"	ג–דקטן האומר יתגדל
D–Saves his father from punishment.[154]	ד–מציל אביו מן הפורענות:

---

liturgy, some were willing to give these recitations to those who were under age. We saw a similar suggestion in regard to *Anim Zemirot*. The process in regard to *Kaddish* would have been helped along by this story of the son posthumously redeeming his father through recitation of *Kaddish*. See Rabbi Isaac Tyrnau (14th–15th century). *Sefer ha-Minhagim* (Tyrnau): *Dinei Kaddish Yatom*; *Sefer Maharil: Hilkhot Tefillah*; Rabbi Joseph Ben Moses (15th century). *Sefer Leket Yosher* 1:56:3; Rabbi Yaakov ben Yehuda Landa. Sefer Ha-Agur *Hilkhot Tefilat Arvit* #334.

153 There are many who have commented on this question over the generations, and – not surprisingly, in light of our discussion here – the further we go in history, the more acceptable is the idea of someone other than a son reciting *Kaddish*. On the negative side, see *Or Zaru'a* (see next note), *Sefer Leket Yosher*, ad. loc, Ramo (16th century) *Yoreh Deah*: 376:4, who also records positions that accept this practice; Rabbi Benjamin ben Mattathias, (16th century), Responsa *Binyamin Ze'ev* #201–202; Rabbi Jacob ben Joseph Reischer (17th–18th centuries), *Shevut Ya'akov*: 2:93–94. On the positive side, see Rabbi Joseph ben Solomon Colon (15th century): Responsa *Maharik* #30 and *Piskei Maharik* #290 principle #30; Rabbi Joseph Chaim Ben Elijah Al-Khakam (19th century), *Rav Pe'Alim* 3 *Yoreh De'ah* #32 and 4 *Orah Hayim* #7; Rabbi Ben-Zion Meir Chai Uzziel (19th–20th centuries): *Mishpetei Uzziel* 1 Orah Hayim #2 and Moses Feinstein (20th century), *Orah Hayim* 5:3 and *Yoreh De'ah* 4:60. The tipping point seems to be the 16th century, when mystical practices became more popular and more accepted.

154 *Or Zaru'a* 2: *Hilkhot Shabbat* #50.

He then tells us that in his day, specifically because of this story, *Kaddish* has become a prayer for mourners in some parts of the world, but not in others.

Part of the reason I highlighted *Rokeah's* version is that it is among the most complete presentations of the story in the literature. There is also another reason that is far more challenging to what we have said so far. It also raises profound questions about this comment by Yitshak ben Moshe.

The presentation of this story in *Rokeah* begins with an outline of the paragraphs that make up *Mourner's Kaddish* and the question of why orphans recite this liturgy. Nonetheless, in lines V-Y, when advice is first given as to how this individual who has died can be freed from his posthumous suffering, *two* choices are offered. The second choice is for his son to recite *Kaddish*, but the first choice is for him to recite – and have the congregation respond to – *Barekhu*.[155]

In addition, and most importantly, I did not present *Rokeah's* description of what the son said when he finally comes to the synagogue. Instead, I left an ellipsis in its place.

If we now fill in that ellipsis, we find something quite interesting. This is how that part of the text reads:

A–And he caused him to stand before the congregation	א–והעמידו לפני הקהל
B–And he said, "Blessed is God, Who is blessed."	ב–ואמר ברכו את ה' המבורך
C–And the congregation responded: "Bless God Who is blessed.	ג–וענו הקהל ברוך ה' המבורך,
D–May [His Name] be magnified, May His great Name…"	ג–יתגדל, יהא שמיה רבא.

In other words, despite the introduction to the story presented in *Rokeah*, and despite Yitshak ben Moshe's comments, it is not *Kaddish* alone, but *Kaddish* along with *Barekhu* that has the power to redeem the father's soul.[156] This reference to prayers other than *Kaddish* also exists in the other works that tell this tale. In fact, when we look at these other texts we find that the

---

155 Siddur, p. 84.

156 See Tah-Shmah, Israel. "Ketsat Inyanei Kaddish Yatom Uminhagav." In *Tarbits* 53:4 (1984): pp. 559–568.

prayer recited by the child varies dramatically. Sometimes it is *Barekhu* alone,[157] sometimes it involves *Keriyat Shema*,[158] sometimes it includes reciting the *Haftorah* (the Sabbath and holiday morning reading from the Prophets)[159] or even simply that the boy recites "blessings" publicly.[160] *Kaddish* is not even the most frequently cited liturgy recited by the dead man's son in the extant versions of this story.[161]

Frankly, one can read these sources to say that the particular prayer is not the important issue. Rather, it is when the son can demonstrate to the community that he has reconnected with Jewish practice – so that the family's Jewish identity can continue – that the father is redeemed.[162]

Nonetheless, possibly as a result of the *Heikhalot* text cited above that also tells of redeeming souls from purgatory and only mentions *Kaddish*, possibly because of the use of *Kaddish* as the liturgy recited by the Cantor in the presence of the mourners in *Masekhet Soferim*, possibly because of the wording of *Kaddish* itself (particularly the *Burial Kaddish*), possibly because of the use of the *Burial Kaddish* at a funeral, possibly because *Rokeah* seems to favor it over *Barekhu* in the introduction to his telling of this story or possibly for some combination of all of these reasons, this liturgy emerged in this role.[163] It is *Kaddish* that becomes the prayer through which redemption of the dead can be accomplished in the popular imagination. It is for this reason that many people will go to great lengths to recite *Kaddish* for their deceased relatives or, at least, will arrange for it to be said by someone – though to this point,

---

157 Seder Eliyahu Zutah #117 (the story here is about Rabbi Johanan ben Zakai, not Rabbi Akiva). *Mahzor Vitry* #144; Rabbi Israel ben Rabbi Joseph Al-Nakawa. *Menorat Hamaor*, ch. 11: "*Gidul Banim*," p. 128.

158 *Mahzor Vitry* , ibid.; *Zohar Hadash*: Megillat Ruth 42a.

159 Kol Bo #114. Here, it is Rabbi Ploni (anonymous) who saves the father.

160 *Kallah Rabbati* 2:9.

161 Uzziel, loc. cit. and Yosef, Ovadiah. Responsa *Yehave Da'at* 5:59. Each cite a number of sources that tell this story in different variations.

162 Uzziel, loc. cit. And see Responsa *Binyamin Ze'ev* #201. Also see Genesis Rabbah 49:4.

163 See Yosef, loc. cit., who carries this history into the 16th century and also provides an explanation of different redemptive capacities that can be associated with different prayers. He also cites B. Sanhedrin 104a that "a son can bring merit to a father, but a father cannot do so for a son." This supports the idea that a son reciting *Kaddish* for his father positively affects the deceased, but limits whether that works for other relatives.

that would seem to be the less desirable option, especially when we are dealing with the death of one's parents.[164]

From its origins in King David's Psalm that calls for praising God's saving power; from Daniel's use of the translation of King David's words in response to an event that was significant and salutary in his life; from the likelihood that Daniel's response was the common reaction in his era to similar circumstances of salvation; from Ezekiel's prophecy – from all of these origins to the use of *Kaddish* at the conclusion of a study session; to the claim of mystical power that is said to reside in its central response; to its use as a demarcation that ends sections of the services; to finding it as a response to the words of Torah that are used in a eulogy and in *Tsiduk ha-Din*, to its being recited in the presence of the mourners in the synagogue on the Sabbath; to its finally being recited by those who have suffered a loss themselves as a way to reconcile with God and as an esoteric tool to improve the lot of the soul of a loved one in heaven, *Kaddish* has had a truly spectacular history that is commensurate with its importance in contemporary Jewish practice.

We have chronicled the story of *Kaddish* as it was used and understood across the centuries of Jewish liturgical experience. Nonetheless, there are still a few important issues for us to discuss in regard to this prayer. To begin with, there is the question of how long one who has suffered a loss should recite *Mourner's Kaddish*. The obvious answer would seem to be: for the entire period of mourning.

But that begs the question of how long the mourning period is. In the Bible the normal experience of formal sadness is thirty days and that is the usual Jewish practice.[165] Consequently, this is the time period of mourning for most relatives.[166] That includes one's spouse, one's siblings and even one's children.[167]

Parents are not in the same category, however. There is a different type of connection that people have with their mother and father than they have with anyone else. Parents create us and live inside us – in a psychological sense – in ways that find no parallel in any other relationship.[168]

---

164 See n. 118.

165 The mourning period for Moses was thirty days (Deuteronomy 32:8). That was also true for Aaron (Numbers 20:29). See Maimonides (*Mishneh Torah*: Laws of Mourning 6:1) and Ravad (ad. loc.) for other sources for the thirty-day period.

166 *Shulhan Arukh* 391:2.

167 Ibid., 374:4.

168 See Blidstein, Gerald. *Honor Thy Father and Mother*. Jersey City: 2005.

Honoring parents is an important principle in Jewish law – so important that it is included in the Ten Commandments.[169] The requirements entailed by this law are quite onerous.[170] Part of the burden imposed by this obligation is that the mourning period for a parent lasts for twelve months.[171] Logically *Kaddish* for parents should cover the same period of time.

But once again mysticism enters the picture by way of this source:

The judgment of the wicked in Hell [lasts for] twelve months,[172]	משפט רשעים בגיהנם שנים עשר חדש

This leads to the following discussion in Ramo:

A–They customarily did not recite Kaddish or [lead] the prayer other than for eleven months	א–ונהגו שאין אומרים קדיש ותפלה רק י"א חדשים,
B–In order that they not make their fathers and mothers into wicked people	ב–כדי שלא יעשו אביהם ואמם רשעים,
C–Because the judgment of a wicked individual [lasts for] twelve months.[173]	ג–כי משפט רשע י"ב חדש

In other words, because *Kaddish* is a liturgy that redeems from purgatory, and because even the complete reprobate suffers in Hell for only twelve months, this prayer, when it is offered on behalf of one's parents, is recited for less than the full period of mourning. This is the common practice because the mourner does not want to give people the impression that he is still trying to redeem his parent from divine punishment as the end of the twelve months approaches. That would suggest that the offspring saw his parent as wicked. In short, the honor due to parents that leads to the twelve-month-long period of mourning for one's mother or father also leads to shortening the time during which *Kaddish* is recited for them.[174]

In the end, several different opinions exist as to exactly how long the prayer

---

169 Exodus 20:11; Deuteronomy 5:15.
170 See Blidstein.
171 Cf. Tyrnau, loc. cit.; Isserless. Responsa #118; Rabbi Shabbetai Ben Meir Ha-Kohen (17th century); *Shach* to *Yoreh De'ah* 344:9.
172 M. Eduyot 2:10.
173 *Yoreh De'ah* 376:4.
174 Cf. *Sefer Maharil: Hilkhot Semahot* 2.

should be said.[175] The generally accepted custom is to recite *Kaddish* for one day less than eleven months so that no part of the twelfth month is used for this liturgy. This avoids any suggestion that the child sees the parent as "wicked."[176]

This has led to two consequences that were not at all intended by those who originally developed these customs. First, some people make the mistake of thinking that mourning is over once *Kaddish* ends. When the recitation concludes, there is actually a month and a day left to the period of formal grief. During this time the restrictions and obligations associated with mourning – other than reciting *Kaddish* – continue.[177] Some people do not realize that this is true.

Second, since the eleven- or twelve-month period of saying *Kaddish* is seen as saving the deceased from punishment, the desire to insure that everyone – even those who have no children – is given the respect and mystical impact of an eleven- or twelve-month *Kaddish* recitation has grown. Such a recitation is often arranged (usually through payment or charitable donation) for anyone if there is any doubt whether or not every day of the rather lengthy *Kaddish* period will be covered by someone saying the prayer for this deceased individual. We have made mention of this practice several times in our discussion so far, and raised the question of whether this makes any conceptual sense given that the story that started all of this speaks only of a father and his son.

There is actually a contemporary opinion that *favors* the prayer being said for the full twelve months whenever possible. If someone other than a child of the deceased is the one reciting *Kaddish* – either exclusively or even in addition to the children – since there is no issue of parental honor vis a vis him and the person who has died, this individual can and should recite the prayer for the entire period. Such a recitation provides the full mystical redemptive benefit of *Kaddish* to the one who has passed away – or so this source argues.

Going further, this text makes the point that, since most people are far less than perfect in life, they can use the twelve months of *Kaddish* to help them avoid divine retribution for their sins. It is only children who should not say *Kaddish* for twelve months, because of the disrespectful implications of such a recitation. Nonetheless, children of parents who were not fully observant

---

175 For a list of different opinions, see Goldberg, Hayim. *Mourning in Halachah.* Brooklyn: 1991, p. 352, n. 2. The text of the note (as the entire book) is somewhat confusing to read.

176 *Shulhan Arukh : Yoreh De'ah* 376:4.

177 See *Maharil,* loc. cit.

should also actually say *Kaddish* for the entire twelve-month period of mourning according to this authority, because their parents really need the full benefit of having the prayer said on their behalf for as long as possible.[178]

The logic of this position suggests arranging for a full twelve-month recitation by someone – either a child or someone else – for everyone who dies. If this suggestion becomes the widespread practice, we may be witnessing the dawn of the next stage in the history of *Kaddish*. Despite the fact that the earliest sources that tell us of the positive impact of this prayer on the dead seem to make that positive effect contingent on the *son* reciting the prayer as a sign of Jewish continuity, we have come to a place where someone else offering this liturgy is seen as being, in some ways, the superior option. Again, I doubt that those who first gave *Kaddish* to the mourners ever saw this as a possible outcome.

In point of fact, this approach has already had its impact. If saving the soul of the deceased is the goal of *Kaddish* – and not reconciliation with God before the community or responding to Torah study – then why is there any need to worry about reciting the verses that appear after *Aleinu* and the Song of Glory that we discussed previously? These verses should simply be unnecessary, as they have nothing to do with the mission of the prayer.[179] Also, the recitation of *Kaddish* should certainly not be limited to *Shabbat* and holidays, and even on *Tishah B'Av* why not be in the synagogue saving souls from Hell regardless of the current state of our relationship with God on that day?

Current practice actually follows precisely these parameters. Many communities do not recite the verses after *Aleinu,* and would ignore those after the Song of Glory as well, except for the reasons discussed previously. Further, *Kaddish* is recited on every day of the year. In all of these cases and more, the story of Rabbi Akiva doing outreach and educating the child of the wicked man has come to dominate the understanding and practices surrounding this prayer.

In short, the mystical underpinnings of this prayer have carried us quite far from where we began. From a prayer for protection and messianic redemption recited after a study session that may well have originated during the Hadrianic persecutions, to the need to have someone say *Kaddish* to benefit the deceased in the next world, at each of the three services of the day – every day – for

---

178 Feinstein, loc. cit. *Yoreh De'ah* 4:61:6 and 15.
179 There is no mention of reciting verses in the Rabbi Akiva story.

twelve months, the meaning and understanding of this liturgy has traveled a very long and complicated road as it has been recited by the Jewish community.

Moving now to the next of the remaining miscellaneous, but important items, we begin by asking the question, How many people should recite *Kaddish* at one time? Certainly those *Kaddish* recitations that are done by the Cantor are done only by him. On the other hand, the almost universal custom today is that for any *Kaddish* said by the mourners, everyone present in the synagogue who needs to say the prayer recites it simultaneously.[180] Also, halakhic texts have established a minimum: one who has suffered a loss must recite *Kaddish* as part of this group at least once a day.[181]

This was not always the case. At one time, *Mourner's Kaddish* was recited by only one person each time it appeared.[182] The honor of leading would rotate through the synagogue, with those having a greater requirement (generally those who had lost parents or those at earlier and more intense stages of bereavement) taking precedence.[183] Under that system, many days might pass without a specific individual being chosen as the leader, and even when chosen, the likelihood was that a particular mourner would recite no more than one *Kaddish* per day.[184] This change in practice has again led to two interesting and unintended consequences.

First, beginning with our earliest *Siddurim*, we find various additional psalms – the Psalm of the Day,[185] or psalms for special days such as *Rosh Hodesh* (the

---

180 See Rabbi Abraham Zvi Hirsh Eisenstadt (19th century). *Pitkhei Teshuvah* 376:6.

181 Cf. Rabbi David Tzvi Hoffman (1843–1929). Responsa *Melammed le-Ho'il* 1: *Orah Hayim* 6; Feinstein, op. cit.: *Yoreh De'ah* 1:254.

182 Colon. *Piskei Maharik* #290, Responsa *Maharik* #30. See Feinstein, loc. cit. 4:60:1, who mentions both the older and the current custom, and see Rabbi Eliezer Yehuda Waldenberg (*Tzitz Eliezer* 9:15) for an intermediate practice where some of the recitations are individual and some are mixed.

183 Cf. *Shulhan Arukh: Yoreh De'ah* 376:4 and the various commentaries to this section. See also Rabbi Ezekiel Ben Judah Landau (18th century). Responsa *Noda Bi-Yehudah: Mahadurah Tinyana: Orah Hayim* #8 and Rabbi Israel Meir Ha-Kohen Kagan (1839–1933). *Bi'ur Halakha* #132, sv. *Kuntrus*. According to the last source, sometimes – if no precedence could be established using these criteria – a lottery system was used (cf. Tyrnau, loc. cit.).

184 Feinstein, op. cit.

185 Siddur, pp. 168–177. See *Seder Rav Amram Gaon: Siyum ha-Tefillah* and Rabbi David Ben Rabbi Yosef Abudraham (thirteenth century). *Abudraham: Shir Shel Yom*.

New Moon)[186] or *Hanukah*[187] – added to the end of the services at *Shaharit*.[188] This was true even before *Aleinu* became the universal "concluding" prayer in the 12th or 13th century.[189] A final *Kaddish* was then recited – by the *prayer leader* – after these liturgies.[190]

Once *Aleinu* joined these psalms at the end of services[191] – which is approximately at the same time that *Kaddish* became a prayer for the dead[192] – mourners were asked to recite *Kaddish* after every one of these liturgies.[193]

Originally, that meant there were two recitations: one for *Aleinu* and one for the psalm. In our earliest sources there was only one psalm said each day. The paragraph for a special occasion would replace the usual Psalm of the Day in the liturgy when it was offered.[194] That is why there were always two *Kaddish* recitations at the end of worship each morning.

---

186 *Abudraham : Seder Rosh Hodesh.*

187 *Seder Troyes #7.*

188 See Rabbi Abraham Ben Nathan (12th–13th century). *Sefer Hamanhig Dinei Tefillah*, p. 107. He also mentions Psalms for *Purim* and *Hol ha-Mo'ed* (the intermediary days of Passover and *Sukkot*) and a single repeating psalm for all regular weekdays. There is no Psalm of the Day in this text. He calls the recitation of these prayers "a practice of Toledo and its surroundings" and a "good custom," that is "logical" and that he "like[s]." As discussed below, he, as all the early reporters of this practice, sees the psalms for special days as a replacement for and not as an addition to the weekday paragraph.

189 See the *Aleinu* chapter in this volume, pp. 208–238.

190 See *Seder Rav Amram*, loc. cit.

191 Some of the earliest sources have the prayer leader reciting *Kaddish* before *Aleinu* with no *Kaddish* recited at the end (*Mahzor Vitry* #99, #193 and #232) and *Siddur Rashi* (12th century) #419. By the fourteenth century, we find the *Mourner's Kaddish* after *Aleinu*; see Tyrnau, *Minhag shel Yom Hol*.

192 For *Aleinu* see the chapter discussing that prayer in this volume; for *Kaddish* see the comment of Rabbi Yitshak ben Rabbi Moshe above, that in his time this was the accepted opinion in some communities but not in others. The reasons for adding *Aleinu* and for giving *Kaddish* to mourners do not seem to be related, though both occur in the era of the Crusades when *Aleinu* was used as a martyr's prayer and *Kaddish* began to be used in response to a loss.

193 Sperber, loc. cit.; *Bi'ur Halakhah*, loc. cit. Also see Rabbi Yechiel Michel Ben Rabbi Aaron Halevi Epstein (19th–20th centuries). *Arukh ha-Shulhan: Orah Hayim* 55:4 and 133:2. This source expresses concern about there being too many *Kaddish* recitations in the services.

194 Rabbi Avraham b. Rabbi Yekhiel Mikhel Danziger. *Hayei Adam* (1748–1820) 118:12;

In contrast, in later literature we find the special psalm or psalms[195] being added to the end of the services where they are recited in addition to the daily psalm.[196] In settings where there was only one mourner reciting *Kaddish* at a time, since an additional *Kaddish* was added after each of these texts, this allowed for more opportunities for different individuals to be the one chosen to say the prayer.[197]

Nonetheless, a quick look at almost any contemporary *Siddur* shows that this reality has changed. The stage direction present in contemporary prayer books tells all mourners to recite *Mourner's Kaddish* whenever it appears in the services.[198] This derives from the felt need to have the person who has suffered a loss recite every *Kaddish*, so that the soul of the deceased can be saved from purgatory or otherwise derive benefit in the World to Come to the greatest extent possible.[199]

When *Kaddish* was understood as being an intrinsic part of the services used to demarcate the ending of a section of the liturgy that was then given to mourners to help them heal and reconcile with God, the push to be the one to recite it was nowhere near as great. This restorative process – which, as we have seen, is the historically earlier understanding of the prayer – can be accomplished through occasional public recitation, and it is also helped along by hearing someone else recite the liturgy as in the early *Masekhet Soferim* text. In contrast, if *Kaddish* is a prayer that helps the dead when specifically said on their behalf, the one charged with offering it would feel much more of an imperative to actually recite it at least once every single day.

Recently, in some communities, the Psalm of the Day and the other special

---

Kol Bo #44. Troyes, loc. cit., mentions that this was the custom in Babylonia; also see n. 188.

195 For example, when it is *Hanukah* and *Rosh Hodesh,* both special prayers are added.

196 See Troyes, loc. cit.; *Bi'ur Halakhah* #132; Rabbi Shemuel Halevi Wosner. Responsa *Shevet ha-Levi* 8:252.

197 Epstein, loc. cit.

198 Cf. Siddur, pp. 52 and 160.

199 See Yosef, *Yabi'a Omer* 7: *Orah Hayim* 10, that "according to public opinion, if one misses even one *Kaddish* ... he is viewed as one who belittles the honor of his dead parents." The claim is made in some sources, based on the teachings of Rabbi Isaac Luria (the Ari), that prayers and other positive acts performed in this world do more than just redeem a deceased individual from purgatory. They also improve that person's lot within the positive precincts of the afterlife; see Al-Khakam, op. cit. 3: *Yoreh De'ah* 32.

psalms have been moved to earlier in the services – in some cases, to the very beginning of the prayers – establishing *Aleinu* as the only daily concluding prayer.[200] The prevalent custom of having a group recitation of *Kaddish* has aided in this process. Now that the mourners all get a chance to recite the prayer every time it is said, there is no need to have several opportunities to offer this liturgy specifically at the end of worship when all the mourners are more likely to have arrived in the synagogue.[201] Having one concluding *Mourner's Kaddish* that can be said by anyone who wants to say it is enough. Some may want to say more, but at least the minimal daily requirement is being fulfilled. As a result, moving the Psalm of the Day and the other special Psalms to earlier in the services presents no problem.

Second, when only one mourner recited *Kaddish* at a time, adopted children, who had lost a step-parent, would often be left out.[202] Since biological children have a greater requirement to say the prayer, they would take precedence.[203] Given enough mourners, those who were adopted would never

---

200 Kagan, *Mishnah Berurah* 581:2. I have seen the Psalm of the Day recited as the first prayer in some Israeli congregations.

201 Cf. Responsa *Shevut Yaakov* 2:93. See Al-Khakam, op. cit. 4: *Orah Hayim* 7, that the Ari saw *Kaddish* at the end of the services as the most important recitation for impacting on souls in the World to Come. See also Yosef, *Yabi'a Omer* 6: *Yoreh De'ah* 31.

202 See Rabbi Moses Sofer (1762–1839). Responsa *Hatam Sofer*: *Orah Hayim* 1:164. Reischer (loc. cit. 2:94) disagrees and sees adopted children as the same as biological children for *Kaddish*. So, too, Rabbi Yekutiel Yehuda Halberstam (1904–1995), in *Divrei Yatsiv*: *Yoreh De'ah* 244:2, argues that the prospective reciter of *Kaddish* for one who has taught him Torah can also claim equal status to that of an actual child. This debate has roots in an earlier conceptual disagreement as to whether grandchildren can claim a share in the recitation of *Kaddish* when children who have lost a parent are present. See Isserless, in Responsa *Ramo* #118, who allows them a smaller number of recitations than children, and Responsa *Maharik* #30, who says they should be treated as non-relatives. Based on the prevailing customs with which these two sages were familiar, in practice, there was no difference between them. However, their theoretical debate has a practical impact on whether or not one allows adopted children to take part in the *Kaddish* recitation rotation.

203 Moellin, loc. cit. *Hilkhot Tefillah* #14; Rabbi Chaim Mordechai Margulies (18th–19th centuries). *Sha'arei Teshuvah*: *Orah Hayim* 132: 5; Isserless. *Yoreh De'ah* 376:4. The original story about saving the father from purgatory involves a biological child. There are even some opinions that because this story is about a father and a son, the father may prevent the son from reciting *Kaddish* for his mother, though others disagree;

get a chance to lead the recitation. In order to alleviate this problem, some communities would say an extra psalm and reserve the *Kaddish* that followed this text exclusively for an adopted child who had suffered a loss. Those who fell in this category would then take turns reciting this liturgy.[204] Now that all mourners say *Kaddish* at once this practice has essentially disappeared, as has recitation of a special Psalm for adopted children.

In contemporary times the question of whether a woman in mourning may recite *Kaddish* in the synagogue has become a point of significant controversy. Despite some claims to the contrary, many authorities allow the practice.[205]

Particularly intriguing in this regard is Rabbi Moses Feinstein's treatment of this issue. He does not respond to the question of whether a woman may recite *Kaddish* in his writings. Instead, he simply assumes that the practice is fine and that it has a long pedigree. In a responsum that deals with the question of how many women must be present in the synagogue before a *mekhitsa* or physical separation is required, Rabbi Feinstein writes:

A–And behold, in all of the generations, they were accustomed	א–והנה בכל הדורות נהגו
B–That occasionally would enter . . . a woman in mourning in order to recite *Kaddish*	ב–שלפעמים היתה נכנסת . . . אבלה לומר קדיש . . .
C–But only occasionally is it possible to permit [without a *mehitsa*]	ג–ורק באקראי אפשר להתיר.
D–And it is possible to permit, occasionally, only up to two women and not more.[206]	ד–ואפשר להתיר, באקראי, רק עד ב' נשים ולא יותר.

One of the important sources often cited as being in opposition to women saying *Kaddish* is a responsum of Rabbi Yair Chaim Bacahrach (1638–1702).

Orhot Hayim, loc. cit. #31; Rabbi Samson ben Tsadok (13th–14th centuries) *Tashbetz Katan* #425.

204 See Sofer for this suggestion and see Jacobson, loc. cit., p. 369.

205 See Eisenstadt, loc. cit. 376:7; Uzziel, loc. cit. 3: *Orah Hayim* 23; Waldenberg, loc. cit. 14:7; Rabbi Yisrael Meir Lau (contemporary). Responsa *Yahel Yisrael* #84.

206 *Igrot Moshe: Yoreh De'ah* 3:124. For a similar inter alia comment supportive of women's recitation of *Kaddish*, see *Bet Yosef: Yoreh De'ah* 403:10, who writes, in a discussion about the recitation of *Kaddish*: היתה זקנה שנה נפשה בעיר ולא עזבה בן ולא בת ["There was an old woman who died in (a particular) city, and she did not leave a son or a *daughter* (to recite *Kaddish*)"].

In this text the question is asked about a rich man from the Amsterdam community who had only daughters. He left money so that after he died ten men would be brought to his home to study Torah. When they concluded, his daughters would recite *Kaddish*.

Rabbi Bacharach indicates his opposition to this arrangement. Some have claimed that he was against women saying *Kaddish* in general. The wording of the responsum indicates that this is not true. Among other things, he says the following:

A–There is logic to suggesting that even for a daughter there is a purpose and comfort for the soul because she is his offspring;	א–יש סברא דגם בבת יש תועלת ונחת רוח לנפש כי זרעו היא.
B–Nonetheless, we must be concerned that as a result of this the power of the customs of the children of Israel, which are also Torah, will be weakened	ב–מ"מ יש לחוש שע"י כך יחלשו כח המנהגים של בני ישראל שג"כ תורה הם
C–And each one will build an idolatrous altar [*Bamah*] for himself according to his own logic	ג–ויהיה כל אחד בונה במה לעצמו ע"פ סברתו ...
D–And therefore, in this situation, where there is a gathering and publicity, we must act to prevent.[207]	ד–ולכן בנדון זה שיש אסיפה ופרסום יש למחות.

His opposition was to dividing the community – to creating separate services – not to women's recitation of *Kaddish*. A *Bamah* was an altar built for worship outside the Temple. It parallels the "breakaway" nature of this practice. So, too, his concern in line D that it was a separate "gathering" indicates where the source of his opposition lies. If this were done under the auspices of the synagogue, these concerns would not exist.

Interestingly, in opposition to Bacharach, Rabbi Jacob ben Joseph Reischer says that women may *only* recite *Kaddish* at home in the presence of a *minyan* (a prayer quorum of ten men, which is always needed for its recitation)[208] and not in the synagogue.[209] However, he too, does not conceptually preclude women from reciting *Kaddish*.[210]

---

207 Responsa *Havot Yair* 222, cited by Eisenstadt, Uzziel, Waldenberg and Lau in the sources cited just above.

208 Cf. Rabbi Asher ben Jechiel (*Rosh*, 13th–14th century). Megillah 3:7.

209 Responsa *Shevut Yaakov* 2:93.

210 Al-Khakam (Responsa *Torah Lishmah* #27) and Waldenberg are both opposed to this

Some may object to a woman being the only one reciting *Kaddish* – in effect becoming the prayer leader for the congregation.[211] This objection is based on the fact that women do not count toward a *minyan* because they have no requirement to pray communally.[212] While different reasons are given for this exemption, the bottom line is that one who is not required to recite a particular prayer may not fulfill the obligation of recitation for someone who is so obligated.[213] As such, there would be some concern in traditional circles if one woman were reciting *Kaddish* alone.[214] She would effectively be fulfilling the obligation for men who are required to recite the prayer.[215]

This problem would seem to be resolved by our present group recitation.[216] As long as at least one man is saying *Kaddish*, a woman reciting it at the same time is no different from a woman reciting *Kedushah* – a prayer that also requires a *minyan*[217] – along with the men. There is no one who objects to that. Even if no male mourner is present, asking a man to recite the *Kaddish*, which, as we have seen, should be done anyway, would allow female mourners this opportunity as well.

We come next to the issue of whether the congregation must stand for *Kaddish*. There are several answers to this question, each with its own history.

---

practice. Their objections, like Bacharach's, are not to the recitation of *Kaddish* per se, but are based on concerns about what such a recitation might lead to.

211 Al-Khakam. Responsa *Rav Pe'Alim* 2: *Orah Hayim* 14.

212 Rabbi Menashe Klein (or ha-Katan, contemporary). *Mishneh Halakhot: Tokhen ha-Inyanim* 15: *Orah Hayim* #26.

213 See the chapter, "Women" in my *Contemporary Orthodox Judaism's Response to Modernity* pp. 265–280.

214 There are several articles on this subject. The best and most objective is Wolowelsky, Joel. "Women and Kaddish." In *Judaism* 44:3 (1995): pp. 282–290. He details and supports the view of my great teacher, Rabbi Joseph Soloveitchik, that a woman may say *Kaddish* in the synagogue even if she is the only one offering the prayer. What appears in the text above is a compromise suggestion that meshes with the history of the liturgy described here.

215 Some argue that the various *Kaddish* recitations that one finds after *Kaddish Titkabel* – meaning the appearances of the *Mourner's Kaddish* at the end of services – are not mandatory, but are simply there for the mourners to recite; see Rabbi Avraham ha-Levi Gombiner. *Magen Avraham* 55:5. For opposition, see Rabbi Alush Praji. *Ohev Mishpat: Orah Hayim* #2.

216 Rabbi Yehudah Herzl Henkin. Responsa *Bnei Banim* 2:7.

217 B. Berakhot 21b.

Ramo says:

> One should stand when reciting *Kaddish* and anything involving holiness [*Kedushah*].[218]

ויש לעמוד כשעונין קדיש וכל
דבר שבקדושה.

This opinion is said to go back to the Jerusalem Talmud.[219] However, it does not appear in our extant texts of that work.[220] In fact, Rabbi Hayim Joseph David Azulai (1724–1806) says that it actually originates in a Medieval commentary called *Hagahot Mordekhai*, authored by Mordekhai, son of Hillel, in the thirteenth century.[221] Somehow this opinion seems to have taken on an older and more authoritative attribution as to its origin over time.

Mishnah Beruruah cites two other answers to our question. The first comes with two options:

> A–... until after he concludes, "*Amen,*
> may His great Name ..."
> B–And there are those who say that one should stand until the *Amen* that comes after "May He be blessed [*Yitbarakh*] ... and say, *Amen*."[222]

א–עד אחר שיסיים אמן יהא
שמיה רבה
ב–וי"א שיש לעמוד עד אמן
שלאחר יתברך וכו' ואמרו אמן

These practices are essentially the same. They require standing either through recitation of what we know to be the single most important sentence in *Kaddish* or through recitation of the paragraph in which it appears. Given the remarkable power ascribed to this sentence in rabbinic and mystical texts, it is no wonder that some authorities would expect worshipers to stand for its recitation.

---

218 Isserless. *Shulhan Arukh: Orah Hayim* 56:1.

219 Halevi. *Turei Zahav* 146:1. See also Rabbi Menachem Azariah da Fano (1548–1620). Responsa *Ramo Mipano* #91.

220 Gombiner (op. cit. 56:4) mentions this and tries to explain that it is in the Jerusalem Talmud. However, the quote that he cites is also not in our texts.

221 Responsa *Tov Ayin* #18. See also Yosef. Responsa *Yehave Da'at* 3:4. The text does not appear in our editions of Mordekhai.

222 *Mishnah Beruruah* 56:7. For a summary of different opinions see, Raab, Menachem. "When Standing is Appropriate in Prayer." In *Journal of Jewish Music and Liturgy* 19 (1997): p. 2.

The final approach cited by *Mishnah Berurah* is this:

A–But there are those who say that there is no need to stand.	א–וי"א שא"צ לעמוד
B–But any *Kaddish* that comes upon him while he is standing,	ב–אלא שכל קדיש שתופסו מעומד
C–For example after Hallel,	ג–כגון לאחר הלל
D–He should not sit until he responds, "*Amen* may His great Name . . ."	ד–לא ישב עד שיענה אמן יש"ר

This custom takes us all the way back to the origins of the prayer as a response to something important that has occurred. As a prayer that "responds," it would seem appropriate to recite it while standing if one is responding to something that was said standing, and to sit when responding to something recited while sitting.

Finally, as an indication of how far back in history at least some parts of *Kaddish* go, many scholars have pointed out the parallels between it and the Lord's Prayer found in the Christian Bible. That prayer, which is very important in Christian thought, reads as follows:

Our Father, which art in heaven, *Hallowed be thy name. Thy kingdom come. Thy will be done in earth, as it is in heaven*. Give us this day our daily bread. And forgive us our debts as we forgive our debtors. And lead us not into temptation, but deliver us from evil; For Thine is the kingdom, and the power, and the glory, forever.[223]

This prayer is claimed by the Christian Bible to have been taught by Jesus to his disciples. If so he used at least some phrases (those in italics) that also appear in some way in *Kaddish*.

Nonetheless, I do not think that the words that we find in common are particularly significant. First, what we have called the "core" of *Kaddish* does not appear here. Since every version of that prayer that we know of has this core, and since the central response of *Kaddish* is the name of the liturgy in rabbinic texts, without "let His great Name be blessed . . ." this would not be a form of *Kaddish* as far as the Rabbis were concerned.

Second, the similar wordings are not exact.[224] Third, there are parallels here to other prayers. For example, "for Thine is the kingdom" appears in precisely

---

223 Matthew 6:9–13; There is a similar prayer in Luke 11:2–4.
224 In *Kaddish* it is "Magnified and sanctified," not only "hallowed."

those words toward the end of the second paragraph of *Aleinu*.[225] Also, the entire phrase, "For Thine is the kingdom, and the power, and the glory" is similar to a line that appears in the story of Daniel and the King's dream discussed back at the beginning of our story of *Kaddish*.[226]

It seems that the only thing we can derive from this is that both prayers go back to a time – roughly two millennia ago – when there was a shared tradition of phrases, verses and prayerful aphorisms that were used both by Judaism and an emerging Christianity.[227] Though there are some similarities here, *Kaddish* is, nonetheless, a prayer whose roots and history lie squarely within the Jewish community.

Drawing on some Biblical texts and other sources, *Kaddish*, "the prayer of response," became part of liturgical practice some two millennia ago – probably within a century or so after the destruction of the second Temple in 70 C.E. It may have been composed in reaction to the Hadrianic persecutions in 135–138 C.E. If it is older (as is the somewhat similar Lord's Prayer), we do not have any record of how it was used in Jewish circles at that earlier time.

During Hadrian's reign it was recited after study sessions where it served as a liturgical act of defiance against that emperor's terrible anti-Semitic decrees. Its vision of a renewed world and a messianic future was a hopeful lifeline to Jews during this difficult period in history. In order to allow as many people as possible to understand this liturgy, it was recited in Aramaic.

Over the centuries the connection between *Kaddish* and Torah study has remained, though in some significant ways it has been attenuated and replaced by other understandings of the meaning of the prayer. Nonetheless, the Torah connection has had its impact. Primarily because various texts are often included in funeral eulogies and various verses can be found in *Tsiduk ha-Din*, *Kaddish* became a response recited at the end of a burial service. So, too, the meaning of the prayer fit well with accompanying an individual on his or her last journey.

If one looks at a *Siddur* today, one is likely to find a number of Biblical verses appearing in the text between *Aleinu* and the *Mourner's Kaddish* that follows it. Other verses can be found before the *Mourner's Kaddish* that is said in some places in response to the Song of Glory. These passages are there to

---

225 See the chapter that discusses this prayer in this volume.
226 Daniel 2:37.
227 Betz, Hans Dieter. *The Sermon on the Mount*. Minneapolis: 1995, pp. 372–373.

satisfy the opinion that even this form of *Kaddish* may not be said except in response to a Torah text. Because the Torah connection has been attenuated over time, many communities do not recite these lines. Ironically, one of the verses that follows *Anim Zemirot* has made a comeback and is sung in many congregations for musical reasons having nothing at all to do with *Kaddish*.

There are, today, two different forms of the prayer that have a specific association with study. One, a shorter form commonly recited after studying a rabbinic source, is called *Kaddish de-Rabbanan*. A second and longer version is also extant and it is offered after completion of a Talmudic tractate or other major text. This second form is the same as the one used at a funeral and it is the most overtly eschatological of the *Kaddish* prayers (all of which are fundamentally eschatological). According to Maimonides, this form of the liturgy should be used at any study session and not just at a *siyum*.

At some point *Kaddish* was brought into the prayer service and recited at the end of different sections of it, as well as at the end of the entire service itself. Different forms of the prayer were developed for different uses. We find these different forms of the prayer at various points in contemporary *Siddurim*.

This use of *Kaddish* as a prayer of conclusion can also be found at the end of special liturgical moments such as a circumcision, the Sanctification of the Moon and the Blessing of the Sun. Even ad hoc prayer services such as the recitation of Psalms for someone who is ill traditionally end with the ubiquitous *Kaddish*.[228]

Masekhet Soferim tells us that along with a special Mourner's Blessing, *Kaddish* was used by the prayer leader in the presence of the mourners on *Shabbat* in order for them to help begin the process of reconciliation with God. Eventually, the prayer was given to those who had suffered a loss to say for themselves for the same reason. The older custom of having only one person at a time recite *Kaddish* may reflect this understanding of the meaning of the prayer.

As this understanding of the purpose of the liturgy also began to recede in prominence, the practice changed. Today, in most synagogues, everyone present who wants to say the prayer does so.

---

228 Azulai (*Birkei Yosef* 55:2) says that *Kaddish* should only be said at the "well-known" places in the prayers (במקומות ידועים בתפילות). Maimonides (Responsa *Pe'er ha-Dor* #130) disagrees and encourages the use of *Kaddish* for any and all prayers. See also ha-Levi (*Orah Hayim* 55:3), Margulies (op. cit. #51), Kagan (*Mishnah Berurah* 581:3).

This change in practice had some unintended results. For example, some communities have moved the Psalm of the Day to earlier in the services. Since there is no longer a need for multiple recitations of *Kaddish* at the end of prayer to accommodate different individuals who are in mourning at the same time, the Psalm of the Day and its attendant *Kaddish* can be moved to a different part of the order of worship.

Second, the mixing of different voices in reciting this liturgy makes it easier for women to join in. *Halakhic* literature conceptually supports the idea of women saying *Kaddish*.[229] If there is at least one man reciting this liturgy at the same time, this might well remove any remaining practical *halakhic* concerns.

The change to a group recitation of *Kaddish* is a late-stage development that emerged from the strong mystical underpinnings of this prayer. These underpinnings also go back to the verses in Daniel and Ezekiel that constitute the roots out of which *Kaddish* grew. Daniel receives a vision from God that explains Nebuhadnezzer's eschatological dream. His response to that vision becomes the central line in *Kaddish*. The verse from *Ezekiel* comes at the end of his prophecies concerning Gog and Magog. Two words from that verse become the opening phrase of this liturgy. Both of these Biblical scenarios border on the mystical, if they are not fully in the world of the esoteric.

The verse from Daniel is very similar to the response of the angels in heaven that appears in *Keriyat Shema* and that was also used in the Temple. Once that enters the equation there is no longer any question as to whether this liturgy is mystical or not. In fact, the prayer is not called *Kaddish* in rabbinic texts; it is referred to instead by the central line of the liturgy. In keeping with the esoteric character of the prayer, rabbinic literature ascribes great power to this line – and this liturgy – to affect both this world and the celestial realm.

One of these claimed powers – found in a *Heikhalot* text – is that those suffering in purgatory will eventually redeem themselves from their fate by answering *Amen* to this central line of *Kaddish*. This opens the door to seeing this liturgy as a prayer that can help the dead.

In the Middle ages, a story is told in a number of sources about the newly Jewishly educated son of a wicked man reciting some part of the prayers in the synagogue. This recitation affords his evil father relief from the eternal sufferings that were his "reward" for the terrible things he did during his life on this earth. Although most of the texts that tell this tale describe the son as

---

229 See notes 205 and 206.

offering something other than *Kaddish*, it is the version of this story that has him saying this liturgy that captures the imagination of the Jewish community.

Kaddish now becomes the prayer of the living recited on behalf of the dead, which must be recited in order to help insure that the deceased have a better fate in the World to Come. This leads to having all the mourners recite this prayer at once and to hiring someone to recite this liturgy if there is any doubt whether children or other relatives will be able to do so.

Another mystical source says that the punishment of evil people in purgatory lasts twelve months. In order for children to avoid the appearance of even suggesting that their parent is wicked, they stop reciting *Kaddish* before reaching the twelfth month of mourning. This has led to a recent suggestion that arrangements for a twelve-month-long recitation of this prayer should be made for everyone, regardless of whether a child is saying *Kaddish* simultaneously as well.

Finally, the question of whether one must stand when *Kaddish* is recited is a matter of debate. But more and more, my sense is that worshipers are standing, which reflects the ever-greater importance and more significant meaning that has been invested in this liturgy over the centuries.

In that vein, the power that this prayer possesses to speak to all Jews can be illustrated by the story of former Supreme Court Justice Felix Frankfurter. He lived his life as a self-declared agnostic. Nonetheless, he arranged for *Kaddish* to be said in his memory after he died. He may not have lived as a Jew, but he left this world as a Jew.[230] His story is repeated in different ways by many people as they confront the loss of a loved one or their own mortality.

---

230 Konvitz, Milton. *Nine American Jewish Thinkers*. New Brunswick: 2000, p. 105.

ABOUT THE AUTHOR

RABBI DR. BARRY FREUNDEL is the author of *Contemporary Orthodox Judaism's Response to Modernity* (Ktav) and the Rabbi of Congregation Kesher Israel at the Georgetown Synagogue located in downtown Washington DC. Rabbi Freundel serves as vice president of the Rabbinical Council of America (RCA) and chair of its Geirus Policies and Standards Committee, where he helped create and administer the RCA's network of North American conversion courts. He is also Associate Professor of Religion at Towson University and Adjunct Professor of Law at Georgetown University. Rabbi Freundel is married to Sharon Freundel, the director of Hebrew and Judaic studies at a Jewish day school in Washington DC and a registered nurse, and they have three children.